FIVE MINUTES A DAY

FIVE MINUTES
A DAY

By
Robert E. Speer

THE WESTMINSTER PRESS
Philadelphia

ISBN 0-664-24139-5

Library of Congress Catalog Card No 43-16427

9 8 7 6 5 4 3 2 1

Published by The Westminster Press®
Philadelphia, Pennsylvania

PRINTED IN THE UNITED STATES OF AMERICA

PREFACE

The MATERIAL of this little book was prepared entirely for personal and private use and not for publication. It is printed now because The Westminster Press learned of it and wanted to make it available for the help of other common Christian folk — lay people, men and women, in our Churches — in the pressure of our daily life and work. It has been cast in form suitable for individual use or for use in family worship or in connection with grace at meals. The book does not contain homilies or meditations. It simply provides for each day some Bible verses and a poem embodying one central thought, and an appropriate prayer. It does not pretend to enter into rivalry with the great books of devotion like Thomas à Kempis' *Imitation of Christ,* or *Daily Strength for Daily Needs,* or *A Chain of Prayers Across the Ages,* or *Great Souls at Prayer.* It is a simple, homely affair for busy people who can find, because they must, a little time at the beginning or ending of the day for a bit of quiet thought and prayer.

In the preparation of the material for the author's own use, great liberty was taken in the alteration of the prayers and in abbreviation of the poems, and it is regretted that in the case of some of the prayers the author has lost trace of their origin or was unable to discover it. The poems are in large part fugitive verse rescued from papers and magazines, but many are from the poets who are well known and loved. Wherever possible, due credit has been given. If there have been any errors or omissions in this regard, the author and the publisher would express their deep regret and would be grateful for any help in locating the source of any of the poems or prayers that are not duly credited.

The book is sent out with the hope and prayer that it may help those who use it to enter into the joy and strength which follow an obedience to Paul's admonition, "Whatsoever things are true, whatsoever things are honorable, whatsoever things are just, whatsoever things are pure, whatsoever things are lovely, whatsoever things are of good report; if there be any virtue, and if there be any praise, think on these things," and to his counsel in the first letter that he wrote, "Rejoice always; pray without ceasing; in everything give thanks: for this is the will of God in Christ Jesus to you-ward."

ROBERT E. SPEER.

FIVE MINUTES A DAY

And he spake a parable unto them to the end that they ought always to pray, and not to faint. *Luke 18:1.*

Rejoice always; pray without ceasing; in everything give thanks: for this is the will of God in Christ Jesus to you-ward. *1 Thess. 5:16–18.*

Is any among you suffering? let him pray. *James 5:13.*

I desire therefore that the men pray in every place. *1 Tim. 2:8.*

We . . . pray always for you. *II Thess. 1:11.*

Evening, and morning, and at noonday, will I complain, and moan; and he will hear my voice. *Ps. 55:17.*

> Be not afraid to pray — to pray is right.
> Pray, if thou canst, with hope, but ever pray
> Though hope be weak or sick with long delay:
> Pray in the darkness if there be no light.
> Far is the time remote from human sight,
> When war and discord on the earth shall cease,
> Yet every prayer for universal peace
> Avails the blessed time to expedite.
> Whate'er is good to wish, ask that of Heaven,
> Though it be what thou canst not hope to see.
> Pray to be perfect, though material leaven
> Forbid the spirit so on earth to be:
> But if for any wish thou dar'st not pray,
> Then pray to God to cast that wish away.
>
> *Hartley Coleridge.*

ALMIGHTY GOD, the Father of our Lord Jesus Christ and our Father: help us as we seek through our prayers to draw near unto Thee; to bow our wills to Thine and to yield our spirits to the influence of Thy Holy Spirit. Help us to trust Thine assurance through Thy dear Son our Lord that if we ask we shall receive, that Thou art more ready to give to us all that we need than any earthly father can be to meet the wants of his children. Help us as we worship Thine eternal goodness; meditate on Thine unwearied mercy; confess our shortcomings and sins; and give ourselves up to be led by Thee in the ways of purity and peace. In Thine infinite love, be found of our seekings. [*Devotional Services* (Altered).]

VISION

There was no frequent vision. *1 Sam. 3:1.*

Where there is no vision, the people cast off restraint. *Prov. 29:18.*

Thy gates also shall be open continually; they shall not be shut day nor night; that men may bring unto thee the wealth of the nations, and their kings led captive. *Isa. 60:11.*

(Now his windows were open in his chamber toward Jerusalem); and he kneeled upon his knees three times a day, and prayed, and gave thanks before his God, as he did aforetime. *Dan. 6:10.*

We all, with unveiled face beholding as in a mirror the glory of the Lord, are transformed into the same image from glory to glory, even as from the Lord the Spirit. *II Cor. 3:18.*

An idle poet, here and there,
  Looks round him; but, for all the rest,
The world, unfathomably fair,
  Is duller than a witling's jest.
Love wakes men once a life time each;
  They lift their heavy lids and look;
And lo, what one sweet face can teach,
  They read with joy, then shut the book.   *Coventry Patmore.*

Whene'er, O ever present Lord!
  These ancient chronicles I read
Of them, Thy human speech who heard,
Who touched Thy human hands indeed,

Forbid that all my faith be spent
  To find them true, and free from flaw,
Or idly pitch my slothful tent
  Upon the truth they knew they saw!

Nay, hold not thus Thyself aloof,
  But come, and bide and walk with me,
That I may cry, on equal proof,
  Not, "Yes, they saw," but "Lo! I see!"
    Rossiter W. Raymond (Altered).

O THOU whom we seek in all our need and through all the mystery of life and without whom we cannot live bravely or well, forgive us that we so often miss Thee. Show us Thy paths already at our feet. Give us courage and vision to follow in faith Thy ways of love and right until our own lives become Thy revelation and Thy Spirit transforms our deeds. As we thus draw near to Thee, do Thou graciously draw near to us until we become more sure of Thee than the light. In His Name in whose life Thy love becomes light and life. [Gaius Glenn Atkins.]

THE FATHER OF JESUS CHRIST

Blessed be the God and Father of our Lord Jesus Christ. *Eph. 1:3.*

No man hath seen God at any time; the only begotten Son, who is in the bosom of the Father, he hath declared him. *John 1:18.*

It is God, that said, Light shall shine out of darkness, who shined in our hearts, to give the light of the knowledge of the glory of God in the face of Jesus Christ. *II Cor. 4:6.*

The Spirit of this Age spoke on a certain day,
" Rise up my child and cast thy early faith away."
I rose to go: my freedom seemed complete.
In vain! Once more, O Lord, behold me at Thy feet.
Thou art the very life which beats within my heart.
I have no power to choose: from Thee I cannot part.
O Light of all the world, that gladdened weary eyes! . . .
The awful unknown Power that in the darkness lies
Thou saidst could be revealed through Thee to mortal eyes:
And what tho' earth and sea His glory do proclaim
Tho' on the stars is writ that great and dreadful Name —
Yea, hear me. Son of Man, — with tears my eyes are dim
I cannot read the word which draws me close to Him.
I say it after Thee with faltering voice and weak,
" Father of Jesus Christ " — this is the God I seek.
                     Notes and Queries, *December 31, 1881.*

*M*ost merciful Father, Giver of every good gift, who hast given us Thy servants so many and great blessings, forgive us, we beseech Thee, our sins; sanctify us with Thy truth, O Thou who art the most merciful Sanctifier of all. Kindle our hearts with the fire of Thy love; grant us ever to walk in the light of Thy Divine Presence; and that seeking Thee alone, we may attain unto Thee, and taught by Thee, we may teach others Thy paths, so that we may together hasten unto Thee, the true Shepherd of our souls. And do Thou, Lord Jesus, vouchsafe to bear us on Thy shoulders, as whom Thou hast redeemed with Thy most precious blood, and to place us in Thy green pastures; who liveth and reigneth, ever one God, world without end. [E. B. Pusey.]

What hast thou that thou didst not receive? but if thou didst receive it, why dost thou glory as if thou hadst not received it? *1 Cor. 4:7.*

The time past may suffice to have wrought the desire of the Gentiles. *1 Peter 4:3.*

Ask now of the days that are past, which were before thee, since the day that God created man upon the earth. *Deut. 4:32.*

And thou shalt say to the rebellious, even to the house of Israel, . . . let it suffice you. *Ezek. 44:6.*

He was to learn that rebellion is a road to wisdom because it is a species of excess. Excess teaches a man to know what is enough, and when Blake knew the exact value of rebellion he was prepared to read the past afresh, and find that its treasury contained priceless jewels that he never even suspected while he was passionately searching for some new thing. [Gardner, *William Blake, the Man.*]

Do you hear a deep voice calling —
Calling persistently?
Like the sound of God's great wa-
ters, —
Calling insistently?
'Tis the voice of our dead, our myriad
dead,
Calling to you and me: —
  " We call you from your trifling
With the petty things of life;

We cry aloud for a new world
vowed
To a world-redeeming strife.
Take God once more as Counsellor
Work with Him, hand in hand,
Build surely in His Grace and
Power,
The nobler things that shall endure,
And having done all — Stand."
John Oxenham.

O GOD, before whose face the generations rise and pass away, the Strength of those who labor and suffer, and the Repose of the holy and blessed dead, we rejoice in the communion of Thy saints. We remember all who have faithfully lived; all who have peacefully died, and espe-cially those most dear to us. Lift us into light and love; give us at last our portion with those who have trusted in Thee and striven in all things to do Thy holy will. And unto Thy Name, with the Church on earth and the Church in heaven would we ascribe all honour and glory, world without end. [*Devotional Services.*]

He [Jehovah] raiseth up the poor. . . . He lifteth up the needy . . . to make them . . . inherit the throne of glory. *1 Sam. 2:8.*

The wise shall inherit glory. *Prov. 3:35.*

He that overcometh shall inherit these things; and I will be his God, and he shall be my son. *Rev. 21:7.*

But unto the tribe of Levi Moses gave no inheritance. *Josh. 13:33.*

Jehovah is the portion of mine inheritance. *Ps. 16:5.*

Ye were sealed with the Holy Spirit of promise, which is an earnest of our inheritance, unto the redemption of God's own possession, unto the praise of his glory . . . ; having the eyes of your heart enlightened, that ye may know what is the hope of his calling, what the riches of the glory of his inheritance in the saints. *Eph. 1:13, 14, 18.*

> How seldom, friends, a good, great man inherits
> Honor and wealth, with all his worth and pains!
> It seems a story from the world of spirits
> When any man obtains that which he merits,
> Or any merits that which he obtains.
>
> For shame, my friend! Renounce this idle strain!
> What would'st thou have a good, great man obtain?
> Wealth, title, dignity, a golden chain,
> Or heap of corpses which his sword hath slain?
> Goodness and greatness are not means but ends.
> Hath he not always treasures, always friends,
> The good, great man? Three treasures, love and light
> And calm thoughts equable as infant's breath:
> And three fast friends more sure than day or night,
> Himself, his Maker and the angel Death.   *Coleridge.*

*A*ND, O Lord, from whom all things do come, grant to us Thy humble servants that by Thy holy inspiration we may think those things that be good, and by Thy merciful guiding may perform the same; through Jesus Christ our Lord. [*Gelasian Sacramentary.*]

They wandered in the wilderness in a desert way; . . . Then they cried unto the Lord in their trouble, and he delivered them out of their distresses, he led them also by a straight way, that they might go to a city of habitation. *Ps. 107:4, 6, 7.*

Let not your heart be troubled, neither let it be fearful. *John 14:27.*

The Lamb that is in the midst of the throne shall be their shepherd, and shall guide them unto fountains of waters of life: and God shall wipe away every tear from their eyes. *Rev. 7:17.*

I do not ask, O Lord, that life may be
    A pleasant road:
I do not ask that Thou shouldst take from me
    Aught of the load; . . .
For one thing only, Lord, dear Lord, I plead,
    Lead me aright:
Though strength should falter and though heart should bleed,
    Through peace to light.
I do not ask, O Lord, that Thou shouldst shed
    Full radiance here;
Give but a ray of peace, that I may tread
    Without a fear.
I do not ask my cross to understand,
    My way to see —
Better in darkness just to feel Thy Hand
    And follow Thee.
Joy is like restless day, but peace divine
    Like quiet night:
Lead me, O Lord, till perfect day shall shine
    Through Peace to Light.   *Adelaide Procter.*

O GOD, by whom the meek are guided in judgment, and light riseth up in darkness for the godly; grant us in our doubts and uncertainties, the grace to ask what Thou wouldst have us to do; that the Spirit of wisdom may save us from false choices, and that in Thy light we may see light, and in Thy straight path may not stumble; through Jesus Christ, our Lord. [William Bright.]

He [the Devil] is a liar, and the father thereof. *John 8:44.*
No lie is of the truth. Who is the liar but he that denieth that Jesus is the Christ? *I John 2:21, 22.*
My people, . . . that will not deal falsely. *Isa. 63:8.*
God, who cannot lie. *Titus 1:2.*
The idle soul shall suffer hunger. *Prov. 19:15.*
The high priest [went in] alone. *Heb. 9:7.*

> Lie not, but let thy heart be true to God,
> Thy mouth to it, thy actions to them both:
> Cowards tell lies and those that fear the rod
> The stormie working soul spits lies and froth.
> Dare to be true. Nothing can mend a ly:
> A fault which needs it most grows two thereby.
>
> Flie idlenesse, which yet thou canst not flie
> By dressing, mistressing and compliment.
> If those take up thy day, the sunne will crie
> Against thee, for his light was only lent.
> God gave thy soul brave wings; put not those feathers
> Into a bed, to sleep out all ill weathers.
>
> By all means use some time to be alone.
> Salute thyself: see what thy soul doth wear.
> Dare to look in thy chest; for 'tis thine own:
> And tumble up and down what thou find'st there.
> Who cannot rest till he good fellowes finde,
> He breaks up house, turns out of doores his mind.
> *George Herbert.*

*A*LMIGHTY GOD, who hast sent the Spirit of Truth unto us to guide us into all truth, so rule our lives by Thy power, that we may be truthful in word, and deed, and thought. O keep us, most merciful Saviour, with Thy gracious protection, that no fear or hope may ever make us false in act or speech. Cast out from us whatever loveth or maketh a lie, and bring us all into the perfect freedom of Thy truth; through Jesus Christ, Thy Son, our Lord. [Bishop Westcott.]

Now then do it. *II Sam. 3:18.*

Whatsoever thy hand findeth to do, do it with thy might. *Eccl. 9:10.*

Look therefore carefully how ye walk, not as unwise, but as wise; redeeming the time. *Eph. 5:15, 16.*

Why stand ye here all the day idle. *Matt. 20:6.*

The people had a mind to work. *Neh. 4:6.*

Yet now be strong, O Zerubbabel, saith Jehovah; and be strong, O Joshua, son of Jehozadak, the high priest; and be strong, all ye people of the land, saith Jehovah, and work: for I am with you, saith Jehovah of hosts. *Hag. 2:4.*

Jesus answered, . . . We must work the works of him that sent me while it is day: the night cometh, when no man can work. *John 9:3, 4.*

> Lose this day loitering — 'twill be the same story
> Tomorrow — and the next more dilatory:
> When indecision brings its own delays
> And days are lost lamenting o'er lost days.
> Are you in earnest? Seize this very minute —
> What you can do — or dream you can — begin it.
> Courage has genius, power and magic in it.
> Only engage and then the mind grows heated —
> Begin it and the work will be completed.
>
> *Goethe.*

*W*E pray Thee, Master, today for power to deny ourselves, to lay down our lives for Thee: purge away our weakness, our timidity, our sloth: Set in us hearts gallant and high, hearts that yearn for the God-given hour when life may be yielded, death conquered, immortality put on, through faithful following of Thyself in the service of men: Show us Thy truth, that life must be always laid down if we would live, but that the highest glory and joy of Thy chosen valiant souls is to bear Thy Cross of self-giving, even to death. [J. S. Hoyland.]

THE PERFECT TEACHER

All these things spake Jesus in parables unto the multitudes; and without a parable spake he nothing unto them. *Matt. 13:34.*

The officers answered, Never man so spake. *John 7:46.*

The multitudes were astonished at his teaching: for he taught them as one having authority, and not as their scribes. *Matt. 7:28, 29.*

And the common people heard him gladly. *Mark 12:37.*

I cannot find truth in any one systematic view of it. I find it only in the doctrine of redemption. My object is to make and harmonize a system which shall make Christ the central point of all important religious truth and doctrine. *Henry B. Smith.*

It is not true that a preacher should uniformly accommodate himself to the more ignorant of his hearers. He who spoke as never man spoke adopted a style which confounded the lawyers, and even the disciples wondered what He could mean. . . . Therefore Smith's main difficulty in preaching was to interest the less enlightened of his audience. His main excellence was that he surmounted this difficulty; he became a preacher to the masses; the common people heard him gladly. *Edwards A. Park, on Henry B. Smith.*

Truth in closest words shall fail
  When truth embodied in a tale
Shall enter in at lowly doors.

Which they may read who bind the sheaf

Or build the house, or dig the grave,
Or those wild eyes which watch the wave
In roarings round the coral reef.
  Tennyson.

*L*ET not Thy word have been spoken in vain to us, but O Lord Jesus explain to us as Thou didst explain privately to Thy disciples long ago, the things that are hidden from us and may our hearts be open to Thine unfolding of Thy truth to us. And grant that we may be not hearers only, but doers of the same, and that it may bring forth the true fruits of salvation in our hearts. Turn not Thy face from us, and withdraw not Thy grace; lead us ever in the right way, keep us in the school of Thy instruction, and let Thy Holy Spirit encourage and enlighten us. [Weiss.]

ALL LOSS TO BE MADE UP

We all do fade as a leaf. *Isa. 64:6.*

All flesh is as grass, and all the glory thereof as the flower of grass. The grass withereth, and the flower falleth: But the word of the Lord abideth for ever. *1 Peter 1:24, 25.*

For I reckon that the sufferings of this present time are not worthy to be compared with the glory which shall be revealed to us-ward. For the earnest expectation of the creation waiteth for the revealing of the sons of God. *Rom. 8:18, 19.*

In him dwelleth all the fulness of the Godhead bodily, and in him ye are made full, who is the head of all principality and power. *Col. 2:9, 10.*

> To leave unseen so many a glorious sight,
>   To leave so many lands unvisited,
>   To leave so many worthiest books unread,
> Unrealized so many visions bright;
> O wretched, yet inevitable spite
>   Of our short span, and we must yield our breath
>   And wrap us in the lazy coil of death,
> So much remaining of unproved delight.
>   But hush, my soul, and vain regrets be stilled:
>   Find rest in Him who is the complement
>   Of whatso'er transcends your mortal doom
>   Of broken hope and frustrated intent;
>   In the clear vision and aspect of whom
>   All wishes and all longings are fulfilled.
>   *Richard C. Trench.*

GRANT to us, Lord, we beseech Thee, the spirit to think and do always such things as are right; that we, who cannot do anything that is good without Thee, may by Thee be enabled to live according to Thy will. . . . Grant us, O Lord, not to mind earthly things; but to love things heavenly; and even now, while we are placed among things that are passing away, to cleave to those that shall abide. Be present to our prayers, and protect us by day as well as by night, that in all successive changes of time we may ever be strengthened by Thine unchangeableness. [*Leonine Sacramentary.*]

THE COMMON FELLOWSHIP

And Joseph called the name of the first-born Manasseh: For, said he, God hath made me forget all my toil. *Gen. 41:51.*

Ye had fellowship with my affliction. *Phil. 4:14.*

Ready to distribute, ready to sympathize. *1 Tim. 6:18.*

Others have labored, ye are entered into their labor. *John 4:38.*

We are God's fellow-workers. *1 Cor. 3:9.*

Two are better than one, because they have a good reward for their labor. *Eccl. 4:9.*

None of us liveth to himself, none dieth to himself. *Rom. 14:7.*

Through love be servants one to another. *Gal. 5:13.*

> What are we set on earth for? Say, to toil;
> Nor seek to leave the tending of the vines
> For all the heat of the day till it declines
> And Death's mild curfew shall from work assoil.
> God did anoint thee with His odorous oil
> To wrestle, not to reign: and He assigns
> All thy tears over, like pure crystallines,
> For younger fellow-workers of the soil
> To wear for amulets. So others shall
> Take patience, labor, to their heart and hand
> From thy heart, and thy hand, and thy brave cheer,
> And God's grace fructify through thee to all.
> The least flower with a brimming cup may stand
> And share its dew-drop with another near.
> *E. B. Browning.*

God of our life, there are days when the burdens we carry chafe our shoulders and weigh us down, when the road seems dreary and endless, the skies grey and threatening; when our lives have no music in them, and our hearts are lonely, and our souls have lost their courage. Flood the path with light, we beseech Thee; turn our eyes to where the skies are full of promise; tune our hearts to brave music; give us the sense of comradeship with heroes and saints and the common folk of every age and of our own time; and so quicken our spirit that we may be able to encourage the souls of all who journey with us on the road of life, to Thy honour and glory. [*Acts of Devotion* (Altered).]

THE SHAME OF ASHAMEDNESS

Then all the disciples left him, and fled. *Matt. 26:56.*

Peter saith unto him, Even if I must die with thee, yet will I not deny thee. Likewise also said all the disciples. *Matt. 26:35.*

And [Peter] . . . denied with an oath, I know not the man. *Matt. 26:72.*

I thank him that enabled me, even Christ Jesus our Lord, for that he counted me faithful, appointing me to his service. *I Tim. 1:12.*

Be thou faithful unto death, and I will give thee the crown of life. *Rev. 2:10.*

If I had been in Palestine
A poor disciple I had been.
I had not risked or purse or limb,
All to forsake and follow Him.
   But with the vast and wondering
      throng
   I too had stood and listened long,
   I too had felt my spirit stirred
   When the Beatitudes I heard.
With the glad crowd that sang the
     psalm,
I too had sung, and strewed the palm:
Then slunk away in dastard shame
When the High Priest denounced His
   name.

But when my late companions cried,
   " Away! let Him be crucified! "
I would have begged with tremulous
   Pale lips, " Release Him unto us! "
Beside the cross when Mary prayed,
A great way off I too had stayed:
Not even in that hour had dared,
And for my dying Lord declared:
   But beat upon my craven breast,
   And loathed my coward heart, at
     least,
To think my life I dared not stake
And beard the Roman for His sake.
         Sarah N. Cleghorn.

*E*TERNAL GOD, who committest to us the swift and solemn trust of life; since we know not what a day may bring forth, but only that the hour for serving Thee is always present, may we wake to the instant claims of Thy holy will, not waiting for tomorrow, not faltering before the tests of today. Subdue by the persuasion of Thy Spirit, the resistance of our passion, indolence, or fear. Consecrate with Thy Presence the way our feet should go. Lift us above unrighteous anger, above cowardice and timidity, above mistrust into faith and hope and love and truth by simple and stedfast reliance on Thy sure will and in obedient loyalty. In all things draw us to the mind of Christ, that Thy lost image may be traced again. [James Martineau (Altered).]

THE TENANT OF THE HEART

My heart exulteth in the Lord. *I Sam. 2:1.*

When thou saidst, Seek ye my face; my heart said unto thee, Thy face, Jehovah, will I seek. *Ps. 27:8.*

From the end of the earth will I call unto thee, when my heart is overwhelmed: Lead me to the rock that is higher than I. *Ps. 61:2.*

There is in my heart as it were a burning fire. *Jer. 20:9.*

Spirit of God, descend upon my heart;
Wean it from earth; through all its pulses move;
Stoop to my weakness, mighty as Thou art,
And make me love Thee as I ought to love.

I ask no dream, no prophet ecstasies,
No sudden rending of the veil of clay,
No angel visitant, no opening skies;
But take the dimness of my soul away. . . .

Teach me to feel that Thou art always nigh;
Teach me the struggles of the soul to bear,
To check the rising doubt, the rebel sigh;
Teach me the patience of unanswered prayer.

Teach me to love Thee as Thine angels love,
One holy passion filling all my frame;
The baptism of the heaven-descended Dove,
My heart an altar, and Thy love the flame.   *George Croly.*

O FATHER of all, who art Wisdom and Beauty and Goodness, whose Spirit is ever striving to present Thee and Thy fullness of life and love to us, we thank Thee for the vision of Thyself in Thy Son our Lord and Saviour; for Thy divine compassion which cares for us despite our weakness, cowardice and self-love; for the discipline of life, for the endurance which is learnt through disappointment and drudgery; for the work which is its own reward, with the richness of the reward so often proportionate to the difficulty of our duty; for the difficulties themselves which are the material of victory, Thy victory in us; for Thy Church on earth, for the comfort and encouragement of the blessed company of Thy faithful people; and above all for Thy companionship with us always and in all things. [*The Kingdom, the Power and the Glory* (Adapted).]

He must reign, till he hath put all his enemies under his feet. *1 Cor. 15:25.*

Wherefore also God highly exalted him, and gave unto him the name which is above every name; that in the name of Jesus every knee should bow, of things in heaven and things on earth and things under the earth, and that every tongue should confess that Jesus Christ is Lord, to the glory of God the Father. *Phil. 2:9–11.*

The earth shall be filled with the knowledge of the glory of Jehovah, as the waters cover the sea. *Hab. 2:14.*

These things shall be: a loftier race
Than e'er the world hath known
shall rise
With flame of freedom in their souls
And light of knowledge in their
eyes.

They shall be gentle, brave, and strong,
To spill no drop of blood, but dare
All that may plant man's lordship firm
On earth, and fire, and sea, and
air. . . .

Nation with nation, land with land,
Inarmed shall live as comrades free;
In every heart and brain shall throb
The pulse of one fraternity.

New arts shall bloom of loftier mold,
And mightier music thrill the skies,
And every life shall be a song,
When all the earth is paradise.
J. A. Symonds.

OVERRULE, we pray Thee, O God, the passions and designs of men. Let Thy strong hand control the nations and bring forth out of the present discord a harmony more perfect than we can conceive, a new humility, a new understanding, a new purity and sincerity, a new sense of reality, a new hunger and thirst for Thy love to rule on the earth. [*Per Christum Vinces.*]

Lord, make me an instrument of Thy peace. Where there is hatred, let me sow love; where there is injury, pardon; where there is doubt, faith; where there is despair, hope; where there is darkness, light; and where there is sadness, joy. It is in pardoning that we are pardoned, in forgiving that we are ourselves forgiven, and in producing good will toward others that Thy peace comes to us. [Francis of Assisi (Adapted).]

EARTH AND HEAVEN

And I saw another angel ascend from the sunrising, having the seal of the living God: and he cried with a great voice to the four angels to whom it was given to hurt the earth and the sea, saying, Hurt not the earth, neither the sea, nor the trees, till we shall have sealed the servants of our God on their foreheads. *Rev. 7:2, 3.*

I saw another angel coming down out of heaven, having great authority; and the earth was lightened with his glory. *Rev. 18:1.*

The glory of the God of Israel came from the way of the east: and his voice was like the sound of many waters; and the earth shined with his glory. *Ezek. 43:2.*

God commendeth his own love toward us, in that, while we were yet sinners, Christ died for us. *Rom. 5:8.*

Love your enemies, and do them good, and lend, never despairing; and your reward shall be great, and ye shall be sons of the Most High: for he is kind toward the unthankful and evil. *Luke 6:35.*

> Oh, good gigantic smile o' the brown, old earth
> This autumn morning! How he sets his bones
> To bask i' the sun, and thrusts out knees and feet
> For the ripple to run over in its mirth:
>   Listening the while, where on the heap of stones
>   The white breast of the sealark twitters sweet.
>
> That is the doctrine, simple, ancient, true;
> Such is life's trial, as old Earth smiles and knows.
> If you loved only what were worth your love
> Love were clear gain, and wholly well for you:
>   Make the low nature better by your throes!
>   Give earth yourself, go up for gain above.   *Browning.*

O THOU who hast called us to be Thy guests and touched our temporal lives with the intimation of the Eternal, may the sense of the enduring brighten all the swift passing of time. Hallow our spirits and dignify all our enterprises by the revelation that we sojourn here upon Thine invitation, and may we so conduct ourselves as to be worthy of Thy Divine hospitality. In His Name who came to prepare for us a place in heavenly mansions.   [Gaius Glenn Atkins.]

He giveth unto his beloved sleep. *Ps. 127:2.*
The beloved of the Lord shall dwell in safety by him. *Deut. 33:12.*

Beloved, let us love one another: for love is of God. *I John 4:7.*
They are beloved for the fathers' sake. *Rom. 11:28.*
When he giveth quietness, who then can condemn? *Job 34:29.*
[He] giveth songs in the night. *Job 35:10.*
He giveth grace. *Prov. 3:34.*
[He] giveth the sun. *Jer. 31:35.*
He giveth power to the faint. *Isa. 40:29.*
[He] giveth life unto the world. *John 6:33.*

Of all the thoughts of God that are
Borne inward into souls afar
 Along the Psalmist's music deep,
Now tell me if there any is,
For gift, or grace surpassing this
 " He giveth His beloved sleep "?

What would we give to our beloved?
The hero's heart, to be unmoved,
 The poet's star-tuned harp to sweep,
The patriot's voice to teach and rouse,
The monarch's crown to light the
  brows?
 " He giveth His beloved sleep "?

What do we give to our beloved?
A little faith all undisproved,
 A little dust to overweep,
And bitter memories to make
The whole earth blasted for our sake.
 " He giveth His beloved sleep."

O earth so full of dreary noises!
O men with wailing in your voices!
 O delvéd gold, the wailers' heap!
O strife, O curse, that o'er it fall!
God strikes a silence through you all
 And giveth His beloved sleep.
     E. B. Browning.

O MOST gracious and loving Father, purify our souls from everything that may hide Thee from us. Do Thou who givest sleep give also waking. Let us feel Thy quickening power flowing through us, building us up into strength and goodness. . . .

O living Christ, make us conscious now of Thy healing nearness. Touch our eyes that we may see Thee; open our ears that we may hear Thy voice; enter our hearts that we may know Thy love. Overshadow our souls and bodies with Thy Presence, that we may partake of Thy strength, Thy love, Thy light and Thy healing Life. [*The Healing Messenger.*]

FULL RECOMPENSE

There came a woman having an alabaster cruse of ointment of pure nard very costly; and she brake the cruse, and poured it over his head. *Mark 14:3.*

Mary . . . anointed the feet of Jesus, and wiped his feet with her hair: and the house was filled with the odor of the ointment. *John 12:3.*

Came Mary Magdalene and the other Mary to see the sepulchre. . . . And behold, Jesus met them, saying, All hail. And they came and took hold of his feet, and worshipped him. *Matt. 28:1, 9.*

✦ Who hath first given to him, and it shall be recompensed unto him again? *Rom. 11:35.*

Our Saviour Christ Jesus . . . abolished death, and brought life and immortality to light. *II Tim. 1:10.*

> She brake the box and all the house was filled
>   With waftures from the fragrant store thereof,
> While at His feet a costlier rose distilled
>   The bruiséd balm of penitential love.
>
> And lo! as if in recompense of her
>   Bewildered in the lingering shades of night,
> He breaks anon the sealéd sepulchre,
>   And fills the world with rapture and with light.
>   *J. B. Tabb.*

MERCIFUL GOD, kind and loving Father, from danger to body and soul hast Thou protected us; with kindness beyond our ken hast Thou overwhelmed; Thou hast surpassed the little that we have done in Thy service with Thine own deeds of infinite love for us; Thou hast given us light for darkness and life for death; and with patience and forgiveness hast Thou borne with our faults and sins. We are not worthy of all the mercy and truth which Thou hast shown us, and we pray with hearty repentance for pardon of any evil we have done, or for anything wherein we have misused Thy grace. Lord, we hope in Thee. Let Thy gracious name shield us, and help us unto everlasting life; through Jesus Christ. [*Weimarischer Gesangbuch* (Altered).]

I am already being offered, and the time of my departure is come. I have fought the good fight, I have finished the course, I have kept the faith: henceforth there is laid up for me the crown of righteousness. *II Tim. 4:6–8.*

Though I walk through the valley of the shadow of death, I will fear no evil; for thou art with me. *Ps. 23:4.*

I was ever a fighter, so — one fight more,
  The best and the last!
I would hate that death bandaged my eyes, and forebore,
  And bade me creep past.
No! let me taste the whole of it, fare like my peers
  The heroes of old,
Bear the brunt, in a minute pay glad life's arrears
  Of pain, darkness and cold.
For sudden the worst turns the best to the brave,
  The black minute 's at end,
And the elements' rage, the fiend-voices that rave,
  Shall dwindle, shall blend,
Shall change, shall become first a peace out of pain,
  Then a light, then thy breast,
O thou soul of my soul! I shall clasp thee again,
  And with God be the rest!   *Robert Browning.*

*A*LMIGHTY GOD, keep us ever in mind that this world, with all the glory of it, fadeth and the fashion thereof passeth away. Grant that we may so use Thy gifts and all Thy temporal blessings, as we abuse them not, but may evermore serve Thee in Christian temperance and sobriety, as it becometh those who, living on earth, have their citizenship in heaven, that at the last we may be admitted into Thy Heavenly Kingdom, where we shall never hunger nor thirst again, being satisfied with the plenteousness of Thy house, and filled with the abundance of Thy pleasures for evermore. Take away from us all fear of death. Beyond and through its shadow may we see the everlasting light. We thank Thee that death is the *last* enemy and that beyond its sure defeat is eternal victory, through Jesus Christ, death's conqueror and our blessed Saviour. [Bishop Cosin (Altered).]

DELIVER HIM AND ME

Thou hast delivered my soul from death . . . , that I may walk before God in the light of the living. *Ps. 56:13.*

The Lord is merciful and gracious. *Ps. 103:8.*

I will be merciful to their iniquities, and their sins will I remember no more. *Heb. 8:12.*

And the prayer of faith shall save him that is sick, and the Lord shall raise him up; and if he have committed sins, it shall be forgiven him. *James 5:15.*

This shall turn out to my salvation, through your supplication. *Phil. 1:19.*

Be merciful, be gracious, spare him,
 Lord!
Be merciful, be gracious, Lord, de-
 liver him.
 From the sins that are past:
  From Thy frown and Thine ire:
  From the perils of dying,
  From any complying
  With sin, or denying
  His God, or relying
 On self at the last.
  From the nethermost fire:
  From all that is evil,

From the power of the devil,
 Thy servant deliver
 For once and forever,
By Thy Birth and by Thy Cross
Rescue him from endless loss,
By Thy Death and Burial
Save him from a final fall.
By Thy Rising from the tomb
 By Thy mounting up above,
 By Thy Spirit's gracious love
Save him in the day of doom.
 J. H. Newman.

O GOD, we pray for our kindred and friends, and for all who are dear to us that they may be preserved outwardly in their bodies, and inwardly in their souls, and that doing Thy will and rejoicing in Thy mercy and love here, they may be partakers of Thy joy hereafter. O God, we pray Thee to have compassion on those who are worn with toil; to bless and support all aged persons; to defend and bless all little children; to protect all who travel by land, sea, or air; to comfort all who are suffering in body or in mind; to extend Thy mercy to all who are oppressed, especially those who are "persecuted for righteousness' sake"; to deliver the tempted, and to bring back all who have wandered from Thy way. Hear us, O Heavenly Father, on behalf of all men; for the sake of Jesus Christ, our Lord and Saviour. [J. Hunter (Altered).]

THE GLORY THAT REMAINETH

Whosoever would save his life shall lose it: and whosoever shall lose his life for my sake shall find it. For what shall a man be profited, if he shall gain the whole world, and forfeit his life? or what shall a man give in exchange for his life? *Matt. 16:25, 26.*

I reckon that the sufferings of this present time are not worthy to be compared with the glory which shall be revealed to us-ward. *Rom. 8:18.*

The world passeth away, and the lust thereof: but he that doeth the will of God abideth for ever. *I John 2:17.*

> "Wilt thou trust death or not?" He answered "Yes!
> Hence with life's pale lure!"
> That low man seeks a little thing to do,
> Sees it and does it:
> This high man, with a great thing to pursue,
> Dies ere he knows it.
> That low man goes on adding one to one,
> His hundred 's soon hit:
> This high man, aiming at a million,
> Misses an unit.
> That, has the world here — should he need the next,
> Let the world mind him!
> This, throws himself on God, and unperplexed,
> Seeking shall find him.
>
> *Robert Browning.*

O GOD, in Thee alone can our wearied spirits find full satisfaction and rest, and in Thy love is the highest joy. Strengthen those of us and Thy people who are in any sorrow or perplexity, by the inward comfort of Thy Holy Spirit, and by the powers of the world to come, and bid us all know that our light affliction which is but for a moment, worketh for us a far more exceeding and eternal weight of glory: for there will come a time when Thou wilt bring us to the place of eternal rest, where we shall behold Thy face in righteousness and be satisfied from Thy eternal fulness, through Jesus Christ our Lord. [Melchior Ritter (Altered).]

BUILDING FOR ETERNITY

We know that if the earthly house of our tabernacle be dissolved we have a building from God, a house not made with hands, eternal, in the heavens. *II Cor. 5:1.*

Every one therefore that heareth these words of mine, and doeth them, shall be likened unto a wise man, who built his house upon the rock: and the rain descended, and the floods came, and the winds blew, and beat upon that house; and it fell not: for it was founded upon the rock. *Matt. 7:24, 25.*

What matters it to us who are immortal
Which side o' the grave we stand on, when we know
That what the world calls death is but the portal
Leading to life again? 'Tis but to go
Across a gurgling river in the dark
Hanging on God; and but a moment so
Till we are over, and we disembark
And enter life afresh. 'Tis basely wrong
We should so meanly understrike the mark
As measure life by years; and all along
Busy ourselves arranging little schemes
That death will dash to pieces, when we might
Be building, far above those earthly dreams
Houses that stand forever in God's sight.
Quoted in " A Highland Editor, James Barron."

OUR FATHER, unto Thee, in the light of our Saviour's blessed life and the comfortable assurance of our immortality, we would lift our souls. We thank Thee for all who have walked in that light and especially for those near to us and dear, in whose lives we have seen Thine excellent glory and beauty, who have builded on Thee and in whom Thou hast builded Thy habitation. May we know that in the body and out of the body they are with Thee, and that when these earthly days come to an end, it is not that our service of Thee and of one another may cease, but that it may begin anew and go on forever, in our house not made with hands, in our Father's House, eternal in the heavens. Make us glad in all who have faithfully lived: make us glad in all who have peacefully died. [Rufus Ellis (Altered).]

Having loved his own that were in the world, he loved them unto the end. *John 13:1.*

Love is strong as death; . . . many waters cannot quench love, neither can floods drown it. *S. of Sol. 8:6, 7.*

Herein is love made perfect with us, that we may have boldness in the day of judgment; because as he is, even so are we in this world. *1 John 4:17.*

Let love . . . continue. *Heb. 13:1.*

Love never faileth. *1 Cor. 13:8.*

They err who tell us love can die.
With life all other passions fly —
All others are but vanity.
In heaven ambition cannot dwell,
Nor avarice in the vaults of hell;
Earthly these passions of the earth,
They perish where they have their
   birth:
But love is indestructible.
Its holy flame forever burneth,

From heaven it came, to heaven re-
   turneth,
Too oft on earth a troubled guest,
At times deceived, at times opprest,
It here is tried and purified,
Then hath in heaven its perfect rest:
It soweth here with toil and care,
But the harvest time of love is there.
        Southey.

O BLESSED LORD and Saviour, who hast commanded us to love one another, grant us grace that, having received Thine undeserved bounty, we may love every man in Thee and for Thee. We beseech Thy blessing for all; but especially for the friends whom Thy love has given us. Love Thou them, O Thou fountain of love, and make them to love Thee with all their heart, with all their mind, and with all their soul, that those things only which are pleasing to Thee they may will and speak and do. And may their love and our love be made like Thy love, constant, unchanging, unchangeable which no waters can quench and which is stronger than death and every other enemy of love. Though our prayer is cold because our love is so little fervent and pure, yet Thou art rich in mercy. Measure not Thy goodness to us and to those we love by the dulness of our devotion; but as Thy kindness surpasseth all human affection, so let Thy hearing transcend our prayer. [Saint Anselm (Altered).]

THE CHILDREN IN HEAVEN

Then was fulfilled that which was spoken through Jeremiah the prophet saying,

A voice was heard in Ramah, weeping and great mourning, Rachel weeping for her children; and she would not be comforted, because they are not. *Matt. 2:17, 18.*

He will gather the lambs in his arm, and carry them in his bosom. *Isa. 40:11.*

Great shall be the peace of thy children. *Isa. 54:13.*

They scarcely waked before they slept,
They scarcely wept before they laughed
They drank indeed death's bitterest
  draught,
But all its bitterest dregs were kept
And drained by mothers while they
  wept.

From Heaven the speechless infants
  speak:
Weep not (they say), our mothers dear,
For swords nor sorrows come not here.
Now we are strong who were so weak
And all is ours we could not seek.

We bloom among the blooming flow-
  ers
We sing among the singing birds;
Wisdom we have who wanted words;
Here morning knows not evening
  hours
All's rainbow here without its show-
  ers.

And softer than our mother's breast,
And closer than our mother's arm,
Is here the love that keeps us warm
And broods above our happy nest.
Dear mothers, come, for heaven is best.
                    Christina Rossetti.

*H*EAVENLY FATHER, hear our voice out of the deep sorrow which Thou in Thy mysterious wisdom hast brought upon us. Thou gavest and Thou hast taken away, blessed be Thy Name. Our children are safe and happy in Thy keeping. We are content and glad to think of them as they follow their Shepherd in the green fields of Paradise. Keep our souls from all the temptations of unworthy and unfaithful mourning, that we may neither sorrow as those without hope, nor lose our trust in Thee. And grant that the remnant of this our family, O Lord, still being upon earth, may be steadfast in faith, joyful through hope, and rooted in love, and that finally we may come to the land of everlasting life, there to meet again all that we have loved and there to reign with Thee, world without end: through Jesus Christ our Lord. [L. Tuttiett (Altered).]

For indeed we that are in this tabernacle do groan, being burdened; not for that we would be unclothed, but that we would be clothed upon, that what is mortal may be swallowed up of life. *II Cor. 5:4.*

Looking for the blessed hope and appearing of the glory of the great God and our Saviour Jesus Christ. *Titus 2:13.*

What was their tale of some one on a summit
　　Looking, I think, upon the endless sea, —
One with a fate and sworn to overcome it,
　　One who was fettered and who should be free?

Round him a robe, for shaming and for searing,
　　Ate with impoisonment and stung with fire.
He through it all was to his Lord uprearing
　　Desperate patience of a brave desire.

Ay and for me there shot from the beginning
　　Pulses of passion, broken with my breath;
O thou poor soul, enwrapped in such a sinning,
　　Bound in the shameful body of thy death!

Well, let me sin, but not with my consenting,
　　Well, let me die, but willing to be whole.
Never, O Christ, so stay me from relenting,
　　Shall there be truce between my flesh and soul. . . .

So even I, and with a pang more thrilling,
　　So even I, and with a hope more sweet,
Yearn for the sign, O Christ! of Thy fulfilling,
　　Faint for the flaming of Thine advent feet.　　*F. W. H. Myers.*

Aʟᴍɪɢʜᴛʏ ɢᴏᴅ, our Heavenly Father, who hast given us in Thy Son Jesus Christ a fountain of life, which, springing up within us, can make all things new, we thank Thee for the deeper meaning which He gives to life. . . . In the power of His Spirit may our griefs be transformed into consolations, our infirmities into strength to do well, our sins into repentance, our fainting and halting spirits into a heavenly mind; and finally the doubts, the discouragements, the trials of this earthly life, into the full assurance and unclouded bliss of an eternal life with Thee, through the same Jesus Christ our Lord.　[Henry W. Foote.]

And the common people heard him gladly. *Mark 12:37.*

Behold, . . . a friend of publicans and sinners! *Matt. 11:19.*

All that which the Father giveth me shall come unto me; and him that cometh to me I will in no wise cast out. *John 6:37.*

If a man love me, he will keep my word: and my Father will love him, and we will come unto him, and make our abode with him. *John 14:23.*

His teaching "was no narrow doctrine, designed for a narrow circle of the initiated; nor was it a scholastic or scientific doctrine, designed for the scholarly and the cultured. It was a message of universally intelligible import, designed for all classes of people, rich and poor, young and old, if they would but hearken and receive it." [Wendt, *The Teaching of Jesus.*]

Lord Christ, beneath Thy starry dome
We light this flickering lamp of home,
And where bewildering shadows throng
Uplift our prayer and evensong.
Dost Thou, with heaven in Thy ken
Seek still a dwelling place with men,
Wandering the world in ceaseless quest?
O Man of Nazareth, be our guest!

Lord Christ, the bird his nest has found,
The fox is sheltered in his ground,
But dost Thou still this dark earth tread
And have no place to lay Thy head?
Shepherd of mortals, here behold
A little flock, a wayside fold
That wait Thy Presence to be blest —
O Man of Nazareth, be our guest!

Daniel Henderson.

O LORD JESUS CHRIST, who when Thou wast here upon the earth in the days of Thy flesh didst love to talk with common folk just like us who now speak to Thee, and to visit them in their homes, come now to us, we pray Thee. We hear Thee gladly and we have room for Thee in our homes and in our hearts. Thou needest not now to wander homeless. There is warm and waiting room in our hearts for Thee. Be pleased to enter, Lord. Whatever Thou dost find uncongenial to Thy Presence cast out from us — all uncharitableness and pride and selfishness and sin. Take full possession for Thyself alone and fill the place of Thine abode with Thine own holiness and joy and love. [R. E. S.]

DAVID LIVINGSTONE

I delivered the poor that cried, the fatherless also, that had none to help him. The blessing of him that was ready to perish came upon me; and I caused the widow's heart to sing for joy. I put on righteousness, and it clothed me: my justice was as a robe and a diadem. I was eyes to the blind, and feet was I to the lame. I was a father to the needy: and the cause of him that I knew not I searched out. And I brake the jaws of the unrighteous and plucked the prey out of his teeth. *Job 29:12–17.*

Droop, half mast colors, bow, bare-headed crowds.
   As this plain coffin o'er the side is slung,
To pass by woods of masts and ratlined shrouds
   As erst by Afric's trunks, liana hung.

'Tis the last mile of many thousands, trod
   With failing strength, but never failing will
By the worn frame, now at its rest with God
   That never rested in its strife with ill.

He knew not that the trumpet he had blown
   Out of the darkness of that dismal land
Had reached and roused an army of its own,
   To strike the chains from the slave's fettered hand.

Open the Abbey doors and bear him in,
   To sleep with king and statesmen, chief and sage,
The missionary come of weaver kin
   But great by work which brooks no lower wage.

He needs no epitaph to guard a name
   Which men shall prize while worthy work is known.
He lived and died for good, be this his fame.
   Let marble crumble, this is Living-stone.
   Punch, *on Livingstone's Burial in Westminster Abbey.*

O JESUS, Thou King of Saints, whom all Adore: I Admire to see Thy Cross in every Understanding, Thy Passion in every Memory, Thy Crown of Thorns in every Eye, and Thy Bleeding, Naked Wounded Body in every Soul. [Thomas Traherne.]

THE SIGNIFICANCE OF THE SMALL

God chose the weak things of the world, that he might put to shame the things that are strong; . . . yea and the things that are not, that he might bring to nought the things that are: that no flesh should glory before God. *I Cor. 1:27-29.*

And he [Gideon] said unto him [Jehovah], Oh, Lord, wherewith shall I save Israel? behold, my family is the poorest in Manasseh, and I am the least in my father's house. And Jehovah said unto him, Surely I will be with thee, and thou shalt smite the Midianites as one man. *Judg. 6:15, 16.*

But thou Beth-lehem Ephrathah, which art little to be among the thousands of Judah, out of thee shall one come forth unto me that is to be ruler in Israel; whose goings forth are from of old, from everlasting. *Micah 5:2.*

As for me my bed is made: I am against bigness and greatness in all their forms, and with the invisible, molecular, moral forces that work from individual to individual, stealing in through the crannies of the world like so many soft rootlets, or like the capillary oozing of water, and yet rending the hardest monuments of man's pride, if you give them time. The bigger the unit you deal with, the hollower, the more brutal, the more mendacious is the life displayed. So I am against all big organizations as such . . . and in favor of the eternal forces of truth which always work in the individual and immediately unsuccessful way, underdogs always until history comes, after they are long dead, and puts them on top. *William James.*

O GOD, our Father, to whose thought and love all things are of concern, both great and small, who hast chosen the weak things of the world that Thou mightst put to shame the things that are strong, we thank Thee that our little lives are great in Thy sight, so that for us men and for our salvation Thou didst give Thine only-begotten Son, the Lord of Glory, and art able to use us to establish His Kingdom, and we rejoice that Thy wisdom and righteousness and sanctification and redemption are to be wrought out in us, small and unworthy as we are, through Him and His greatness and infinite worth. [R. E. S.]

And working together with him we entreat also that ye receive not the grace of God in vain . . . but in everything commending ourselves as ministers of God . . . ; as unknown, and yet well known; as dying, and behold, we live; as chastened, and not killed; as sorrowful, yet always rejoicing; as poor, yet making many rich; as having nothing, and yet possessing all things. *Il Cor. 6:1, 4, 9, 10.*

Far be it from me to glory, save in the cross of our Lord Jesus Christ, through which the world hath been crucified unto me, and I unto the world. *Gal. 6:14.*

Lo, the kingdom of God is within you. *Luke 17:21.*

If we have become united with him in the likeness of his death, we shall be also in the likeness of his resurrection. *Rom. 6:5.*

> O gain that lurk'st ungained in all gain!
> O love we just fall short of in all love!
> O height that in all heights art still above!
> O beauty that dost leave all beauty pain!
> Thou unpossessed that mak'st possession vain!
> See these strained arms that fright the simple air
> And say what ultimate fairness holds thee, Fair!
> They girdle Heaven, and girdle Heaven in vain;
> They shut, and lo! but shut in their unrest.
> Thereat a voice in me that voiceless was: —
> "Whom seekest thou through the unmarged arcane
> And not discern'st to thine own bosom prest? "
> I looked. My claspéd arms athwart my breast
> Framed the august embraces of the Cross.
>
> *Francis Thompson.*

ALMIGHTY and everlasting God, we most heartily thank Thee that Thou dost vouchsafe to feed us with the food of the most precious body and blood of Thy Son our Saviour Jesus Christ, who died for us upon the Cross, and that Thou dost assure us thereby of Thy favor and goodness toward us, and that united to Him in His death we are also one with Him in His risen life and very members incorporate in the mystical body of Thy Son which is the blessed company of all faithful people. [*The Book of Common Prayer* (Altered).]

THE SERVICE OF PATIENCE

And she [Martha] had a sister called Mary, who also sat at the Lord's feet, and heard his word. But Martha was cumbered about much serving; and she came up to him, and said, Lord, dost thou not care that my sister did leave me to serve alone? bid her therefore that she help me. But the Lord answered and said unto her, Martha, Martha, thou art anxious and troubled about many things: but one thing is needful: for Mary hath chosen the good part, which shall not be taken away from her. *Luke 10:39-42.*

Jehovah is good unto them that wait for him, to the soul that seeketh him. It is good that a man should hope and quietly wait for the salvation of Jehovah. *Lam. 3:25, 26.*

I John, your brother and partaker with you in the tribulation and kingdom and patience which are in Jesus. *Rev. 1:9.*

> When I consider how my light is spent
> Ere half my days, in this dark world and wide,
> And that one talent, which is death to hide,
> Lodged with me useless, though my soul more bent
> To serve therewith my Maker, and present
> My true account lest He returning chide;
> "Doth God exact day-labor, light denied?"
> I fondly ask. But patience to prevent
> That murmur, soon replies, God doth not need
> Either man's work or His own gifts; who best
> Bear His mild yoke, they serve Him best: His state
> Is kingly. Thousands at His bidding speed
> And post o'er land and ocean without rest:
> They also serve who only stand and wait.
> *John Milton, On His Blindness.*

O FAITHFUL, ever-blessed Father, who dost keep us in an holy fellowship, grant, we pray Thee, to all of Thy servants the support of Thy steadfastness. Assist us in our warfare against sin and in the fulfillment of our daily duty. . . . And, O God of peace, who hast taught us that in returning and rest we shall be saved, that in quietness and confidence shall be our strength, by the might of Thy Spirit uphold and strengthen us that we may be still and know that Thou art God.

And he will destroy in this mountain the face of the covering that covereth all peoples, and the veil that is spread over all nations. *Isa. 25:7.*

Whensoever a man shall turn to the Lord, the veil is taken away. *II Cor. 3:16 and margin.*

I came to cast fire upon the earth; and how would I that it were already kindled! *Luke 12:49 and margin.*

Was not our heart burning within us, while he spake to us in the way, while he opened to us the scriptures? *Luke 24:32.*

> Fain would I wish what my heart cannot will.
>   Between it and the fire a veil of ice
>   Deadens the fire, so that I deal in lies;
> My words and actions are discordant still,
> I love Thee with my tongue, then mourn my fill;
>   For love warms not my heart, nor can I rise,
>   Or open the doors of grace, who from the skies
> Might flood my soul, and pride and passion kill.
> Rend Thou the veil, dear Lord! Break Thou that wall
>   Which with its stubbornness retards the rays
>   Of that bright sun this earth hath dulled for me!
> Send down Thy promised light to cheer and fall
>   On Thy fair spouse, that I with love may blaze,
>   And, free from doubt, my heart feel only Thee.
>   *J. A. Symonds.*

MY heart needs Thee, O Lord, my heart needs Thee. *No* part of my being needs Thee like my heart. All else within me can be filled by Thy *gifts.* But no outward thing can make my *heart* pure. The calmest day will not calm my passions. This world has not provided for my *heart.* Provide Thou for my heart, O Lord! Be *Thou* the strength of my heart. Be Thou its fortress in temptation, its shield in remorse, its covert in the storm, its star in the night, its voice in the solitude! Guide it in the gloom; help it in its heat; direct it in its doubt; calm it in its conflict; fan it in its faithfulness; prompt it in its perplexity; lead it through its labyrinths; raise it from its ruins! *I* cannot rule this heart of mine; keep it under the shadow of Thine own wings. [George Matheson (Altered).]

CAN THE ANCIENT LEISURE
BE REGAINED?

Know therefore that Jehovah thy God, he is God, the faithful God, who keepeth covenant and lovingkindness with them that love him and keep his commandments to a thousand generations. *Deut. 7:9.*

Lord, thou hast been our dwelling-place in all generations. . . . Even from everlasting to everlasting, thou art God. . . . For a thousand years in thy sight are but as yesterday when it is past. *Ps. 90:1, 2, 4.*

I have considered the days of old, the years of ancient times. *Ps. 77:5.*

I am he; I am the first, I also am the last. Yea, my hand hath laid the foundation of the earth, and my right hand hath spread out the heavens: when I call unto them, they stand up together. . . . Come ye near unto me, hear ye this; from the beginning I have not spoken in secret; from the time that it was, there am I. *Isa. 48:12, 13, 16.*

Man's life was spacious in the early world:
It paused, like some slow ship with sail unfurled,
Waiting in seas by scarce a wavelet curled:
Behind the slow star spaces of the skies,
And grew from strength to strength through centuries:
Saw infant trees fill out their giant limbs
And heard a thousand times the sweet birds' marriage hymns.
Time was but leisure to their lingering thought,
There was no need for haste to finish aught:
But sweet beginnings were repeated still,
Like infant babblings that no task fulfill,
For love, that loved not change, constrained the simple will.
George Eliot.

HEAVENLY FATHER, we are thankful because Thou hast put into our minds a remembrance of Thee. We know how far we have gone away from the light and joy and peace which belong in Thy Presence. We see ourselves, although dimly, through Thy revelation and we understand more clearly what poverty is ours since we deserted Thee. In utter loneliness and despair we desire, O God, to come back unto Thy house. Forgive us, we pray Thee, and receive us once again in Thy love.

Consider the lilies of the field. *Matt. 6:28.*

And he will destroy in this mountain the face of the covering that covereth all peoples, and the veil that is spread over all nations. He hath swallowed up death for ever; and the Lord Jehovah will wipe away tears from off all faces; and the reproach of his people will he take away from off all the earth. *Isa. 25:7, 8.*

A veil lieth upon their heart. But whensoever a man shall turn to the Lord, the veil is taken away. *II Cor. 3:15, 16 and margin.*

To a Daisy

Slight as thou art, thou art enough to hide,
    Like all created things, secrets from me,
    And stand a barrier to eternity.
And I, how can I praise thee well and wide

From where I dwell — upon the hither side?
    Thou little veil for so great mystery,
    When shall I penetrate all things and thee,
And then look back? For this I must abide,

Till thou shalt grow and be unfurled
Literally between me and the world,
    Then I shall drink from in beneath a spring,

And from a poet's side shall read his book.
O daisy mine, what will it be to look
    From God's side even of such a simple thing?
                                        Alice Meynell.

O GOD, of whose gift come sunshine and friendship and the glory of spring time, who in the common things of daily life givest to us Thy very self, making of bread and wine the sacrament of Thy sustaining Presence, strengthen and refresh us that we may seek Thee eagerly, find Thee surely, and serve Thee faithfully, discovering in common occasions and in small things our opportunity to live unto Thee, to serve and love Thee, to do good to our fellows and to glorify the Lord and Master who did always in little things and in great that which pleased Thee. [*The Abiding Presence* (Altered).]

The whole world. For God so loved the world, that he gave his only begotten Son, that whosoever believeth on him should not perish, but have eternal life. *John 3:16.*

The single soul. Who loved me, and gave himself up for me. *Gal. 2:20.*

The single sheep. What man of you, having a hundred sheep, and having lost one of them, doth not leave the ninety and nine in the wilderness, and go after that which is lost, until he find it? *Luke 15:4.*

The multitude. And he came forth and saw a great multitude, and he had compassion on them. *Mark 6:34.*

> The human race
> To you, means such a child or such a man
> You saw one morning waiting in the cold
> Beside that gate, perhaps. . . . Why I call you hard
> To general suffering. . . .
>
> Does one of you
> Stand still from dancing, stop from stringing pearls
> And pine and die because of the great sum
> Of universal anguish? . . . You cannot count
> That you should weep for this account; not you.
> You weep for what you know. A red-haired child,
> Sick in a fever, if you touch him once,
> Though but so little as with a single tip,
> Will set you weeping; but for a million sick,
> You could as soon weep for the rule of three
> Or compound fractions.   *E. B. Browning.*

O LORD JESUS CHRIST, we thank Thee that Thy love is a love for the whole world of men and also for each single child of Thy Father's human family. Help us to love with like love to Thine, to see both human need and human needs and the very bodies of the needy, not altogether only but also one by one; to be moved both by human hunger and wrong and also by the hungers and wrongs of persons whom we can know and whom we can serve and in whom we can find Thee and minister to Thee according to Thy word. " Inasmuch as ye have done it unto these, ye have done it unto Me." [R. E. S.]

Thus saith Jehovah, Hast thou seen all this great multitude? behold, I will deliver it into thy hand this day; and thou shalt know that I am Jehovah. And Ahab said, By whom? And he [Elisha] said, Thus saith Jehovah, By the young men of the princes of the provinces. Then he said, Who shall begin the battle? And he answered, Thou. *1 Kings 20:13, 14.*

Curse ye Meroz, said the angel of Jehovah, curse ye bitterly the inhabitants thereof, because they came not to the help of Jehovah, to the help of Jehovah against the mighty. *Judg. 5:23.*

This charge I commit unto thee, my child Timothy, according to the prophecies which led the way to thee, that by them thou mayest war the good warfare, holding faith and a good conscience. *1 Tim. 1:18, 19.*

God's trumpet wakes the slumbering
    world;
  Now each man to his post!
The red-cross banner is unfurled:
  Who joins the glorious host? . . .

He who, no anger on his tongue,
  Nor any idle boast,
Bears steadfast witness against
    wrong —
  He joins the sacred host.

He who with calm undaunted will
  Ne'er counts the battle lost,
But, though defeated, battles still —
  He joins the faithful host.

He who is ready for the cross,
  The cause despised loves most,
And shuns not pain or shame or
    loss —
  He joins the martyr host.
              Samuel Longfellow.

Thou wast their Rock, their Fortress, and their Might;
Thou, Lord, their Captain in the well-fought fight;
Thou, in the darkness drear, their one true Light.
O may Thy soldiers, faithful, true, and bold,
Fight as the saints who nobly fought of old,
And win with them the victor's crown of gold. . . .
And when the strife is fierce, the warfare long,
Steals on the ear the distant triumph-song,
And hearts are brave again, and arms are strong.
The golden evening brightens in the west;
Soon, soon to faithful warriors comes their rest;
Sweet is the calm of Paradise the blest. Alleluia!
              William Walsham How.

THE CONQUEROR

Have this mind in you, which was also in Christ Jesus: who, existing in the form of God, counted not the being on an equality with God a thing to be grasped, but emptied himself, taking the form of a servant, being made in the likeness of men; and being found in fashion as a man, he humbled himself, becoming obedient even unto death, yea, the death of the cross. Wherefore also God highly exalted him, and gave unto him the name which is above every name; that in the name of Jesus every knee should bow, of things in heaven and things on earth and things under the earth, and that every tongue should confess that Jesus Christ is Lord, to the glory of God the Father. *Phil. 2:5–11.*

Who is the blessed and only Potentate, the King of kings, and Lord of lords. *1 Tim. 6:15.*

No longer of Him be it said,
"He hath no place to lay His head."

In every land a constant lamp
Flames by His small and mighty camp.

There is no strange and distant place
That is not gladdened by His face.

And every nation kneels to hail
The splendor shining through its veil.

Cloistered beside the shouting street,
Silent, He calls me to His feet.

Imprisoned for His love of me,
He makes my spirit greatly free.

And through my life that uttered sin
The King of Glory enters in.
                                    Joyce Kilmer.

Our blessed Lord Jesus Christ, who for the love of man didst lay aside the glory which Thou hadst with the Father before the world was and didst humble Thyself to be born of a Virgin and to take on Thee our human flesh and to live our human life, and to drink the cup of our human suffering and death, we thank Thee that by Thy humility Thou art exalted and art raised over death as the Prince of Life, and art yet to reign in power and glory over all things as Lord of lords and King of kings. Be pleased, we beseech Thee, to set Thine authority in our minds and hearts, that Thy Kingdom may begin in us. For us Thou didst humble Thyself. In us now, O blessed Saviour, be Thou exalted. Hear us, we pray Thee, as we bow before Thee and in joy and love confess that Thou art Lord, to the glory of God the Father. [R. E. S.]

Seek ye the Lord while he may be found; call ye upon him while he is near. *Isa. 55:6.*

To-day, oh that ye would hear his voice! Harden not your heart. *Ps. 95:7, 8.*

Behold, now is the acceptable time; behold, now is the day of salvation. *II Cor. 6:2.*

It is appointed unto men once to die, and after this cometh judgment. *Heb. 9:27.*

Opportunity

Master of human destinies am I!
Fame, love and fortune on my footsteps wait.
Cities and fields I walk. I penetrate
Deserts and seas remote, and passing by
Hovel and mart and palace, soon or late,
I knock unbidden once at every gate!
If sleeping, wake! If feasting, rise before
I turn away. It is the hour of fate,
And they who follow me reach every state
Mortals desire, and conquer every foe
Save death: but those who doubt or hesitate,
Condemned to failure, penury and woe
Seek me in vain and uselessly implore.
I answer not and I return no more.   *John J. Ingalls.*

ALMIGHTY and most merciful Father; We have erred, and strayed from thy ways like lost sheep. We have followed too much the devices and desires of our own hearts. We have offended against thy holy laws. We have left undone those things which we ought to have done; And we have done those things which we ought not to have done; And there is no health in us. But thou, O Lord, have mercy upon us, miserable offenders. Spare thou those, O God, who confess their faults. Restore thou those who are penitent; According to thy promises declared unto mankind In Christ Jesus our Lord. And grant, O most merciful Father, for his sake; That we may hereafter live a godly, righteous, and sober life, To the glory of thy holy Name. [*The Book of Common Prayer.*]

God hath spoken once, twice have I heard this, that power belongeth unto God. *Ps. 62:11.*

The Lord thy God . . . will return and gather thee. . . . And thou shalt return and obey the voice of the Lord, and do all his commandments. . . . For the Lord will again rejoice over thee for good, . . . if thou turn unto the Lord thy God with all thy heart, and with all thy soul. *Deut. 30:3, 8–10.*

Answer to " Opportunity "

They do me wrong who say I come no more
 When once I knock and fail to find you in;
For every day I stand outside your door,
 And bid you wake and rise to fight and win. . . .

Though deep in mire, wring not your hands and weep.
 I lend my arm to all who say " I can."
No shame-faced outcast ever sank so deep
 But might arise and be again a man.

Dost thou behold thy lost youth all aghast?
 Dost reel from righteous retribution's blow?
Then turn from blotted archives of the past
 And find the future's pages white as snow.

Art thou a mourner? Rouse thee from thy spell;
 Art thou a sinner? Sins may be forgiven.
Each morning gives thee wings to flee from hell,
 Each night a star to guide thy feet to heaven.
         Walter Malone.

GIVE ear, O Lord, unto my prayer; attend unto the voice of my supplication. In the day of trouble will I call upon Thee, for Thou wilt answer me. Lord, I cry unto Thee: make haste to help me. Forsake me not, my God, be not far from me; make haste to help me, O Lord, my salvation. Preserve me, O God, for in Thee do I put my trust. O keep my soul, and deliver me; let me not be ashamed, for I put my trust in Thee. Show Thy marvelous lovingkindness, O Thou that savest them which put their trust in Thee. [*The Devotional Companion.*]

MUTUAL OWNERSHIP

Know ye not that your body is a temple of the Holy Spirit which is in you, which ye have from God? and ye are not your own; for ye were bought with a price: glorify God therefore in your body. *1 Cor. 6:19, 20.*

Ye were redeemed . . . with precious blood, . . . even the blood of Christ. *1 Peter 1:18, 19.*

God, being rich in mercy, for his great love wherewith he loved us, even when we were dead through our trespasses, made us alive together with Christ (by grace have ye been saved), and raised us up with him, and made us to sit with him in the heavenly places, in Christ Jesus. *Eph. 2:4-6.*

> Lord, I am Thine, and Thou art mine;
> So mine Thou art, that something more
> I may presume Thee mine then Thine,
> For Thou didst suffer to restore
> Not Thee, but me, and to be mine:
> And with advantage mine the more,
> Since Thou in death wast none of Thine,
> Yet then as mine didst me restore:
> O be mine still! still make me Thine!
> Or rather make me Thine and mine!
>
> *George Herbert.*

Let Thy love so warm our souls, O Lord, that we may gladly surrender ourselves with all we are and have unto Thee. Let Thy love fall as fire from heaven upon the altar of our hearts; teach us to guard it heedfully by continual devotion and quietness of mind, and to cherish with anxious care every spark of its holy flame with which Thy good Spirit would quicken us, so that neither height nor depth, nor things present nor things to come, may ever separate us therefrom. Strengthen Thou our souls; awaken us from the deathly sleep which holds us captive; animate our cold hearts with Thy warmth and tenderness, that we may no more live as in a dream, but walk before Thee as pilgrims in earnest to reach their home. And grant us all at last to meet with Thy holy saints before Thy throne, and there rejoice in Thy love for ever and ever. [Gerhard Tersteegen.]

ALONE AND NOT ALONE

At my first defence no one took my part, but all forsook me. . . .
But the Lord stood by me, and strengthened me; that through me the
message might be fully proclaimed. . . . The Lord will deliver me from
every evil work, and will save me unto his heavenly kingdom. *II Tim.
4:16–18.*

Putting away therefore all wickedness, and all guile, and hypocri-
sies, and envies, and all evil speakings, as newborn babes, long for the
spiritual milk which is without guile, that ye may grow thereby unto
salvation; if ye have tasted that the Lord is gracious; unto whom coming,
a living stone, rejected indeed of men, but with God elect, precious, ye
also, as living stones, are built up a spiritual house, to be a holy priesthood, to offer up spiritual sacrifices, acceptable to God through Jesus
Christ. *I Peter 2:1–5.*

He came to the desert of London town
  Grey miles long;
He wandered up and he wandered down,
  Singing a quiet song.

There were thousands and thousands of human kind
  In this desert of brick and stone:
But some were deaf, and some were blind,
  And he was there alone.

At length the good hour came; he died
  As he had lived, alone:
He was not missed from the desert wide,
  Perhaps he was found at the throne.
                              James Thomson, on William Blake.

O JESUS CHRIST, the Lord of all good life, who hast called us to
build the City of God, do Thou enrich and purify our lives and deepen
in us our discipleship. Help us daily to know more of Thee, and through
us, by the power of Thy Holy Spirit, show forth Thyself to other men.
Make us humble, brave and loving: make us ready for adventure. We
do not ask that Thou wilt keep us safe but that Thou wilt keep us loyal,
who for us didst face death unafraid and dost live and reign forever
and ever. [From *The Kingdom, the Power and the Glory.*]

THE GOOD FIGHT

And I saw the heaven opened; and behold, a white horse, and he that sat thereon called Faithful and True; and in righteousness he doth judge and make war. *Rev. 19:11.*

Suffer hardship with me, as a good soldier of Christ Jesus. No soldier on service entangleth himself with the affairs of this life; that he may please him who enrolled him as a soldier. *II Tim. 2:3, 4.*

> Long since, in sore distress, I heard one pray:
> " Lord, who prevailest with resistless might,
> Ever from war and strife keep me away;
> My battles fight! "
>
> I know not if I play the Pharisee,
> And if my brother after all be right;
> But mine shall be the warrior's plea to Thee —
> Strength for the fight.
>
> I do not ask that Thou shalt front the fray,
> And drive the warring foeman from my sight;
> I only ask, O Lord, by night, by day,
> Strength for the fight.
>
> When foes upon me press, let me not quail,
> Nor think to turn me into coward flight.
> I only ask, to make mine arms prevail,
> Strength for the fight.
>
> And when, at eventide, the fray is done,
> My soul to Death's bed-chamber do Thou light,
> And grant me, be the field or lost or won,
> Rest from the fight.   *Paul Lawrence Dunbar.*

ALMIGHTY GOD, who seest that we have no power of ourselves to help ourselves; Keep us both outwardly in our bodies, and inwardly in our souls; that we may be defended from all adversities which may happen to the body, and from all evil thoughts which may assault and hurt the soul; through Jesus Christ our Lord. [*The Book of Common Prayer.* Collect for Second Sunday in Lent.]

IN GOD'S HOLY KEEPING

Look therefore carefully how ye walk, not as unwise, but as wise; redeeming the time, because the days are evil. *Eph. 5:15, 16.*

All things that are mine are thine, and thine are mine: and I am glorified in them. . . . And the glory which thou hast given me I have given unto them; that they may be one, even as we are one; I in them, and thou in me, that they may be perfected into one. . . . Father, I desire that they also whom thou hast given me be with me where I am, that they may behold my glory, which thou has given me. *John 17:10, 22–24.*

I have been crucified with Christ; and it is no longer I that live, but Christ liveth in me: and that life which I now live in the flesh I live in faith, the faith which is in the Son of God, who loved me, and gave himself up for me. *Gal. 2:20.*

> These Houres and that which hovers o'er my End
> Into Thy hands and hart, Lord, I commend.
>
> Take both to Thine account, that I and mine
> In that Hour, and in these, may be all Thine.
>
> That as I dedicate my devoutest Breath
> To make a kind of Life for my Lord's Death,
>
> So from His living, and life-giving Death
> My dying Life may draw a new and never fleeting Breath.
> *Richard Crashaw.*

O LORD, grant that our hearts may be truly cleansed, and filled with Thy Holy Spirit, and that we may arise to serve Thee, in entire confidence and submission to Thy will, ready to do and to endure whatsoever Thou hast appointed for us. Let us live for the day, not overcharged with worldly cares, but feeling that our treasure is not here, and desiring truly to be joined to Thee in Thy heavenly kingdom, and to those who are already gone to Thee. O Lord, save us from sin, and guide us with Thy Spirit, and keep us in faithful obedience to Thee, through Jesus Christ our Lord. [*The Book of Common Worship,* Revised.]

Now hath Christ been raised from the dead, the firstfruits of them that are asleep. *1 Cor. 15:20.*

Christ being raised from the dead dieth no more; death no more hath dominion over him. *Rom. 6:9.*

There ariseth another . . . after the power of an endless life. *Heb. 7:15, 16.*

The word of God is living. *Heb. 4:12.*

We doubted our God in secret,
  We scoffed in the market-place,
We held our hearts from His keeping,
  We held our eyes from His face;
We looked to the ways of our fathers,
  Denying where they denied,
And we said as He passed, "He is stilled at last,
  And a man is crucified."

We buried our God in darkness,
  In secret and all affright;
We crept on a path of silence,
  Fearful things in the night;
We buried our God in terror,
  After the fashion of men;
As we said each one, "The deed is done,
  And the grave is closed again."

But now I give you certain news
  To bid a world rejoice:
Ye may crush Truth to silence,
  Ye may cry above His voice,
Ye may close your ears before Him,
  Lest ye tremble at the word,
But late or soon, by night or noon,
  The living Truth is heard.

But now I give you certain news
  To spread by land and sea;
Ye may scourge Truth naked,
  Ye may nail Him to the tree,
Ye may roll the stone above Him,
  And seal it priestly-wise.
But against the morn, unmaimed, new-born,
  The living Truth shall rise!
    Theodosia Garrison.

O THOU who makest the stars, and turnest the shadow of death into the morning; on this day of days we meet to render Thee, our Lord and King, the tribute of our praise; for the Resurrection of our Lord Jesus Christ, for the new life of the spring time, for the sure triumph of truth, for the victory of light over darkness, for the everlasting hopes that rise within the human heart, and for the Gospel which hath brought life and immortality to light. Receive our thanksgiving, reveal Thy Presence, and send into our hearts the Spirit of the Risen Christ. [*Divine Service* (Altered).]

TREES AND THE MASTER

• He went forth with his disciples over the brook Kidron, where was a garden, into which he entered, himself and his disciples. Now Judas also, who betrayed him, knew the place: for Jesus oft-times resorted thither with his disciples. *John 18:1, 2.*

And the most part of the multitude spread their garments in the way; and others cut branches from the trees, and spread them in the way. *Matt. 21:8.*

Every good tree bringeth forth good fruit; but the corrupt tree bringeth forth evil fruit. *Matt. 7:17.*

Who his own self bare our sins in his body upon the tree. *1 Peter 2:24.*

And on this side of the river and on that was the tree of life, bearing twelve manner of fruits, yielding its fruit every month: and the leaves of the tree were for the healing of the nations. *Rev. 22:2.*

Into the woods my Master went,
Clean forspent, forspent.
Into the woods my Master came
Forspent with love and shame.
But the olives they were not blind to
    Him,
The little grey leaves were kind to
    Him
The thorn-tree had a mind to Him
When into the woods He came.

Out of the woods my Master went,
And He was well-content.
Out of the woods my Master came,
Content with death and shame.
When Death and Shame would woo
    Him last
From under the trees they drew Him
    last
'Twas on a tree they slew Him — last,
When out of the woods He came.

Sidney Lanier.

ALMIGHTY GOD, who hast shown us in the life and teaching of Thy son the true way of blessedness, Thou hast also showed us in His suffering and death that the path of love may lead to the cross, and the reward of faithfulness may be a crown of thorns. Give us grace to learn these hard lessons. May we take up our cross and follow Christ, in the strength of patience and the constancy of faith; and may we have such fellowship with Him in His sorrow, that we may know the secret of His strength and peace, and see, even in our darkest hour of trial and anguish, the shining of the eternal light. [*A Book of Prayers for Students.*]

WORDS AND THE WORD

In the beginning was the Word, and the Word was with God, and the Word was God. . . . And the Word became flesh, and dwelt among us. *John 1:1, 14.*

And if any man hear my sayings, and keep them not, I judge him not. . . . The word that I spake, the same shall judge him in the last day. *John 12:47, 48.*

If ye abide in me, and my words abide in you, ask whatsoever ye will, and it shall be done unto you. *John 15:7.*

With a measure of light and a measure of shade,
The world of old by the Word was made;
By the shade and light was the Word concealed,
And the Word in flesh to the world revealed
Is by outward sense and its forms obscured:
The spirit within is the long lost Word,
Besought by the world of the soul in pain
Through a world of words which are void and vain.
O never while shadow and light are blended
Shall the world's Word-quest or its woe be ended,
And never the world of its wounds made whole
Till the Word made flesh be the Word made soul.
Arthur Edward Waite.

O GOD, who hast made us in Thine own image and given us the gift of thought that we may be able to understand the meaning of Thy handiwork and to use it aright, be with us now, we beseech Thee, as with reverent hearts and receptive spirits we draw near to Thee to receive the illumination we need. We thank Thee for every word Thou hast spoken to us and art speaking today, in nature, in history, in the Bible, through Thy Church, in the familiar experiences of every day. But most of all we thank Thee for Jesus Christ, the Word made flesh, through whom Thou hast translated all Thy other words into the language of life, and art drawing us to Thyself by the contagion of love. Help us to understand what we see in Him, interpret to us what we feel concerning Him. Be Thou our teacher as with expectant faith we seek to enter into the mind of Christ. [William Adams Brown.]

IN AND WITH

Abide in me, and I in you. As the branch cannot bear fruit of itself, except it abide in the vine; so neither can ye, except ye abide in me. I am the vine, ye are the branches: He that abideth in me, and I in him, the same beareth much fruit: for apart from me ye can do nothing. *John 15:4, 5.*

I have been crucified with Christ; and it is no longer I that live, but Christ liveth in me: and that life which I now live in the flesh I live in faith, the faith which is in the Son of God, who loved me, and gave himself up for me. *Gal. 2:20.*

For to me to live is Christ. *Phil. 1:21.*

> Oh, turn me, mold me, mellow me for use!
> Pervade my being with Thy vital force,
> That this else inexpressive life of mine
> May become eloquent and full of power,
> Impregnated with life and strength divine. . . .
> I cannot raise the dead, nor from this soil
> Pluck precious dust, nor bid the sleepers wake,
> Nor still the storm, nor bend the lightning back,
> Nor muffle up the thunder,
> Nor bind the Evil One, nor bid the chain
> Fall from creation's long-enfettered limbs;
> But I can live a life that tells on other lives, and makes
> This world less full of evil and of pain —
> A life, which like a pebble dropped at sea,
> Sends its wide circles to a hundred shores.
> Let such be mine! Creator of true life!
> Thyself the life Thou givest, give Thyself,
> That Thou mayst dwell in me, and I in Thee.
>
> *H. Bonar.*

O GOD, Holy Ghost, Sanctifier of the faithful, visit us, we pray thee, with thy love and favour; enlighten our minds more and more with the light of the everlasting Gospel; graft in our hearts a love of the truth; increase in us true religion; nourish us with all goodness; and of thy great mercy keep us in the same, O blessed Spirit, whom, with the Father and the Son together, we worship and glorify as one God, world without end. [*The Book of Common Prayer* (Altered).]

ONLY CHRIST

I am the way, and the truth, and the life: no man cometh unto the Father, but by me. *John 14:6.*

In none other is there salvation: for neither is there any other name under heaven that is given among men, wherein we must be saved. *Acts 4:12.*

Ye have heard that it was said, Thou shalt love thy neighbor, and hate thine enemy: but I say unto you, Love your enemies, and pray for them that persecute you; that ye may be sons of your Father who is in heaven. *Matt. 5:43-45.*

"Only through Me!" . . . The clear, high call comes pealing,
Above the thunders of the battle-plain; —
"Only through Me can Life's red wounds find healing;
Only through Me shall Earth have peace again.

Only through Me! . . . Love's Might, all might transcending,
Alone can draw the poison-fangs of Hate.
Yours the beginning! — Mine a nobler ending, —
Peace upon Earth, and Man regenerate!

Only through Me can come the great awaking;
Wrong cannot right the wrongs that Wrong hath done;
Only through Me, all other gods forsaking,
Can ye attain the heights that must be won." . . .

Can we not rise to such great height of glory?
Shall this vast sorrow spend itself in vain?
Shall future ages tell the woeful story, —
"Christ by His own was crucified again"?   *John Oxenham.*

O CHRIST, our Lord, who art the way, the truth, and the life, guide our feet in Thy path, illumine our minds with Thy light, feed our souls with Thy living bread, and satisfy our thirst with Thy living water. Thou alone art all we want. More than all in Thee we find. May we live in Thee and in Thy Lordship and lay aside all evil and forsake the ways of darkness and hate, and for ourselves and for all mankind seek Thy mind and Thy glory and walk in love of Thee and of all men, to do Thy will and to hasten Thy Kingdom.

Behold, the Lamb of God, that taketh away the sin of the world! *John 1:29.*

The Lamb that hath been slain. *Rev. 13:8.*

A Lamb goes uncomplaining forth
  The guilt of all men bearing;
Laden with all the sin of earth,
  None else the burden sharing!
Goes patient on, grows weak and faint,
To slaughter led without complaint,
  That spotless life to offer
Bears shame and stripes and wounds and death,
Anguish and mockery and saith
  " Willing all this I suffer."

That Lamb is Lord of death and life
  God over all forever;
The Father's Son, whom to that strife
  Love doth for us deliver!
O mighty Love, what hast Thou done!
The Father offers up His Son —
  The Son content descendeth
O Love, O Love! how strong art Thou!
In shroud and grave Thou layest Him low,
  Whose word the mountain rendeth.

From the German.

O LAMB of God, that takest away the sins of the world, have mercy on us.

O Lamb of God, that takest away the sins of the world, receive our prayer.

O Lord Jesus, we praise Thee, that Thou didst come among us, a gracious gift to the ungrateful race of men, and, undismayed by our sin and blindness didst live out Thy life of holiness and power, bringing health and peace to all who came to Thee.

O Lamb of God, that takest away the sin of the world, for Thy loneliness and failure, for Thy stress of spirit and Thy strong prayer, for Thy Cross upon the hill, for Thy death that giveth life, for Thy life that overcometh death, we worship Thee our Lord and Master, our Saviour and Redeemer. [*A Book of Prayers for Students.*]

THE LAMB AND HIS LAMBS

The Lord God the Almighty, and the Lamb, are the temple. *Rev. 21:22.*

I saw in the midst of the throne and of the four living creatures, and in the midst of the elders, a Lamb standing. *Rev. 5:6.*

He will feed his flock like a shepherd, he will gather the lambs in his arm, and carry them in his bosom, and will gently lead those that have their young. *Isa. 40:11.*

Now will Jehovah feed them as a lamb. *Hos. 4:16.*

The Lord is my shepherd. *Ps. 23:1.*

I am the good shepherd: the good shepherd layeth down his life for the sheep. *John 10:11.*

Little lamb, who made thee?
Dost thou know who made thee,
Gave thee life and bade thee feed
By the stream and o'er the mead;
Gave thee clothing of delight,
Softest clothing, woolly, bright;
Gave thee such a tender voice,
Making all the vales rejoice?
  Little lamb, who made thee?
  Dost thou know who made thee?

Little lamb, I'll tell thee;
Little lamb, I'll tell thee.
He is calléd by thy name,
For He calls Himself a Lamb;
He is meek and He is mild,
He became a little child.
I a child and thou a lamb,
We are calléd by His name.
  Little lamb, God bless thee!
  Little lamb, God bless thee!
    William Blake.

*C*HRIST, Holy and Strong, Holy and Immortal, God from God, Light from Light, born of woman, crucified, risen, in whom are fulfilled all human possibilities and all the treasures of God revealed, receive the adoration of Thy people. Above our failure and bewilderment and sin, our ignorance, and our anxieties, we lift up our hearts to Thy perfections; we love and reverence and worship Thee; Thou hast won eternal redemption for us and Thou art ever present with Thy people. Manifest Thyself to the world which waits for Thee, and show us, O Lord, the way that we should walk in: for we lift up our hearts unto Thee. [F. R. Barry.]

We would not have you ignorant, brethren, concerning them that fall asleep; that ye sorrow not, even as the rest, who have no hope. . . . Them also that are fallen asleep in Jesus will God bring with him. *1 Thess. 4:13, 14.*

In Christ shall all be made alive. *1 Cor. 15:22.*

For whether we live, we live unto the Lord; or whether we die, we die unto the Lord: whether we live, therefore, or die, we are the Lord's. For to this end Christ died and lived again, that he might be Lord of both the dead and the living. *Rom. 14:8, 9.*

I go and prepare a place for you, I come again, and will receive you unto myself; that where I am, there ye may be also. *John 14:3.*

> Though he that ever kind and true
> Kept slowly step by step with you
> Your whole long, gusty life time through,
>   Be gone awhile before —
> Be now a moment gone before,
> Yet doubt not; anon the seasons shall restore
>   Your friend to you. . . .
>
> He is not dead, this friend, not dead,
> But in the path we mortals tread
> Got some few trifling steps ahead,
>   And nearer to the end.
> So that you, too, once past this bend,
> Shall meet again, as face to face, this friend
>   You fancy dead.   *Robert Louis Stevenson.*

*A*LMIGHTY GOD, with whom do live the spirits of those who depart hence in the Lord, and with whom the souls of the faithful, after they are delivered from the burden of the flesh, are in joy and felicity; We give thee hearty thanks for the good examples of all those thy servants, who, having finished their course in faith, do now rest from their labours. And we beseech thee, that we, with all those who are departed in the true faith of thy holy Name, may have our perfect consummation and bliss, both in body and soul, in thy eternal and everlasting glory, through Jesus Christ our Lord. [*The Book of Common Prayer.*]

THE SAVIOUR OF THE WORLD, JESUS OF NAZARETH

Christ died for the ungodly. For scarcely for a righteous man will one die: for peradventure for the good man some one would even dare to die. But God commendeth his own love toward us, in that, while we were yet sinners, Christ died for us. *Rom. 5:6–8.*

Jesus of Nazareth . . . God anointed. *Acts 10:38.*

We have found him, of whom Moses in the law, and the prophets, wrote, Jesus of Nazareth, the son of Joseph. *John 1:45.*

He came to Nazareth, where he had been brought up. *Luke 4:16.*

And Pilate wrote a title also, and put it on the cross. And there was written, JESUS OF NAZARETH, THE KING OF THE JEWS. *John 19:19.*

Jesus of Nazareth, a man approved of God. *Acts 2:22.*

Suddenly there shone from heaven a great light. . . . And he said unto me, I am Jesus of Nazareth. *Acts 22:6, 8.*

A boy was born at Bethlehem
  That knew the haunts of Galilee.
He wandered on Mount Lebanon
  And learned to love each forest tree.

But I was born at Marlborough
  And love the homely faces there:
And for all other men besides
  'Tis little love I have to spare.

I should not mind to die for them,
  My own dear downs, my comrades true.
But that great heart of Bethlehem,
  He died for men He never knew.

And yet I think at Golgotha
  As Jesus' eyes were closed in death
They saw with love most passionate
  The village street at Nazareth.
        E. Hilton Young.

O FATHER, whose dwelling place is our soul's true home, toward which our hearts are ever turning, we thank Thee for the dear memories of those earthly homes where our lives began, for childhood's scenes and friends, for the plays and tasks, the sorrows and joys, the freedoms and restraints by which we were disciplined for life, and its work and duty. And we beseech Thee of whom every family in heaven and on earth is named to bless all the friends of our childhood days, and all who remain of the loved ones of long ago and grant that we may ever be knit together in the bonds of mutual love, and above all that we may be members together of the mystical body of Christ, through the same Jesus Christ, Thy Son our Lord.

Five barley loaves, and two fishes: but what are these among so many? *John 6:9.*

And Jehovah said unto him, What is that in thy hand? And he said, A rod. *Ex. 4:2.*

And he [David] took his staff in his hand, and chose him five smooth stones out of the brook, and put them in the shepherd's bag which he had, even in his wallet; and his sling was in his hand: and he drew near to the Philistine. *1 Sam. 17:40.*

God chose the weak things of the world, that he might put to shame the things that are strong. *1 Cor. 1:27.*

This I beheld, or dreamed it in a dream: —
There spread a cloud of dust along a plain;
And underneath the cloud, or in it, raged
A furious battle, and men yelled, and swords
Shocked upon swords and shields. A prince's banner
Wavered, then staggered backward, hemmed by foes.
A craven hung along the battle's edge,
And thought, "Had I a sword of keener steel —
That blue blade that the king's son bears, — but this
Blunt thing — ! " he snapped and flung it from his hand,
And lowering crept away and left the field.
Then came the king's son, wounded, sore bestead,
And weaponless, and saw the broken sword,
Half buried in the dry and trodden sand,
And ran and snatched it, and with battle shout
Lifted afresh, he hewed his enemy down,
And saved a great cause that heroic day.   *E. R. Sill.*

O LIVING Christ, make us conscious now of Thy healing nearness. Touch our eyes that we may see Thee; open our ears that we may hear Thy voice; enter our hearts that we may know Thy love. Overshadow our souls and bodies with Thy presence, that we may partake of Thy strength, Thy love, and Thy healing life. Help us to find in life's common implements and occasions our opportunity to live unto Thee and to accomplish the work which Thou hast given us to do.

And he shall wipe away every tear from their eyes; and death shall be no more; neither shall there be mourning, nor crying, nor pain, any more: the first things are passed away. *Rev. 21:4.*

For we have not here an abiding city, but we seek after the city which is to come. *Heb. 13:14.*

Ye are come unto mount Zion, and unto the city of the living God, . . . and to God the Judge of all, and to the spirits of just men made perfect, and to Jesus. *Heb. 12:22–24.*

Our citizenship is in heaven; whence also we wait for a Saviour, the Lord Jesus Christ: who shall fashion anew the body of our humiliation, that it may be conformed to the body of his glory. *Phil. 3:20, 21.*

> Fierce was the wild billow, dark was the night,
> Oars labored heavily, foam glimmered white,
> Trembled the mariners, peril was nigh,
> Then said the God of God, " Peace, it is I."
>
> Ridge of the mountain wave, lower thy crest,
> Wail of Euroclydon, be thou at rest!
> Sorrow can never be, darkness must fly
> When saith the Light of Light, " Peace, it is I."
>
> Jesus, Deliverer, come Thou to me,
> Soothe Thou my voyaging over life's sea.
> Then when the storm of death roars sweeping by,
> Whisper, O Truth of Truth, " Peace, it is I "
>
> *Anatolius.*

O GOD, who hast made the most glorious Name of our Lord Jesus Christ, Thine only-begotten Son, to be exceedingly precious and supremely lovable to Thy faithful servants, and a protection against all evil; mercifully grant that all who devoutly venerate the Name of Jesus on earth may in this life receive the sweetness of holy comfort, and in the life to come attain the joy of great gladness and never-ending praise through the same Jesus Christ our Lord. [*The Devotional Companion.*]

A NEW LIFE

Are ye ignorant that all we who were baptized into Christ Jesus were baptized into his death? We were buried therefore with him through baptism into death: that like as Christ was raised from the dead through the glory of the Father, so we also might walk in newness of life. For if we have become united with him in the likeness of his death, we shall be also in the likeness of his resurrection. *Rom. 6:3–5.*

If Christ is in you, the body is dead because of sin; but the spirit is life because of righteousness. But if the Spirit of him that raised up Jesus from the dead dwelleth in you, he that raised up Christ Jesus from the dead shall give life also to your mortal bodies through his Spirit that dwelleth in you. *Rom. 8:10, 11.*

Blessed be the God and Father of our Lord Jesus Christ, who according to his great mercy begat us again unto a living hope by the resurrection of Jesus Christ from the dead, unto an inheritance incorruptible, and undefiled, and that fadeth not away. *1 Peter 1:3, 4.*

> Now am I too come even unto Bethlehem
> There to be born again in the shadow of my Lord.
>
> Now am I too come even unto Calvary,
> There to taste the mighty wine for me outpoured.
>
> Now am I risen again out of hours dark as death,
> Risen to wear a living faith as Christ His person wore.
>
> It is enough, O Jesus, never a miracle
> Could move me more than this Thy beauty to adore.
> *Marguerite Wilkinson.*

ALMIGHTY and everlasting God, who, of Thy tender love toward mankind, hast sent Thy Son, our Saviour Jesus Christ, to take upon Him our flesh, and that in the form of a servant, and to suffer death, even the death of the cross, for our redemption, mercifully grant that this mind may be in us that was also in Christ Jesus that we may not only follow the example of His humble obedience and patient suffering but also in very truth die with Him and in Him to all sin and rise with Him and in Him to a new life of purity and holiness here in our mortal flesh and hereafter be made partakers of His glory, to live with Thee forever. [*Gelasian Sacramentary* (Altered).]

NO UNBELIEF

If we are faithless, he abideth faithful; for he cannot deny himself. *II Tim. 2:13.*

Ye ought to say, If the Lord will, we shall both live, and do this or that. *James 4:15.*

And he [Jesus] marvelled because of their unbelief. *Mark 6:6.*

Take heed, brethren, lest haply there shall be in any one of you an evil heart of unbelief. *Heb. 3:12.*

The demons also believe. *James 2:19.*

Ye believe not, because ye are not of my sheep. *John 10:26.*

I believe; help thou mine unbelief. *Mark 9:24.*

> There is no unbelief!
> Whoever plants a seed beneath the sod,
> And waits to see it push away the clod,
>   He trusts in God.
>
> Whoever says, when clouds are in the sky,
> " Be patient, heart, light breaketh by and by,"
>   Trusts the Most High. . . .
>
> Whoever lies down on his couch to sleep,
> Content to lock each sense in slumber deep,
>   Knows God will keep. . . .
>
> There is no unbelief:
> And still by day and night, unconsciously,
> The heart lives by the faith the lips decry.
>   God knoweth why.   *Elizabeth York Case.*

LORD, increase our faith. We believe; help Thou our unbelief. Give us a true child's trust in Thee in all Thy strength and goodness. Cause us to rest with perfect confidence in all Thy purposes and ways. Enable us to confide all our interests for time and for eternity to Thy keeping. Give us, heavenly Father, the substance of things hoped for and the evidence of things unseen, that we may walk by faith, not by sight, looking not at the things which are seen and temporal but at those things which are not seen and eternal. Through Jesus Christ our Lord by whom we believe in Thee.

DAILY DEATH

I die daily. *1 Cor. 15:31.*

If we have become united with him in the likeness of his death, we shall be also in the likeness of his resurrection. . . . But if we died with Christ, we believe that we shall also live with him; knowing that Christ being raised from the dead dieth no more; death no more hath dominion over him. For the death that he died, he died unto sin once: but the life that he liveth, he liveth unto God. *Rom. 6:5, 8–10.*

That I may know him, and the power of his resurrection, and the fellowship of his sufferings, becoming conformed unto his death; if by any means I may attain unto the resurrection from the dead. Not that I have already obtained, or am already made perfect: but I press on. *Phil. 3:10–12.*

Pausing a moment ere the day was done
   While yet the earth was scintillant with light,
   I backward glanced. From valley, plain and height,
At intervals, where my life-path had run,
Rose cross on cross; and nailed upon each one
   Was my dead self. And yet that gruesome sight
   Lent sudden splendor to the falling night,
Showing the conquests that my soul had won.

Up to the rising stars I looked and cried,
   There is no death! For year on year, re-born
   I wake to larger life; to joy more great.
So many times have I been crucified,
   So often seen the resurrection morn
   I go triumphant, though new Calvaries wait.
                    Ella Wheeler Wilcox.

ALMIGHTY GOD, who hast given thine only Son to be unto us both a sacrifice for sin, and also an example of a godly life; Give us grace that we may always most thankfully receive that his inestimable benefit, and also daily endeavour ourselves to follow the blessed steps of his most holy life; through the same thy Son Jesus Christ our Lord. [*The Book of Common Prayer.* Collect for Second Sunday After Easter.]

HEREDITY

I Jehovah thy God am a jealous God, visiting the iniquity of the fathers upon the children, upon the third and upon the fourth generation of them that hate me, and showing lovingkindness unto thousands of them that love me and keep my commandments. *Ex. 20:5, 6.*

Flesh and blood cannot inherit the kingdom of God; neither doth corruption inherit incorruption. *I Cor. 15:50.*

In those days they shall say no more, The fathers have eaten sour grapes, and the children's teeth are set on edge. But every one shall die for his own iniquity: every man that eateth the sour grapes, his teeth shall be set on edge. *Jer. 31:29, 30.*

I thank God, . . . having been reminded of the unfeigned faith that is in thee; which dwelt first in thy grandmother Lois, and thy mother Eunice; and, I am persuaded, in thee also. *II Tim. 1:3, 5.*

Lord, I find the genealogy of my Saviour strangely checkered with four remarkable changes in four immediate generations:

1. Roboam begat Abia; that is a bad father begat a bad son.
2. Abia begat Asa; that is a bad father a good son.
3. Asa began Josaphat; that is a good father a good son.
4. Josaphat begat Joram; that is a good father a bad son.

I see, Lord, from hence that my father's piety cannot be entailed; that is bad news for me. But I see also that actual impiety is not always hereditary; that is good news for my son. *Thomas Fuller.*

O GOD of all generations, by whose ordinance we have received the bequest of the past and who hast laid on us responsibility for the inheritance of our children, deliver us, we pray, from the guilt of transmitting an evil burden to those who come after us. Purify us in flesh and spirit, that the stream of life may flow through us clean and undefiled. O blessed Jesus, who, by the shining of a star, didst manifest Thyself to them that sought Thee, show Thy heavenly light in us and give us grace to follow until we find Thee; finding to rejoice in Thee, and rejoicing to present to Thee ourselves, our souls and bodies, and our children and our children's children for Thy service evermore, for Thine honor and glory.

THE WALK OF LIFE

Look therefore carefully how ye walk, not as unwise, but as wise; redeeming the time, because the days are evil. *Eph. 5:15.*

Walk while ye have the light, that darkness overtake you not: and he that walketh in the darkness knoweth not whither he goeth. *John 12:35, 36.*

Wherefore girding up the loins of your mind, be sober and set your hope perfectly on the grace that is to be brought unto you at the revelation of Jesus Christ; as children of obedience, not fashioning yourselves according to your former lusts in the time of your ignorance: but like as he who called you is holy, be yourselves also holy in all manner of living; because it is written, Ye shall be holy; for I am holy. And if ye call on him as Father, who without respect of persons judgeth according to each man's work, pass the time of your sojourning in fear: knowing that ye were redeemed, not with corruptible things, with silver or gold, from your vain manner of life handed down from your fathers; but with precious blood. *I Peter 1:13-19.*

> We live in deeds, not years; in thoughts, not breaths;
> In feelings, not in figures on a dial.
> We should count time by heart-throbs. He most lives
> Who thinks most, feels the noblest, acts the best.
> And he whose heart beats quickest lives the longest:
> Lives in one hour more than in years do some
> Whose fat blood sleeps as it slips along their veins.
> Life's but a means unto an end; that end,
> Beginning, mean, and end to all things — God.
> The dead have all the glory of the world.   *P. J. Bailey.*

O MERCIFUL God, lest through our own frailty, or the temptations which encompass us, we be drawn into sin, vouchsafe us, we beseech Thee, the direction and assistance of Thy Holy Spirit. Reform whatever is amiss in the temper and disposition of our souls, that no unclean thoughts, unlawful designs or inordinate desires may rest there. Purge our hearts from envy, hatred and malice; that we may never suffer the sun to go down upon our wrath, but may always go to our rest in peace, charity and good will, with a conscience void of offense towards Thee and towards men.

IN ONE PEACE, OF ONE BLOOD

And suddenly there was with the angel a multitude of the heavenly host praising God, and saying, Glory to God in the highest, and on earth peace among men in whom he is well pleased. *Luke 2:13, 14.*

Blessed are the peacemakers: for they shall be called sons of God. *Matt. 5:9.*

Peace I leave with you; my peace I give unto you. *John 14:27.*

God hath called us in peace. *I Cor. 7:15.*

For he is our peace . . . : and he came and preached peace to you that were far off, and peace to them that were nigh: for through him we both have our access . . . unto the Father. *Eph. 2:14, 17.*

Blessed are the meek: for they shall inherit the earth. *Matt. 5:5.*

O black and unknown bards of long ago,
 How came your lips to touch the sacred fire?
How, in your darkness, did you come to know
 The power and beauty of the minstrel's lyre?

Heart of what slave poured out such melody
 As " Steal Away to Jesus "? On its strains
His spirit must have nightly floated free,
 Though still about his hands he felt his chains.

What merely living clod, what captive thing,
 Could up toward God through all its darkness grope,
And find within its deadened heart to sing
 These songs of sorrow, love and faith, and hope?

You sang far better than you knew; the songs
 That for your listeners' hungry hearts sufficed
Still live, — but more than this to you belongs:
 You sang a race from wood and stone to Christ.
James Weldon Johnson.

ALMIGHTY and everlasting God, who, of Thy tender love towards mankind, hast sent Thy Son, our Saviour Jesus Christ, to take upon Him our flesh, and to suffer death upon the cross, that all mankind should follow the example of His great humility; . . . mercifully grant, that we may both follow the example of His patience, and also be made partakers of His resurrection; through the same Jesus Christ our Lord. [*Gelasian Sacramentary.*]

Let both grow together until the harvest: and in the time of the harvest I will say to the reapers, Gather up first the tares, and bind them in bundles to burn them; but gather the wheat into my barn. *Matt. 13:30.*

Every idle word that men shall speak, they shall give account thereof in the day of judgment. For by thy words thou shalt be . . . condemned. *Matt. 12:36, 37.*

We must all be made manifest before the judgment-seat of Christ; that each one may receive the things done in the body, according to what he hath done, whether it be good or bad. *II Cor. 5:10.*

We scatter seeds with careless hand,
   And dream we ne'er shall see them
      more.
   But for a thousand years
    Their fruit appears
In weeds that mar the land,
   Or hearthful store.

The deeds we do, the words we say,
   Into still air they seem to float.
   We count them ever past,

But they shall last.
In the dread judgment they
   And we shall meet.

I charge thee by the years gone by,
   For the love's sake of brethren dear,
   Keep thou the one true way,
    In work and play,
Lest, in that world, their cry
   Of woe thou hear.
            John Keble.

O MERCIFUL Lord, enlighten Thou me with a clear, shining inward light, and remove away all darkness from the habitation of my heart. Repress Thou my many wandering thoughts, and break in pieces those temptations which violently assault me. Fight Thou for me, and vanquish the evil beasts; that so peace may be obtained by Thy power, and that Thine abundant praise may resound in Thy holy court, that is, in a pure conscience. Send out Thy light and Thy truth, that they may shine upon the earth; for, until Thou enlighten me, I am but as earth without form and void. Lift Thou up my mind which is pressed down by a load of sins, for no created thing can give full comfort and rest to my desires. Join Thou me to Thyself with an inseparable band of love; for Thou ever alone dost satisfy him that loveth Thee. [Thomas à Kempis.]

THE TESTING

To you it hath been granted in the behalf of Christ, not only to believe on him, but also to suffer in his behalf: having the same conflict which ye saw in me, and now hear to be in me. *Phil. 1:29, 30.*

I rejoice in my sufferings for your sake, and fill up on my part that which is lacking of the afflictions of Christ in my flesh for his body's sake, which is the church. *Col. 1:24.*

Fight the good fight of the faith. *1 Tim. 6:12.*

I therefore so run, as not uncertainly; so fight I, as not beating the air: but I buffet my body, and bring it into bondage. *1 Cor. 9:26, 27.*

That I may know him [Christ], and the power of his resurrection, and the fellowship of his sufferings, becoming conformed unto his death; if by any means I may attain unto the resurrection from the dead. Not that I have already obtained, or am already made perfect: but I press on. *Phil. 3:10–12.*

> And so I live, you see,
> Go through the world, try, prove, reject,
> Prefer, still struggling to effect
> My warfare; happy that I can
> Be crossed and thwarted as a man,
> Not left in God's contempt apart,
> With ghostly smooth life, dead at heart,
> Tame in earth's paddock as her prize.
> Thank God, no paradise stands barred
> To entry, and I find it hard
> To be a Christian, as I said.
> *Robert Browning.*

Holy father, whose chosen way of manifesting Thyself to Thy children is by the discipline of trial and pain, we rejoice that we can turn to Thee in the midst of great anxiety, and commit all our troubles to Thy sure help. As Thou art with us in the sunlight, oh, be Thou with us in the cloud. In the path by which Thou guidest us, though it be through desert and stormy sea, suffer not our faith to fail, but sustain us by Thy near Presence, and let the comforts which are in Jesus Christ fill our hearts with peace. And, O God, grant that the fiery trial which trieth us may not be in vain, but may bear us to a cheerful courage, and a holy patience; and let patience have her perfect work, that we may be perfect and entire, wanting nothing, wholly consecrate to Thee, through Jesus Christ our Lord. [Henry W. Foote.]

SOLDIER, FIGHT ON

Suffer hardship with me, as a good soldier of Christ Jesus. No soldier on service entangleth himself in the affairs of this life; that he may please him that enrolled him as a soldier. *II Tim. 2:3, 4.*

This charge I commit unto thee, . . . that thou mayest war the good warfare. *I Tim. 1:18.*

We do not war according to the flesh (for the weapons of our warfare are not of the flesh, but mighty before God to the casting down of strongholds). *II Cor. 10:3, 4.*

And I saw the heaven opened; and behold, a white horse, and he that sat thereon called Faithful and True; and in righteousness he doth judge and make war. *Rev. 19:11.*

Wherefore take up the whole armor of God, that ye may be able to withstand in the evil day, and, having done all, to stand. *Eph. 6:13.*

O may Thy soldiers, faithful, true, and bold,
Fight as the saints who nobly fought of old,
And win with them the victor's crown of gold.

And when the strife is fierce, the warfare long,
Steals on the ear the distant triumph-song,
And hearts are brave again, and arms are strong.

The golden evening brightens in the west;
Soon, soon to faithful warriors comes their rest;
Sweet is the calm of Paradise the blest. Alleluia!
W. W. How.

O GOD, the Father of our Saviour Jesus Christ, whose Name is great, whose nature is blissful, whose goodness is inexhaustible, God and Ruler of all things, who art blessed forever; before whom stand thousands and thousands, and ten thousand times ten thousand, the hosts of holy angels and archangels; sanctify, O Lord, our souls and bodies and spirits, search our consciences, and cast out of us every evil thought, every base desire, all envy and pride, all wrath and anger, and all that is contrary to Thy holy will. And grant us, O Lord, lover of men, with a pure heart and contrite soul, to call upon Thee, our Holy God, and Father who art in Heaven. *[Liturgy of St. James.]*

NO LIE IS WHITE

No lie is of the truth. *I John 2:21*.
God . . . cannot lie. *Titus 1:2*.
It is impossible for God to lie. *Heb. 6:18*.
There shall in no wise enter into . . . [that City] anything unclean or he that maketh an abomination and a lie. *Rev. 21:27*.

Truth is always consistent with itself and needs nothing to help it out; it is always near at hand and sits upon our lips, and is ready to drop out before we are aware; whereas a lie is troublesome, and sets a man's invention upon the rack, and one trick needs a great many more to make it good. It is like building upon a false foundation, which constantly stands in need of props to shore it up, and proves at last more chargeable than to have raised a substantial building at first upon a true and solid foundation; for sincerity is firm and substantial, and there is nothing hollow and unsound in it, and, because it is plain and open, fears no discovery; of which the crafty man is always in danger. . . . Whatsoever convenience may be thought to be in falsehood and dissimulation it is soon over, but the inconvenience of it is perpetual, because it brings a man under an everlasting jealousy and suspicion, so that he is not believed when he speaks the truth, nor trusted when perhaps he means honestly. When a man has once forfeited the reputation of his integrity, he is set fast, and nothing will then serve his turn, neither truth nor falsehood. *Tillotson*.

O DEAREST Friend, who hast so loved and saved us, the thought of whom is so sweet and always growing sweeter, come with Christ and dwell in our hearts; then Thou wilt keep a watch over our lips, our steps, our deeds, and we shall not need to be anxious either for our souls or our bodies. Build us into Truth, we pray; and build Truth in us. Unite us more perfectly to Christ who made it His meat and drink to do Thy will and whom the zeal of Thine House consumed. O most loving Father of Jesus Christ, from whom floweth all love, who art Love and Truth, let our hearts, frozen in sin, cold to Thee and cold to others, be warmed by Thy fire and brightened by Thy light. So help and bless us in Thy Son. [Saint Anselm (Altered).]

THERE IS A REST

There remaineth therefore a sabbath rest for the people of God. For he that is entered into his rest hath . . . also rested from his works, as God did from his. Let us therefore give diligence to enter into that rest. *Heb. 4:9–11.*

Ye shall find rest unto your souls. *Matt. 11:29.*

I . . . accomplished the work . . . thou hast given me to do. *John 17:4.*

And there shall be no curse any more: and the throne of God and of the Lamb shall be therein: and his servants shall serve him; and they shall see his face. *Rev. 22:3, 4.*

There's a fancy some lean to and others hate
    That, when this life is ended begins
New work for the soul in another state,
    Where it strives and gets weary, loses and wins:
Where the strong and the weak, this world's congeries,
    Repeat in large what they practiced in small
Through life after life in unlimited series,
    Only the scale's to be changed, that's all.

Yet I hardly know. When a soul has seen
    By the means of Evil that God is best,
And through earth and its noise what is heaven's serene —
    When our faith in the same has stood the test —
Why the child turned man, you burn the rod,
    The uses of labor are surely done.
There remaineth a rest for the people of God:
    And I have had trouble enough, for one. *Browning.*

O MY Father, I have moments of deep unrest — moments when I know not what to ask by reason of the very excess of my wants. I have in these hours no words for Thee, no conscious prayers for Thee. Yet all the time Thou hast accepted my unrest as a prayer. I know not what I ask. But Thou knowest what I ask, O my God. Thou knowest that, because I am made in Thine image, I can find rest only in what gives rest to Thee; therefore Thou hast counted my unrest for righteousness and hast called my groaning Thy Spirit's prayer. [George Matheson (Abbreviated).]

And why call ye me, Lord, Lord, and do not the things which I say? *Luke 6:46.*

Every one therefore who shall confess me before men, him will I also confess before my Father who is in heaven. But whosoever shall deny me before men, him will I also deny before my Father who is in heaven. *Matt. 10:32, 33.*

A disciple is not above his teacher, nor a servant above his lord. It is enough for the disciple that he be as his teacher, and the servant as his lord. *Matt. 10:24, 25.*

Be ye imitators of me, even as I also am of Christ. *I Cor. 11:1.*

These are they that follow the Lamb whithersoever he goeth. *Rev. 14:4.*

Thus speaketh Christ our Lord to us:
Ye call Me Master, and obey Me not;
Ye call Me Light, and see Me not;
Ye call Me Way, and walk Me not;
Ye call Me Life, and desire Me not;
Ye call Me Wise, and follow Me not;
Ye call Me Fair, and love Me not;
Ye call Me Rich, and ask Me not;
Ye call Me Eternal, and seek Me not;
Ye call Me Gracious, and trust Me not;
Ye call Me Noble, and serve Me not;
Ye call Me Mighty, and honor Me not;
Ye call Me Just, and fear Me not;
If I condemn you, blame Me not.

Inscription in Lübeck Cathedral.

O LOVER of men, very tenderly pitiful, Father of mercies, rich in mercy toward all that call upon Thee: I have sinned against heaven and before Thee, neither am I worthy to be called a son, neither am I worthy to be made an hired servant, no, not the lowest of them all. But I repent, alas, I repent; help Thou my impenitence: be merciful to me a sinner. Deep calleth unto deep, the deep of our misery unto the deep of Thy mercy. Where sin abounded, let grace much more abound: overcome our evil with Thy good: let Thy mercy rejoice against Thy justice in our sins: Thou that takest away the sins of the world, take away my sins: Thou that didst come to redeem that which was lost, suffer not that to be lost which hath been redeemed of Thee: I have deserved death, but even now I appeal from the seat of Thy justice to the throne of Thy grace. [Bishop Andrewes.]

JOY IN WORK

Abide in me, and I in you. *John 15:4.*

Let the peace of Christ rule in your hearts, to the which also ye were called in one body; and be ye thankful. Let the word of Christ dwell in you richly; in all wisdom teaching and admonishing one another with psalms and hymns and spiritual songs, singing with grace in your hearts unto God. *Col. 3:15, 16.*

The Lord is my strength and song. *Ex. 15:2.*

He hath put a new song in my mouth, even praise unto our God. *Ps. 40:3.*

> The woman singeth at her spinning wheel
> A pleasant chant, ballad or barcarole,
> She thinketh of her song, upon the whole,
> Far more than of her flax; and yet the reel
> Is full, and artfully her fingers feel
> With quick adjustment, provident control,
> The lines, too subtly twisted to unroll,
> Out to a perfect thread. I hence appeal
> To the dear Christian Church that we may do
> Our Father's business in these temples merk
> Thus swift and steadfast, thus intent and strong;
> While thus apart from toil, our souls pursue
> Some high, calm spheric tune, and prove our work
> The better for the sweetness of our song.
> *E. B. Browning.*

O GOD, our Heavenly Father, we Thy children come now to Thy feet with our supplications. We cannot live without Thy blessing. Life is too hard for us and duty is too large. We come to Thee with our weakness, asking Thee for strength. Help us always to be of good cheer. Give us grace to be encouragers of others, never discouragers. Let us not go about with sadness or fear among men, but may we be a benediction to every one we meet, always making life easier, never harder for those who come within our influence. Help us to be as Christ to others, that they may see something of His love in our lives and learn to love Him in us. [J. R. Miller (Abbreviated).]

THE UNCHANGING

I, Jehovah, change not. *Mal. 3:6.*

They shall perish; but thou continuest: And they all shall wax old as doth a garment; and as a mantle shalt thou roll them up, as a garment, and they shall be changed: But thou art the same, and thy years shall not fail. *Heb. 1:11, 12.*

The heavens shall vanish away like smoke, and the earth shall wax old like a garment; and they that dwell therein shall die in like manner: but my salvation shall be for ever, and my righteousness shall not be abolished. *Isa. 51:6.*

Jesus Christ is the same yesterday and today, yea and for ever. *Heb. 13:8.*

The One remains, the Many change and pass:
  Heaven's light forever shines, Earth's shadows fly:
Life like a dome of many colored glass
  Stains the white radiance of Eternity —
Until Death tramples it to fragments.

Shelley.

It fortifies my soul to know
That though I perish, Truth is so;
That howso'er I stray and range,
Whate'er I do, Thou dost not change.
I steadier step, when I recall
That if I slip, Thou dost not fall.

Clough.

*A*BIDE with me: fast falls the eventide; The darkness deepens; Lord, with me abide: . . . Swift to its close ebbs out life's little day; Earth's joys grow dim, its glories pass away; Change and decay in all around I see; O Thou who changest not, abide with me. . . . I fear no foe, with Thee at hand to bless: Ills have no weight, and tears no bitterness; Where is death's sting? where, grave, thy victory? I triumph still, if Thou abide with me. Hold Thou Thy cross before my closing eyes; Shine through the gloom, and point me to the skies: Heaven's morning breaks, and earth's vain shadows flee: In life, in death, O Lord, abide with me. [Henry F. Lyte.]

THE JUDGMENT IS GOD'S

Do ye not make distinctions among yourselves, and become judges with evil thoughts? *James 2:4.*

Ye shall not be afraid of the face of man; for the judgment is God's. *Deut. 1:17.*

Being confident of this very thing, that he who began a good work in you will perfect it until the day of Jesus Christ. *Phil. 1:6.*

Time was when I believed that wrong   Now better taught by Thee, O Lord!
   In others to detect   This truth dawns on my mind —
Was part of genius, and a gift   The best effect of heavenly light
   To cherish, not reject.   Is earth's false eyes to blind.

Faber.

The best men, doing their best,
Know peradventure least of what they do:
Men usefullest in the world are simply used:
The nail that holds the wood must pierce it first,
And he alone who wields the hammer sees
The work advanced by the earliest blows.

E. B. Browning.

*W*E confess unto Thee, O God, how weak we are in ourselves, how powerless to do the work of life, how prone to uncharitable judgments of others, to selfishness and to sin. We beseech Thee to grant us strength and charity, the strength of Thy Spirit and the charity of Christ wherein we can think and do what is right and true and kind. Enable us to refuse every selfish inclination, every wilful purpose, every unkind feeling, every thought and end and deed of anger and impatience, and to cherish perfect love, constant kindness, to think pure thoughts, to speak gentle words, to do helpful and gracious deeds. Deliver us from all judgment of our fellows remembering that with what measure we judge we shall be judged. Deliver us from all fear of man's judgment of ourselves. Raise our minds to the contemplation of Thy beloved Son alone, that seeing His divine beauty, we may be drawn near unto Him, and changed into His image, and empowered to bring every thought into obedience to Christ, into harmony with His Spirit and His immortal life. [Thomas C. Stone (Altered).]

Rejoice in the Lord always: and I will say, Rejoice. *Phil. 4:4.*
Ye shall rejoice in all that ye put your hand unto. *Deut. 12:7.*
Thou hast loved righteousness, and hated iniquity; therefore God, thy God, hath anointed thee with the oil of gladness above thy fellows. *Heb. 1:9.*
I will see you again, and your heart shall rejoice, and your joy no one taketh away from you. *John 16:22.*
Ye shall be sorrowful, but your sorrow shall be turned into joy. *John 16:20.*

I thank Thee, too, that Thou hast
    made
  Joy to abound;
So many gentle thoughts and deeds
    Circling us round,
That in the darkest spot of earth
    Some love is found.

I thank Thee more that all our joy
  Is touched with pain;
That shadows fall on brightest hours,
  That thorns remain;
So that earth's bliss may be our guide,
  And not our chain.

For Thou who knowest, Lord, how
    soon
  Our weak heart clings,
Hast given us joys tender and true,
  Yet all with wings;
So that we see, gleaming on high,
  Diviner things.
              Adelaide Procter.

O SOURCE of Life and Strength! Many of Thy mercies do we plainly see, and we believe in a boundless store behind. No morning stars that sing together can have deeper call than we for grateful joy. Thou hast given us a life of high vocation, and Thine own breathing in our hearts interprets for us its sacred opportunities. Thou hast cheered the way with many dear affections and glimpses of solemn beauty and everlasting truth. Not a cloud of sorrow, but Thou hast touched with glory: not a dusty atmosphere of care, but Thy light shines through! And lest our spirits should fail before Thine unattainable perfections, Thou hast set us in the train of Thy saints who have learned to take up the cross of sacrifice. Let the time past suffice to have wrought our own will, and now make us consecrate to Thine. [James Martineau.]

CHILDREN OF LIGHT

With thee is the fountain of life: In thy light shall we see light. *Ps. 36:9.*

Again therefore Jesus spake unto them, saying, I am the light of the world: he that followeth me shall not walk in the darkness, but shall have the light of life. *John 8:12.*

Ye are all sons of light, and sons of the day. *I Thess. 5:5.*

Oh, we're sunk enough here, God
  knows!
  But not quite so sunk that mo-
    ments,
Sure tho' seldom, are denied us,
  When the spirit's true endowments
Stand out plainly from the false ones
  And apprise it if pursuing
Or the right way, or the wrong way,
  To its triumph or undoing.

There are flashes struck from mid-
  nights,
  There are fire-flames noondays kin-
    dle,
Whereby piled up honors vanish,
  Whereby swollen ambitions dwin-
    dle
While just this or that poor impulse
  Which for once had play unstifled
Seems the whole work of a life-time
  That away the rest have trifled.
            Robert Browning.

*T*HOU makest darkness and it is night, yet the darkness and the light are both alike to Thee. Make us children of the light. Help us to escape the condemnation that light is come into the world and yet men love darkness rather than light because their deeds are evil. Make us of the company of those who, doing the truth, come to the light without fear, that their works may be made manifest that they have been wrought in God. Make us lovers of the light, our lives kept in the open and unconcealed, knowing that nothing is hid from Thee. Illumine us with truth; may we so look unto Thee that we shall be radiant. Give us eyes to see the glory of God in the face of Jesus Christ who hath brought life and immortality to light and who is the lamp of the Eternal City. Teach us out of Thy Word. May it be a lamp to our feet, a guide to our path. Bring us all home at last to the Lord of Light, away from the outer darkness and let us see Thy Face. [Boyd Edwards (Altered).]

God chose the foolish things of the world, that he might put to shame them that are wise; and God chose the weak things of the world, that he might put to shame the things that are strong; and the base things of the world, . . . and the things that are not, that he might bring to nought the things that are: that no flesh should glory before God. *1 Cor. 1:27–29.*

And after the fire a still small voice. *1 Kings 19:12.*

Who hath despised the day of small things? *Zech. 4:10.*

The little one shall become a thousand, and the small one a strong nation: I, Jehovah, will hasten it in its time. *Isa. 60:22.*

From "Chinese" Gordon's letters to his sister:

Soudan, 1875. We are much more important than we have any idea of. Nothing is trivial that is unseen; it is only the material things of life that are of no import.

Aden, 1880. What we need is a profound faith in God's ruling all things. It is not the Duke nor Lord Beaconsfield; it is He alone who rules. Napoleon, in a book lent me by Watson, says, " The smallest trifles produce the greatest results."

Jaffa, 1883. Every one is doing work quite as important as any one else, whether on a sick bed or as Viceroy of India; it is our folly which makes us think otherwise.

*F*ATHER of spirits, who hast made us in Thine image, we come to Thee this day conscious of our weakness, that Thou mayest make us strong; aware of our ignorance, that Thou mayest make us wise. Free us, we beseech Thee, from all error of false proportion in our judgments, from any contempt for that which seems small and any deference to that which appears great; from the haste that is too busy to enjoy and the restlessness that can bring nothing to completion and the lethargy that longs for no change, and the fear that change may bring loss outweighing its gain. May we realize that beneath all changes of time and space, all limits of knowledge, all instability of will, the foundation of God standeth sure: The Lord knoweth them that are His. Help us to be still and know that Thou art God. [William Adams Brown (Alt.).]

GOD THE SEEKER, NOT MAN

Herein is love, not that we loved God, but that he loved us, and sent his Son to be the propitiation for our sins. *I John 4:10.*

We love, because he first loved us. *I John 4:19.*

Thus saith the Lord Jehovah: Behold, I myself, even I, will search for my sheep, and will seek them out. As a shepherd seeketh out his flock in the day that he is among his sheep that are scattered abroad, so will I seek out my sheep. *Ezek. 34:11, 12.*

The Son of man came to seek and to save that which was lost. *Luke 19:10.*

Ye did not choose me, but I chose you. *John 15:16.*

> I sought the Lord and afterward I knew
> He moved my soul to seek Him, seeking me:
> It was not I that found, O Saviour true,
> No, I was found of Thee.
>
> Thou didst reach forth Thine hand and mine enfold,
> I walked and sank not on the storm-vexed sea, —
> 'Twas not so much that I on Thee took hold
> As Thou, dear Lord, on me.
>
> I find, I walk, I love, but O the whole
> Of love is but my answer, Lord, to Thee;
> For Thou wast long beforehand with my soul.
> Always Thou lovedst me.

O GOD, our Father, the author and giver of life, all that we have that is good we owe to Thee. Our faith in Thee is only the fruitage of Thy faith in us. We love because Thou hast first loved us. All our good is the fruitage of Thy grace. We come to Thee because Thou hast come to us. Every outreaching of our souls to Thee is only response to Thy Spirit whispering "Father" within our hearts. We bless Thee for Thy sovereignty and for our peace therein. Forgive us when we repel the advances of Thy love, for our coldness before the glow of Christ's devotion to our souls, for our blindness and wilfulness and unbelief. Thou who hast made us guardians of the doors, help us to accept the grace that Thou art giving and to let Thee in. [*R. E. S.*]

79

Not that I speak in respect of want: for I have learned, in whatsoever state I am, therein to be content. I know how to be abased, and I know also how to abound: in everything and in all things have I learned the secret both to be filled and to be hungry, both to abound and to be in want. *Phil. 4:11, 12.*

Godliness with contentment is great gain: for we brought nothing into the world, for neither can we carry anything out; but having food and covering we shall be therewith content. *I Tim. 6:6–8.*

My mind to me a kingdom is,
    Such perfecte joy therein I find,
As farre exceeds all earthly blisse
    That God or nature hath assignde:
Though much I want, that most would have,
Yet still my mind forbids to crave.

Content I live, this is my stay:
    I seek no more than may suffice:
I press to bear no haughtie sway;
    Look what I lack my minde supplies
Loe; thus I triumph like a king
Content with that my mind doth bring.

I see how plentie surfeits oft
    And hastie clymbers soonest fall;
I see that such as sit aloft
    Mishap doth threaten most of all;
These get with toil and keep with feare.
Such cares my mind could never bear.

Some have too much, yet still they crave,
    I little have, yet seek no more:
They are but poore, tho' much they have,
    And I am rich with little store.
They poor, I rich; they beg, I give;
They lack, I lend; they pine, I live.
                    Edward Dyer.

My Lord, in Thine arms I am safe; keep me and I have nothing to fear; give me up and I have nothing to hope for. I know nothing about the future, but I rely upon Thee. I pray Thee to give me what is good for me; I pray Thee to take from me whatever may imperil my salvation. I leave it all to Thee, because Thou knowest and I do not. If Thou bringest pain or sorrow on me, give me grace to bear it well, keep me from fretfulness and selfishness. If Thou givest me health and strength and success in this world, keep me ever on my guard lest these great gifts carry me away from Thee. Give me to know Thee, to believe on Thee, to love Thee, to serve Thee, to live to and for Thee. [John Henry Newman.]

Then they cry unto Jehovah in their trouble, and he bringeth them out of their distresses. He maketh the storm a calm, so that the waves thereof are still. Then they are glad because they are quiet; so he bringeth them unto their desired haven. *Ps. 107:28–30.*

There remaineth therefore a . . . rest for the people of God. *Heb. 4:9.*

In my Father's house are many mansions; if it were not so, I would have told you; for I go to prepare a place for you. *John 14:2.*

We are of good courage, and are willing rather to be absent from the body, and to be at home with the Lord. *II Cor. 5:8.*

While he was yet afar off, his father saw him, and was moved with compassion, and ran, and fell on his neck, and kissed him. *Luke 15:20.*

How much more . . . your heavenly Father. *Luke 11:13.*

Does the road wind uphill all the way?
"Yes, to the very end."
Will the day's journey take the whole long day?
"From morn to night, my friend."

But is there for the night a resting place?
A roof for when the slow, dark hours begin?
May not the darkness hide it from my face?
"You cannot miss that inn."

Shall I meet other wayfarers at night?
Those who have gone before?
Then must I knock, or call when just in sight?
"They will not keep you standing at the door."

Shall I find comfort, travelsore and weak?
"Of labor you shall find the sum."
Will there be beds for me and all who seek?
"Yea, beds for all who come." *Christina Rossetti.*

O LORD, support us all the day long . . . , until the shadows lengthen and the evening comes, and the busy world is hushed, and the fever of life is over, and our work is done. Then in Thy mercy grant us a safe lodging, and a holy rest, and peace at the last. [John Henry Newman.]

UNDERSHEPHERDS

What man of you, having a hundred sheep, and having lost one of them, doth not leave the ninety and nine in the wilderness, and go after that which is lost, until he find it? And when he hath found it, he layeth it on his shoulders, rejoicing. *Luke 15:4, 5.*

For I could wish that I myself were anathema from Christ for my brethren's sake, my kinsmen according to the flesh. *Rom. 9:3.*

I am the good shepherd: the good shepherd layeth down his life for the sheep. *John 10:11.*

Greater love hath no man than this, that a man lay down his life for his friends. *John 15:13.*

But God commendeth his own love toward us, in that, while we were yet sinners, Christ died for us. *Rom. 5:8.*

But thou would'st not alone
Be saved, my father! alone
Conquer and come to thy goal,
Leaving the rest in the wild.
We were weary, and we
Fearful, and we in our march
Fain to drop down and to die.
Still thou turnedst, and still
Beckonedst the trembler, and still
Gavest the weary thy hand.
If, in the paths of the world,
Stones might have wounded thy feet,
Toil or dejection have tried
Thy spirit, of that we saw
Nothing — to us thou wast still
Cheerful, and helpful, and firm!
Therefore to thee it was given
Many to save with thyself;
And, at the end of thy day,
O faithful shepherd! to come,
Bringing thy sheep in thy hand.
Matthew Arnold.

ALMIGHTY and Most Merciful Father, who hast given us a new commandment that we should love one another, give us also grace that we may fulfill it. Make us gentle, courteous, and forbearing. Direct our lives so that we may look each to the good of the other in word and deed. And hallow all our friendships by the blessing of Thy Spirit. Help us by Thy great love to succour the afflicted, to relieve the needy and destitute, to share the burdens of the heavy laden, and ever to see Thee in all who are poor and desolate: for His sake who loved us and gave Himself for us, Jesus Christ our Lord. [Bishop Westcott.]

That he would grant you, according to the riches of his glory, that ye may be strengthened with power through his Spirit in the inward man; that Christ may dwell in your hearts through faith; to the end that ye, being rooted and grounded in love, may be strong to apprehend with all the saints what is the breadth and length and height and depth, and to know the love of Christ which passeth knowledge, that ye may be filled unto all the fulness of God. *Eph. 3:16–19.*

> I am so weak, dear Lord, I cannot stand
>   One moment without Thee;
> But, oh, the tenderness of Thy enfolding,
> And, oh, the faithfulness of Thy upholding,
> And, oh, the strength of Thy right hand —
>   That Strength is enough for me.
>
> I am so needy, Lord, and yet I know
>   All fullness dwells in Thee;
> And, hour by hour, that never-failing treasure
> Supplies and fills in overflowing measure
> My last and greatest need, and so
>   Thy Grace is enough for me. . . .
>
> There were strange soul-depths, restless, vast, and broad,
>   Unfathomed as the sea —
> And infinite craving for some infinite stilling;
> But now Thy perfect love is perfect filling;
> Lord Jesus Christ, my Lord, my God,
>   Thou, Thou art enough for me.   *George Macdonald.*

O LORD JESUS, we praise Thee, that Thou didst come amongst us, a gracious gift to the ungrateful race of men, and, undismayed by our sin and blindness, didst live out Thy life of holiness and power, bringing health and peace to all who came to Thee. O Lamb of God, that takest away the sin of the world, for Thy loneliness and failure, for Thy stress of spirit, and Thy strong prayer, for Thy Cross upon the hill, for Thy death that giveth life, for Thy life that overcometh death, we worship Thee, our Lord and Master, our Saviour and Redeemer. [*A Book of Prayers for Students.*]

O magnify Jehovah with me, and let us exalt his name together.
Ps. 34:3.

The glory of Lebanon shall come unto thee, the fir-tree, the pine,
and the box-tree together, to beautify the place of my sanctuary; and I
will make the place of my feet glorious.   *Isa. 60:13.*

God so loved the world.   *John 3:16.*

My blessing fall on this fair world,
 On mountain, valley, forest, ocean.
The clarion winds in ceaseless motion
 And heaven's blue banner high unfurled.
And bless the staff that higher bore me,
 The alms that helped me on my way,
The boundless plain that lies before me,
 The glowing morn, the evening gray!
The very path by which I wander
 Shows glorious, golden, bathed in light.
No blade of grass that glistens yonder
 But seems a star from heaven's height.
God's boundless love to His creation
 Speaks through this beauty to my heart!
Fain would I in rare exaltation
 Sound through the world the wondrous message
Of boundless love to all creation
 To all His love and joy impart!

Tolstoi.

O GOD, purify our hearts that we may entirely love Thee, and
rejoice in being beloved by Thee. Make us kindly affectioned one to
another with brotherly love, delighting to do good, and ever showing
all meekness to all men. May we rejoice to owe no man anything, but
to love one another. And help us to pray always and not faint; in everything giving thanks, offering up the sacrifice of praise continually; possessing our souls in patience, and learning in whatsoever state we are
therewith to be content, for the sake of Jesus Christ, our Lord and
Master. [Fielding Ould (Abbreviated).]

THE GOOD FAITH OF GOD

I know him whom I have believed, and I am persuaded that he is able to guard that which I have committed unto him against that day. *II Tim. 1:12.*

If we are faithless, he abideth faithful; for he cannot deny himself. *II Tim. 2:13.*

Jehovah will keep thee from all evil; he will keep thy soul. Jehovah will keep thy going out and thy coming in from this time forth and for evermore. *Ps. 121:7, 8.*

Now unto him that is able to guard you from stumbling, and to set you before the presence of his glory without blemish in exceeding joy. *Jude 24.*

> Thou Christ, my soul is hurt and bruised;
>   With words the scholars wear me out.
> Brain of me weary and confused,
>   Thee and myself and all I doubt.
>
> And must I back to darkness go
>   Because I cannot say their creed?
> I know not what I think, I know
>   Only that Thou art all I need.
>
> Oh, let me live in Thy realities,
> Nor substitute my notions for Thy facts
> Notion with notion making leagues and pacts,
> They are to Truth as dream-deeds are to acts,
> And questioned, make me doubt of everything.
> "O Lord, my God," my soul gets up and cries,
> "Come Thy own self and with Thee my faith bring."
>   *George Macdonald.*

O THOU Hope of all holy and humble men of heart, and the Saviour of them that trust in Thee in time of trouble, give us not over as captives, in spiritual chains, but recover us that we may awake to do Thy will. Give us wisdom to abound, or patience to suffer need; and where the Master placed us there to be content. Let all our work be done well before we come to die; and let us be gathered into Thine arms, as the harvesters gather a shock in full season. [Rowland Williams.]

LIFE IN GOD'S GOOD WILL

And we know that to them that love God all things work together for good, . . . to them that are called according to his purpose. *Rom. 8:28.*

Be ye transformed by the renewing of your mind, that ye may prove what is the good and acceptable and perfect will of God. *Rom. 12:2.*

Who gave himself for our sins, that he might deliver us out of this present evil world, according to the will of our God and Father. *Gal. 1:4.*

The God of peace . . . make you perfect in every good thing to do his will. *Heb. 13:20, 21.*

Let nothing make thee sad or fretful
  Or too regretful,
    Be still.
What God hath ordered must be right,
Then find in this thine own delight
    His will.

Why shouldst thou fill today with sorrow
  About tomorrow,
    My heart?

One watches all with care most true;
Doubt not that He will give thee too
    Thy part.

Only be steadfast; never waver
  Nor seek earth's favour;
    But rest.
Thou knowest what God's will must be
For all His children, so for thee,
    The best.   *Paul Fleming.*

O LORD, this is all my desire — to walk along the path of life that Thou hast appointed me, even as Jesus my Lord would walk along it, in steadfastness of faith, in meekness of spirit, in lowliness of heart, in gentleness of love. And because outward events have so much power in scattering my thoughts and disturbing the inward peace in which alone the voice of Thy Spirit is heard, do Thou, gracious Lord, calm and settle my soul by that subduing power which alone can bring all thoughts and desires of the heart into captivity to Thyself. All I have is Thine; do Thou with all as seems best to Thy divine will; for I know not what is best. Let not the cares or duties of this life press on me too heavily; but lighten my burden that I may follow Thy way in quietness, filled with thankfulness for Thy mercy, and rendering acceptable service unto Thee. [Maria Hare.]

I therefore, the prisoner in the Lord, beseech you to walk worthily of the calling wherewith ye were called. *Eph. 4:1.*

Walk worthily of the Lord unto all pleasing, bearing fruit in every good work, and increasing in the knowledge of God. *Col. 1:10.*

To the end that ye may be counted worthy of the kingdom of God. *II Thess. 1:5.*

We also pray always for you, that our God may count you worthy of your calling, and fulfil every desire of goodness and every work of faith, with power. *II Thess. 1:11.*

Whether we live, we live unto the Lord; or whether we die, we die unto the Lord: whether we live therefore, or die, we are the Lord's. *Rom. 14:8.*

They shall walk with me in white; for they are worthy. *Rev. 3:4.*

I may not reach the heights I seek,
  My untried strength may fail me:
Or, half-way up the mountain's peak,
  Fierce tempest may assail me:
But though that place I never gain,
Herein lies comfort for my pain —
  I will be worthy of it.

I may not triumph in success,
  Despite my earnest labor:
I may not grasp results that bless
The efforts of my neighbor:
But though my goal I never see
This thought shall always dwell with
  me —
  I will be worthy of it. *Anon.*

Nor deem that acts heroic wait on
  chance!
The man's whole life preludes the
  single deed.
                              Lowell.

Almighty and merciful God, who dost grant unto Thy faithful people the grace to make every path of life temporal the straight and narrow way which leadeth unto life eternal, grant that we who know that we have no strength as of ourselves to help ourselves, and therefore do put all our trust in Thine almighty power, may, by the assistance of Thy heavenly grace, always prevail in all things, against whatsoever shall arise to fight against us, through Jesus Christ. [Roman Breviary.]

THE SECOND TOUCH

The second [foundation of the wall was] sapphire. *Rev. 21:19.*

The second face was the face of a man. *Ezek. 10:14.*

A second [commandment] like unto it is this, Thou shalt love thy neighbor. *Matt. 22:39.*

The second man is of heaven. *I Cor. 15:47.*

So Christ . . . shall appear a second time. *Heb. 9:28.*

The Second Touch: Mark 8:25

The blind man, bowed in sordid helplessness,
  A sound of footsteps caught.
"The Healer comes," they cried, and through the press
  The hapless wretch they brought.
With wild hope born of uttermost distress,
  The healing touch he sought.
A hand reached forth in potent tenderness —
  The miracle was wrought.

Strangely he stares. "What dost thou see?" they cry.
  "I see men walk as trees."
Again the cool hand strokes each aching eye,
  The last dim shadow flees:
Not moving shapes but live men, drawing nigh,
  Now far and clear he sees.
To each he tells how God's own Son came by
  And healed his dire disease.

Dungeoned by self, we too besought His hand
  Our shuttered eyes to free.
His touch bestowed, dumb, stricken crowds we scanned,
  And guessed their misery.
Lord Christ, Thy second touch our hearts demand,
  Each separate soul to see.
His wounds to salve, his wants to understand,
  And lead him home to Thee.   *Howard Arnold Walter.*

O MOST merciful Father, open our eyes, that with fulness of sight we may behold Thy glory in the face of Christ and the face of Christ in every man.

The heavens declare the glory of God; and the firmament show-eth his handiwork. . . . His going forth is from the end of the heavens, and his circuit unto the ends of it. *Ps. 19:1, 6.*

The earth is Jehovah's, and the fulness therof; the world, and they that dwell therein. *Ps. 24:1.*

In the cool of the evening, when the low sweet whispers waken,
    When the laborers turn them homeward, and the weary have their
        will,
When the censers of the roses o'er the forest aisles are shaken,
    Is it but the wind that cometh o'er the far green hill? . . .

In the beauty of the twilight, in the Garden that He loveth
    They have veiled His lovely vesture with the darkness of a name!
Thro' His Garden, thro' His Garden, it is but the wind that moveth,
    No more! But O the miracle, the miracle is the same.

In the cool of the evening, when the sky is an old story,
    Slowly dying, but remembered, ay, and loved with passion still. . . .
Hush! . . . the fringes of His garment, in the fading golden glory
    Softly rustling as He cometh o'er the far green hill.

                                                                Alfred Noyes.

O GOD, we thank thee for this universe, our great home; for its vastness and its riches, and for the manifoldness of the life which teems upon it and of which we are part. We praise thee for the arching sky and the blessed winds, for the driving clouds and the constellations on high. We praise thee for the salt sea and the running water, for the everlasting hills, for the trees, and for the grass under our feet. We thank thee for our senses by which we can see the splendor of the morning, and hear the jubilant songs of love, and smell the breath of the spring-time. Grant us, we pray thee, a heart wide open to all this joy and beauty, and save our souls from being so steeped in care or so darkened by pas-sion that we pass heedless and unseeing when even the thornbush by the wayside is aflame with the glory of God. [Walter Rauschenbusch.]

Let them also that suffer according to the will of God commit their souls in well-doing unto a faithful Creator. *1 Peter 4:19.*

Jesus Christ, . . . the faithful witness, the firstborn of the dead, and the ruler of the kings of the earth. *Rev. 1:5.*

Be thou faithful unto death, and I will give thee the crown of life. *Rev. 2:10.*

Consider . . . Jesus; who was faithful to him that appointed him. *Heb. 3:1, 2.*

The Lord is faithful, who shall establish you, and guard you from the evil one. *II Thess. 3:3.*

> The drowsy lions of Trafalgar lie
> With pride and conquest sated, round about
> The hero's column: travelers pass by
> With careless glance, and oftener without
> A thought of all the glory storied there
> That makes the Lion-Island's fame so fair.
>
> Thou solitary Lion of Lucerne
> Defeated, gasping on an alien shield —
> To thee the stranger's steps with fondness turn.
> Thou dying majesty! To thee we yield
> The tribute due to loyalty and love
> Unshaken as the solid cliff above.   *Irving Browne.*

ALMIGHTY and merciful God, who art the Strength of the weak, the Refreshment of the weary, the Comfort of the sad, the Help of the tempted, the Life of the dying, the God of patience and of all consolation; Thou knowest full well the inner weakness of our nature, how we tremble and quiver before pain, and cannot bear the Cross without Thy divine help and support. Help me, then, O eternal and pitying God, help me to possess my soul in patience, to keep faith with Thee even unto death; so shall I be strengthened with power according to Thy glorious might, in all patience and long suffering; I shall be enabled to endure pain and temptation and, in the depth of my suffering and discipline, hold fast and be true, and by Thy grace to praise Thee with a joyful and steadfast heart. [Johann Habermann (Altered).]

THE LADDER OF ANGELS

And he [Jacob] lighted upon a certain place, and tarried there all night, because the sun was set; and he took one of the stones of the place, and put it under his head, and lay down in that place to sleep. And he dreamed; and, behold, a ladder set up on the earth, and the top of it reached to heaven; and, behold, the angels of God ascending and descending on it. *Gen. 28:11, 12.*

And he [Jesus] saith unto him, Verily, verily, I say unto you, Ye shall see the heaven opened, and the angels of God ascending and descending upon the Son of man. *John 1:51.*

> Not where the wheeling systems darken,
> And our benumbed conceiving soars! —
> The drift of pinions, would we harken,
> Beats at our own clay-shuttered doors.
>
> The angels keep their ancient places; —
> Turn but a stone and start a wing!
> 'Tis ye, 'tis your estrangéd faces,
> That miss the many-splendoured thing.
>
> But (when so sad thou canst not sadder)
> Cry; — and upon thy so sore loss
> Shall shine the traffic of Jacob's ladder
> Pitched betwixt Heaven and Charing Cross.
>
> Yea, in the night, my Soul, my daughter,
> Cry, — clinging Heaven by the hems;
> And lo, Christ walking on the water
> Not of Gennesareth, but Thames!   *Francis Thompson.*

*S*ANCTIFY, O Lord, our souls, bodies and spirits, and touch our apprehensions and search out our consciences, and cast out of us every evil thought, every base desire, all envy and pride and hypocrisy, all falsehood, all deceit, all worldly anxiety, all covetousness, vainglory and sloth, all malice, all wrath, all anger, all remembrance of injuries, every motion of the flesh and spirit that is contrary to Thy holy will; and grant us, O Lord, the Lover of men, with freedom, with a pure heart, and a contrite soul, without confusion of face, and with sanctified lips, boldly to call upon Thee, our holy God and Father, who art in heaven. [*Liturgy of St. James.*]

For the word of God is living, and active, and sharper than any two-edged sword. *Heb. 4:12.*

And they sing a new song, saying, Worthy art thou to take the book, and to open the seals thereof: for thou wast slain, and didst purchase unto God with thy blood men of every tribe, and tongue, and people, and nation, and madest them to be unto our God a kingdom and priests; and they reign upon the earth. *Rev. 5:9, 10.*

God . . . gave unto him the name which is above every name. *Phil. 2:9.*

O God, the Father of all,
O God, the Brother of all,
O God, the Friend of all,
   Turn our hearts to Thee.

From greed and covetousness,
From pride and boastfulness,
From hate and violence,
   Deliver us, good Lord.

I know of a land that knows a lord
That's neither brave nor true;
But I know of a sword, a sword, a sword
Can cut a chain in two.
Its edge is sharp and its blade is broad;
I know of a sword, a sword, a sword
Will cut a chain in two.

I know of a land that's sunk in shame
And hearts that faint and tire,
And I know of a name, a name, a name
Can set the land on fire.
Its sound is a brand, its letters flame;
I know of a name, a name, a name
Will set the land on fire.

I know of hearts that loathe the wrong,
That still are leal and true;
And I know of a song, a song, a song
Can break a fetter through.
Oh, you who long, and long, and long,
I'll give you a song, a song, a song
Will break your fetters through.

Songs from the Book of Jaffir.

GOD ONLY

Thou meetest him that rejoiceth and worketh righteousness, those that remember thee in thy ways. *Isa. 64:5.*

Against thee, thee only, have I sinned, and done that which is evil in thy sight; that thou mayest be justified when thou speakest, and be clear when thou judgest. *Ps. 51:4.*

All my fountains are in thee. *Ps. 87:7.*

Our sufficiency is from God. *II Cor. 3:5.*

Father, into thy hands I commend my spirit. *Luke 23:46.*

To me to live is Christ. *Phil. 1:21.*

> Thou art the source and center of all minds,
> Their only point of rest, Eternal Word!
> From Thee departing, they are lost, and rove
> At random, without honor, hope or peace.
> From Thee is all that soothes the life of man,
> His high endeavor, and his glad success,
> His strength to suffer, and his will to serve.
> But, O; Thou bounteous giver of all good,
> Thou art of all Thy gifts Thyself the crown!
> Give what Thou canst, without Thee we are poor:
> And with Thee rich, take what Thou wilt away.
>
> *Cowper.*

O LORD, lift up the light of Thy countenance upon us: let Thy peace rule in our hearts; and may it be our strength and our song, in the house of our pilgrimage. We commit ourselves to Thy care and keeping this day; let Thy grace be mighty in us and sufficient for us, and let it work in us both to will and to do of Thine own good pleasure, and grant us strength for all the duties of the day. Keep us from sin; give us the rule over our own spirits; and keep us from speaking unadvisedly with our lips. May we live together in peace and holy love, and do Thou command Thy blessing upon us, even life forevermore. Prepare us for all the events of the day: for we know not what a day may bring forth. Give us grace to deny ourselves; to take up our cross daily, and to follow in the steps of our Lord and Master. [Matthew Henry.]

Wherefore we faint not; but though our outward man is decaying, yet our inward man is renewed day by day. For our light affliction which is for the moment, worketh for us more and more exceedingly an eternal weight of glory; while we look not at the things which are seen, but at the things which are not seen: for the things which are seen are temporal; but the things which are not seen are eternal. *II Cor. 4:16–18.*

And he spake a parable unto them to the end that they ought always to pray, and not to faint. *Luke 18:1.*

He giveth power to the faint; and to him that hath no might he increaseth strength. *Isa. 40:29.*

And let us not be weary in well-doing, for in due season we shall reap, if we faint not. *Gal. 6:9.*

I will not faint, but trust in God,
  Who this my lot hath given;
He leads me by the thorny road
  Which is the road to heaven.
Though sad my day that lasts so long,
At evening I shall have a song;
Though dim my day until the night,
At evening time there shall be light.

My life is but a waking day
  Whose tasks are set aright;

Awhile to work, awhile to pray,
  And then a quiet night,
And then, please God, a quiet night
Where saints and angels walk in white:
One dreamless sleep from work and sorrow,
But reawakening on the morrow.
        Christina Rossetti.

GLORY be to Thee, O Lord; glory be to Thee. That this day, and every day, may come on, perfect, holy, peaceable, healthful and without sin, grant, Lord, we beseech Thee. What things are good and profitable to our souls, together with peace in this world, grant, Lord, we beseech Thee. Whatsoever things are true, whatsoever things are honest, whatsoever things are just, whatsoever things are pure, whatsoever things are of good report, — that we may think on these things to do them, grant, Lord, we beseech Thee. A Christian end of our life, without sin, without shame, and, if Thou thinkest good, without pain; when Thou wilt and as Thou wilt, grant, Lord, we beseech Thee. [Lancelot Andrews.]

OUR LORD'S RETURN

I come again. *John 14:3.*

Ye men of Galilee, why stand ye looking into heaven? this Jesus, who was received up from you into heaven, shall so come in like manner as ye beheld him going into heaven. *Acts 1:11.*

Watch therefore: for ye know not when the lord of the house cometh, whether at even, or at midnight, or at cockcrowing, or in the morning; lest coming suddenly he find you sleeping. And what I say unto you I say unto all, Watch. *Mark 13:35-37.*

And not be ashamed before him at his coming. *I John 2:28.*

So I am watching quietly
   Every day.
Whenever the sun shines brightly,
   I rise and say,
Surely it is the shining of His face!
And look unto the gates of His high place
   Beyond the sea.
For I know He is coming shortly
   To summon me.
And when a shadow falls across the threshold
   Of my room
Where I am working my appointed task,
I lift my head to watch the door and ask,
   If He is come.
And the angel answers sweetly
   In my home —
"Only a few more shadows
   And He will come." *Barbara MacAndrew.*

O LORD Jesus Christ who didst send forth with Thy Father the Holy Spirit that He might bring to our remembrance all that Thou didst say to Thy disciples, help us by His aid ever to keep in recollection the promise of Thy coming again. Grant that no doubt or confusion may rob us of this blessed hope but may we ever live as those who are watching for their Lord's return that they may, without amaze but with great joy, welcome Him at His appearing. Even so, come, Lord Jesus. [R. E. S.]

He who testifieth these things saith, Yea: I come quickly. Amen: come, Lord Jesus. *Rev. 22:20.*

Looking for and earnestly desiring the coming of the day of God. *II Peter 3:12.*

If we believe that Jesus died and rose again, even so them also that are fallen asleep in Jesus will God bring with him. *I Thess. 4:14.*

Waiting for the revelation of our Lord Jesus Christ; who shall also confirm you unto the end, that ye be unreprovable in the day of our Lord Jesus Christ. *I Cor. 1:7, 8.*

> Lo! as some wanderer from his stars receiving
>   Promise and presage of sublime emprize,
> Wears evermore the seal of his believing
>   Deep in the dark of solitary eyes, —
>
> So even I, and with a heart more burning,
>   So even I, and with a hope more sweet,
> Yearn for the hour, O Christ, of Thy returning,
>   Faint for the flaming of Thine advent feet. . . .
>
> Surely He cometh, and a thousand voices
>   Shout to the saints and to the deaf are dumb;
> Surely He cometh, and the earth rejoices,
>   Glad in His coming who hath sworn " I come."
>   *F. W. H. Myers.*

O LORD Jesus Christ, we thank Thee that we have besides the story of Thine earthly life and the experience of Thy constant presence, the blessed hope of Thy coming again, when we shall see Thee as Thou art, and when Thou wilt bring with Thee all whom we love who have left our mortal sight and are safe with Thee. Forbid that we should lose the joy and strength of the daily expectancy of Thy return. May our eyes be ever toward Thy coming, not in memory of the past alone, and not alone in common human experience or in the mystery of death, but in Thy visible, personal appearing, remembering Thy most sure word, " I will come again. Watch therefore, lest coming suddenly I find you sleeping." [R. E. S.]

ONE WITH ALL MEN

Wherefore it behooved him in all things to be made like unto his brethren. . . . He is not ashamed to call them brethren. *Heb. 2:17, 11.*

Bear ye one another's burdens, and so fulfil the law of Christ. *Gal. 6:2.*

We are members one of another. *Eph. 4:25.*

But speaking truth in love, may grow up in all things into him, who is the head, even Christ; from whom all the body fitly framed and knit together through that which every joint supplieth, according to the working in due measure of each several part, maketh the increase of the body unto the building up of itself in love. *Eph. 4:15, 16.*

> Give me a heart that beats
> In all its fulness with the common heart
> Of human kind, which the same things make glad,
> The same make sorry! Give me grace enough
> Even in their first beginnings to detect
> The endeavors which the proud heart still is making
> To cut itself from off the common root,
> To set itself upon a private base,
> To have wherein to glory of its own,
> Beside the common glory of the kind!
> Each such attempt in all its hateful pride
> And meanness give me to detect and loathe, —
> A man and claiming fellowship with men! *Trench.*

O GOD, the Father of the forsaken, the Help of the weak, the Supplier of the needy, who hast diffused and proportioned Thy gifts to body and soul, in such sort that all may acknowledge and perform the joyous duty of mutual service, who teachest us that love towards the race of man is the bond of perfectness, and the imitation of Thy blessed self; that it is our Christian life to serve one another, and to love men even as Christ loved us; that we are so wholly one with all mankind that we suffer or are in honor with all others; open our eyes and touch our hearts, that we may see and do, both for this world and for that which is to come, the things that belong to the peace of all men. [Earl of Shaftesbury (Altered).]

THE TRUE COMPANION

Lo, I am with you always, even unto the end of the world. *Matt. 28:20.*

Watch therefore: for ye know not when the lord of the house cometh, whether at even, or at midnight, or at cockcrowing, or in the morning; lest coming suddenly he find you sleeping. And what I say unto you I say unto all, Watch. *Mark 13:35-37.*

Behold, I stand at the door and knock: if any man hear my voice and open the door, I will come in to him, and will sup with him, and he with me. *Rev. 3:20.*

Whosoever shall do the will of my Father who is in heaven, he is my brother, and sister, and mother. *Matt. 12:50.*

If a man love me, he will keep my word: and my Father will love him, and we will come unto him, and make our abode with him. *John 14:23.*

When thou turn'st away from ill
Christ is this side of thy hill.
When thou turnest toward good,
Christ is walking in thy wood.
When thy heart says, " Father, pardon! "
Then the Lord is in thy garden.
When stern Duty wakes to watch,
Then His hand is on the latch.
But when Hope thy song doth rouse,
Then the Lord is in the house.
When to love is all thy wit,
Christ doth at thy table sit.
When God's will is thy heart's pole,
Then is Christ thy very soul.
George Macdonald.

O GOD, who hast made man in Thine own likeness, and who dost love all whom Thou hast made, teach us the unity of Thy family, and the breadth of Thy love. By the example of Thy Son, Jesus our Saviour, enable us, while loving and serving our own, to enter into the fellowship of the whole human family; and forbid that from pride or hardness of heart, we should despise or neglect any for whom Christ died or injure any in whom He lives. And, O Son of Man, as we thus seek with Thy help to walk in Thy ways, fulfill unto us Thy promise. In the hungry whom we feed, and the naked whom we clothe, may we indeed meet Thee, of a surety recognizing Thy presence, and rejoicing in Thy loving word, Inasmuch as ye have done it to these, ye have done it to Me. [Mornay Williams (Altered).]

A MORE STATELY MANSION

So then ye are no more strangers and sojourners, but ye are fellow-citizens with the saints, and of the household of God, being built upon the foundation of the apostles and prophets, Christ Jesus himself being the chief corner stone; in whom each several building, fitly framed together, groweth into a holy temple in the Lord; in whom ye also are builded together for a habitation of God in the Spirit. *Eph. 2:19-22.*

This is the ship of pearl, which, poets feign,
   Sails the unshadowed main, —
   The venturous bark that flings
On the sweet summer wind its purple wings
In gulfs enchanted, where the Siren sings,
   And coral reefs lie bare.
Where the cold sea-maids rise to sun their streaming hair. . . .

Year after year behold the silent toil
   That spread his lustrous coil;
   Still, as the spiral grew,
He left the past year's dwelling for the new,
Stole with soft step its shining archway through
   Built up its idle door,
Stretched in his last found home, and knew the old no more. . . .

Build thee more stately mansions, O my soul,
   As the swift seasons roll!
   Leave thy low-vaulted past!
Let each new temple, nobler than the last,
Shut thee from heaven with a dome more vast
   Till thou at length art free,
Leaving thine outgrown shell by life's unresting sea.
                 Oliver Wendell Holmes.

GRANT unto us, Almighty God, that by increase of love of that which is true, by increase of vision of that which is fair, we may know Thee more, and rising by Thy Spirit's gifts into spiritual pureness, may behold Thee, the Spirit, in spirit and in truth: and so, passing on from strength to strength of human endeavor and human reaching, come to the beatific vision of God, which shall give us perfect peace. [George Dawson.]

LIBERATORS AND LIGHT BEARERS

The Spirit of the Lord is upon me, because he anointed me to preach good tidings to the poor: He hath sent me to proclaim release to the captives, and recovering of sight to the blind, to set at liberty them that are bruised, to proclaim the acceptable year of the Lord. *Luke 4:18, 19.*

To lift the sombre fringes of the Night,
To open lands long darkened to the Light,
To heal grim wounds, to give the blind new sight,
   Right mightily wrought he. . . .

He passed like light across the darkened land,
And dying, left behind him this command,
" The door is open! So let it ever stand! "
   Full mightily wrought he.

Forth to the fight he fared,
High things and great he dared,
In His Master's might, to spread the Light,
Right mightily wrought he.
He greatly loved —
He greatly lived —
And died right mightily.
      John Oxenham, on David Livingstone.

O LORD, who by Thy holy apostle hast taught us to do all things in the Name of the Lord Jesus and to Thy glory; give Thy blessing to this our work, that we may do it in faith and heartily as to the Lord and not unto men. All our powers of body and mind are Thine, and we would fain devote them to Thy service. Sanctify them and the work in which we are engaged; let us not be slothful, but fervent in spirit, and do Thou, O Lord, so bless our efforts that they may bring forth in us the fruit of true wisdom. Teach us to seek after truth, and enable us to gain it; where men are in darkness may we be ready to bear Thy light; wherever in any land, among children or the poor, or anywhere in Thy human family there is suffering or need, there may we be ready to render service in the Name of Christ. [Thomas Arnold (Altered).]

And I will bring the blind by a way that they know not: in paths that they know not will I lead them; I will make darkness light before them, and crooked places straight. *Isa. 42:16.*

And in that day shall the deaf hear the words of the book, and the eyes of the blind shall see out of obscurity and out of darkness. *Isa. 29:18.*

The Spirit of the Lord is upon me, because he . . . hath sent me to proclaim . . . recovering of sight to the blind. *Luke 4:18.*

We look not at the things which are seen, but at the things which are not seen: for the things which are seen are temporal; but the things which are not seen are eternal. *II Cor. 4:18.*

> Thus with the year
> Seasons return, but not to me returns
> Day or the sweet approach of even or morn,
> Or sight of vernal bloom or summer's rose,
> Or flocks or herds, or human face divine;
> But cloud instead and ever during dark
> Surrounds me, from the cheerful ways of men
> Cut off, and for the book of knowledge fair
> Presented with a universal blank
> Of nature's works, to me expunged and rased,
> And wisdom at one entrance quite shut out.
> So much the rather Thou, celestial light,
> Shine inward and the mind through all her powers
> Irradiate; there plant eyes, all must from thence
> Purge and disperse, that I may see and tell
> Of things invisible to mortal sight.
>
> *John Milton* (*On His Blindness*).

LATE have I loved Thee, O Thou Eternal Truth and Goodness! . . . But Thou didst seek me, and when Thou shinedst forth upon me, then I knew Thee and learnt to love Thee. I thank Thee, O my Light, that Thou didst thus shine upon me. . . . When I loved darkness, I knew Thee not, but wandered on from night to night. But Thou didst lead me out of that blindness; Thou didst take me by the hand and call me to Thee, and now I can thank Thee, and Thy mighty voice which hath penetrated to my inmost heart. [Saint Augustine.]

DARKNESS GIVES LIGHT

Even the darkness hideth not from thee, but the night shineth as the day: the darkness and the light are both alike to thee. *Ps. 139:12.*

Jehovah spake . . . out of . . . the thick darkness. *Deut. 5:22.*

Night unto night showeth knowledge. *Ps. 19:2.*

The night following the Lord stood by him, and said, Be of good cheer. *Acts 23:11.*

There stood by me this night an angel of the God whose I am. *Acts 27:23.*

And the light about me shall be night. *Ps. 139:11.*

It is God, that said, Light shall shine out of darkness. *II Cor. 4:6.*

> Mysterious Night! when our first parent knew
> Thee, from report divine, and heard thy name,
> Did he not tremble for this lovely frame, —
> This glorious canopy of light and blue?
> Yet 'neath a curtain of translucent dew,
> Bathed in the rays of the great setting flame,
> Hesperus, with the host of heaven came,
> And lo! creation widened in man's view.
> Who could have thought such darkness lay concealed
> Within thy beams, O Sun! or who could find
> Whilst fly and leaf and insect stood revealed
> That to such countless orbs thou mad'st us blind!
> Why do we then shun death with anxious strife!
> If light can thus deceive, wherefore not life?
> *Joseph Blanco White.*

WE give Thee thanks, Almighty God, for that inward light by which in the midst of outward darkness and outward light, we may behold, as far as may be, Thy purposes and Thy doings, and see under all things Thy judgments, and being upheld by perfect trust in Thee, in times of evil we may rejoice, and in days of darkness be fearless and in times of light be unbewildered and undeceived, and pass on through life in safety, led by Thy sure guidance. Forgive us when we forget or fall away from Thee, when the lights of time hide the lights of eternity. [George Dawson (Altered).]

GOD AND HIS CHILDREN

Jesus saith, . . . Little children. *John 13:31, 33.*

Verily I say unto you, Whosoever shall not receive the kingdom of God as a little child, he shall in no wise enter therein. *Mark 10:15.*

Love your enemies, and pray for them that persecute you; that ye may be sons of your Father who is in heaven. *Matt. 5:44, 45.*

Verily I say unto you, Except ye turn, and become as little children, ye shall in no wise enter into the kingdom of heaven. *Matt. 18:3.*

We are children of God. *Rom. 8:16.*

Ye are all sons of light, and sons of the day. *I Thess. 5:5.*

Jesus spake unto them, saying, I am the light of the world: he that followeth me shall not walk in the darkness, but shall have the light of life. *John 8:12.*

A tender child of summers three
Seeking her little bed at night,
Paused on the dark stair timidly.
"O Mother, take my hand," said she,
"And then the dark will all be light."

We older children grope our way
From dark behind to dark before;
And only when our hands we lay

Dear Lord, in Thine, the night is day,
And there is darkness nevermore.

Reach downward to the sunless days
Wherein our guides are blind as we,
And faith is small, and hope delays;
Take Thou the hands of prayer we raise,
And let us feel the light of Thee.
J. G. Whittier.

*W*E beseech Thee, O Lord, let our hearts be graciously enlightened by Thy holy radiance, that we may serve Thee without fear in holiness and righteousness all the days of our life; that so we may escape the darkness of this world, and by Thy guidance attain the land of eternal brightness; through Thy mercy, O blessed Lord, who dost live and govern all things, world without end. [*Sarum Breviary.*]

O God, by whom the meek are guided in judgment and light riseth up in darkness for the godly; grant us in all our doubts and uncertainties, the grace to ask what Thou wouldst have us do; that the Spirit of wisdom may save us from all false choices, and that in Thy light we may see light, and in Thy straight path may not stumble, through Jesus Christ our Lord. [William Bright.]

THE CITY THAT IS TO COME

I know that my Redeemer liveth, and at last he will stand up upon the earth. *Job 19:25.*

Repent ye therefore, and turn again, that your sins may be blotted out, that so there may come seasons of refreshing from the presence of the Lord; and that he may send the Christ who hath been appointed for you, even Jesus: whom the heaven must receive until the times of restoration of all things. *Acts 3:19–21.*

And I saw the holy city, new Jerusalem, coming down out of heaven from God, made ready as a bride adorned for her husband. *Rev. 21:2.*

And the city hath no need of the sun, neither of the moon, to shine upon it: for the glory of God did lighten it, and the lamp thereof is the Lamb. *Rev. 21:23.*

And did those feet in ancient time
　Walk upon England's mountains green?
And was the holy Lamb of God
　On England's pleasant pastures seen?

And did the Countenance Divine
　Shine forth upon our clouded hills?
And was Jerusalem builded here
　Among these dark Satanic mills?

Bring me my bow of burnished gold,
　Bring me my arrows of desire,
Bring me my spear: O clouds, unfold!
　Bring me my chariot of fire.

I will not cease from mental fight
　Nor shall my sword sleep in my hand
Till we have built Jerusalem
In England's green and pleasant land.
William Blake.

O THOU whose eye is over all the children of men, and who hast called them by Thy Prince of Peace into a Kingdom not of this world, send forth Thy Spirit into all the dark places of life. Let Him still the noise of our strife, and the tumult of the people, carry faith to the doubting, hope to the fearful, strength to the weak, light to the mourners, and more and more increase the pure in heart who see their God. Commit Thy Word, O Lord, to the lips of faithful servants that soon the knowledge of Thee may cover the earth as the waters cover the channels of the deep, and so let Thy Kingdom come and Thy will be done on earth as it is in heaven; through Jesus Christ our Lord. [James Martineau.]

NO HIDING PLACE FROM GOD

Whither shall I go from thy Spirit? Or whither shall I flee from thy presence? If I ascend up into heaven, thou art there: If I make my bed in Sheol, behold, thou art there. If I take the wings of the morning, and dwell in the uttermost parts of the sea; even there shall thy hand lead me, and thy right hand shall hold me. *Ps. 139:7-10.*

Deliver me, O Jehovah, from mine enemies: I flee unto thee to hide me. *Ps. 143:9.*

He was fleeing from the presence of Jehovah. *Jonah 1:10.*

If there had anywhere appeared in space
    Another place of refuge where to flee,
Our hearts had taken refuge in that place
    And not with Thee.

For we against creation's bars had beat
    Like prisoned eagles; through great worlds had sought
Though but a foot of ground to plant our feet,
    Where Thou wert not.

And only when we found in earth and air,
    In heaven or hell, that such might nowhere be —
That we could not flee from Thee anywhere,
    We fled to Thee.   *Trench.*

O GOD, before whose face the generations rise and pass away, age after age the living seek Thee and find that of Thy faithfulness there is no end. Our fathers in their pilgrimage walked by Thy guidance and rested on Thy compassion. Thou wast their Refuge, their Rock, their Fortress, and their Might. Still to their children be all that Thou wast to them, the cloud by day, the fire by night. Where but in Thee have we a covert from the storm, or shadow from the heat of life? In our manifold temptations Thou alone knowest and art ever nigh; in sorrow, Thy pity revives the fainting soul. O Thou sole source of peace and righteousness take now the evil from every heart and join us in one communion with Thy prophets and saints who have trusted in Thee and were not ashamed, O Lord our Refuge and our Redeemer. [James Martineau (Altered).]

THE EYES OF THE HEART

That the God of our Lord Jesus Christ, the Father of glory, may give unto you a spirit of wisdom and revelation in the knowledge of him; having the eyes of your heart enlightened, that ye may know what is the hope of his calling, what the riches of the glory of his inheritance in the saints. *Eph. 1:17, 18.*

> I can see as well as ever, in my dreams
> Then my sight was never better, so it seems:
> But awaking, I'm reminded
> That I am for all time blinded.
> So let me dream.
>
> Toward the sleep that knows no waking,
> Now my steps are ever taking —
> Steps that quicken in their pace,
> As they near my resting place.
> There let me rest. . . .
>
> But this thought brings me no fear,
> For my faith is strong and clear,
> That be it life or be it rest,
> That which will be, will be best,
> And I'm content.
>
> Content indeed, I've had my share
> Of this world's blessing, grief and care,
> And when my summons comes to join
> The countless myriads, who have gone,
> I will be ready.

Written by an Old Man of Eighty Who Had Become Blind in Both Eyes.

ALMIGHTY GOD, Maker of heaven and earth, Giver of light and life, so teach us those things that belong to the heavenly kingdom, and those duties which are of the earth, that we, stirred by the light and life of the peace of God, may be enabled faithfully to do the things committed, and courageously to bear all that we are called to suffer and endure, that being lifted above ourselves, the light of God in the heart and the life of God in the soul of man may be ours. [George Dawson (Altered).]

And I saw the heaven opened; and behold, a white horse, and he that sat thereon called Faithful and True; and in righteousness he doth judge and make war. . . . And he is arrayed in a garment sprinkled with blood: and his name is called The Word of God. . . . And out of his mouth proceedeth a sharp sword, that with it he should smite the nations: and he shall rule them with a rod of iron. . . . And he hath on his garment and on his thigh a name written, KING OF KINGS, AND LORD OF LORDS. *Rev. 19:11, 13, 15, 16.*

O Captain of the wars, whence won Ye so great scars?
  In what fight did Ye smite, and what manner was the foe?
Was it on a day of rout they compassed Thee about,
  Or gat Ye these adornings when Ye wrought their overthrow?

" 'Twas on a day of rout they girded Me about,
  They wounded all My brow, and they smote Me through the side;
My hand held no sword when I met their armed horde,
  And the conqueror fell down, and the conquered bruised his pride."

What is this, unheard before, that the unarmed make war,
  And the slain hath the gain, and the victor hath the rout?
What wars, then, are these, and what the enemies,
  Strange Chief, with the scars of Thy conquest trenched about?

" The Prince I drave forth held the Mount of the North,
  Girt with the guards of flame that roll around the pole.
I drave him with My wars from all his fortress-stars,
  And the sea of death divided that My march might strike its goal. . . ."

What is *Thy* Name? O show! — " My Name ye may not know;
  'Tis a going forth with banners, and a baring of much swords:
But My titles that are high, are they not upon My thigh?
  ' King of Kings! ' are the words, ' Lord of Lords ';
It is written, ' King of Kings, Lord of Lords.' "   *Francis Thompson.*

O THOU whose eternal love for our weak and struggling race was most perfectly shown forth in the blessed life and death of Jesus Christ, our Lord, enable me now so to meditate upon my Lord's passion that, having fellowship with Him in His sorrow, I may also learn the secret of His strength and peace. [John Baillie.]

PRAY AND STILL PRAY

Rejoice always, pray without ceasing; in everything give thanks: for this is the will of God in Christ Jesus to you-ward. *I Thess. 5:16–18.*

In nothing be anxious; but in everything by prayer and supplication with thanksgiving let your requests be made known unto God. And the peace of God, which passeth all understanding, shall guard your hearts and your thoughts in Christ Jesus. *Phil. 4:6, 7.*

O thou that hearest prayer, unto thee shall all flesh come. *Ps. 65:2.*

And he kneeled down and prayed. And there appeared unto him an angel from heaven, strengthening him. *Luke 22:41, 43.*

Lord, what a change within us one short hour
Spent in Thy Presence will prevail to make!
What heavy burdens from our bosoms take!
What parchéd grounds refresh as with a shower!
We kneel and all around us seems to lower,
We rise, and all, the distant and the near,
Stands forth in sunny outline, bright and clear.
We kneel how weak, we rise how full of power!
Why therefore should we do ourselves this wrong,
Or others, that we are not always strong,
That we are ever overborne with care,
That we should ever weak or heartless be,
Anxious or troubled, when with us is prayer,
And joy and strength and courage are with Thee.
Trench.

*O*UR FATHER, grant us, this day, the sense of Thy Presence to cheer, and Thy light to direct us, and give us strength for Thy service. And yet more, Father, give us Thine own help and blessing in our sorrows, our faintness, our failure and sin. Thou knowest that we cannot bear our burdens alone. We are only little children, and the world seems very dark to us, and our path very hard, if we are alone. But we are Thy little children; and so we know we can come to our Father, to ask Thee to help us, and enliven us and strengthen us, and give us hope. [*The Altar of Home.*]

Love is strong as death; . . . a very flame of Jehovah. Many waters cannot quench love, neither can floods drown it. *S. of Sol. 8:6, 7.*

And thou shalt be called The repairer of the breach, The restorer of paths to dwell in. *Isa. 58:12.*

Lord, to whom shall we go? Thou hast the words of eternal life. *John 6:68.*

Jesus said unto her, I am the resurrection, and the life: he that believeth on me, though he die, yet shall he live; and whosoever liveth and believeth on me shall never die. *John 11:25, 26.*

Through the resurrection of Jesus Christ. *I Peter 3:21.*

> Though I have watched so many mourners weep
> O'er the real dead, in dull earth laid asleep —
> Those dead seemed but the shadows of my days
> That passed and left me in the sun's bright rays.
> Now though you go on smiling in the sun
> Our love is slain, and you and love were one.
> You are the first, you I have known so long,
> Whose death was deadly, a tremendous wrong.
> Therefore I seek the faith that sets it right
> Amid the lilies and the candle light.
> I think on Heaven, for in that air so clear
> We two may meet, confused and parted here.
> Oh, when man's dearest dies, 'tis then he goes
> To that old balm that heals the centuries' woes.
> Then Christ's wild cry in all the streets is rife: —
> " I am the Resurrection and the Life."
>
> *Vachel Lindsay.*

BEFORE Thee, O Heavenly Father, we remember those who have passed from us into the fuller light of Thy eternal Presence, into the Life Everlasting. We thank Thee for their loyalty to duty, and their power of self-surrender, by Thy grace, and for the discipline by which Thou hast made them fit in a short time for the higher service in Thy Kingdom. May we have the assurance of their continued fellowship in Thee, and realize that there is no separation between those that love. [John Hunter.]

If any man buildeth on the foundation gold, silver, costly stones, wood, hay, stubble, each man's work shall be made manifest: for the day shall declare it, because it is revealed in fire; and the fire itself shall prove each man's work of what sort it is. If any man's work shall abide which he built thereon, he shall receive a reward. *I Cor. 3:12–14.*

William Tyndale, the first translator of the Bible from the original languages into English speech, was strangled and his body burned at the stake near Brussels, on October 6, 1536. His only crime was making the Bible accessible to every Englishman in his mother tongue. His version comprised all the New Testament and all the Old through Second Chronicles and The Book of Jonah. And his work abides. He built upon the foundation of the apostles and prophets, Jesus Christ being the chief Cornerstone. Our present Authorized Version of the Bible contains, it is estimated, eighty per cent of Tyndale's Old Testament and ninety per cent of his New. Death had no power over him. In the immortal speech of the English Bible he lives on and his voice is clearer and stronger, and reaches farther today than when he moved on the earth.

> How firm a foundation, ye saints of the Lord,
> Is laid for your faith in His excellent Word! . . .
> When through fiery trials thy pathway shall lie,
> My grace, all-sufficient, shall be thy supply;
> The flame shall not hurt thee; I only design
> Thy dross to consume, and thy gold to refine.
> *George Keith.*

O HEAVENLY FATHER, the Father of all wisdom, understanding and true strength, we beseech Thee look mercifully upon Thy servants, and send Thy Holy Spirit into their hearts, and when they must join to fight for the glory of Thy Holy Name, then they, being strengthened with the defence of Thy right hand, may manfully stand in the confession of Thy faith, and of Thy truth, and continue in the same unto the end of their lives, through Jesus Christ our Lord. [Bishop Nicholas Ridley.]

The heavens declare the glory of God; and the firmament showeth his handiwork. Day unto day uttereth speech, and night unto night showeth knowledge. *Ps. 19:1, 2.*

Consider the lilies of the field, how they grow; they toil not, neither do they spin: yet I say unto you, that even Solomon in all his glory was not arrayed like one of these. But if God so clothe the grass of the field, which today is, and tomorrow is cast into the oven, shall he not much more clothe you, O ye of little faith? *Matt. 6:28-30.*

Let thy work appear unto thy servants, and thy glory upon their children. And let the beauty of the Lord our God be upon us. *Ps. 90:16, 17 and margin.*

Thine eyes shall see the king in his beauty: they shall behold a land that reacheth afar. *Isa. 33:17.*

He that speaketh from himself seeketh his own glory: but he that seeketh the glory of him that sent him, the same is true. *John 7:18.*

> God give me speech, in mercy touch my lips,
>   I cannot bear Thy beauty and be still,
> Watching the red-gold majesty that tips
>   The crest of yonder hill,
> And out to sea smites on the sails of ships,
>
> That flame like sudden stars across the deep,
>   Calling their silver comrades from the sky,
> As long, and even longer, shadows creep
>   To sing their lullaby,
> And soothe the tired eyes of earth to sleep.
>   *G. A. Studdert-Kennedy.*

ALMIGHTY GOD, we thank Thee for all that Thou unfoldest and revealest through the veil of earthly things, and for thoughts which have strengthened us to work patiently, to endure stedfastly, and to continue in the doing of Thy will. We also bless and praise Thee, O Lord our God, that when we are in darkness and we see Thee not, Thy heaven remaineth full of light, and we beseech Thee to help us at all times to remember that the darkness and the light are both alike to Thee: grant this through Jesus Christ our Lord. [*A Chain of Prayer.*]

OUR CONTENTMENT IN CARE
FOR OTHERS

And Jesus looking upon him loved him, and said unto him, One thing thou lackest: go, sell whatsoever thou hast, and give to the poor, and thou shalt have treasure in heaven: and come, follow me. *Mark 10:21.*

I rejoice in the Lord greatly, that now at length ye have revived your thought for me; wherein ye did indeed take thought, but ye lacked opportunity. Not that I speak in respect of want: for I have learned, in whatsoever state I am, therein to be content. *Phil. 4:10, 11.*

I exhort therefore, first of all, that supplications, prayers, intercessions, thanksgivings, be made for all men. *I Tim. 2:1.*

These all with one accord continued stedfastly in prayer. *Acts 1:14.*

Not looking each of you to his own things, but . . . to the things of others. *Phil. 2:4.*

Dear Lord! kind Lord!
  Gracious Lord! I pray
Thou wilt look on all I love,
  Tenderly to-day!
Weed their hearts of weariness;
  Scatter every care
Down a wake of angel-wings
  Winnowing the air.

Bring unto the sorrowing
  All release from pain;
Let the lips of laughter
  Overflow again;
And with all the needy
  O divide, I pray,
This vast treasure of content
  That is mine to-day!
       James Whitcomb Riley.

KEEP, O Lord, we beseech Thee, under the shadow of Thy wings, ourselves, our relations and friends, that we may obey Thy will, and enjoy Thy Presence always. Compass us about with Thy holy angels. Shield us with the armor of Thy righteousness upon the right hand and upon the left. Deliver us from the snares of the evil one, and grant us to pass this day, and all the days of our life, without stumbling and without offence; for Thine it is, O Lord, to pity and to save, through Jesus Christ our Lord. [Dean Goulburn.]

NEVER ALONE

And when ye pray, ye shall not be as the hypocrites: for they love to stand and pray in the synagogues and in the corners of the streets, that they may be seen of men. Verily I say unto you, They have received their reward. But thou, when thou prayest, enter into thine inner chamber, and having shut thy door, pray to thy Father who is in secret, and thy Father who seeth in secret shall recompense thee. *Matt. 6:5, 6.*

Ye have heard that it was said, Thou shalt love thy neighbor, and hate thine enemy: but I say unto you, Love your enemies, and pray for them that persecute you; that ye may be sons of your Father who is in heaven. *Matt. 5:43–45.*

> And so I find it well to come
> For deeper rest to this still room;
> For here the habit of the soul
> Feels less the outer world's control.
> And from the silence multiplied
> By these still forms on every side,
> The world that time and sense has known
> Falls off and leaves us God alone.
>
> *J. G. Whittier.*

By words and works we can but touch or influence a few; by our prayers we may benefit the whole world, and every individual of it, high and low, friend, stranger, and enemy. Is it not fearful then to look back on our past lives even in this one respect? *J. H. Newman.*

O THOU Keeper of mankind, leave us not when we go alone. Come to us in the midst of our inward thoughts, where we are alone even among our fellows, that there we may be saved from hurting both Thyself and ourselves. We fear the strife of the open far less than the wrestling with our thoughts in our room or in the fields and forests. Here Thou alone art the helper of the helpless. May our secret place be unknown to our soul's foes that we may be at peace there with Thee, and inasmuch as our worst foes are those who seek lodgment in the soul that they may know its secret places, O conquer these foes for us and be Thou Thyself in sole possession of us and only Companion in our solitude. [Peter Ainslie (Altered).]

Though he was a Son, yet he learned obedience. *Heb. 5:8.*

Whatsoever he saith unto you, do it. *John 2:5.*

To obey is better than sacrifice, and to hearken than the fat of rams. *I Sam. 15:22.*

We must obey God rather than men. *Acts 5:29.*

Through the obedience of the one shall the many be made righteous. *Rom. 5:19.*

> For Knowledge is a steep which few may climb,
> While Duty is a path which all may tread.
> And if the soul of Life and Thought be this, —
> How best to speed the mighty scheme, which still
> Fares onward day by day — the Life of the World,
> Which is the sum of petty lives, — how then shall each
> Of that great multitude of faithful souls,
> Who walk not on the heights, fulfill himself?
> But by the duteous Life which looks not forth
> Beyond its narrow sphere, and finds its work,
> And works it out? — content, this done, to fall
> And perish, if Fate will, — so the great scheme
> Goes forward.   *L. Morris.*

PRESERVE us blameless, O Lord, in our goings out and comings in this day. Fill us with the simplicity of a divine purpose, that we may be inwardly at one with Thy holy will, and lifted above vain wishes of our own. Set free from every detaining desire or reluctance, may we heartily surrender all our powers to the work which Thou hast given us to do; rejoicing in any toil, and fainting under no hardness that may befall us as good soldiers of Jesus Christ; and counting it as our crown of blessing if we may join the company of the faithful who have accomplished their duty and kept Thy Name and witnessed to Thy Kingdom in every age. Fulfill to us the words of Thy Son; grant us His rest and His peace and teach us in the school of His obedience, and then receive us unto Thyself, to mingle with the glorious company of those who have sought to follow Him who is Faithful and True. [James Martineau (Altered).]

REPORTING FOR THE DAY

Have mercy upon me, O God, according to Thy lovingkindness: According to the multitude of thy tender mercies blot out my transgressions. Wash me thoroughly from mine iniquity, and cleanse me from my sin. For I know my transgressions; and my sin is ever before me. *Ps. 51:1–3.*

Come unto me, all ye that labor and are heavy laden, and I will give you rest. *Matt. 11:28.*

Though your sins be as scarlet, they shall be as white as snow; though they be red like crimson, they shall be as wool. *Isa. 1:18.*

Can a woman forget her sucking child, that she should not have compassion on the son of her womb? yea, these may forget, yet will not I forget thee. Behold, I have graven thee upon the palms of my hands. *Isa. 49:15, 16.*

Take unto Thyself, O Father,
  This folded day of Thine,
  This weary day of mine,
Its ragged corners cut me yet,
O, still the jar and fret!
Father, do not forget
  That I am tired
  With this day of Thine.

Breathe Thy pure breath, watching
  Father,
  On this marred day of Thine,
  This wandering day of mine;
Be patient with its blur and blot,
Wash it white of stain and spot.
Reproachful eyes! Remember not
  That I have grieved Thee
  On this day of Thine.
       E. S. P. Ward.

LORD, I offer unto Thee all my sins and offences, which I have committed before Thee, from the day wherein I first could sin even unto this hour, that Thou mayest consume and burn them one and all, with the fire of Thy love, and do away all the stains of my sins, and cleanse my conscience from all offences, and restore to me Thy grace, fully forgiving me all, and admitting me mercifully to the kiss of peace. I offer up also unto Thee all that is good in me, though it be very small and imperfect, in order that Thou mayest amend and sanctify it, that Thou mayest make it grateful and acceptable unto Thee, and always be perfecting it more and more; and bring me also, slothful and unprofitable poor creature as I am, to a good and blessed end. [Thomas à Kempis.]

We are not of them that shrink back unto perdition; but of them that have faith unto the saving of the soul. Now faith is assurance of things hoped for, a conviction of things not seen. *Heb. 10:39 to 11:1.*

For in hope were we saved: but hope that is seen is not hope: for who hopeth for that which he seeth? But if we hope for that which we see not, then do we with patience wait for it. *Rom. 8:24, 25.*

Behind him lay the gray Azores,
  Behind the Gates of Hercules
Before him not the ghost of shores,
  Before him only shoreless seas.
The good mate said, "Now must we pray,
  For lo! the very stars are gone.
Brave Adm'r'l, speak; what shall I say?"
"Why say, 'Sail on! Sail on! and on!'"

They sailed and sailed, as winds might blow,
  Until at last the blanched mate said:
"Why, now not even God would know
Should I and all my men fall dead.
These very winds forget their way
  For God from these dread seas is gone.
Now speak, brave Adm'r'l; speak and say — "
He said, "Sail on! Sail on! and on!"

Then pale and worn he kept his deck
And peered through darkness. Ah! that night
Of all dark nights! And then a speck —
  A light! a light! a light! a light!
It grew, a star-lit flag unfurled!
  It grew to be Time's burst of dawn,
He gained a world; he gave that world
  Its grandest lesson: "On! and on!"
  Joaquin Miller, on Columbus.

O THOU ever blessed Fountain of life, I bless Thee that Thou hast infused into me Thine own vital breath, so that I may become a living soul. It is my earnest desire that I may not only live, but grow; grow in grace and in the knowledge of my Lord and Saviour Jesus Christ. May I grow in patience and fortitude of soul, in humility and zeal, in spirituality and a heavenly disposition of mind. In a word, as Thou knowest I hunger and thirst after righteousness, make me whatever Thou wouldst delight to see me. [Philip Doddridge.]

OURS ARE OURS FOREVER

If we believe that Jesus died and rose again, even so them also that are fallen asleep in Jesus will God bring with him. *1 Thess. 4:14.*

In my Father's house are many mansions; if it were not so, I would have told you; for I go to prepare a place for you. And if I go and prepare a place for you, I come again, and will receive you unto myself; that where I am, there ye may be also. *John 14:2, 3.*

God himself shall be with them, and be their God: and he shall wipe away every tear from their eyes; and death shall be no more; neither shall there be mourning, nor crying, nor pain, any more. *Rev. 21:3, 4.*

I cannot think of them as dead
  Who walk with me no more.
Along the path of life I tread;
  They have but gone before.

The Father's house is mansioned fair
  Beyond my vision dim;
All souls are His and here or there
  Are living unto Him.

And still their silent ministry
  Within my heart hath place,
As when on earth they walked with me
  And met me face to face.

Their lives are made forever mine,
  What they to me have been
Hath left henceforth its seal and sign
  Engraven deep within.

Mine are they by an ownership
  Nor time nor death can free,
For God gives me to love and keep
  Mine own eternally.
                 F. L. Hosmer.

Our heavenly father, we rejoice in the blessed communion of all Thy saints, wherein Thou givest us also to have part. We remember before Thee all who have departed this life in Thy faith and love, and especially those most dear to us. We thank Thee for our present fellowship with them, for our common hope, and for the promise of future joy. . . .

O Eternal God, who holdest all souls in life, impart, we beseech Thee, to Thy whole Church in Paradise and on earth Thy light and Thy peace; and grant that we, following the good examples of those who have served Thee here and are at rest, may at the last enter with them into Thine unending joy; through Jesus Christ, our Lord. [*Prayers from Many Sources,* Page and Laidlaw.]

Where two or three are gathered together in my name, there am I in the midst of them. *Matt. 18:20.*

The kingdom of God is . . . righteousness and peace and joy in the Holy Spirit. *Rom. 14:17.*

Be perfected; be comforted; be of the same mind; live in peace: and the God of love and peace shall be with you. *II Cor. 13:11.*

God is love; and he that abideth in love abideth in God, and God abideth in him. *I John 4:16.*

The kingdom of God is within you. *Luke 17:21.*

O thou not made with hands,
Not throned above the skies,
Nor walled with shining walls
Nor framed with stones of price,
    More bright than gold or gem,
    God's own Jerusalem.

Where'er the gentle heart
Finds courage from above;
Where'er the heart forsook
Warms with the breath of love;
    Where faith bids fear depart,
    City of God! thou art.

Where in life's common ways
With cheerful feet we go;
Where in His steps we tread
Who trod the way of woe:
    Where He is in the heart,
    City of God! thou art.

Not throned above the skies,
Nor golden walled afar,
But where Christ's two or three
In His name gathered are,
    Be in the midst of them
    God's own Jerusalem.
                    Francis Turner Palgrave.

*B*LESS us, O God, with the vision of Thy being and beauty, that in the strength of it and in the joy of it, we may work without haste and without rest. Deepen and quicken in us the sense of Thy presence and refresh us with Thy power. Quiet our understandings and give ease to our hearts by bringing us close to things infinite and eternal: grant us dignity by taking us into Thy service; humble us by laying bare before us our littleness and our sin, and then exalt us by revealing Thyself to us as our Counselor, our Father, and our Friend; and do Thou make us springs of strength and joy to those whom Thou hast sent us to serve.

THE SHADOW AND THE SUBSTANCE

Ye men of Athens, in all things I perceive that ye are very religious. For as I passed along, and observed the objects of your worship, I found also an altar with this inscription, To an Unknown God. What therefore ye worship in ignorance, this I set forth unto you. *Acts 17:22, 23.*

The law having a shadow of the good things to come, not the very image of the things, can never with the same sacrifices year by year, which they offer continually, make perfect them that draw nigh. *Heb. 10:1.*

For if the blood of goats and bulls, and the ashes of a heifer sprinkling them that have been defiled, sanctify unto the cleanness of the flesh: how much more shall the blood of Christ, who through the eternal Spirit offered himself without blemish unto God, cleanse your conscience from dead works to serve the living God? *Heb. 9:13, 14.*

I will shake all nations; and the precious things of all nations shall come. *Hag. 2:7.*

Christ and the Pagan

I had no God but these,
The sacerdotal Trees,
And they uplifted me.
"I hung upon a Tree." . . .

Within a lifeless Stone —
All other gods unknown —
I sought Divinity.
"The Corner-stone am I."

For sacrificial feast
I slaughtered man and beast,
Red recompense to gain.
"So I, a Lamb, was slain."

"Yea, such My hungering Grace
That whereso'er My face
Is hidden, none may grope
Beyond eternal Hope."

John B. Tabb.

THINE, O Lord, is the greatness, and the power and the glory and the victory and the majesty, for all that is in the heaven and the earth is Thine; Thine is the Kingdom, O Lord, and Thou art exalted as head above all. Let all creatures serve Thee, for Thou speakest and they were made. Thou didst send forth Thy Spirit and they were created. O God, Thou art worthy to be praised with all pure and holy praise, therefore let Thy saints praise Thee with all Thy creatures, and let all Thine angels and Thine elect praise Thee forever. [St. Chrysostom.]

GOD AND THE SMALL

Consider the lilies of the field, how they grow; they toil not, neither do they spin: yet I say unto you, that even Solomon in all his glory was not arrayed like one of these. *Matt. 6:28, 29.*

One of his disciples, Andrew, Simon Peter's brother, saith unto him, There is a lad here, who hath five barley loaves, and two fishes: but what are these among so many? *John 6:8, 9.*

He . . . said unto them, . . . bring me a denarius, that I may see it. *Mark 12:15.*

Neither present your members unto sin as instruments of unrighteousness; but present yourselves unto God, as alive from the dead, and your members as instruments of righteousness unto God. *Rom. 6:13.*

Thy loveliness is meek and free
  From arrogance and yet I find
A certain stately pride in thee
  That wakens reverie in my mind.

And well I guess why it is so! —
  A lily once the Master took
His lesson from, then let it go.
  But first He blessed it with a look.

Oh! Who can doubt the flower was thrilled
  With tremblings strange, and raised its head
With joy, its lovesome body filled
  With sense of what the Master said?

And lilies since, forevermore
  Do hold them high, do bear them well,
Do raise their cups more proudly, for
  The lily of the parable. *Richard Burton.*

O LORD, I have a busy world around me. Eye, ear and thought will be needed for my work done in the midst of that world. Now, ere I enter upon it, I would commit eye, ear, thought and wish to Thee. Do Thou bless them and keep their work Thine, that as through Thy natural laws my heart beats and my blood flows without my thought for them, so my spiritual life may hold on its course at those times when my mind cannot consciously turn to Thee to commit each particular thought to Thy service. Hear my prayer for my dear Redeemer's sake. [Thomas Arnold.]

LET THE FIRE BURN

I came to cast fire upon the earth. *Luke 12:49.*

I counsel thee to buy of me gold refined by fire, that thou mayest become rich. *Rev. 3:18.*

That the proof of your faith, being more precious than gold that perisheth though it is proved by fire, may be found unto praise and glory and honor at the revelation of Jesus Christ. *I Peter 1:7.*

Each man's work shall be made manifest: for the day shall declare it, because it is revealed in fire; and the fire itself shall prove each man's work of what sort it is. *I Cor. 3:13.*

He shall baptize you in the Holy Spirit and in fire. *Luke 3:16.*

Out of heaven he made thee to hear his voice, that he might instruct thee: and upon earth he made thee to see his great fire; and thou heardest his words out of the midst of the fire. *Deut. 4:36.*

Who can abide the day of his coming? and who shall stand when he appeareth? for he is like a refiner's fire and like fullers' soap: and he will sit as a refiner and purifier of silver, and he will purify the sons of Levi, and refine them as gold and silver; and they shall offer unto Jehovah offerings in righteousness. *Mal. 3:2, 3.*

Lay me to sleep in sheltering flame,
　O Master of the Hidden Fire!
Wash pure my heart, and cleanse for
　me
　My soul's desire.

In flame of sunrise bathe my mind,
　O Master of the Hidden Fire,
That when I wake, clear-eyed may be
　My soul's desire.
　　　　　　　William Sharp.

O THOU who art of purer eyes than to behold iniquity, who dost require of those who would truly worship Thee clean hands and a pure heart, what can we do, whom sin has stained but cast ourselves upon Thy mercy and accept the purifying discipline of Thy burning love? We thank Thee for the fire that consumes our dross, for the blood of Jesus Christ Thy Son which cleanses us from all sin, for the pain that purifies, for the despairs of earth from which the sure hope of heaven is born, for the light out of darkness, and for the Everlasting Day beyond our mortal night. [R. E. S.]

THE WORLD'S RELIANCE AND LIFE'S CONTEMPT

Money answereth all things. *Eccl. 10:19.*

They build up Zion with blood, and Jerusalem with iniquity. The heads thereof judge for reward, and the priests thereof teach for hire, and the prophets thereof divine for money. *Micah 3:10, 11.*

Now when Simon saw that through the laying on of the apostles' hands the Holy Spirit was given, he offered them money, saying, Give me also this power, that on whomsoever I lay my hands, he may receive the Holy Spirit. But Peter said unto him, Thy silver perish with thee. *Acts 8:18-20.*

Ho, every one that thirsteth, come ye to the waters, and he that hath no money; come ye, buy, and eat; yea, come, buy wine and milk without money and without price. *Isa. 55:1.*

I am the good shepherd: the good shepherd layeth down his life for the sheep. *John 10:11.*

> Then sovereigns, statesmen, north and south
> Rose up in wrath and fear,
> And cried, protesting by one mouth,
> What monster have we here,
> A great deed at this hour of day,
> A great, just deed, and not for pay?
> Absurd or insincere. *E. B. Browning.*

O GOD, who hast shown us in the life and words and deeds of Thy Son the true way of blessedness, Thou hast also showed us in His suffering and death that the path of love may lead to the Cross and the reward of faithfulness be a crown of thorns. Give us grace to learn these hard lessons. Forgive us for our selfishness, for our misuse of Thy gifts, for our unfaithfulness to the trusts Thou hast committed to us, for our mercenary minds, for our unlikeness to Thee in Thy generous, forgiving and impartial love. May we take up our cross and follow Christ in the strength of patience, in the constancy of faith, and the self-forgetfulness of love, and may we have such fellowship with Christ in His suffering that we may know also the power of His resurrection and share with Him in the glory which He has with Thee.

His face did shine as the sun, and his garments became white as the light. *Matt. 17:2.*

Now are we children of God, and it is not yet made manifest what we shall be. We know that, if he shall be manifested, we shall be like him; for we shall see him even as he is. *I John 3:2.*

There was a Man who saw Life face to face
    And ever as He walked from day to day
    The deathless mystery of being lay
Plain as the path He trod in loneliness;
And each deep-hid inscription could He trace;
    How men have fought and loved and fought again;
    How in lone darkness souls cried out for pain;
How each green foot of sod from sea to sea
    Was red with blood of men slain wantonly;
    How tears of pity, warm as summer rain,
Again and ever washed the stains away,
        Leaving to love at last the victory,
    Above the strife and hate and fever pain,
The squalid talk and walk of sordid men,
    He saw the vision changeless as the stars
    That shone through temple gates or prison bars,
        Or to the body nailed upon the tree,
    Through each mean action of the life that is,
        The marvel of the life that yet shall be.
                                    David Starr Jordan.

Most gracious God, who in our best moments dost give us foretastes of those good things which Thou hast prepared for those that love Thee, increase our faith, we beseech Thee, in Thy power and in Thy will to do for us exceedingly abundantly above all that we ask or even think. Thou who in time past hast visited Thy people with Thy blessing, pour forth Thy Spirit upon us in this latter day. May those of us who are young see visions of the better world Thou hast in store; may those of us who are old be refreshed with dreams of the endless life to which Thou art inviting us. [William Adams Brown (Abbreviated).]

And I saw the holy city, new Jerusalem, coming down out of heaven from God, made ready as a bride adorned for her husband. And I heard a great voice out of the throne saying, Behold, the tabernacle of God is with men, . . . and they shall be his peoples, and God himself shall be with them, and be their God. *Rev. 21:2, 3.*

Awake, awake, put on thy strength, O Zion; put on thy beautiful garments, O Jerusalem, the holy city. *Isa. 52:1.*

His foundation is in the holy mountains. Jehovah loveth the gates of Zion more than all the dwellings of Jacob. Glorious things are spoken of thee, O city of God. *Ps. 87:1–3.*

According to his promise, we look for new heavens and a new earth, wherein dwelleth righteousness. *II Peter 3:13.*

I give you the end of a golden string;
　Only wind it into a ball,
It will lead you in at heaven's gate,
　Built in Jerusalem's wall.

England! awake! awake! awake!
　Jerusalem thy sister calls!
Why wilt thou sleep the sleep of death,
　And close her from thy ancient
　　walls?

Thy hills and valleys felt her feet
　Gently upon their bosoms move:
Thy gates beheld sweet Zion's ways;
　Then was a time of joy and love.

And now the time returns again:
　Our souls exult, and London's towers
Receive the Lamb of God to dwell
　In England's green and pleasant bowers.

William Blake.

ALMIGHTY GOD, who turnest the heart of the fathers to the children and of the children to their fathers, receive, we pray Thee, our unfeigned thanks for the good land which Thou hast given us. Forgive us our transgressions; cleanse us from all things that defile our national life, and grant that this people which Thou hast abundantly blessed may keep Thy commandments, walk in Thy ways, and fear Thee. Be gracious to our times, that by Thy bounty both national quietness and Christian devotion may be duly maintained. Let Thy work appear unto Thy servants and Thy glory unto their children; and let the beauty of the Lord our God be upon us; yea the work of our hands, establish Thou it, through Jesus Christ our Lord. [*The Book of Common Worship* (Alt.).]

ONCE AND FOREVER

I have set the Lord always before me: Because he is at my right hand, I shall not be moved. *Ps. 16:8.*

Lo, I am with you always, even unto the end of the world. *Matt. 28:20.*

The Lord loved Israel for ever. *1 Kings 10:9.*

He shall abide before God for ever. *Ps. 61:7.*

I trust in the lovingkindness of God for ever and ever. *Ps. 52:8.*

I know that, whatsoever God doeth, it shall be for ever: nothing can be put to it, nor anything taken from it; and God hath done it, that men should fear before him. That which is hath been long ago; and that which is to be hath long ago been: and God seeketh again that which is passed away. *Eccl. 3:14, 15.*

All things once are things forever:
Soul, once living, lives forever;
Blame not what is only once,
When that once endures forever;
Love once felt, though soon forgot,
Moulds the heart to good forever,
Once betrayed from childly faith,

Man is conscious man forever;
Once the void of life revealed,
It must deepen on forever,
Unless God fill up the heart
With Himself for once and ever:
Once made God and man at one
God and man are one forever.

Richard Monckton Milnes.

*A*LMIGHTY and most merciful Father, in Whom we live and move and have our being, to whose tender compassion we owe our safety in days past, together with all the comforts of this present life, and the hopes of that which is to come, we praise Thee, O God, our Creator and Preserver, unto Thee do we give thanks, O God, our exceeding joy. From everlasting to everlasting Thou art God, and daily Thou pourest Thy benefits upon us. Grant, we beseech Thee that Jesus our Lord, the same yesterday, today and forever, the hope of glory, may even now be formed in us, in all humility, meekness, patience, contendedness and absolute surrender of our souls and bodies to Thy holy will and pleasure. Leave us not, nor forsake us, O Father, but conduct us safe through all changes of our condition here in an unchangeable love to Thee, and in holy quietness of mind in Thy unchanging love to us, till we come to dwell with Thee and rejoice in Thee forever. [Simon Patrick (Alt.).]

SIN NOT WORTH THE PRICE

The wages of sin is death. *Rom. 6:23.*

For if we sin wilfully after that we have received the knowledge of the truth, there remaineth no more a sacrifice for sins, but a certain fearful expectation of judgment. *Heb. 10:26, 27.*

And Cain saith unto Jehovah, My punishment is greater than I can bear. *Gen. 4:13.*

Be not deceived; God is not mocked: for whatsoever a man soweth, that shall he also reap. For he that soweth unto his own flesh shall of the flesh reap corruption. *Gal. 6:7, 8.*

Repent therefore; or else I come to thee quickly. *Rev. 2:16.*

Thy way and thy doings have procured these things unto thee; this is thy wickedness; for it is bitter, for it reacheth unto thy heart. My anguish, my anguish! I am pained at my very heart; my heart is disquieted in me. *Jer. 4:18, 19.*

I have had my will,
  Tasted every pleasure.
I have drunk my fill
  Of the purple measure.
Life has lost its zest
Sorrow is my quest,
  O the lees are bitter, bitter,
Give me rest.

Love once filled the bowl
  Running o'er with blisses,
Made my very soul
  Drunk with crimson kisses.
But I drank it dry,
Love has passed me by.
  O the lees are bitter, bitter,
Let me die.   *George Arnold.*

ALMIGHTY GOD, Father of our Lord Jesus Christ, Maker of all things, Judge of all men; We acknowledge and bewail our manifold sins and wickedness, Which we, from time to time, most grievously have committed, By thought, word, and deed, Against thy Divine Majesty, Provoking most justly thy wrath and indignation against us. We do earnestly repent, And are heartily sorry for these our misdoings; The remembrance of them is grievous unto us; The burden of them is intolerable. Have mercy upon us, Have mercy upon us, most merciful Father; For thy Son our Lord Jesus Christ's sake, Forgive us all that is past; And grant that we may ever hereafter Serve and please thee In newness of life, To the honour and glory of thy Name; Through Jesus Christ our Lord. [*The Book of Common Prayer.*]

GOD THE BUILDER AND CONSERVER

Know ye not that ye are a temple of God, and that the Spirit of God dwelleth in you? If any man destroyeth the temple of God, him shall God destroy; for the temple of God is holy, and such are ye. *I Cor. 3:16, 17.*

For we know that if the earthly house of our tabernacle be dissolved, we have a building from God, a house not made with hands, eternal, in the heavens. *II Cor. 5:1.*

[Christ's] house are we. *Heb. 3:6.*

Ye are . . . God's building. *I Cor. 3:9.*

Therefore to whom turn I but to Thee, the ineffable Name?
Builder and maker, Thou, of houses not made with hands!
What, have fear of change from Thee who art ever the same?
Doubt that Thy power can fill the heart that Thy power expands?
There shall never be one lost good! What was, shall live as before.
The evil is null, is nought, is silence implying sound:
What was good shall be good, with, for evil, so much good more;
On the earth the broken arcs; in the heaven a perfect round.

All we have willed or hoped or dreamed of good, shall exist;
Not its semblance but itself; no beauty, no good, nor power
Whose voice has gone forth, but each survives for the melodist
When eternity affirms the conception of an hour.
The high that proved too high, the heroic for earth too hard,
The passion that left the ground to lose itself in the sky
Are music sent up to God by the lover and the bard:
Enough that He heard it once: we shall hear it by and by.
                                        Robert Browning.

O EVER-BLESSED Father who dost keep Thy faithful in one holy fellowship, grant, we pray Thee, to us Thy servants the support of Thine everlasting love. Assist us in the great fight against sin, and keep us safe amid the dangers and temptations of this mortal life. Grant that we may never faint or fail through weariness of spirit, but so strengthen us through Thine eternal power, that we, persevering in all good works, may finally receive the crown of everlasting glory, through the merits of Christ Jesus our Lord. [*Prayers from Ancient and Modern Sources.*]

THE WHOLE IN THE SMALLEST PART

The light of the knowledge of the glory of God in the face of Jesus Christ. *II Cor. 4:6.*

I fear, lest . . . your minds should be corrupted from the simplicity and purity that is toward Christ. *II Cor. 11:3.*

I proclaimed a fast there, at the river Ahava, that we might humble ourselves before our God, to seek of him a straight way for us, and for our little ones. *Ezra 8:21.*

Thou, Beth-lehem Ephrathah, which art little to be among the thousands of Judah, out of thee shall one come forth unto me that is to be ruler in Israel; whose goings forth are from of old, from everlasting. *Micah 5:2.*

Martha, Martha, thou art anxious and troubled about many things: but one thing is needful: for Mary hath chosen the good part, which shall not be taken away from her. *Luke 10:41, 42.*

Clasp thou of truth the central core!
Hold fast that centre's central sense!
An atom there shall fill thee more
Than realms on Truth's circumference.

That cradled Saviour, mute and small
Was God — is God while worlds endure!

Who holds Truth truly holds it all
In essence, or in miniature.

Know what thou know'st! He knoweth much
Who knows not many things: and he
Knows most whose knowledge has a touch
Of God's divine simplicity.
Aubrey Thomas de Vere.

O LORD, let us walk before Thee in childlike simplicity, stedfast in prayer, looking ever unto Thee that whatsoever we do or abstain from doing, we may in all things follow the least indication of Thy will. Become Lord of our hearts and spirits, that the whole inner man may be brought under Thy rule, and that Thy life of love and righteousness may pervade all our thoughts and energies, and the very ground of our souls; that we may be wholly filled with it. Grant us grace to rest from all sinful deeds and thoughts, to surrender ourselves wholly unto Thee and to keep our souls still before Thee like a still lake; that so the beams of Thy grace may be mirrored therein, and may kindle in our hearts the glow of faith and love and prayer. [Gerhard Tersteegen (Altered).]

For this God is our God for ever and ever: He will be our guide even unto death. *Ps. 48:14.*

Thou wilt guide me with thy counsel, and afterward receive me to glory. *Ps. 73:24.*

And Jehovah will guide thee continually, and satisfy thy soul in dry places, and make strong thy bones; and thou shalt be like a watered garden, and like a spring of water, whose waters fail not. *Isa. 58:11.*

My witness is true; for I know whence I came, and whither I go. *John 8:14.*

Teach me thy way, O Jehovah; and lead me in a plain path. *Ps. 27:11.*

Thy way, O God, is in holiness. *Ps. 77:13 and margin.*

To a Waterfowl

Whither midst falling dew,
While glow the heavens with the last steps of day,
Far, through their rosy depths, dost thou pursue
    Thy solitary way? . . .

There is a Power whose care
Teaches thy way along that pathless coast, —
The desert and illimitable air, —
    Lone wandering but not lost. . . .

Thou'rt gone, the abyss of heaven
Hath swallowed up thy form; yet on my heart
Deeply hath sunk the lesson thou hast given,
    And shall not soon depart.

He who, from zone to zone,
Guides through the boundless sky thy certain flight,
In the long way that I must tread alone,
    Will lead my steps aright. *William Cullen Bryant.*

O GOD, by whom the meek are guided in judgment, and light riseth up in darkness for the godly; grant us, in all our doubts and uncertainties, the grace to ask what Thou wouldst have us to do; that the Spirit of wisdom may save us from all false choices, and that in Thy light we may see light, and in Thy straight path may not stumble; through Jesus Christ our Lord. [William Bright.]

THE PERFECT TEACHER

He taught them as one having authority, and not as their scribes. *Matt. 7:29.*

Never man so spake. *John 7:46.*

And he opened his mouth and taught them saying, Blessed. *Matt. 5:2, 3.*

Jesus was pre-eminently a teacher. This is one of our first glimpses of him: And Jesus went about in all Galilee, teaching in their synagogues, *Matt. 4:23.* Luke summarizes his ministry as a work of doing and teaching: The former treatise I made, O Theophilus, concerning all that Jesus began both to do and to teach. *Acts 1:1.* He was constantly addressed as " Teacher," by Nicodemus, *John 3:2,* by his enemies, *Matt. 12:38,* by his disciples, *John 11:28,* and he called himself by the same title, *Matt. 23:8.*

Tho' truths in manhood darkly join,
Deep seated in our mystic frame
We yield all blessing to the Name
Of Him that made them current coin.

For Wisdom dealt with mortal powers,
When truth is closest words shall fail,
When truth embodied in a tale
Shall enter in at lowly doors.

And so the Word had breath, and wrought
With human hands the creed of creeds
In loveliness of perfect deeds,
More strong than all poetic thought.

Tennyson.

Almighty god, the inspirer of prophets and apostles, and of ᷉very true and good thought and feeling in all men; we would join the Christian Church throughout the world in thanking Thee for the gift of Thy Spirit by which Thou hast enabled some in all ages to be the teachers of their brethren. Most of all we thank Thee for the Perfect Teacher, Thy Son Jesus Christ our Lord, who came into the world as the Light and the Truth, and who by what He was and what He did taught us the truth about Thee and about ourselves. And we pray Thee so to pour out His Spirit on us that we may know and understand the deep things of God, and that love and goodness and all the fruits of righteousness may abound in our lives to Thy praise and glory. [*Devotional Services* (Altered).]

ALL OUR DAYS ARE IN GOD'S CARE

Be not . . . anxious, saying, What shall we eat? or, What shall we drink? or, Wherewithal shall we be clothed? . . . ; for your heavenly Father knoweth that ye have need of all these things. . . . Be not therefore anxious for the morrow. *Matt. 6:31, 32, 34.*

I, even I, am he that blotteth out thy transgressions for mine own sake; and I will not remember thy sins. *Isa. 43:25.*

Look therefore carefully how ye walk, not as unwise, but as wise; redeeming the time. *Eph. 5:15, 16.*

Take heed, brethren, lest haply there shall be in any one of you an evil heart of unbelief, in falling away from the living God: but exhort one another day by day, so long as it is called To-day; lest any one of you be hardened by the deceitfulness of sin: for we are become partakers of Christ, if we hold fast the beginning of our confidence firm unto the end. *Heb. 3:12–14.*

With every rising of the sun
Think of your life as just begun.

The past has shrivelled and buried deep
All yesterdays, then let them sleep.

Nor seek to summon back one ghost
Of that innumerable host.

Concern yourself with but today,
Woo it, and teach it to obey.

You will and wish. Since time began,
Today has been the friend of man;

But in his blindness and his sorrow
He looks to yesterday and tomorrow.

You and today! A soul sublime
And the great pregnant hour of time.

With God Himself to bind the twain!
Go forth, I say, Attain! Attain!
British Weekly.

*L*ORD, I know not what I ought to ask of Thee; Thou only knowest what I need; Thou lovest me better than I know how to love myself. O Father! give to Thy child that which he himself knows not how to ask. I dare not ask either for crosses or consolations; I simply present myself before Thee, I open my heart to Thee. Behold my needs which I know not myself; see and do according to Thy tender mercy. Smite, or heal; depress me, or raise me up; I adore all Thy purposes without knowing them; I am silent; I offer myself in sacrifice; I yield myself to Thee today; I would have no other desire than to accomplish Thy will. Teach me to pray. Pray Thyself in me. [Fénelon (Altered).].

FOLLOW ME

And passing along by the sea of Galilee, he saw Simon and Andrew the brother of Simon casting a net in the sea; for they were fishers. And Jesus said unto them, Come ye after me, and I will make you to become fishers of men. *Mark 1:16, 17.*

And as Jesus passed by from thence, he saw a man called Matthew, sitting at the place of toll: and he saith unto him, Follow me. And he arose, and followed him. *Matt. 9:9.*

And when they had brought their boats to land, they left all and followed him. *Luke 5:11.*

Peter therefore seeing him saith to Jesus, Lord, and what shall this man do? Jesus saith unto him, If I will that he tarry till I come, what is that to thee? follow thou me. *John 21:21, 22.*

Let us follow after things which make for peace. *Rom. 14:19.*

Always follow after that which is good. *I Thess. 5:15.*

Follow after righteousness. *I Tim. 6:11.*

I heard Him call —
  "Come, follow," that was all.
My gold grew dim
My soul went after Him.
  I rose and followed, that was all.
Who would not follow
If they heard Him call?

Him evermore I behold
  Walking in Galilee,

Through the corn-fields' waving gold,
In hamlet, or grassy wold,
  By the shores of the Beautiful Sea.
He toucheth the sightless eyes
  Before Him the demons flee;
To the dead He sayeth, Arise!
  To the living, Follow Me!
And that Voice still soundeth on
From the centuries that are gone
  To the centuries that shall be.
          H. W. Longfellow.

O CHRIST, the true Vine and the Source of life, ever giving Thyself that the world may live, who also hast called us to follow Thee and who hast taught us that those who would follow Thee must drink of Thy cup and be baptized with Thy baptism, and will to lose their lives for Thy sake; Grant us so to receive within our souls the power of Thine eternal sacrifice that in sharing Thy cup and Thy baptism we may show Thy glory and at the last be made perfect in Thy love, and losing our lives for Thy sake and the Gospel's find them unto life eternal. [*The Kingdom, the Power and the Glory* (Altered).]

The Father . . . seeketh. *John 4:23, margin.*

And Jehovah God called unto the man, and said unto him, Where art thou? *Gen. 3:9.*

For thus saith the Lord Jehovah: Behold, I myself, even I, will search for my sheep, and will seek them out. As a shepherd seeketh out his flock in the day that he is among his sheep that are scattered abroad, so will I seek out my sheep. *Ezek. 34:11, 12.*

The Lord is . . . not wishing that any should perish, but that all should come to repentance. *II Peter 3:9.*

Hereby know we love, because he laid down his life for us. *I John 3:16.*

O Love that wilt not let me go,
  I rest my weary soul in Thee;
I give Thee back the life I owe,
That in Thy ocean depths its flow
  May richer, fuller be.

O Joy that seekest me through pain,
  I cannot close my heart to Thee;
I trace the rainbow through the rain,
And feel the promise is not vain
  That morn shall tearless be.

O Light that followest all my way,
  I yield my flickering torch to Thee;
My heart restores its borrowed ray,
That in Thy sunshine's blaze its day
  May brighter, fairer be.

O Cross that liftest up my head,
  I dare not ask to fly from Thee;
I lay in dust life's glory dead,
And from the ground there blossoms
  red
Life that shall endless be.
  George Matheson.

*A*LMIGHTY GOD, Father of all mercies, we Thine unworthy servants do give Thee most humble and hearty thanks for all Thy goodness and loving kindness to us and to all men. We bless Thee for our creation, preservation, and all the blessings of this life; but, above all, for Thine inestimable love in the redemption of the world by our Lord Jesus Christ; for the means of grace and for the hope of glory. And we beseech Thee, give us that due sense of all Thy mercies, that our hearts may be unfeignedly thankful; and that we may show forth Thy praise, not only with our lips, but in our lives; by giving up ourselves to Thy service, and by walking before Thee in holiness and righteousness all our days. [Bishop Reynolds.]

THE HAPPY MAN

Blessed are the poor in spirit: for theirs is the kingdom of heaven. . . . Blessed are the meek: for they shall inherit the earth. . . . Blessed are the pure in heart: for they shall see God. *Matt. 5:3, 5, 8.*

He that overcometh shall inherit these things; and I will be his God, and he shall be my son. *Rev. 21:7.*

For behold your calling, brethren, that not many wise after the flesh, not many mighty, not many noble, are called: but God chose . . . the weak things of the world, that he might put to shame the things that are strong. *1 Cor. 1:26, 27.*

I have learned, in whatsoever state I am, therein to be content. *Phil. 4:11.*

> He is the happy man whose life even now
> Shows somewhat of that happier life to come;
> Who, doomed to an obscure but tranquil state
> Is pleased with it, and, were he free to choose
> Would make his fate his choice; whom place, the fruit
> Of virtue, and whom virtue, fruit of faith
> Prepare for happiness; bespeak him one
> Content indeed to sojourn while he must
> Below the skies, but having there his home
> The world o'er looks him in her busy search
> Of objects, more illustrious in her view;
> And occupied as earnestly as she,
> Though more sublimely, he o'er looks the world.
>
> *William Cowper.*

O GOD, our Lord, the stay of all them that put their trust in Thee, wherever Thou leadest we would go, for Thy ways are perfect wisdom and love. We would be Thine; let us never fall away from Thee. We would accept all things without murmuring from Thy hand, for whatever Thou dost is right. Blend our wills with Thine, and then we need fear no evil, nor death itself, for all things must work together for our good. Lord, keep us in Thy love and truth; comfort us with Thy light; and guide us by Thy Holy Spirit. [S. Weiss (Abbreviated).]

THE CHILD HEART

See that ye despise not one of these little ones: for I say unto you, that in heaven their angels do always behold the face of my Father who is in heaven. *Matt. 18:10.*

Then were there brought unto him little children, that he should lay his hands upon them, and pray: and the disciples rebuked them. But Jesus said, Suffer the little children, and forbid them not, to come unto me: for to such belongeth the kingdom of heaven. *Matt. 19:13, 14.*

I will write upon him the name of my God, and the name of the city of my God, the new Jerusalem, which cometh down out of heaven from my God, and mine own new name. *Rev. 3:12.*

Verily I say unto you, Except ye turn, and become as little children, ye shall in no wise enter into the kingdom of heaven. Whoso shall cause one of these little ones that believe on me to stumble, it is profitable for him that a great millstone should be hanged about his neck, and that he should be sunk in the depth of the sea. *Matt. 18:3, 6.*

> Jesus, permit Thy gracious Name to stand
> As the first effort of a youthful hand
> And as her fingers o'er the canvass move
> Engage her tender heart to seek Thy love.
> With Thy dear children may she have a part,
> And write Thy Name Thyself upon her heart.
> *An Old Sampler by Mary Wilson.*

O LORD, prepare my heart, I beseech Thee, to reverence Thee, to adore Thee, to love Thee; to hate, for love of Thee, all my sins, imperfections, shortcomings, whatever in me displeaseth Thee; and to love all which Thou lovest and whom Thou lovest. Give me, Lord, fervor of love, shame for my unthankfulness, sorrow for my sins, longing for Thy grace, and to be wholly united with Thee. Let my very coldness call for the glow of Thy love; let my emptiness and dryness, like a barren and thirsty land, thirst for Thee, call on Thee to come into my soul, who refreshest those who are weary. Let my heart ache to Thee and for Thee, who stillest the aching of the heart. Let my mute longings praise Thee, crave to Thee, who satisfiest the empty soul, that waits on Thee. [E. B. Pusey.]

THE WITNESSES

Therefore let us also, seeing we are compassed about with so great a cloud of witnesses, lay aside every weight, and the sin which doth so easily beset us, and let us run with patience the race that is set before us, looking unto Jesus. *Heb. 12:1, 2.*

Angels came and ministered unto him. *Matt. 4:11.*

Who maketh his angels winds, and his ministers a flame of fire. *Heb. 1:7.*

And he [Elisha] answered, Fear not; for they that are with us are more than they that are with them. And Elisha prayed, and said, Jehovah, I pray thee, open his eyes, that he may see. And Jehovah opened the eyes of the young man; and he saw: and, behold, the mountain was full of horses and chariots . . . about Elisha. *II Kings 6:16, 17.*

> O may I join the choir invisible
> Of those immortal dead who live again
> In minds made better by their presence; live
> In pulses stirred to generosity,
> In deeds of daring rectitude, in scorn
> Of miserable aims that end with self,
> In thoughts sublime that pierce the night like stars
> And with their mild persistence urge men's minds
> To vaster issues. . . .   *George Eliot.*

Open the eyes of faith and thou shalt behold a theatre of spectators, for if the air is filled with angels much more the church.
Chrysostom.

ALMIGHTY GOD, Father of all who live, Inspirer of all who labor, Comforter of all who suffer, in Thy rest may we remain, feeling that beneath us and around us there is a mystery which no thought of ours may fathom, but which is to us full of friendliness and hope. For out of that deep mystery we have come, as have all whom we have loved and known, all who have made our lives beautiful. And so we take their lives as the revealing of powers that are eternal. Knowing their love, their truth, their heroism, we take heart, for Thou from whom they came and in whom they have lived will sustain us in our hours of need. [Samuel M. Crothers.]

LIVING AND DYING

We must work the works of him that sent me, while it is day: the night cometh, when no man can work. *John 9:4.*

Then was our mouth filled with laughter, and our tongue with singing: Then said they among the nations, Jehovah hath done great things for them. Jehovah hath done great things for us, whereof we are glad. *Ps. 126:2, 3.*

[Dr. S. Hall Young, pioneer missionary in Alaska, was killed by an interurban car at Clarksburg, West Virginia, on September 2, 1927. The record of his heroic service in the North is one of the most inspiring stories of modern Christian service. In Dr. Young's papers his daughter found, after his death, these lines of an unfinished poem.]

> Let me die, working.
> Still tackling plans unfinished, tasks undone!
> Clean to its end, swift may my race be run.
> No laggard steps, no faltering, no shirking;
> Let me die, working!
>
> Let me die, thinking.
> Let me fare forth still with an open mind,
> Fresh secrets to unfold, new truths to find,
> My soul undimmed, alert, no question blinking;
> Let me die, thinking!
>
> Let me die, laughing.
> No sighing o'er past sins; they are forgiven.
> Spilled on this earth are all the joys of Heaven;
> The wine of life, the cup of mirth quaffing.
> Let me die, laughing!

O LORD Jesus Christ, . . . send out Thy Light and Thy Truth, and enlighten the eyes of our minds to understand Thy Divine Word. Give us grace to be bearers of it, and not hearers only, but doers of the Word, that we may bring forth good fruit abundantly, and be counted worthy of the Kingdom of Heaven. And to Thee, O Lord our God, we ascribe glory and thanksgiving, saying: Holy, Holy, Holy, Father, Son, and Holy Spirit, now and forever. [*Liturgy of the Greek Church.*]

THE FORGIVENESS OF THE MARTYRS

Looking unto Jesus the author and perfecter of our faith, who for the joy that was set before him endured the cross, despising shame, and hath sat down at the right hand of the throne of God. *Heb. 12:2.*

If, when ye do well, and suffer for it, ye shall take it patiently, this is acceptable with God. For hereunto were ye called: because Christ also suffered for you, leaving you an example, that ye should follow his steps: who did no sin, neither was guile found in his mouth: who, when he was reviled, reviled not again; when he suffered, threatened not; but committed himself to him that judgeth righteously. *I Peter 2:20-23.*

A disciple is not above his teacher, nor a servant above his lord. It is enough for the disciple that he be as his teacher, and the servant as his lord. *Matt. 10:24, 25.*

And they stoned Stephen, calling upon the Lord, and saying, Lord Jesus, receive my spirit. And he kneeled down, and cried with a loud voice, Lord, lay not this sin to their charge. *Acts 7:59, 60.*

In Memory of John E. Williams, Killed in Nanking, China,
March 24, 1927

He waited for their coming with a smile:
Their torture too he answered smilingly;
And with a smile he met their final thrusts.
What secret did he carry in his heart
That kept his lips curved through death's cruelties?
Was it that down the centuries he gazed,
Past the mob's fury and its stupid greed,
To where a radiant Face smiled out at fear?
And did he see, beyond the hate the Love —
Beyond the Crucifix the opening skies?   *Katherine Burton.*

O JESU, who hast known what troubles and sorrows are, have compassion upon us in our trouble. . . . O Jesu, who now sittest on the right hand of God, to succour all those who suffer for righteousness' sake, be Thou our advocate unto God for grace that in all our sufferings and trials we may follow Thy example, and be supported in all difficulties and discouragements with which God shall see fit to exercise the patience and fidelity of His servants: for Thine honour and glory. [Bishop Thomas Wilson.]

GOD AND OUR FOLLY

The fool hath said in his heart, There is no God. *Ps. 14:1.*

Who forgiveth all thine iniquities; who healeth all thy diseases. *Ps. 103:3.*

Father, forgive them . . . they know not what they do. *Luke 23:34.*

For thou, Lord, art good, and ready to forgive, and abundant in lovingkindness unto all them that call upon thee. *Ps. 86:5.*

> Thou whose deep way is in the sea,
> Whose footsteps are not known,
> Tonight a world that turned from Thee
> Is waiting at Thy throne.
>
> The towering Babels that we raised
> Where scoffing sophists brawl,
> The little antichrists we praised, —
> The night is on them all. . . .
>
> Grant us the single heart once more,
> That mocks no sacred thing,
> The sword of truth our fathers wore,
> When Thou wast Lord and King.
>
> Let darkness unto darkness tell
> Our deep unspoken prayer,
> For, while our souls in darkness dwell,
> We *know* that Thou art there.   *Alfred Noyes.*

ALMIGHTY GOD, Father of our Lord Jesus Christ, we humbly acknowledge our manifold sins and offenses against Thee, by thought and deed. . . . We now come to thee as those whom Thou wilt not cast out. Hear, O Lord, and have mercy upon us, O Almighty God, Heavenly Father, who forgivest iniquity and transgression. O Lord Jesus Christ, Lamb of God, who takest away the sin of the world; O Holy Spirit, who helpest the infirmities of those who pray, receive our humble confession. Give us true repentance and sincere faith in Thee. Do away with our offences, and give us grace to live hereafter more worthily of our Christian calling; for the glory of Thy great Name. [Bishop Westcott (Abbreviated).]

I call heaven and earth to witness against you this day, that I have set before thee life and death, the blessing and the curse: therefore choose life, that thou mayest live, thou and thy seed; to love Jehovah thy God, to obey his voice, and to cleave unto him; for he is thy life, and the length of thy days. *Deut. 30:19, 20.*

Thou hidest thy face, they are troubled. *Ps. 104:29.*

How long, O Jehovah? wilt thou hide thyself for ever. *Ps. 89:46.*

And ye shall seek me, and find me, when ye shall search for me with all your heart. And I will be found of you, saith Jehovah. *Jer. 29:13, 14.*

> When in the dim beginning of the years
> God mixed in man the raptures and the tears
> And scattered through his brain the starry stuff,
> He said, " Behold, yet this is not enough,
> For I must test his spirit to make sure
> That he can dare the vision and endure.
>
> " I will withdraw my face
> Veil me in shadow for a certain space
> And leave behind only a broken clue,
> A crevice where the glory glimmers through,
> Some whisper from the sky
> Some foot print in the road to track me by.
>
> " I will leave man to make the fateful guess,
> Will leave him torn between the ' No ' and ' Yes,'
> Leave him unresting till he rests in Me,
> Drawn upward by the choice that makes him free —
> Leave him in tragic loneliness to choose,
> With all in life to win or all to lose."   *Edwin Markham.*

*S*PIRIT DIVINE, why is it that I am at war with Thee? . . . I am the only thing in creation which strives with Thee, which needs to be reconciled with Thee. They say that to believe in Thee is to believe in that which contradicts reason; no, it is to find something which destroys the contradiction. Spirit of Christ, conquer my will, that the miracle may be destroyed. Reconcile my heart to Thy heart, that there may be no more violation of Thy law.   [George Matheson.]

DEATH NOT SUNDOWN BUT DAWN

The righteous hath a refuge in his death. *Prov. 14:32.*

He hath swallowed up death for ever; and the Lord Jehovah will wipe away tears from off all faces. *Isa. 25:8.*

I am persuaded, that neither death, nor life, nor angels, nor principalities, nor things present, nor things to come, nor powers, nor height, nor depth, nor any other creature, shall be able to separate us from the love of God, which is in Christ Jesus our Lord. *Rom. 8:38.*

Yea, though I walk through the valley of the shadow of death, I will fear no evil; for thou art with me. *Ps. 23:4.*

Seek him that . . . turneth the shadow of death into the morning. *Amos 5:8.*

> The smoke ascends
> In a rosy and golden haze. The spires
> Shine and are changed. In the valley
> Shadows rise. The lark sings on. The sun,
> Closing his benediction,
> Sinks, and the darkening air,
> Thrills with a sense of the triumphing night —
> Night with her train of stars
> And her great gift of sleep.
>
> So be my passing!
> My task accomplished and the long day done,
> My wages taken and in my heart
> Some late lark singing,
> Let me be gathered to the quiet west,
> The sundown splendid and serene,
> Death!   *W. E. Henley.*

O ALMIGHTY and everlasting God, in whose hands are the issues of life and whose infinite wisdom ordereth all things for the best to them that love Thee, help us Thy servants when we come to the last hour. Support us by Thy grace, confirm our faith, increase our faith and perfect our love. And when it shall please Thee to call us to Thyself, carry us safely through the valley of the shadow of death, through which our loving Saviour has passed before us. And finally receive us into those heavenly mansions which our blessed Lord has gone to prepare.

The eleven disciples went into Galilee, unto the mountain where Jesus had appointed them. And when they saw him, they worshipped him; but some doubted. And Jesus came to them and spake unto them. *Matt. 28:16–18.*

From of old men have not heard, nor perceived by the ear, neither hath the eye seen a God besides thee, who worketh for him that waiteth for him. Thou meetest him that rejoiceth and worketh righteousness, those that remember thee in thy ways. *Isa. 64:4, 5.*

There I will meet with thee, and I will commune with thee from above the mercy-seat. *Ex. 25:22.*

Jesus himself drew near, and went with them. But their eyes were holden that they should not know him. *Luke 24:15, 16.*

When He appoints to meet thee, go
   thou forth —
  It matters not
If south or north,
  Bleak waste or sunny flat.
Nor think, if He thou seek'st be late
He does thee wrong.
To stile or gate
  Lean thou thy head, and long!

It may be that to spy thee He is mount-
   ing
  Upon a tower,
Or in thy counting
  Thou hast mista'en the hour.
But if He comes not, neither do thou
  go
  Till vesper chime.
Belike thou then shall know
  He hath been with thee all the time.
      Thomas Edward Brown.

LORD, we are not worthy that Thou shouldst come under our roof, but speak the word only and Thy servants shall be healed. Foxes have holes and birds of the air have nests but in our souls the Son of Man hath not a fit place wherein to lay His head. But as Thou didst vouchsafe to be laid in the stall and manger of brute beasts; so Thou didst not disdain to be received into the house of Simon the leper; as Thou didst not reject the woman that was a sinner when she approached and touched Thee, nor abhor her lips when she kissed Thy feet, neither the thief on the cross when he confessed Thee, even so vouchsafe to admit us also, bruised and sinful creatures, to the communion of Thy body and spirit. Come and meet with us, we pray Thee, and abide in us. [Saint Chrysostom.]

WISDOM

To know wisdom and instruction . . . that the man of understanding may attain unto sound counsels: . . . The words of the wise, and their dark sayings. The fear of Jehovah is the beginning of knowledge. *Prov. 1:2, 5-7.*

God has us in discipline and not in hospitality.
God is doing facts and we are thinking dangers.
There can be no labor where there is no want.
Industry is the natural teacher and guardian of virtue.
Real life must have some heroic force in it, else it only breathes, but does not live.
To bear and dare — these two great lessons are among the chief moral uses of life.
Pain is a kind of general sacrament for the world.
The world is but the shadow of God.
God is always letting things come into the world that He will not let stay in it.
No prayer takes hold of God until it first takes hold of the man.
Deem every sin a sacrilege.
The life of man is in his heart, and if he does not live there, he does not live.
The soul of all improvement is the improvement of the soul.

Bushnell.

O GOD, our Lord and Christ, who hast been our word and our truth and our very life, We pray Thee, walk with us through our days, that every morning's rise may be as the beginning of life and every evening at its close may be well-done for Thee. But keep us, we pray Thee, O Christ, in that good way that leads from now until that great tomorrow. We pray Thee, give us our daily work, that we may earn our daily bread, a little hardship that we may grow lusty souls, a little sorrow that our tears may run for others' griefs, a little task that we may do for Thee to make our journey worthwhile. So help us, Lord, to journey all our days with Thee and love Thee more each day because Thou art to us the way, the truth, and the life. Amen. [Isabel Dress (Abbreviated).]

There was evening and there was morning, one day. *Gen. 1:5.*

All chastening seemeth for the present to be not joyous but grievous; yet afterward it yieldeth peaceable fruit unto them that have been exercised thereby, even the fruit of righteousness. *Heb. 12:11.*

Weeping may tarry for the night, but joy cometh in the morning. *Ps. 30:5.*

When the day was now breaking, Jesus stood on the beach. *John 21:4.*

'Tis first the true, and then the beautiful
Not first the beautiful and then the true.
First the wild moor, with rock and fen and pool
Then the gay garden rich in scent and hue. . . .

Not first the glad and then the sorrowful
But first the sorrowful and then the glad,
Tears for a day, for earth of tears is full,
Then we forget that we were ever sad.

Not first the bright and after that the dark
But first the dark and after that the bright;
First the thick cloud, and then the rainbow's arc,
First the dark grave, then resurrection light.

'Tis first the night, stern night of storm and war
Long night of heavy clouds and veiléd skies,
Then the far sparkle of the Morning Star
That bids the saints awake and dawn arise.

Horatius Bonar.

W E thank Thee, O God, that Thou dost answer the complaints of our tormented soul. Through the veil of tears comes the vision of the Christ bearing the cross for the sins of the world; of Thyself struggling with us in our feeble efforts inspiring the discontent with what is; and of Thy saints through the ages, who amidst strife and suffering have fixed their eyes upon the fulfilment of Thy purpose, and who in life and in death, have labored for the day when mercy and truth shall meet, righteousness and peace kiss each other, and nations walk in the way of the Lord. [Tsu.]

If thy right eye causeth thee to stumble, pluck it out, and cast it from thee. *Matt. 5:29.*

Bringing every thought into captivity to the obedience of Christ. *II Cor. 10:5.*

Every idle word that men shall speak, they shall give account thereof in the day of judgment. For by thy words thou shalt be justified and by thy words thou shalt be condemned. *Matt. 12:36, 37.*

That Christ may dwell in your hearts. *Eph. 3:17.*

> O that mine eyes might closed be
> To what concerns me not to see;
> That deafness might possess mine ear
> To what concerns me not to hear;
> That truth my tongue might always tie
> From ever speaking foolishly;
> That no vain thought might ever rest
> Or be conceived within my breast;
> That by each deed and word and thought
> Glory may to my God be brought!
> But what are wishes! Lord, mine eye
> On Thee is fixed, to Thee I cry!
> Wash, Lord, and purify my heart,
> And make it clean in every part;
> And when 'tis clean, Lord, keep it too,
> For that is more than I can do.
>
> *Thomas Elwood.*

O THOU who knowest our most secret thoughts and before whom all the hidden places of our souls are open, make clean our hearts within us. And grant, we pray Thee, that the words of our mouths and the meditations out of which they speak may be acceptable in Thy sight. Save us from wrong thoughts and vain imaginations, from stained desire and idle dreaming. May we think only what we may rightly dare to say and dream only of what we may worthily hope to be and do. Forgive all that we may have ever said that was untrue or unkind. Lay Thy spirit upon our minds and Thy finger on our lips that we may always think and say only those things that please Thee through Jesus Christ who is Truth and Love. [*The Fellowship of Prayer,* 1933 (Altered).]

If therefore the Son shall make you free, ye shall be free indeed. *John 8:36.*

Now being made free from sin and become servants to God, ye have your fruit unto sanctification, and the end eternal life. *Rom. 6:22.*

Ye shall receive power, when the Holy Spirit is come upon you. *Acts 1:8.*

He that was called in the Lord being a bondservant is the Lord's freedman: likewise he that was called being free, is Christ's bondservant. *1 Cor. 7:22.*

Make me a captive, Lord,
And then I shall be free;
Force me to render up my sword,
And I shall conqueror be.
I sink in life's alarms
When by myself I stand;
Imprison me within Thine arms,
And strong shall be my hand.

My heart is weak and poor
Until it master find;
It has no spring of action sure —
It varies with the wind.
It cannot freely move
Till Thou hast wrought its chain;
Enslave it with Thy matchless love,
And deathless it shall reign.

My power is faint and low
Till I have learned to serve;
It wants the needed fire to glow,
It wants the breeze to nerve;
It cannot drive the world
Until itself be driven;
Its flag can only be unfurled
When Thou shalt breathe from heaven.

My will is not my own
Till Thou hast made it Thine;
If it would reach a monarch's throne
It must its crown resign;
It only stands unbent
Amid the clashing strife,
When on Thy bosom it has leant
And found in Thee its life.

George Matheson.

O GOD, who deliverest Thy servants from every sort of bondage and dost rescue those who trust in Thee from the darkness of their imprisonment, grant, we beseech Thee, that our faith may endure through the long watches and triumph over every doubt; that when Thy Light shineth and Thine angel cometh, we may be ready to accept the deliverance which Thou Thyself hast prepared for us in Thy great mercy, through Jesus Christ our Lord. [*The Fellowship of Prayer.* 1932.]

LEAVING WHAT IS BEHIND

Leaving the doctrine of the first principles of Christ, let us press on unto perfection; not laying again a foundation of repentance from dead works, and of faith toward God. *Heb. 6:1.*

We know in part, and we prophesy in part; but when that which is perfect is come, that which is in part shall be done away. *I Cor. 13:9, 10.*

Not that I have already obtained, or am already made perfect: but I press on. *Phil. 3:12.*

Grow up in all things into him. *Eph. 4:15.*

> Man was made to grow, not stop;
> That help, he needed once, and needs no more,
> Having grown but an inch by, is withdrawn:
> For he hath new needs, and new helps to these.
> This imports solely, man should mount on each
> New height in view; the help whereby he mounts,
> The ladder-rung his foot has left, may fall,
> Since all things suffer change save God the Truth.
> Man apprehends him newly at each stage
> Whereat earth's ladder drops, its service done;
> And nothing shall prove twice what once was proved. . . .
>
> Man knows partly but conceives beside,
> Creeps ever on from fancies to the fact,
> And in this striving, this converting air
> Into a solid he may grasp and use,
> Finds progress, man's distinctive mark alone,
> Not God's, and not the beasts': God is, they are,
> Man partly is and wholly hopes to be.   *Browning.*

O LORD GOD ALMIGHTY, who givest power to the faint, and increaseth strength to them that have no might; without Thee we can do nothing, but by Thy gracious assistance we are enabled for the performance of every duty laid upon us. . . . O our God, let Thy grace be sufficient for us, and ever present with us, that we may do all things as we ought. . . . Be Thou our helper, to carry us on beyond our own strength, and to make all that we think, and speak, and do, acceptable in Thy sight, through Jesus Christ. [Benjamin Jenks.]

He leadeth me. *Ps. 23:2.*

Oh that thou hadst hearkened to my commandments! then had thy peace been as a river, and thy righteousness as the waves of the sea. *Isa. 48:18.*

He was seen upon the wings of the wind. *II Sam. 22:11.*

Who bringeth forth the wind out of his treasures. *Ps. 135:7.*

They . . . got into the boats, and came to Capernaum, seeking Jesus. *John 6:24.*

I feel the winds of God today;
  Today my sail I lift,
Though heavy oft with drenching
    spray,
And torn with many a rift:
If hope but light the water's crest,
  And Christ my bark will use,
I'll seek the seas at His behest
  And brave another cruise.

It is the wind of God that dries
  My vain, regretful tears,
Until with braver thoughts shall rise
  The purer, brighter years:

If cast on shores of selfish ease
  Or pleasure I should be,
Lord, let me feel Thy freshening
    breeze
And I'll put back to sea.

If ever I forget Thy love
  And how that love was shown,
Lift high the blood-red flag above:
  It bears Thy Name alone.
Great Pilot of my onward way,
  Thou wilt not let me drift:
I feel the winds of God today,
  Today my sail I lift.
                    Jessie Adams.

O GOD, who bestowest Thy mercy at all times on them that love Thee, and in no place art distant from those that serve Thee: Direct the ways of Thy servants in Thy will, that, having Thee for their Protector and Guide, they may walk without stumbling in the paths of righteousness. Raise up, we pray Thee, Thy power, and come among us, and with great might succour us; that whereas through our sins and wickedness, we are sore let and hindered in running the race that is set before us, Thy bountiful grace and mercy may speedily help and deliver us. [*Gelasian Sacramentary.*]

I speak in regard of Christ and of the church. *Eph. 5:32.*

That he might present the church to himself a glorious church, not having spot or wrinkle or any such thing; but that it should be holy and without blemish. *Eph. 5:27.*

The kingdom of the world is become the kingdom of our Lord, and of his Christ: and he shall reign for ever and ever. *Rev. 11:15.*

O Lily of the King! low lies thy silver wing,
  And long has been the hour of thine enqueening;
And thy scent of Paradise on the night wind spill its sighs,
  Nor any take the secrets of its meaning.
O Lily of the King! I speak a secret thing,
  O patience, most sorrowful of daughters,
Lo, the hour is at hand for the troubling of the land,
  And red shall be the breaking of the waters. . . .

O Lily of the King! I shall not see, that sing,
  I shall not see the hour of thy queening!
But my song shall see, and wake like a flower that dawn winds shake,
  And sigh with joy the odors of its meaning.
O Lily of the King, remember then the thing,
  That this dead mouth sang; and thy daughters,
As they dance before His way, sing there on the day
  What I sang when the night was on the waters!
                        Francis Thompson.

*A*RISE and have mercy on Thy Church, O Lord: let the time to favor her, yea, the set time come. Bring her up from the wilderness, leaning on her Beloved; and make her the perfection of beauty. When her enemy comes in like a flood, do Thou lift up a standard against him. Be Thou as a wall of fire round about her, and a glory in the midst of her. Hast Thou not purchased her with Thy blood; and wilt Thou not grave her on the palms of Thy hands, and set her walls continually before Thee? O King of Kings, do Thou marshal, and discipline, and strengthen, and multiply the sacramental host and lead it on conquering and to conquer, until the kingdoms of this world shall become the Kingdom of our Lord and His Christ, and He shall reign forever and ever. [*A Manual of Prayer.*]

THE HUMILITY OF LOVE

Jesus . . . riseth from supper, and layeth aside his garments; and he took a towel, and girded himself. Then he poureth water into the basin, and began to wash the disciples' feet, and to wipe them with the towel wherewith he was girded. *John 13:3–5.*

Through love be servants one to another. *Gal. 5:13.*

Which is greater, he that sitteth at meat, or he that serveth? is not he that sitteth at meat? but I am in the midst of you as he that serveth. *Luke 22:27.*

Love made me welcome; yet my soul drew back,
    Guilty of dust and sin.
But quick-eyed love, observing me grow slack
    From my first entrance in,
Drew near to me, sweetly questioning
    If I lacked anything.

"A guest," I answered, "worthy to be here."
    Love said, "You shall be he!"
"I the unkind, ungrateful? Ah, my dear,
    I cannot look on Thee."
Love took my hand, and smiling, did reply
    "Who made the eyes but I?"

"Truth, Lord, but I have marr'd them; let my shame
    Go where it doth deserve."
"And know you not?" says Love, "Who bore the blame?"
    "My dear, then I will serve."
"You must sit down," says Love, "and taste my meat."
    So I did sit and eat.

Christopher Harvey.

*B*E Thou favorable unto me, O Merciful Jesu, sweet and gracious Lord, and grant to me, Thy poor, needy creature, sometimes at least in this holy communion, to feel if it be but a small portion of Thy hearty love, that my faith may become more strong, my hope in Thy goodness may be increased, and that charity once perfectly kindled within me after the tasting of this heavenly manna may never decay. [Thomas à Kempis.]

LIVING BEFORE DYING

If ye live after the flesh, ye must die; but if by the Spirit ye put to death the deeds of the body, ye shall live. *Rom. 8:13.*

Who his own self bare our sins in his body upon the tree, that we, having died unto sins, might live unto righteousness. *I Peter 2:24.*

And Jesus saith unto him, Verily I say unto thee, that thou today, even this night, before the cock crow twice, shalt deny me thrice. But he spake exceeding vehemently, If I must die with thee, I will not deny thee. *Mark 14:30, 31.*

But he denied before them all. *Matt. 26:70.*

So he died for his faith. That is fine —
　More than most of us do.
But say, can you add to that line
　That he lived for it, too?

It is easy to die. Men have died
　For a wish or a whim —
From bravado or passion or pride.
　Was it harder for him?

In his death he bore witness at last
　As a martyr to truth.
Did his life do the same in the past
　From the days of his youth?

But to live: every day to live out
　All the truth that he dreamt,
While his friends met his conduct
　　with doubt,
　And the world with contempt —

Was it thus that he plodded ahead,
　Never turning aside?
Then we'll talk of the life that he led.
　Never mind how he died.
　　　Ernest H. Crosby.

O GOD, how often we have prayed for the coming of Thy Kingdom, yet when it has sought to come through us we have barred the way; we have wanted it without in others, but not in our own hearts. We feel it is we who stand between man's need and Thee; between ourselves and what we might be; and we have no trust in our own strength, or loyalty or courage.

O give us to love Thy will, and seek Thy Kingdom first of all. Sweep away our fears, our compromise, our weakness. Help us to live, to live now, to live to Thee.　[W. E. Orchard (Altered).]

Philip saith unto him, Lord, show us the Father, and it suf-ficeth us. Jesus saith unto him, Have I been so long time with you, and dost thou not know me, Philip? *John 14:8, 9.*

As the hart panteth after the water brooks, so panteth my soul after thee, O God. My soul thirsteth for God, for the living God: When shall I come and appear before God? *Ps. 42:1, 2.*

Lord, when saw we thee? *Matt. 25:44.*

Lo, I am with you always. *Matt. 28:20.*

We place Thy sacred Name upon our brows;
Our cycles from Thy natal day we score:
Yet spite of all our songs and all our vows,
We thirst, and ever thirst to know Thee more.

For Thou art Mystery and Question still:
Even when we see Thee lifted as a sign
Drawing all men unto that hapless hill
With the resistless power of Love Divine.

Still Thou art Question — while rings in our ears
Thine outcry to a world discord-beset;
*Have I been with thee all these many years,
O World, — dost thou not know Me even yet?*
Martha Foote Crow.

Our heavenly father, we thank Thee for the times and for the experiences when we feel the need of Thee most deeply. We know that the only true life is life that is aware of Thee and of its need of Thee. Forgive us that we have so often ceased to live by forgetting our absolute dependence upon Thee; and deliver us from the pride of our strength which is weakness and the folly of our self-confidence which is death. Give us the mind of Christ who did always the things that pleased Thee and who was one with Thee in all things, and make us also one with Thee in Him. Help us by Thy Holy Spirit to use mem-ory and imagination, will and affection, to make Him and Thee our greatest reality, and by Thy power fulfill in us the sense of Thy Presence and the purity and joy of Thy Life. [R. E. S.]

Wherefore if any man is in Christ, he is a new creature: the old things are passed away; behold, they are become new. *II Cor. 5:17.*

My God shall supply every need of yours according to his riches in glory in Christ Jesus. *Phil. 4:19.*

In him dwelleth all the fulness of the Godhead bodily, and in him ye are made full. *Col. 2:9, 10.*

He who began a good work in you will perfect it until the day of Jesus Christ. *Phil. 1:6.*

For morning sun and evening dew,
For every bud that April knew,
For storm and silence, gloom and light,
And for the solemn stars at night;
For fallow field, and burdens byre,
For rooftree, and the hearthside fire,
For everything that shines and sings,
For dear familiar daily things —
The friendly trees, and in the sky
The white cloud-squadrons sailing by;
For Hope that waits, for Faith that dares;
For Patience that still smiles and bears;
For Love that fails not nor withstands;
For healing touch of children's hands;
For happy labor, high intent,
For all life's blessed sacrament —
O Comrade of our nights and days,
Thou givest all things, take our praise. *Arth. Ketchum.*

WITH humble thankfulness. O God, we acknowledge Thine unspeakable love to us, Thy most unworthy children. We bless Thee, we praise Thee, we worship Thee, we glorify Thee, we give thanks to Thee for Thy great goodness. We are not worthy of the least of these Thy mercies, but Thou art the same and Thy love towards us cannot fail. Therefore not trusting in our own righteousness, but only in Thy grace, we offer once again to Thee the devotion of our hearts, which Thou wilt accept because we offer it through Jesus Christ, Thy Son our Lord. [*A Book of Prayers for Students.*]

In thy light shall we see light. *Ps. 36:9.*

As servants of Christ, doing the will of God from the heart. *Eph. 6:6.*

As therefore ye received Christ Jesus the Lord, so walk in him, rooted and builded up in him, and established in your faith, even as ye were taught, abounding in thanksgiving. *Col. 2:6, 7.*

> Have you and I today
> Stood silent as with Christ, apart from joy or fray
> Of life, to see by faith His face;
> To look, if but a moment, at its grace,
> And grow, by brief companionship, more true,
> More nerved to lead, to dare to do,
> For Him at any cost? Have we today
> Found time, in thought, our hand to lay
> In His, and thus compare
> His will with ours, and wear
> The impress of His wish? Be sure
> Such contact will endure
> Throughout the day; will help us walk erect
> Through storm and flood; detect
> Within the hidden life, sin's dross, its stain;
> Revive a thought of love for Him again;
> Steady the steps which waver, help us see
> The footpath meant for you and me.   *George Klingle.*

GRANT us, O God of peace and truth, the gracious help of Thy Spirit, that we may amid the things seen which are temporal have knowledge of the unseen things which are eternal. Especially we pray Thee to help us to find in the toil and tumult of life the rest of Christ, that we may know Him and the strength of His fellowship and the guidance of His love. Forgive us that we are so little like Him who perfectly stooped to be made in the likeness of men, and by Thy grace and the power of His resurrection lift us up, we beseech Thee, into His purity and goodness, His faithfulness and obedience, that we may walk even as He walked and work even as He worked who did always the things that pleased Thee and finished the work that Thou gavest Him to do. In His name.

THE GAIN OF LOSS

He that findeth his life shall lose it; and he that loseth his life for my sake shall find it. *Matt. 10:39.*

Except a grain of wheat fall into the earth and die, it abideth by itself alone; but if it die, it beareth much fruit. He that loveth his life loseth it; and he that hateth his life in this world shall keep it unto life eternal. *John 12:24, 25.*

Insomuch as ye are partakers of Christ's sufferings, rejoice; that at the revelation of his glory also ye may rejoice with exceeding joy. *1 Peter 4:13.*

We also rejoice in our tribulations: knowing that tribulation worketh stedfastness; and stedfastness, approvedness; and approvedness, hope. *Rom. 5:3, 4.*

It became him, . . . to make the author of their salvation perfect through sufferings. *Heb. 2:10.*

> The Vine from every living limb bleeds wine.
> Is it the poorer for that spirit shed?
> The drunkard and the wanton drink thereof.
> Are they the richer for that gift's excess?
> Measure thy life by loss instead of gain,
> Not by the wine drunk, but the wine poured forth;
> For love's strength standeth in love's sacrifice
> And whoso suffers most, hath most to give.
> *Harriet E. King.*

*A*ccomplish Thy perfect work in our souls, O Father; let us become day by day purer, freer, more heavenly, more happy and preserve us unto eternal life. The road is rough, our Father. But we are not dismayed, for we are more than earth and dust, we are akin to Thee who hast made us in Thine own image and we are aware of Thy loving and constant care and we know that Thou art the God of all grace, who hast called us unto Thine eternal glory in Christ and who, after that we have suffered a little while, will Thyself perfect, establish, strengthen us. Unite us more closely to Thyself and to the company of faithful hearts whom Thou art sanctifying and preparing for that which Thou hast in store for them; fill us with their faith and love and hope and with Thy grace. [V. R. Reinhard (Altered).]

Now are we children of God, and it is not yet made manifest what we shall be. We know that, if he shall be manifested, we shall be like him; for we shall see him even as he is. And every one that hath this hope set on him purifieth himself, even as he is pure. *I John 3:2, 3.*

I know that my Redeemer liveth, and at last he will stand up upon the earth: and after my skin, even this body, is destroyed, then without my flesh shall I see God; whom I, even I, shall see, on my side, and mine eyes shall behold, and not as a stranger. *Job 19:25–27.*

From of old men have not heard, nor perceived by the ear, neither hath the eye seen a God besides thee, who worketh for him that waiteth for him. Thou meetest him that rejoiceth and worketh righteousness, those that remember thee in thy ways. *Isa. 64:4, 5.*

> So with the wan waste grasses on my spear
> I ride forever seeking after God.
> My hair grows whiter than my thistle plume
> And all my limbs are loose, but in my eyes
> The star of an unconquerable praise,
> For in my soul one hope forever sings,
> That at the next white corner of a road
> My eyes may look on Him.   *G. K. Chesterton.*

OUR FATHER, we thank Thee that it is not we who are seeking Thee but Thou who art seeking us. Herein is love, not that we love Thee, but that Thou dost love us and didst send forth Thy Son to be our Saviour. We rejoice that it is Thy Son, the Son of Man, who is seeking to save us who have been lost. Forgive us for our unresponsiveness to the solicitations of Thy love, for our incredible reluctance to accept Thy grace, and help us now, in this moment, to open ourselves to Thee, to give over our quest for Thee as though Thou wert far away and needed to be sought for by us, to see that Thou art not far from any one of us, that in Thee we live and move and have our being. Thou art here and henceforth we are assured that neither death nor life, nearness nor distance, nor angels, nor principalities, nor things present nor things to come, nor powers nor weaknesses, nor height nor depth, nor any other creature shall be able to separate us from Thy love which is in Christ Jesus our Lord. [R. E. S.]

THE BOY JESUS

And he [Jesus] went down with them, and came to Nazareth; and he was subject unto them: and his mother kept all these sayings in her heart. And Jesus advanced in wisdom and stature, and in favor with God and men. *Luke 2:51, 52.*

Consider the lilies. *Matt. 6:28.*

And he went forth again by the sea side. *Mark 2:13.*

I am meek and lowly in heart. *Matt. 11:29.*

A man of sorrows, and acquainted with grief. *Isa. 53:3.*

I think He was a blithesome boy.
  I think His words were clear and
    free.
I think He was as straight and brown
  As some young tree. . . .

I think He lingered on the hills
  And learned the magic of the grass;
And knew the heart of every tree
  That saw Him pass. . . .

I think He came to Mary's door
  With eager homeward-running feet,
And to His hungry human mouth
  Her bread was sweet.

Yet He Himself was bread, and wine,
  And olive branch, and cedar tree,
And grass, and star, and shining
    depths
  Of Galilee.

Oh, He was laughter and delight.
  And He was pain, and tears, and
    death,
And every suffering and joy
  Of Nazareth.

He was all silence, and all song:
  He was a cross; a diadem;
The Man of Sorrows; and the lovely
    Babe
  Of Bethlehem.   *Barbara Young.*

Our father, we thank Thee for the human life of Jesus, for the simple, natural boyhood; for His love of out-of-doors, of the mountains and the sky, of the flowers and the sheep, of the lake and the brooks and the garden; for His friendships; for His gentleness and His courage and His faithfulness; that He trod the full pathway of our human lot and bare our sins in His own body on the tree. We thank Thee that in the man Christ Jesus and in His human life Thou dost give Thyself to us, convincing us of Thy forgiveness and love, and issuing us into Thy redemption, the freedom of the souls that are in communion with Thee through Jesus Christ, Thy Son our Lord. [R. E. S.]

DARKNESS AND LIGHT

Ye are not come unto . . . blackness, and darkness, and tempest, . . . but . . . to God the Judge of all, and to the spirits of just men made perfect, and to Jesus. *Heb. 12:18, 22–24.*

Who delivered us out of the power of darkness, and translated us into the kingdom of the Son of his love. *Col. 1:13.*

If I say, Surely the darkness shall overwhelm me, and the light about me shall be night; even the darkness hideth not from thee, but the night shineth as the day: The darkness and the light are both alike to thee. *Ps. 139:11, 12.*

The night is far spent, and the day is at hand: let us therefore cast off the works of darkness, and let us put on the armor of light. Let us walk becomingly, as in the day. *Rom. 13:12, 13.*

> Die down, O dismal day, and let me live:
> And come, blue deeps, magnificently strewn
> With colored clouds, — large, light and fugitive, —
> By upper winds through pompous motions blown.
> Now it is death in life, — a vapor dense
> Creeps round my window till I cannot see
> The far snow-shining mountains, and the glens
> Shagging the mountain-tops. O God! make free
> This barren shackled earth, so deadly cold, —
> Breathe gently forth Thy spring, till winter flies
> In rude amazement, fearful and yet bold,
> While she performs her customed charities:
> I weigh the loaded hours till life is bare, —
> O God! for one clear day, a snowdrop and sweet air.
>   *David Gray.*

O GOD, our Father, who dost exhort us to pray, and who dost grant what we ask, according to Thy wise and loving will, hear us who are weary of this darkness, and stretch forth Thy hand unto us; hold forth Thy light before us; recall us from our wanderings; and Thou being our Guide may we be restored to ourselves and to Thee. Let all the darkness of our souls vanish before the beams of Thy brightness. Fill us with Thy holy love, and open to us the treasures of Thy wisdom. [Augustine (Altered).]

DEATH UNFEARED

Having the desire to depart and be with Christ; for it is very far better. *Phil. 1:23.*

Death is swallowed up in victory. O death, where is thy victory? Thanks be to God, who giveth us the victory through our Lord Jesus Christ. *1 Cor. 15:54, 55, 57.*

Our Saviour Christ Jesus . . . abolished death, and brought life and immortality to light through the gospel. . .*II Tim. 1:10.*

For if we believe that Jesus died and rose again, even so them also that are fallen asleep in Jesus will God bring with him. *1 Thess. 4:14.*

Why be afraid of Death as though your life were breath?
Death but anoints your eyes with clay. O glad surprise!

Why should you be forlorn? Death only husks the corn.
Why should you fear to meet the thresher of the wheat? . . .

Why should it be a wrench to leave your wooden bench,
Why not with happy shout run home when school is out?

The dear ones left behind! O foolish one and blind.
A day — and you will meet, — A night — and you will greet!

This is the death of Death, to breathe away a breath
And know the end of strife, and taste the deathless life.
                                        Maltbie D. Babcock.

THANKS be to Thee, O God, that Thy Son, Jesus Christ our Lord, conquered death and brought life and immortality to light through the gospel. We praise Thee for His assurance of Thy house of many mansions, where He has prepared a place for us, that where He is, there we may be also. . . . Wherefore we rejoice in this hour for those whom we have lost on earth, but who are now with Thee. . . . By Thy grace comfort our hearts with the thought of their safety and joy, and help us so to walk before Thee in faith and love, that in Thy good time, we may be joined to them in Thy heavenly presence evermore; through Jesus Christ our Lord. [*The Book of Common Worship,* Revised.]

He that findeth his life shall lose it; and he that loseth his life for my sake shall find it. *Matt. 10:39.*

I have been crucified with Christ; and it is no longer I that live, but Christ liveth in me: and that life which I now live in the flesh I live in faith, the faith which is in the Son of God, who loved me, and gave himself up for me. *Gal. 2:20.*

Wretched man that I am! who shall deliver me out of the body of this death? I thank God through Jesus Christ our Lord. *Rom. 7:24, 25.*

We have found the . . . Christ. *John 1:41.*

Resolve to be thyself; and know that he
Who finds himself loses his misery.   *Matthew Arnold.*

"Who finds himself," the poet saith,
    "Shall lose his misery"; ah, no!
For long ago I found myself,
    Yet still went companied by woe. . . .

This was my self: compact of faults,
    Of failure, foolishness, and sins
Nor could I see the end of them
    Nor knew I where the list begins.

Then, weary of the futile strife,
    Heart sick of bondage and defeat,
I sought another self than mine;
    One strong enough my foes to meet; . . .

With Whom my sin-stained soul could leave
    Its burden of iniquity.
I found them all, oh, Christ and Lord,
    And lost myself in finding Thee!   *Annie Johnson Flint.*

O LORD, who hast promised a blessing to those who first seek Thy kingdom and righteousness, enlighten, we pray Thee, our hearts, that we be not entangled among the things of this world. Teach us, as those who are risen with Thee, so to set our affection upon things above, that our life even now may be truly hid with Thee, O Christ, in God. [*A Chain of Prayer Across the Ages.*]

THE LIGHT SHALL NOT FAIL

Then shall thy light break forth as the morning. *Isa. 58:8.*

He shall be as the light of the morning, when the sun riseth. *II Sam. 23:4.*

The path of the righteous is as the dawning light, that shineth more and more unto the perfect day. *Prov. 4:18.*

> Say not the struggle nought availeth,
> The labour and the wounds are vain,
> The enemy faints not, nor faileth,
> And as things have been they remain.
>
> If hopes were dupes, fears may be liars;
> It may be, in yon smoke concealed,
> Your comrades chase e'en now the fliers
> And, but for you, possess the field.
>
> For while the tired waves, vainly breaking,
> Seem here no painful inch to gain,
> Far back, through creeks and inlets making,
> Comes silent, flooding in, the main.
>
> And not by eastern windows only,
> When daylight comes, comes in the light,
> In front, the sun climbs slow, how slowly
> But westward look, the land is bright.
> *Arthur Hugh Clough.*

GIVE us grace, O God, to listen to Thy call, to obey Thy voice and to follow Thy guiding. Thou leadest us to pleasures that never fade, to riches which no moth nor rust can corrupt or destroy. Unsearchable riches are in Thy hand: O give us grace to know Thy value of them and to covet them. Thou leadest us to fountains of living water: suffer us not to wander or turn aside till we attain unto the pleasures which are at Thy right hand forevermore. Establish, settle, strengthen us, that our goodness may not be like the early dew, which passeth away, but make us stedfast, immovable, alway abounding in the work of the Lord, forasmuch as we know that our labor is not in vain in the Lord. Grant this, we beseech Thee, for Thy dear Son, Jesus Christ's sake. [Ludovicus Vives.]

LIFE AND LIFE FOREVERMORE

For I am already being offered, and the time of my departure is come. I have fought the good fight, I have finished the course, I have kept the faith: henceforth there is laid up for me the crown of righteousness, which the Lord, the righteous judge, shall give me at that day; and not to me only, but also to all them that have loved his appearing. *II Tim. 4:6–8.*

Fear not, little flock; it is your Father's good pleasure to give you the kingdom. *Luke 12:32.*

Fear thou not, for I am with thee; be not dismayed, for I am thy God; I will strengthen thee; yea, I will help thee; yea, I will uphold thee with the right hand of my righteousness. *Isa. 41:10.*

Giving thanks unto the Father, who made us meet to be partakers of the . . . saints in light; who delivered us out of the power of darkness, and translated us into the kingdom of the Son of his love. *Col. 1:12, 13.*

I know the night is near at hand,
   The mists lie low on hill and bay,
The Autumn leaves are drifting by,
   But I have had the day.

Yes, I have had, dear Lord, the day:
   When at Thy call I have the night,
Brief be the twilight as I pass
   From light to dark, from dark to light.

          S. Weir Mitchell.

*B*LESSED art Thou, O Lord our God, the God of our fathers, who turnest the shadow of death into the morning; who hast lightened mine eyes that I sleep not in death. O Lord, blot out as a night-mist mine iniquities. Scatter my sins as a morning cloud. Grant that I may become a child of the light and of the day. Vouchsafe to keep me this day without sin. Uphold me when I am falling, and lift me up when I am down. Preserve this day from any evil of mine, and me from the evil of the day. Let this day add some knowledge, a good deed, to yesterday. Oh, let me hear Thy loving kindness in the morning, for in Thee is my trust. Teach me to do the thing that pleaseth Thee, for Thou art my God. Let Thy loving spirit lead me forth into the land of righteousness. [Lancelot Andrewes.]

THE PEACE OF CHRIST

Peace I leave with you; my peace I give unto you: not as the world giveth, give I unto you. *John 14:27.*

These things have I spoken unto you, that in me ye may have peace. In the world ye have tribulation: but be of good cheer; I have overcome the world. *John 16:33.*

Being therefore justified by faith, we have peace with God through our Lord Jesus Christ. *Rom. 5:1.*

But now in Christ Jesus ye that once were far off are made nigh in the blood of Christ. For he is our peace. *Eph. 2:13, 14.*

Let the peace of Christ rule in your hearts. *Col. 3:15.*

Insomuch as ye are partakers of Christ's sufferings, rejoice; that at the revelation of his glory also ye may rejoice with exceeding joy. *1 Peter 4:13.*

> There is a Peace that cometh after sorrow,
> Of hope surrendered, not of hope fulfilled;
> A Peace that looketh not upon tomorrow,
> But calmly on a tempest that is stilled.
>
> A Peace which lives not now in joy's excesses,
> Nor in the happy life of love secure;
> But in the unerring strength the heart possesses
> Of conflicts won while learning to endure.
>
> A Peace there is in sacrifice secluded;
> A life subdued, from will and passion free: —
> 'Tis not the Peace which over Eden brooded,
> But that which triumphed in Gethsemane.
>
> *Jessie Rose Gates.*

LET me not seek out of Thee what I can find only in Thee, O Lord, peace and rest and joy and bliss, which abide only in Thine abiding joy. Lift up my soul above the weary round of harassing thoughts to Thy eternal Presence. Lift up my soul to the pure, bright, serene, radiant atmosphere of Thy Presence, that there I may breathe freely, there repose in Thy love, there be at rest from myself, and from all things that weary me; and thence return, arrayed with Thy peace, to do and bear what shall please Thee. [E. B. Pusey.]

THE WAY OF THE CROSS

By this shall all men know that ye are my disciples, if ye have love one to another. *John 13:35.*

That they all may be one; even as thou, Father, art in me, and I in thee, that they also may be in us: that the world may believe that thou didst send me. *John 17:21.*

If any man would come after me, let him deny himself, and take up his cross, and follow me. For whosoever would save his life shall lose it: and whosoever shall lose his life for my sake shall find it. *Matt. 16:24, 25.*

> Would you win all the world for Christ?
>   One way there is and only one;
> You must live Christ from day to day,
>   And see His will be done. . . .
>
> No easy way, — rough — strewn with stones,
>   And wearisome, the path He trod.
> But His way is the only way
>   That leads man back to God.
>
> And lonesome oft, and often dark
>   With shame, and outcastry, and scorn;
> And, at the end, perchance a cross,
>   And many a crown of thorn.
>
> But His lone cross and crown of thorn
>   Endure when crowns and empires fall,
> The might of His undying love
>   In dying conquered all.
>
> Only by treading in His steps.
>   The all-compelling ways of Love,
> Shall earth be won, and man made one
>   With that Great Love above.   *John Oxenham.*

O JESUS, Thou King of Saints, . . . Thou wholly communicatest Thyself to every Soul in all Kingdoms, and art wholly seen in every Saint, and wholly fed upon by every Christian. It is my Privilege that I can enter with Thee into every Soul, and in every Living Temple of Thy manhood and Thy Godhead, behold again and enjoy Thy glory. [Thomas Traherne.]

JUDGMENT SURE AND JUST

We must all be made manifest before the judgment-seat of Christ; that each one may receive the things done in the body, according to what he hath done, whether it be good or bad. *II Cor. 5:10.*

The three ghosts on the lonesome road
  Spoke each to one another
" Whence came that stain about your mouth
  No lifted hand may cover? "
" From eating of forbidden fruit,
  Brother, my brother."

The three ghosts on the sunless road
  Spoke each to one another
" Whence came that red burn on your foot
  No dust or ash may cover? "
" I stamped a neighbor's hearth flame out,
  Brother, my brother."

The three ghosts on the windless road
  Spoke each to one another
" Whence came that blood upon your hand
  No other hand may cover? "
" From breaking of a woman's heart,
  Brother, my brother."

" Yet on the earth clean men we walked
  Glutton and thief and lover;
White flesh and fair it hid our stains
  That no man might discover."
Naked the soul goes up to God
  Brother, my brother.   *Theodosia Garrison.*

ALMIGHTY and Most Merciful Father, . . . enter not into judgment with Thy servants, but be Thou merciful unto us, and wash away all our sins with that precious blood which our Saviour shed for us. Purify our hearts by Thy Holy Spirit, and as Thou dost add days to our lives, so good Lord, we beseech Thee, to add repentance to our days, that when we have passed this mortal life we may be partakers of Thine everlasting Kingdom; through the merits of Jesus Christ our Lord. [King Charles I.]

CHRIST'S SELF-RESTRAINT

Jesus therefore said unto Peter, Put up the sword into the sheath: the cup which the Father hath given me, shall I not drink it? *John 18:11.*

Thinkest thou that I cannot beseech my Father, and he shall even now send me more than twelve legions of angels. *Matt. 26:53.*

He saved others; himself he cannot save. *Matt. 27:42.*

Therefore doth the Father love me, because I lay down my life, that I may take it again. No one taketh it away from me, but I lay it down of myself. I have power to lay it down, and I have power to take it again. This commandment received I from my Father. *John 10:17, 18.*

He might have reared a palace at a word
   Who sometimes had not where to lay His head,
   Time was when He who nourished crowds with bread
Would not one meal unto Himself afford.
   He healed another's scratch, His own side bled,
Side, hands and feet with cruel piercings gored.
   Twelve legions, girded with angelic sword,
   Stood at his beck, the scorned and buffeted.
O wonderful the wonders left undone
   And not less wonderful than those He wrought!
   O self-restraint, surpassing human thought,
To have all power, yet be as having none
O self-denying love that thought alone
For needs of others, never for His own!   *Trench.*

O MOST Merciful Jesus, grant to me Thy grace, that it may be with me and work with me, and continue with me even to the end. Grant that I may always desire and will that which is to Thee most acceptable and most dear. Let Thy will be mine and let my will ever follow Thine, and agree perfectly with it. . . . Grant to me above all things that I can desire, to desire to rest in Thee and in Thee to have my heart at peace. Thou art the true peace of the heart: Thou art its only rest; out of Thee all things are full of trouble and unrest. In this peace, that is, in Thee, the one chiefest eternal Good, I will lay me down and sleep. [Thomas à Kempis.]

THE GOOD WARFARE

Watch ye, stand fast in the faith, quit you like men, be strong.
I Cor. 16:13.
War the good warfare. *I Tim. 1:18.*
Be ye stedfast, unmovable. *I Cor. 15:58.*

There's a breathless hush in the Close tonight —
Ten to make and the match to win —
A bumping pitch and a blinding light,
An hour to play and the last man in.
And it's not for the sake of a ribboned coat,
Or the selfish hope of a season's fame,
But his Captain's hand on his shoulder smote —
"Play up! play up! and play the game!"

The sand of the desert is sodden red —
Red with the wreck of a square that broke; —
The Gatling's jammed and the Colonel dead,
And the regiment blind with dust and smoke.
The river of death has brimmed his banks,
And England's far, and Honor a name,
But the voice of a schoolboy rallies the ranks:
"Play up! play up! and play the game!"

This is the word that year by year,
While in her place the School is set,
Every one of her sons must hear,
And none that hears it dare forget.
This they all with joyful mind
Bear through life like a torch in flame,
And falling fling to the host behind —
"Play up! play up! and play the game!"   *H. Newbolt.*

Give us, O Lord, a steadfast heart, which no unworthy affection may drag down; give us an unconquered heart, which no tribulation can wear out; give us an upright heart, which no unworthy purpose may tempt aside. Bestow upon us also, O Lord our God, understanding to know Thee, diligence to seek Thee, wisdom to find Thee, and a faithfulness that may finally embrace Thee; through Jesus Christ our Lord. [Thomas Aquinas.]

THE TENANT

Behold, I stand at the door and knock: if any man hear my voice and open the door, I will come in to him, and will sup with him, and he with me. *Rev. 3:20.*

If a man love me, he will keep my word: and my Father will love him, and we will come unto him, and make our abode with him. *John 14:23.*

Whosoever shall confess that Jesus is the Son of God, God abideth in him, and he in God. *I John 4:15.*

He will himself show you a large upper room furnished and ready. *Mark 14:15.*

> Come in, O come! the door stands open now!
> I knew Thy voice; Lord Jesus, it was Thou;
> The sun has set long since; the storms begin;
> 'Tis time for Thee, my Saviour, O come in!
>
> Alas! ill-ordered shows the dreary room;
> The household stuff lies heaped amidst the gloom;
> The table empty stands, the couch undressed;
> Ah, what a welcome for the Eternal Guest!
>
> Yet welcome; and today; this doleful scene
> Is e'en itself my cause to hail Thee in;
> This dark confusion e'en at once demands
> Thine own bright Presence, Lord, and ordering hands. . . .
>
> Come, not to find but make this troubled heart
> A dwelling worthy of Thee as Thou art;
> To chase the gloom, the terror and the sin:
> Come, all Thyself, yea come, Lord Jesus, in!
> *H. C. G. Moule.*

Soul of Christ, sanctify me. Body of Christ, save me. Blood of Christ, refresh me. Water from the side of Christ, wash me. Passion of Christ, strengthen me. O good Jesus, hear me. Within Thy wounds, hide me. Permit me not to be separated from Thee. From the evil enemy defend me. In the hour of death call me, and bid me come to Thee, that with Thy saints I may praise Thee forever and ever. [Ignatius Loyola.]

THE END OF THE JOURNEY

There remaineth therefore a sabbath rest for the people of God. *Heb. 4:9.*

But now they desire a better country, that is, a heavenly: wherefore God is not ashamed of them, to be called their God; for he hath prepared for them a city. *Heb. 11:16.*

An inheritance incorruptible, and undefiled, and that fadeth not away, reserved in heaven for you. *I Peter 1:4.*

The hope which is laid up for you in the heavens. *Col. 1:5.*

He that overcometh shall inherit these things; and I will be his God, and he shall be my son. *Rev. 21:7.*

> If this poor vale, with helpless sorrow teeming
> Is so fair-seeming, ah! What shall it be,
> Th' unstinted glee of yonder home-land blest,
> Our lonely soul's safe nest!
>
> If this unrestful sea of stormy weeping
> At times is sleeping, when in vessel frail
> We spread our sail, to course it o'er and o'er, —
> How calm the sheltered shore! . . .
>
> Oh! let us leave this valley grey and dreary,
> For we are weary with vain journeying,
> And Christ our King points out: " O sheep astray!
> Behold the only way!
>
> " Take up your cross with me, and leave the byway,
> I am the Highway, and their only guide
> Who gain, betide what will, yon City white
> Of endless pure delight! "
> *Italian Hymn, Translated by Father John O'Connor.*

*B*LESSED are all Thy saints, my God and King, who have travelled over the tempestuous sea of mortality, and have at last made the desired port of peace and felicity. Oh, cast a gracious eye upon us who are still in our dangerous voyage. Remember and succour us in our distress, and think on them that lie exposed to the rough storms of troubles and temptations. Grant, O Lord, that we may bring our vessel safe to shore, unto our desired haven. [Saint Augustine.]

THE HAND OF GOD

The hand of our God is upon all them that seek him, for good. *Ezra 8:22.*

Even there shall thy hand lead me, and thy right hand shall hold me. *Ps. 139:10.*

I, Jehovah, have called thee in righteousness, and will hold thy hand, and will keep thee. *Isa. 42:6.*

Be not thou far off, O Lord. *Ps. 22:19.*

> The way is dark, my Father! Cloud on cloud
> Is gathering thickly o'er my head, and loud
> The thunders roar above me. See, I stand
> Like one bewildered! Father, take my hand,
>   And through the gloom
>   Lead safely home Thy child!
>
> The day goes fast, my Father! and the night
> Is drawing darkly down. My faithless sight
> Sees ghostly visions. Fears, a spectral band,
> Encompass me. O Father! take my hand,
>   And from the night
>   Lead up to light Thy child! . . .
>
> The throng is great, my Father! Many a doubt
> And fear and danger compass me about;
> And foes oppress me sore. I cannot stand
> Or go alone. O Father! take my hand,
>   And through the throng
>   Lead safe along Thy child!
>
> The cross is heavy, Father! I have borne
> It long, and still do bear it. Let my worn
> And fainting spirit rise to that blest land
> Where crowns are given. Father, take my hand,
>   And reaching down,
>   Lead to the crown Thy child!   *Henry N. Cobb.*

O LORD GOD in whom we live and move and have our being, open our eyes that we may behold Thy Fatherly presence ever about us. Draw our hearts to Thee with the power of Thy love. Help us to feel Thy hand clasping our hand. [Bishop Westcott (Altered).]

THE FINALITY OF CHRIST

Heaven and earth shall pass away, but my words shall not pass away. *Matt. 24:35.*

I am the Alpha and the Omega, the first and the last, the beginning and the end. . . . I am the root and offspring of David, the bright, the morning star. *Rev. 22:13, 16.*

God, having of old time spoken unto the fathers in the prophets by divers portions and in divers manners, hath at the end of these days spoken unto us in his Son, whom he appointed heir of all things, through whom also he made the worlds; who being the effulgence of his glory, and the very image of his substance, and upholding all things by the word of his power, when he had made purification of sins, sat down on the right hand of the Majesty on high. *Heb. 1:1-3.*

Christ's thought after two thousand years needs no revision. His conceptions of God, of man and human society are ultimate conceptions; intellectual power cannot go beyond them, can never even master their entire content. His Spirit has upon it the mark of finality. His character is the full impression upon humanity of the moral perfection of the Deity. The ultimateness of Christ's thought and the finality of His Spirit differentiate His transcendence from that of the greatest and best of mankind, and ground His being in the Godhead in a way solitary and supreme. *G. A. Gordon,* The Christ of Today.

O GOD, who hast proven Thy love for mankind by sending us Jesus Christ, our Lord, and hast illumined our human life by the radiance of His Presence, we give Thee thanks for this Thy greatest gift.

For our Lord's days upon earth:
For the record of His deeds of love:
For the words He spake for our guidance and help:
For His obedience unto death:
For His triumph over death:
For the Presence of His Spirit with us now:
    We thank Thee, O God!

Grant that the remembrance of the blessed Life that once was lived out on this common earth under these ordinary skies may remain with us in all the tasks and duties of this day. [John Baillie (Altered).]

THE CITY WALL

The Lord is gracious: unto whom coming, a living stone, rejected indeed of men, but with God elect, precious, ye also, as living stones, are built up a spiritual house, to be a holy priesthood. *I Peter 2:3–5.*

And I saw the holy city, new Jerusalem, coming down out of heaven from God, made ready as a bride adorned for her husband. . . . And the wall of the city had twelve foundations, and on them twelve names of the twelve apostles of the Lamb. *Rev. 21:2, 14.*

In November, 1913, Julia Richman who had been for years a Jewish teacher in the public schools of New York City finished her work of singular devotion and usefulness. At the time of her death she was principal of one of the schools subsequently named for her. At the memorial meeting, one friend bore tribute to the work she had done as one of the builders of the city in the following sonnet:

> Come all who serve the City, all who serve
> The glorious golden City of our dream
> With true heart service that can never swerve,
> How faint soe'er the strength, or far the gleam;
> Come, sorrow proudly for our comrade passed
> Into the silence; one who served indeed
> In all things even unto the least and last,
> Spending herself to meet the moment's need.
> Share memories of that strong, illumined face,
> Keen speech, and courage springing to the test,
> And all the fervor of the ancient race;
> That finds its longed-for East in this young West,
> Be this the sum, the last word best of all;
> She built her life into the City wall.

O GOD we pray Thee for our city. Help us to make it the workshop of our people, where every one will find his place and task, in daily achievement, building his own life in truth and service into the walls of the city, keen to do his best with hand and mind, and where no one will be unemployed. Help us to make our city a true home for all its people where all may live their lives in comfort, unafraid, loving their loves in peace and fulfilling their years in strength and joy. [Walter Rauschenbusch (Abbreviated).]

And he will judge between the nations, and will decide concerning many peoples; and they shall beat their swords into plowshares, and their spears into pruning-hooks; nation shall not lift up sword against nation, neither shall they learn war any more. *Isa. 2:4.*

And the fruit of righteousness is sown in peace for them that make peace. *James 3:18.*

Follow after peace with all men. *Heb. 12:14.*

I cannot see the Christ-Child for the soldiers marching past:
I cannot hear the angels for the bugle's angry blast.
But I know the Bells are ringing
And that Faith and Hope are clinging
To the Day when Love shall crown the world at last.

I cannot see the Christ-Child, for the smoke is in my eyes,
I cannot hear the Shepherds for the little children's cries:
But I know the Bells are ringing
And I think I hear the singing
Of the Day when Peace like Morning Dawn shall rise.

I cannot see the Christ-Child, for the clouds hang dark and low
I cannot hear the Wise Men, for the conflict rages so:
But I know the Bells are ringing,
And that Christmas Morn is bringing
In the Golden Day, Foretold so long ago.   *Hugh T. Kerr.*

OUR Father, forgive us that we have called ourselves Thy children and have not been like our Father. Forgive us if instead of making peace, we have stirred up strife. Help us to realize how much nobler it is to pass by a transgression against ourselves than to be ready to take offence. We pray that Thou wouldst make us more like Jesus. May His mind be in us. May we learn from Him to be willing to take the lowest place and not to think too highly of ourselves. We thank Thee for the joy that comes through a sense of Thy forgiveness. We thank Thee for the peace which comes through Thy forgiveness. We have peace with God through our Lord Jesus Christ. May there be peace and good will among all men. [*Morning and Evening Prayers* (Altered).]

And behold, there talked with him two men, who were Moses and Elijah; who appeared in glory. *Luke 9:30, 31.*

This mortal must put on immortality. *I Cor. 15:53.*

[God] will render to every man according to his works: to them that by patience in well-doing seek for glory and honor and incorruption, eternal life. *Rom. 2:6, 7.*

For to this end Christ died and lived again, that he might be Lord of both the dead and the living. *Rom. 14:9.*

If we died with Christ, we believe that we shall also live with him; knowing that Christ being raised from the dead dieth no more; death no more hath dominion over him. For the death that he died, he died unto sin once: but the life that he liveth, he liveth unto God. Even so reckon ye also yourselves to be dead unto sin, but alive unto God in Christ Jesus. *Rom. 6:8–11.*

> Call me not dead when I, indeed, have gone
> Into the company of the ever-living
> High and most gracious poets! Let thanksgiving
> Rather be made. Say: " He at last hath won
> Rest and release, converse supreme and wise,
> Music and song and light of immortal faces;
> Today, perhaps, wandering in starry places,
> He hath met Keats, and known him by his eyes.
> Tomorrow (who can say!) Shakespeare may pass,
> And our lost friend may catch one syllable
> Of that three-centuried wit that kept so well;
> Or Milton: or Dante, looking on the grass
> Thinking of Beatrice, and listening still
> To chanted hymns that sound from the heavenly hill."
>   *Richard Watson Gilder.*

Our Heavenly Father, we rejoice in the blessed communion of all Thy saints, wherein Thou givest us also to have part. We remember before Thee all who have departed this life in Thy faith and love, and especially those most dear to us. We thank Thee for our present fellowship with them, for our common hope, and for the promise of future joy. [*Prayers,* Compiled by Page and Laidlaw.]

LIVING INTO KNOWLEDGE

He that looketh into the perfect law, the law of liberty, and so continueth, being not a hearer that forgetteth but a doer that worketh, this man shall be blessed in his doing. *James 1:25.*

For whosoever would save his life shall lose it: and whosoever shall lose his life for my sake shall find it. For what shall a man be profited, if he shall gain the whole world, and forfeit his life? or what shall a man give in exchange for his life? *Matt. 16:25, 26.*

Jesus therefore said to those Jews that had believed him, If ye abide in my word, then are ye truly my disciples; and ye shall know the truth, and the truth shall make you free. *John 8:31, 32.*

Where wast thou, little song,
That didst delay so long
  To come to me?
Mute in the mind of God,
Till where thy foot had trod
  I followed thee.
                John B. Tabb.

Oh righteous doom, that they who make
  Pleasure their only end
Ordering the whole life for its sake,
  Miss that whereto they tend:
While they who bid stern duty lead,
  Content to follow — they
Of duty only taking heed
  Find pleasure by the way.
                R. C. Trench.

O LORD, my Maker and Protector, who hast graciously sent me into this world, to work out my salvation, enable me to drive from me all such unquiet and perplexing thoughts as may mislead or hinder me in the practice of those duties which Thou hast required. When I behold the works of Thy hands and consider the course of Thy providence, give me Grace always to remember that Thy thoughts are not my thoughts, nor Thy ways my ways. And while it shall please Thee to continue me in this world where much is to be done and little to be known, teach me by Thy Holy Spirit to withdraw my mind from unprofitable and dangerous inquiries, from difficulties vainly curious, and doubts impossible to be solved. Let me rejoice in the light which Thou hast imparted, let me serve Thee with active zeal, and humble confidence, and wait with patient expectation for the time in which the soul which Thou receivest shall be satisfied with knowledge. Grant this, O Lord, for Jesus Christ's sake. [Samuel Johnson.]

Therefore let us also, seeing we are compassed about with so great a cloud of witnesses, lay aside every weight, and the sin which doth so easily beset us, and let us run with patience the race that is set before us. *Heb. 12:1.*

After he had in his own generation served the counsel of God, he fell asleep, and was laid unto his fathers. *Acts 13:36.*

John Meigs, of the Hill School, Pottstown, Pennsylvania, one of the greatest of American schoolmasters, is buried in the cloister of the school chapel.

> The sun sets red behind the tower
> Small clouds, pink-rimmed, float light above,
> The quiet of the evening hour
> Gives evidence of God's great love.
>
> A light burns dim above that grave —
> The holiest place upon the Hill —
> Where rests the man whose life-work gave
> Us inspiration — gives it still.
>
> And though Time, flying year by year,
> Brings those who never knew his power,
> His Spirit always hovers near
> And sanctifies the evening hour.   *Hill School Record.*

ALMIGHTY and eternal God, . . . give unto us courage and faith and hope and love that we, in our day and generation, may do all that Thou requirest of us in Thy fear and with an eye single to Thine honor and Thy glory. May we never be discouraged or disheartened because the right seems to fail and the wrong seems to prevail, assured that Thou wilt cause all things at last to work together, so that Thy Kingdom of peace and righteousness may prevail throughout all the earth. We beseech Thee to have mercy on us in all our iniquities, Thou just and righteous One. Overcome the strife of opposing foes. Teach men better co-operation, that they may remember that they are all members of one great family in Thee and may all be considerate of each other's interests. Help us to bear one another's burdens and so fulfill Thy law. [L. Clark Seelye.]

THE CHIEF

Looking unto Jesus the author and perfecter of our faith, who for the joy that was set before him endured the cross, despising shame, and hath sat down at the right hand of the throne of God. *Heb. 12:2.*

He that followeth me shall not walk in darkness, but shall have the light of life. *John 8:12.*

We have not a high priest that cannot be touched with the feeling of our infirmities; but one that hath been . . . tempted like as we are, yet without sin. *Heb. 4:15.*

It became him, for whom are all things, and through whom are all things, . . . to make the author of their salvation perfect through sufferings. *Heb. 2:10.*

> Our Chief has blazed the path and climbed the way.
> His sacred feet have found for us a ford.
> Press forward, men, fear not the leaping spray.
> See on the peak the day break of His sword!
>
> For Christ is Freedom and the light within,
> The only hold of reason and of hope;
> He is the Stillness in the world's mad din,
> The Foothold where the blind feet slide and grope.
>
> He knows the loneliness; He knows the road.
> Barefoot and hungry, He has traveled it.
> He knows the brute betrayal, the dead load,
> The cry of worlds, the laughter of the pit.
> *Edwin Markham.*

Glory to our ascended Lord, that He is with us always. Glory to the Word of God, going forth with His armies, conquering and to conquer. Glory to Him who has led captivity captive, and given gifts for the perfecting of His saints. Glory to Him who has gone before to prepare a place in His Father's Home for us. Glory to the Author and Finisher of our Faith; that God in all things may be glorified through Jesus Christ, to whom be all worship and praise, dominion and glory; now, and forever and ever. [*Sursum Corda.*]

They were intrusted with the oracles of God. *Rom. 3:2.*

I delivered unto you first of all that which also I received. *I Cor. 15:3.*

Now they know that all things whatsoever thou hast given me are from thee: for the words which thou gavest me I have given unto them. . . . I have given them thy word. *John 17:7, 8, 14.*

For we are not as the many, corrupting the word of God: but as of sincerity, but as of God, in the sight of God, speak we in Christ. *II Cor. 2:17.*

We cannot but speak the things which we saw and heard. *Acts 4:20.*

Lord, at Thy Word opens yon door, inviting
Teacher and taught to feast this hour with Thee;
Opens a Book where God in human writing
Thinks His deep thoughts, and dead tongues live for me.

Too dread the task, too great the duty calling,
Too heavy far the weight is laid on me;
O if mine own thought should on Thy words falling
Mar the great message, and men hear not Thee!

Give me Thy voice to speak, Thine ear to listen,
Give me Thy mind to grasp Thy mystery;
So shall my heart throb, and my glad eyes glisten,
Rapt with the wonders Thou dost show to me.
J. H. Moulton.

*A*LMIGHTY GOD by whose word all things work, so order our inward life, that we may be enabled to understand the things that we see; and by Thy guidance in the spiritual life and in charity, so order what there is disordered in our lives, so bring our minds to the truth, and our hearts to Thy true love, that we may hear the music of the heavenly will. So give us hope that we may pass on through time, into the higher and better education of the eternal life to come, and that at last we may know those things that are hidden, and learn the glorious beauty and the glorious living of the eternal years. [George Dawson (Abbreviated).]

THE FATHER'S FACE

By his light I walked through darkness. *Job 29:3.*

The darkness hideth not from thee, but the night shineth as the day: the darkness and the light are both alike to thee. *Ps. 139:12.*

Thou . . . settest me before thy face for ever. *Ps. 41:12.*

See that ye despise not one of these little ones: for I say unto you, that in heaven their angels do always behold the face of my Father who is in heaven. *Matt. 18:10.*

"Is your face turned toward me, father?"
  Eyes that were used to daylight opened in the dark,
Closing at twilight, waking with the morn
  They knew not what it was, no single spark
Or glimmer in the room. Frightened, forlorn,
  The boy moved restless, and the father said,
"Lie still and sleep again." "Father," he cried,
  "Is your face turned toward me?" and the dear head
Pillowed itself in peace, nor longer tried
  To look the dark through, for the answered "Yes"
Brought calm assurance, banishing all fear.
  O Father, turn Thy Face towards me, and bless
Each darkest hour — knowing Thou art near.
  I will not try dark things to comprehend
Nor shall my heart in sorrow's darkness fear,
  But rest on Thee, my Father and my Friend.
                                    William Croswell Doane.

O LORD, we beseech Thee, listen now to the prayer of Thy servants who desire to fear Thy Name. Prosper us, we pray Thee, this day in our work. Help us ever to remember that Thou art a God at hand, that no secret place is hidden from Thee, but that all our thoughts and words and actions are seen and known by Thee. Make us truthful in all our words, holy in all our thoughts, and honest in every act. Make Thy presence a happiness to us. Let us often think of Thee as our Father and Friend and our Helper in every hour of need. Bless all who are dear to us and teach them the paths of goodness and truth; for the sake of Jesus Christ, our Saviour. [O. H. C.]

PEACE, PERFECT PEACE

The peace of God, which passeth all understanding, shall guard your hearts and your thoughts in Christ Jesus. *Phil. 4:7.*

Now the God of hope fill you with all joy and peace in believing, that ye may abound in hope, in the power of the Holy Spirit. *Rom. 15:13.*

And let the peace of Christ rule in your hearts, to which also ye were called in one body; and be ye thankful. Let the word of Christ dwell in you richly. *Col. 3:15, 16.*

> And when we dwell in darkness of the mind, 'tis we
> That turn our faces from Thy radiancy.
>
> *Fraser-Tytler.*

It lives not on the sunlit hill
Nor on the sunlit plain;
Nor even on any running stream
Nor on the unclouded main —
But sometimes, through the soul of man
Slow moving o'er his pain,
The moonlight of a perfect peace
Floods heart and brain.

William Sharp.

O LORD who never failest to help and govern those whom Thou dost bring up in Thy steadfast fear and love; Keep us, we beseech Thee, under the protection of Thy good providence, and make us to have a perpetual fear and love of Thy Holy Name. Grant, we beseech Thee, Merciful Lord, to Thy faithful people pardon and peace, that they may be cleansed from all their sins, and serve Thee with a quiet mind. O Almighty God who alone canst order the unruly wills and affections of sinful men; Grant unto Thy people that they may love the thing which Thou commandest, and desire that which Thou dost promise, that so, among the sundry and manifold changes of the world, our hearts may surely there be fixed, where true joys are to be found.

Let Thy continual pity cleanse and defend Thy Church and, because it cannot continue in safety without Thy succour, preserve it evermore by Thy help and goodness. [*Gelasian Sacramentary.*]

Ye also helping together on our behalf by your supplication. *Il Cor. 1:11.*

Pray for us: for we are persuaded that we have a good conscience, desiring to live honorably in all things. And I exhort you the more exceedingly to do this, that I may be restored to you the sooner. *Heb. 13:18, 19.*

I beseech you, brethren, by our Lord Jesus Christ, and by the love of the Spirit, that ye strive together with me in your prayers to God for me. *Rom. 15:30.*

> The weary ones had rest, the sad had joy
> That day, and wondered "how?"
> A plowman singing at his work had prayed,
> "Lord, help them now."
>
> Away in foreign lands, they wondered "how"
> Their simple word had power.
> At home, the gleaners, two or three had met
> To pray an hour.
>
> Yes, we are always wondering "how?"
> Because we do not see
> Someone, unknown perhaps, and far away
> On bended knee.

O GOD, most merciful, who healest those that are broken in heart, and turnest the sadness of the sorrowful to joy; let Thy fatherly goodness be upon all that Thou hast made. Especially we beseech Thee to remember in pity such as are this day destitute, homeless, or forgotten of their fellow men. Uplift those who are cast down, mightily befriend innocent sufferers, and sanctify to them the endurance of their wrongs. Cheer with hope all discouraged and unhappy people, and by Thy heavenly grace preserve from falling those whose penury tempteth them to sin. Though they be troubled on every side, suffer them not to be distressed; though they be perplexed, save them from despair. Grant this, O Lord, for the love of Him who for our sakes became poor, Thy Son, our Saviour Jesus Christ. [*The Book of Common Worship,* Revised.]

SEEKERS AND SOUGHT

And they found him, and say unto him, All are seeking thee. *Mark 1:37.*

If then ye were raised together with Christ, seek the things that are above, where Christ is, seated on the right hand of God. Set your mind on the things that are above, not on the things that are upon the earth. For ye died, and your life is hid with Christ in God. When Christ, who is our life, shall be manifested, then shall ye also with him be manifested in glory. *Col. 3:1-4.*

> The world uprose as a man to find Him —
> Ten thousand methods, ten thousands ends —
> Some bent on treasure; the more on pleasure;
> And some on the chaplet which fame attends:
> But the great deep's voice in the distance dim
> Said: Peace, it is well; they are seeking Him.
> *Arthur Edward Waite.*

I bind my heart this tide
To the Galilean's side,
To the wounds of Calvary,
To the Christ who died for me.

I bind my heart in thrall
To the God, the Lord of all,
To the God, the poor man's Friend,
And the Christ whom He did send.

I bind my soul this day
To the brother far away,
And the brother near at hand,
In this town, and in this land.

I bind myself to peace,
To make strife and envy cease;
God, knit Thou sure the cord
Of my thralldom to my Lord!
L. M. Watt.

*A*LMIGHTY GOD, from whom all thoughts of Truth and Peace proceed; kindle, we pray Thee, in the hearts of all men the true love of peace, and guide with Thy pure and peaceable wisdom those who take counsel for the nations of the earth; that in tranquillity Thy Kingdom may grow till the earth is filled with the knowledge of Thy love. [*Acts of Devotion* (Altered).]

HIDDEN MEANING

No prophecy of Scripture is of private interpretation. For no prophecy ever came by the will of man: but men spake from God, being moved by the Holy Spirit. *II Peter 1:20, 21.*

Not unto themselves, but unto you, did they minister these things, which now have been announced unto you through them that preached the gospel unto you by the Holy Spirit sent forth from heaven. *I Peter 1:12.*

And I heard, but I understood not. *Dan. 12:8.*

Therefore have I uttered that which I understood not, things too wonderful for me, which I knew not. *Job 42:3.*

> From end to end we glance: from Adam's fall
> To Christ's triumphant death and victory
> At once: those mysteries that between them be
> By man are known but scantly, if at all:
> And thus in time our marvel waxes small;
> Thus gazing down into an air-like sea,
> Its depth eludes us from its purity,
> And treasures ours so cheaply vainly call
> For gratitude or gladness. On we go,
> Unmoved beneath a heaven of awe-struck eyes,
> While purer beings, angel minds that know
> The cost of that great boon which we despise,
> Look down on us suspended from their skies,
> With deeper awe than men on God bestow.
> *Aubrey de Vere.*

O GOD who didst speak unto the fathers by the prophets, we thank Thee that still by these same prophets Thou art speaking to us today, by Thy Holy Spirit revealing to us in their words depths of meaning which were hidden from them. Open our eyes to behold these wonderful things concealed even from those who uttered them. Especially we pray for such light of understanding of Thy dear Son, the Word made flesh, as shall enable us to apprehend His mystery which in other generations was only dimly seen and not yet made known unto the sons of men as it hath now been revealed unto us. In His light may we see light even in the dark places of the ancient days. [R. E. S.]

I know in part. *1 Cor. 13:12.*

And this is life eternal, that they should know thee the only true God, and him whom thou didst send, even Jesus Christ. *John 17:3.*

Increasing in the knowledge of God. *Col. 1:10.*

In everything ye were enriched in him, in all utterance and in all knowledge. *1 Cor. 1:5.*

> We have but faith; we cannot know;
>   For knowledge is of things we see;
>   And yet we trust it comes from Thee,
> A beam in darkness, let it grow.
>
> Let knowledge grow from more to more,
>   But more of reverence in us dwell;
>   That mind and soul according well,
> May make one music as before,
>
> But vaster. We are fools and slight;
>   We mock Thee when we do not fear:
>   But help Thy foolish ones to bear;
> Help Thy vain worlds to bear Thy light. *Tennyson.*

O GOD, forasmuch as without Thee we are not able to please Thee; mercifully grant that Thy Holy Spirit may in all things direct and rule our hearts; and because through the weakness of our mortal nature, we can do no good thing without Thee, grant us the help of Thy grace, that in keeping Thy commandments we may please Thee, both in will and deed. Graft in our hearts the love of Thy Name, increase in us true religion, nourish us with all goodness, and of Thy great mercy keep us in the same. O God, the protector of all that trust Thee, the fountain of light, the beginning and the end of truth, without whom nothing is strong, nothing is holy; by whose illumination we truly know though we know now but in part; Increase and multiply upon us Thy mercy, that in Thy light we may see light, that, Thou being our ruler and guide, we may so pass through things temporal, that we finally lose not things eternal, and may come thither at last where we no longer see through a glass darkly but face to face. [*Gelasian Sacramentary* (Altered).]

WE SHALL SEE

And there shall be no curse any more: and the throne of God and of the Lamb shall be therein: and his servants shall serve him; and they shall see his face. *Rev. 22:3, 4.*

But as for me I know that my Redeemer liveth, and at the last he will stand upon the earth: and after my skin, even this body, is destroyed, then without my flesh, shall I see God; whom I, even I, shall see, on my side, and mine eyes shall behold, and not as a stranger. *Job 19:25–27.*

Blessed are the pure in heart: for they shall see God. *Matt. 5:8.*

He is not the God of the dead, but of the living: for all live unto him. *Luke 20:38.*

Jesus answered and said unto him, Verily, verily, I say unto thee, Except one be born anew, he cannot see the kingdom of God. *John 3:3.*

> O Lord of work and peace! O Lord of life!
> O Lord, the awful Lord, of will! Though late
> E'en yet renew this soul with duteous breath;
> That, when the peace is garnered in from strife,
> The work retrieved, the will regenerate,
> This soul may see Thy face, O Lord of Death.
> *Dante Gabriel Rossetti.*

O GOD, who hast delivered us from the power of darkness and translated us into the Kingdom of Thy dear Son; Pour Thy Spirit into our hearts, that He may show us things to come; so that every face however furrowed by sorrow, or distorted by passion, or stupefied by self-indulgence, may be a witness to us of eternity; that we may remember that Thy Son Jesus Christ died to redeem that man and us; that we may look not for a new heaven only, but a new earth wherein dwelleth righteousness. Lift up, we beseech Thee, our hearts and our spirits above the false shows of things, above fear and melancholy, above laziness and despair, above custom and fashion, up to the everlasting Truth and Order that Thou art; that so we may live joyfully and freely, in the faith and trust that Thou hast given us Thy Son to be our King and our Saviour, our Example and our Judge. [Charles Kingsley (Altered).]

Behold, I will bring them from the north country, and gather them from the uttermost parts of the earth, and with them the blind and the lame, the woman with child and her that travaileth with child together: a great company shall they return hither. They shall come with weeping; and with supplications will I lead them: I will cause them to walk by rivers of waters, in a straight way wherein they shall not stumble; for I am a father to Israel, and Ephraim is my first-born. *Jer. 31:8, 9.*

Teach me thy way, O Jehovah; and lead me in a plain path. *Ps. 27:11.*

> I go to prove my soul!
> I see my way as birds their trackless way.
> I shall arrive! what time, what circuit first,
> I ask not: but unless God send his hail
> Or blinding fireballs, sleet or stifling snow,
> In some time, his good time, I shall arrive:
> He guides me and the bird. In his good time!
> *Browning.*

We have millions of ideas, each of which has its influence on our character, but only a true ideal can lead us to the completeness for which we crave. Ideas are like pebbles which disturb the wave on the shore; the ideal like the celestial body which dominates the tides. *Hadfield.*

O GOD, who hast promised that if any lack wisdom and ask it of Thee, Thou wilt give it; Give us that Spirit without whom we cannot will or having willed cannot perform anything acceptable to Thee. Give us the Spirit of wisdom and understanding, the Spirit of counsel and might, the Spirit of knowledge and love and of Thy holy fear. When we are strong, do Thou uphold us; When we are weak do Thou strengthen us; Govern our thoughts; direct our ways; fill us with holy desires. Enlighten us with wisdom; fortify us with purity; teach us true humility; comfort us when we are in pain; arm us when we are in temptation. Guard all that we say; sanctify all that we do; accept all that we suffer. Make us Thine, O God, and keep us Thine, so that we may be Thine forever; through Jesus Christ our Lord. [*Manual of the Guild of St. Barnabas for Nurses.*]

I see a different law in my members, warring against the law of my mind, and bringing me into captivity under the law of sin which is in my members. Wretched man that I am! who shall deliver me out of the body of this death? I thank God through Jesus Christ our Lord. *Rom. 7:23–25.*

For what the law could not do, in that it was weak through the flesh, God, sending his own Son in the likeness of sinful flesh and for sin, condemned sin in the flesh. *Rom. 8:3.*

God, being rich in mercy, for his great love wherewith he loved us, even when we were dead through our trespasses, made us alive together with Christ (by grace have ye been saved), and raised us up with him, and made us sit with him in the heavenly places, in Christ Jesus. *Eph. 2:4–6.*

O Thou who didst grant me that day
And before it not seldom has granted Thy help to essay,
Carry on and complete my adventure, my Shield and my Sword,
In that act where my soul was Thy servant, Thy word was my word, —
So be with me, who thus at the summit of human endeavor
And scaling the highest man's thought could, gazed hopeless as ever
On the new stretch of heaven above me — till, mighty to save,
Just one lift of Thy hand cleared the distance — God's throne from man's grave.   *Robert Browning.*

O LORD GOD, heavenly Father, we thank Thee for Thy grace that Thou hast sent us Thy Son and hast appointed Him to be the King of Righteousness and our Saviour and Redeemer, who should rescue us from the dominion of darkness and bestow on us righteousness, salvation and blessedness. May He take up His abode among us and within us and may we ever continue in His kingdom and allegiance. . . . Restrain and check all influences that would close the door against Him and forbid Him to come in. But show forth Thy power and mercy on the poor sons of men who are bound in the fetters of oppression, or the dreariness of unbelief, in idolatry, false doctrine or utter careless ungodliness; may Christ now come also unto them and set up His kingdom of light, truth and righteousness. [*Riga Prayer Book.*]

THE FOOL'S PRAYER

O God, thou knowest my foolishness; and my sins are not hid from thee. *Ps. 69:5.*

And Aaron said unto Moses, Oh, my lord, lay not, I pray thee, sin upon us, for that we have done foolishly, and for that we have sinned. *Num. 12:11.*

The royal feast was done; the king
  Sought some new sport to banish care,
And to his jester cried: " Sir Fool,
  Kneel now, and make for us a prayer! "

The jester doffed his cap and bells,
  And stood the mocking court before;
They could not see the bitter smile
  Behind the painted grin he wore.

He bowed his head, and bent his knee
  Upon the monarch's silken stool;
His pleading voice arose: " O Lord,
  Be merciful to me, a fool!

" No pity, Lord, could change the heart
  From red with wrong to white as wool;
The rod must heal the sin; but, Lord,
  Be merciful to me, a fool!

" 'Tis not by guilt the onward sweep
  Of truth and right, O Lord, we stay;
'Tis by our follies that so long
  We hold the earth from heaven away. . . .

" Our faults no tenderness should ask,
  The chastening stripes must cleanse them all;
But for our blunders — oh, in shame
  Before the eyes of heaven we fall.

" Earth bears no balsam for mistakes;
  Men crown the knave, and scourge the tool
That did his will; but Thou, O Lord,
  Be merciful to me, a fool! "

The room was hushed; in silence rose
  The king, and sought his gardens cool,
And walked apart, and murmured low,
  " Be merciful to me, a fool! "
          E. R. Sill.

O LORD of heaven and earth, we are truly sorry for all our misdoings; we utterly renounce whatsoever is contrary to Thy will, and here devote ourselves entirely to the obedience thereof. Accept, O most merciful Father, of this renewed dedication which we make of ourselves, our bodies, souls and spirits unto Thee. [Simon Patrick.]

Thus said the Lord Jehovah, the Holy One of Israel, In returning and rest shall ye be saved; in quietness and in confidence shall be your strength. *Isa. 30:15.*

Study to be quiet, and to do your own business, and to work with your hands, even as we charged you. *I Thess. 4:11.*

Come unto me, all ye that labor and are heavy laden, and I will give you rest. Take my yoke upon you, and learn of me . . . and ye shall find rest unto your souls. *Matt. 11:28, 29.*

> When God at first made man,
> Having a glasse of blessings standing by,
> "Let us," said He, "poure on him all we can;
> Let the world's riches, which dispersed lie,
>   Contract into a span."
>
> So strength first made a way:
> Then beautie flow'd, then wisdome, honour, pleasure;
> When almost all was out, God made a stay,
> Perceiving that, alone of all His treasure,
>   Rest in the bottome lay.
>
> "For if I should," said He,
> "Bestow this jewell also on my creature
> He would adore My gifts instead of Me,
> And rest in Nature, not the God of nature:
>   So both should losers be.
>
> "Yet let him keep the rest,
> But keep them with repining restlessnesse:
> Let him be rich and wearie, that at least,
> If goodness lead him not, yet wearinesse
>   May tosse him to my breast."   *George Herbert.*

GRANT unto us, O heavenly Father, Thy peace that passeth understanding, that we amid the storms and troubles of this our life, may rest in Thee, knowing that all things are in Thee, under Thy care, governed by Thy will, guarded by Thy love; so that with a quiet heart we may face the storms of life, the cloud and the thick darkness; through Jesus Christ our Lord.

All things therefore whatsoever ye would that men should do unto you, even so do ye also unto them. *Matt. 7:12.*

Jesus of Nazareth, how God anointed him with the Holy Spirit and with power: who went about doing good, and healing all that were oppressed of the devil; for God was with him. *Acts 10:38.*

And be ye kind one to another, tender-hearted, forgiving each other, even as God also in Christ forgave you. *Eph. 4:32.*

Put on therefore, as God's elect, holy and beloved, a heart of compassion, kindness, lowliness, meekness, longsuffering; forbearing one another, and forgiving each other, if any man have a complaint against any; even as the Lord forgave you, so also do ye: and above all these things put on love, which is the bond of perfectness. *Col. 3:12-14.*

> The bread that bringeth strength I want to give;
> The water pure that bids the thirsty live;
> I want to help the fainting day by day;
> I'm sure I shall not pass again this way.

> I want to give the oil of joy for tears,
> The faith to conquer crowding doubts and fears,
> Beauty for ashes may I give alway:
> I'm sure I shall not pass again this way. . . .

> I want to give to others hope and faith;
> I want to do all that the Master saith;
> I want to live aright from day to day;
> I'm sure I shall not pass again this way.
>
> *Ellen H. Underwood.*

O BLESSED LORD, who makest all the commandments of the law to consist in love towards God and towards man; grant to us so to love Thee with all our heart, with all our mind and all our soul, and our neighbor as ourselves, that the grace of charity and brotherly love may dwell in us, and all envy, harshness and ill will may die in us. And we beseech Thee, so fill our hearts with true affections, that by constantly rejoicing in the happiness and good success of others, by sympathizing with them in their sorrows, and by putting away all harsh judgments and envious thoughts, we may follow Thee, who art the Way, the Truth and the Life. [*Treasury of Devotion.*]

THE DESIRE AND DUTY OF FAITH

Jesus cometh, the doors being shut, and stood in the midst, and said, Peace be unto you. Then saith he to Thomas, Reach hither thy finger, and see my hands; and reach hither thy hand, and put it into my side: and be not faithless, but believing. Thomas answered and said unto him, My Lord and my God. Jesus saith unto him, Because thou hast seen me thou hast believed: blessed are they that have not seen, and yet have believed. *John 20:26–29.*

But they did not all hearken to the glad tidings. For Isaiah saith, Lord, who hath believed our report? So belief cometh of hearing, and hearing by the word of Christ. But I say, Did they not hear? *Rom. 10:16–18.*

Looking unto Jesus the author and perfecter of our faith. *Heb. 12:2.*

According as God hath dealt to each man a measure of faith. *Rom. 12:3.*

So that your faith and hope might be in God. *I Peter 1:21.*

My faith looks up to Thee,
Thou Lamb of Calvary,
  Saviour divine:
Now hear me while I pray,
Take all my guilt away,
O let me from this day
  Be wholly Thine!   *Ray Palmer.*

ALMIGHTY and everlasting God, who hast given us the faith of Christ for a light to our feet amid the darkness of this world; Have pity upon all who by doubting or denying it are gone astray from the path of safety; bring home the truth to their hearts and grant them to receive it as little children. Grant all who contend for the faith never to injure it by clamor and impatience, but, speaking Thy precious truth in love, so to present it that it may be loved and that men may see in it Thy goodness and beauty. Let Thy Spirit overshadow us in reading Thy Word, and conform our thoughts to Thy revelation, that, learning of Thee with honest hearts, we may be rooted and built up in Thy Son Christ. [William Bright (Altered).]

So teach us to number our days, that we may get us an heart of wisdom. . . . Oh satisfy us in the morning with thy lovingkindness, that we may rejoice and be glad all our days. *Ps. 90:12, 14.*

Jesus therefore said unto them, Yet a little while is the light among you. Walk while ye have the light, that darkness overtake you not: and he that walketh in the darkness knoweth not whither he goeth. While ye have the light, believe on the light, that ye may become sons of light. *John 12:35, 36.*

If we walk in the light, as he is in the light, we have fellowship one with another, and the blood of Jesus his Son cleanseth us from all sin. *I John 1:7.*

The path of the righteous is as the dawning light, that shineth more and more unto the perfect day. *Prov. 4:18.*

> Forenoon and afternoon and night, —
>   Forenoon,
> And afternoon and night, — Forenoon and
>   — What!
> The empty song repeats itself. No more?
> Yea, that is life: make this forenoon sublime,
> This afternoon a psalm, this night a prayer,
> And time is conquered, and thy crown is won. *E. R. Sill.*

The radiant morn hath passed away,
   And spent too soon her golden store;
The shadows of departing day
   Creep on once more.

Our life is but a fading dawn;
   Its glorious noon how quickly past!
Lead us, O Christ, when all is gone,
   Safe home at last.
   Godfrey Thring.

ALMIGHTY GOD, who canst give the light that in darkness shall make us glad, let us live this day in that light, so that we may gain the victory over those things that press us down and over the flesh that so often encumbers us and over death that seemeth for the moment to win the victory. Thus, we being filled with inward peace and light and life may walk all the days of this our mortal life, doing our work as the business of our Father, glorifying it because it is Thy will. [George Dawson (Altered).]

GOD IN THE FLESH OF CHRIST

And the Word became flesh, and dwelt among us. *John 1:14.*

Have this mind in you, which was also in Christ Jesus: who, existing in the form of God, counted not the being on an equality with God a thing to be grasped, but emptied himself, taking the form of a servant, being made in the likeness of men; and being found in fashion as a man, he humbled himself, becoming obedient even unto death, yea, the death of the cross. *Phil. 2:5-8.*

Oh, speak through me now!
Would I suffer for him that I love? So wouldst Thou — so wilt Thou!
So shall crown Thee the topmost, ineffablest, uttermost crown —
And Thy love fill infinitude wholly, nor leave up or down
One spot for the creature to stand in! It is by no breath,
Turn of eye, wave of hand, that salvation joins issue with death!
As Thy Love is discovered almighty, almighty be proved
Thy power, that exists with and for it, of being Beloved!
He who did most, shall bear most; the strongest shall stand the most
weak.
'Tis the weakness in strength, that I cry for! my flesh, that I seek
In the Godhead! I seek and I find it. O Saul, it shall be
A Face like my face that receives thee; a Man like to me,
Thou shalt love and be loved by, forever: a Hand like this hand
Shall throw open the gates of new life to thee! See the Christ stand.
Robert Browning.

O GOD, who, by the birth of Thy Holy One into the world, didst give Thy true Light to dawn upon our darkness; grant that as Thou hast given us to believe in the mystery of His incarnation and hast made us partakers of the divine nature, so we may ever abide with Him in this world and in the glory of His kingdom, through the same Jesus Christ our Lord. And give us grace that we may cast away the works of darkness and put on us the armor of light, now in the time of this mortal life, in which Thy Son Jesus Christ came to visit us in great humility, that when He shall come again in His glorious majesty to judge both the quick and the dead, we may rise to the life immortal through Him who liveth and reigneth with Thee and the Holy Ghost, now and ever. [*The Book of Common Prayer* (Altered).]

THE LOVE THAT PASSETH
KNOWLEDGE

Ye are my friends, if ye do the things which I command you. No longer do I call you servants; for the servant knoweth not what his lord doeth: but I have called you friends; for all things that I heard from my Father I have made known unto you. *John 15:14, 15.*

And I heard a great voice out of the throne saying, Behold, the tabernacle of God is with men, and he shall dwell with them, and they shall be his peoples, and God himself shall be with them, and be their God. *Rev. 21:3.*

Why should I call Thee Lord, who art my God?
Why should I call Thee Friend, who art my Love?
Or King, who art my very Spouse above?
Or call Thy Sceptre on my heart Thy rod?
    Lo, now Thy banner over me is love.
All heaven flies open to me at Thy nod:
For Thou hast lit Thy flame in me a clod,
    Made me a nest for dwelling of Thy Dove.
    What wilt Thou call me in our home above?
Who now hast called me friend? how will it be
    When Thou for good wine settest forth the best?
Now Thou dost bid me come and sup with Thee,
    Now Thou dost make me lean upon Thy breast,
How will it be with me in time of love?

Christina Rossetti.

O GOD, the God of all goodness and all grace, who art worthy of a greater love than we can either give or understand, fill our hearts, we beseech Thee, with such love toward Thee that nothing may seem too hard for us to do or to suffer in obedience to Thy will. And, O Almighty God and most merciful Father, who through Thy dear Son hast given us the new commandment that we should love one another even as Christ Himself has loved us, give us grace to obey and fulfill this word. Make us gentle, courteous, and forbearing. May the fruit of Christ's Spirit be born in us, and mayst Thou find in us, living in such love of Thee and of one another, a place of Thine own indwelling where we may abide with Thee and where Thou wilt abide with us.

LIFE'S CHOICE MUST BE CLEAN AND CLEAR

Choose you this day whom ye will serve; whether the gods which your fathers served that were beyond the River, or the gods of the Amorites, in whose land ye dwell: but as for me and my house, we will serve Jehovah. *Josh. 24:15.*

Butter and honey shall he eat, when he knoweth to refuse the evil, and choose the good. *Isa. 7:15.*

Imitate not that which is evil, but that which is good. He that doeth good is of God: he that doeth evil hath not seen God. *III John 11.*

Woe unto them that call evil good, and good evil; that put darkness for light, and light for darkness. *Isa. 5:20.*

Count it all joy, my brethren, when ye fall into manifold temptations; knowing that the proving of your faith worketh patience. And let patience have its perfect work, that ye may be perfect and entire, lacking in nothing. *James 1:2–4.*

Then, welcome each rebuff
That turns earth's smoothness rough,
Each sting that bids nor sit nor stand but go!
Be our joy three-parts pain!
Strive, and hold cheap the strain;
Learn, nor account the pang; dare, never grudge the throe!

For thence, — a paradox
Which comforts while it mocks, —
Shall life succeed in that it seems to fail:
What I aspired to be,
And was not, comforts me:
A brute I might have been, but would not sink i' the scale.
Robert Browning.

O GOD of light, in whom is no darkness at all, lighten our darkness that we may distinguish the things that look alike in the dark but that are different in the light. And by Thy grace help us to prefer the things that are excellent. Enable us to choose what is right and to right what is wrong, that we may be sincere and void of offense unto the day of Christ.

THE UNENDINGNESS OF LOVE

For love is strong as death; . . . a very flame of Jehovah. Many waters cannot quench love, neither can floods drown it. *S. of Sol. 8:6, 7.*

Having loved his own that were in the world, he loved them unto the end. *John 13:1.*

Love never faileth. *I Cor. 13:8.*

Yea, I have loved thee with an everlasting love: therefore with lovingkindness have I drawn thee. *Jer. 31:3.*

I have this against thee, that thou didst leave thy first love. *Rev. 2:4.*

> Love is not love
> Which alters when it alteration finds,
> Or bends with the remover to remove.
> O, no! it is an ever-fixéd mark
> That looks on tempests and is never shaken;
> It is the star to every wand'ring bark,
> Whose worth's unknown, although his height be taken.
> Love's not Time's fool, though rosy lips and cheeks
> Within his binding sickle's compass come;
> Love alters not with his brief hours and weeks,
> But bears it out even to the edge of doom.
> *Shakespeare.*

O MERCIFUL Lord God, O Lord most merciful, if being Truth Thou canst not deny Thyself, neither being Love canst Thou be other than Thyself. Make us, we beseech Thee, as stedfast and unalterable in our loving as Thou art in Thine. And in this Thine unchangeableness, grant us quiet hearts, assurance of holy hope, peace, patient confidence of love. [Christina G. Rossetti (Altered).]

O Blessed Lord, who hast commanded us to love one another, grant us grace that having received Thine undeserved bounty, we may love every one in Thee and for Thee and with Thy love, true, abiding and deathless, unchanging and unchangeable. [Anselm (Altered).]

CHRIST'S ESTIMATE OF GREATNESS

He that is least among you all, the same is great. *Luke 9:48.*

Jesus . . . said, Ye know that the rulers of the Gentiles lord it over them, and their great ones exercise authority over them. Not so shall it be among you: but whosoever would become great among you shall be your minister; and whosoever would be first among you shall be your servant. *Matt. 20:25-27.*

Thine, O Lord, is the greatness. *I Chron. 29:11.*

Thy right hand hath holden me up, and thy gentleness hath made me great. *Ps. 18:35.*

> He that of such a height has built his mind
> And reared the dwelling of his thoughts so strong
> As neither fear, nor hopes can shake the frame
> Of his resolvéd powers, nor all the wind
> Of vanity or malice pierce to wrong
> His settled peace or to disturb the same —
> What a fair seat hath he, from whence he may
> The boundless wastes and wealds of man survey.
>
> And with how free an eye doth he look down
> Upon these lower regions of turmoil!
> Where all the streams of passion mainly beat
> On flesh and blood; where honor, power, renown,
> Are only gay afflictions, golden toil;
> Where greatness stands upon as feeble feet
> As frailty doth and only great doth seem
> To little minds who do it so esteem.
> *Samuel Daniel, " Epistle to the Countess of Cumberland."*

O THOU divine power of meekness, I bow before Thy marvellous strength. I stand amazed in the presence of that might which could empty itself of all might. Thou art more wonderful to me in Thy cross than in Thy crown. Thou art greater to me in what Thou hast given up than in what Thou possessest. Thy majesty is Thy self-surrender. Thy Kinghood is Thy service. Thou art the Head over the body of humanity, just because without complaining Thou takest the pains of all its members. Thy meekness truly, O Christ, hath inherited the earth. [George Matheson.]

PILGRIMS

They were strangers and pilgrims on the earth. *Heb. 11:13.*

I beseech you as sojourners and pilgrims, to abstain from fleshly lusts, which war against the soul. *1 Peter 2:11.*

Thy statutes have been my songs in the house of my pilgrimage. *Ps. 119:54.*

Unto an inheritance incorruptible, and undefiled, and that fadeth not away, reserved in heaven for you. *1 Peter 1:4.*

He who would valiant be
'Gainst all disaster,
Let him in constancy
Follow the Master.
There's no discouragement
Shall make him once relent
His first avowed intent
To be a pilgrim.

Who so beset him round
With dismal stories,
Do but themselves confound —
His strength the more is.

No lion can him fright;
He'll with a giant fight
But he will have the right
To be a pilgrim.

Since, Lord, thou dost defend
Us with Thy Spirit,
We know we at the end
Shall life inherit.
Then, fancies, flee away!
I'll fear not what men say,
I'll labor night and day
To be a pilgrim.

John Bunyan.

Master of all things, Lord of all, who hast ordained that our life should be a pilgrimage throughout its course, even to the end; so guide and order the conflict within us and our struggle without that what is good may conquer, and all evil be overcome, that all things may be brought into harmony, and God may be all in all. So do Thou guide and govern us, that every day whatsoever betide us, some gain to better things, some more blessed joy in higher things may be ours, that so we, though but weaklings, may yet, God-guided, go from strength to strength, until at last, delivered from that burden of the flesh, through which comes so much struggling, we may complete our pilgrimage in triumph and enter into the land of harmony and eternal peace. Hear us of Thy mercy: through Jesus Christ our Lord. [George Dawson (Altered).]

IN QUIETNESS AND CONFIDENCE

For thus saith the Lord Jehovah, the Holy One of Israel, In returning and rest shall ye be saved; in quietness and in confidence shall be your strength. *Isa. 30:15.*

And the work of righteousness shall be peace; and the effect of righteousness, quietness and confidence for ever. And my people shall abide in a peaceable habitation, and in safe dwellings, and in quiet resting-places. *Isa. 32:17, 18.*

Be ambitious to be quiet, and to do your own business, and to work with your hands, even as we charged you. *I Thess. 4:11, 12.*

That we may lead a quiet and tranquil life in all godliness and gravity. *I Tim. 2:2.*

> One lesson, Nature, let me learn from thee,
> One lesson which in every wind is blown,
> One lesson of two duties kept at one
> Though the loud world proclaim their enmity —
> Of toil unsevered from tranquillity;
> Of labor, that in lasting fruit outgrows
> Far noisier schemes, accomplished in repose,
> Too great for haste, too high for rivalry.
>
> Yes, while on earth a thousand discords ring,
> Man's fitful uproar mingling with his toil,
> Still do thy sleepless ministers move on,
> Their glorious tasks in silence perfecting;
> Still working, blaming still our vain turmoil;
> Laborers that shall not fail, when man is gone.
>
> *Matthew Arnold.*

Grant unto us, O Lord, beyond all objects of desire, to rest in Thee and to still our hearts in Thee to perfect peace in Thee. Out of Thee all is restless and unquiet; in this peace, that is in Thyself alone, may we find true rest, for Thy Name's sake.

O God, who art peace everlasting, whose chosen reward is the gift of peace, and who hast taught us that the peacemakers are Thy children, pour Thy peace into our souls, that everything discordant may utterly vanish, and all that makes for peace be sweet to us forever. Amen. [S. C. H. C.]

AS DYING AND BEHOLD WE LIVE

All we who were baptized into Christ Jesus were baptized into his death. . . . If we died with Christ, we believe that we shall also live with him. . . . Reckon ye . . . yourselves to be dead unto sin, but alive unto God in Christ Jesus. *Rom. 6:3, 8, 11.*

For the love of Christ constraineth us; because we thus judge, that one died for all, therefore all died; and he died for all, that they that live should no longer live unto themselves, but unto him who for their sakes died and rose again. *II Cor. 5:14, 15.*

Set your mind on the things that are above, not on the things that are upon the earth. For ye died, and your life is hid with Christ in God. *Col. 3:2, 3.*

I die daily. *1 Cor. 15:31.*

His eyes behold, his eyelids try, the children of men. *Ps. 11:4.*

Lord when the sense of Thy sweet
  grace
Sends up my soul to seek Thy face,
Thy blessed eyes breed such desire,
I dy in love's delicious Fire.
  O love, I am thy sacrifice.
Be still triumphant, blessed eyes.
Still shine on me, fair suns! that I
Still may behold, though still I dy.

Though still I dy, I live again:
Still longing so to be still slain
So painfull is such loss of breath
I dy even in desire of death.
  Still live in me this loving strife
Of living death and dying life.
For while Thou sweetly slayest me
Dead to myself, I live in Thee.
        Richard Crashaw.

L<small>ET</small> all my passions and affections be so mortified and brought under the dominion of grace, that I may never by deliberation and purpose, nor yet by levity, rashness, or inconsideration offend Thy Divine Majesty. Make me such as Thou wouldst have me to be: strengthen my faith: confirm my hope, and give me a daily increase of charity, that this day and ever I may serve Thee according to all my opportunities and capacities; growing from grace to grace, till at last by Thy mercies I shall receive the consummation and perfection of grace, even the glories of Thy Kingdom in the full fruition of the face and excellencies of God the Father, the Son and the Holy Ghost, to whom be glory and praise, honor and adoration given by all Angels, and by all men, and all creatures, now and to all eternity. Amen. [Jeremy Taylor.]

And he said unto them, Cast the net on the right side of the boat, and ye shall find. They cast therefore, and now they were not able to draw it for the multitude of fishes. That disciple therefore whom Jesus loved saith unto Peter, It is the Lord. *John 21:6, 7.*

Christ may dwell in your hearts through faith. *Eph. 3:17.*

The land is large; for God hath given it into your hand, a place where there is no want of anything that is in the earth. *Judg. 18:10.*

I know . . . a man . . . that . . . was caught up into Paradise, and heard unspeakable words, which it is not lawful for a man to utter. *II Cor. 12:3, 4.*

He satisfieth the longing soul, and the hungry soul he filleth with good. *Ps. 107:9.*

> In strenuous hope I wrought
> And hope seem'd still betrayed:
> Lastly I said,
> " I have labored through the night nor yet
> Have taken aught,
> But at Thy word I will again cast forth the net."
> And lo, I caught
> (Oh quite unlike and quite beyond my thought)
> Not the quick, shining harvest of the Sea
> For food, my wish.
> But Thee!
> Then hiding even in me
> As hid was Simon's coin within the fish,
> Thou sigh'st, with joy, " Be dumb
> Or speak but of forbidden things to far off times to come."
>   *Coventry Patmore.*

LORD, Thou knowest what is best for me to do, according to Thy will. Give me I beseech Thee, what Thou wilt, as much as Thou wilt, and when Thou wilt. Do with me in all things as Thou knowest is best to be done and as it shall please Thee and as may be most for Thy honour; place me where Thou wilt and freely do with me in all things after Thy will and pleasure. Lo, I am Thy servant, ready to do all things that Thou commandest me. [Bishop Hickes.]

A NEW EARTH

According to his promise, we look for new heavens and a new earth, wherein dwelleth righteousness. Wherefore, beloved, seeing that ye look for these things, give diligence that ye may be found in peace, without spot and blameless in his sight. *II Peter 3:13, 14.*

And I saw a new heaven and a new earth: for the first heaven and the first earth are passed away; and the sea is no more. And I saw the holy city, new Jerusalem, coming down out of heaven from God, made ready as a bride adorned for her husband. And I heard a great voice out of the throne saying, Behold, the tabernacle of God is with men, and he shall dwell with them, and they shall be his peoples, and God himself shall be with them, and be their God. *Rev. 21:1-3.*

God grant us wisdom in these coming days,
And eyes unsealed. that we clear visions see
Of that new world that He would have us build,
To Life's ennoblement and His high ministry.

God give us sense, — God-sense of Life's new needs,
And souls aflame with new-born chivalries —
To cope with those black growths that foul the ways, —
To cleanse our poisoned founts with God-born energies. . . .

Not since Christ died upon His lonely cross
Has Time such prospect held of Life's new birth;
Not since the world of chaos first was born
Has man so clearly visaged hope of a new earth.

Not of our own might can we hope to rise
Above the ruts and soilures of the past,
But, with His help who did the first earth build,
With hearts courageous we may fairer build this last.
                                              John Oxenham.

O LORD, make bare Thy Holy Arm in the eyes of all peoples, that all the ends of the earth may see Thy salvation; Establish Thy dominion over all nations. Show forth Thy salvation openly in the sight of all nations, that the Kingdom of Christ may come on earth, and Thy will be done here as it is done in heaven. [Adapted.]

I am the way, and the truth, and the life. *John 14:6.*

Again therefore Jesus spake unto them, saying, I am the light of the world: he that followeth me shall not walk in darkness, but shall have the light of life. *John 8:12.*

I can do all things in him that strengtheneth me. . . . And my God shall supply every need of yours according to his riches in glory in Christ Jesus. *Phil. 4:13, 19.*

I delight in the law of God after the inward man: but I see a different law in my members, warring against the law of my mind, and bringing me into captivity under the law of sin which is in my members. Wretched man that I am! who shall deliver me out of the body of this death? I thank God through Jesus Christ our Lord. *Rom. 7:22-25.*

> The morning breaks, I place my hand in Thine,
> My God, 'tis Thine to lead; to follow, mine.
> No word deceitful shall I speak the while,
> Nor shall I stain my hand with action vile.
>
> Thine be the day with worthy labor filled,
> Strong would I stand to do the duty willed;
> Nor swayed by restless passions let me be
> That I may give the offering pure to Thee:
>
> Else were I shamed when hoary age I see,
> Shamed were this board that bears Thy gifts to me;
> Mine is the impulse; O my Christ I pray,
> Be Thou Thyself to me the Blessed Way.
>
> *Gregory of Nazianzus.*

WE thank Thee, Saviour Christ, for Thy hand ever strongly guiding us forward, smoothing the path for our feeble feet, thrusting aside the briers and thorns that seem too thick to be passed, in time of danger encircling us very securely, lifting us up and away into peace and joy, from the heart of turmoil. Even when darkness surrounds us, black, rayless, impenetrable, when in folly we loose our grasp of Thy hand, and wander away, to stumble wounded, despairing, and to fall in the waste, even then Thou art there at our side, Thou art there, to uplift, to restore, to forgive, to heal. [J. S. Hoyland (Abbreviated).]

Because I live, ye shall live also. *John 14:19.*

If we died with Christ, we believe that we shall also live with him. *Rom. 6:8.*

I have been crucified with Christ; and it is no longer I that live, but Christ liveth in me: and that life which I now live in the flesh I live in faith, the faith which is in the Son of God, who loved me, and gave himself up for me. *Gal. 2:20.*

Ye were raised together with Christ. *Col. 3:1.*

So shall we ever be with the Lord. *I Thess. 4:17.*

Come let us drink the water new
  Not from the rock divinely springing,
But from that pure, immortal stream
  That from His tomb our Lord is bringing.

With Thee, O Christ, I lay entombed,
  Ere light upon this day was falling;
With Thee I leave death's dark abode,
  For Thou hast risen and Thou art calling.

With Thee upon the Cross I hung
  When Thou wast weak and faint and sighing:
Lord with Thyself Thy servant bless,
  In Thy bright realm through years undying.
                    John of Damascus.

O GOD, our Father, shew Thou us the way that we should walk in, for we lift up our souls unto Thee: Keep our feet upon that strait and narrow way which will lead us to the more abundant life. When we hunger for a fuller life, be Thou to us the living bread: when our spirits are parched, be Thou within us a spring of living water, refreshing the dry surfaces of life. When we look forward with dread to the days that are to come, show Thyself to us as our exceeding great reward. Teach us . . . that no power can sever us from the blessed companionship of love, until we wake up after Thy likeness and are satisfied with it in Thy Kingdom, where all good things are fulfilled and continued in Thee, O Father of everlasting love. Amen. [*New Every Morning.*]

I determined not to know anything among you, save Jesus Christ, and him crucified. *I Cor. 2:2.*

Not with eye-service, as men-pleasers, but in singleness of heart, fearing the Lord: whatsoever ye do, work heartily, as unto the Lord, and not unto men; knowing that from the Lord ye shall receive the recompense of the inheritance: ye serve the Lord Christ. *Col. 3:22–24.*

Ye . . . have a Master in heaven. *Col. 4:1.*

Walk by the Spirit, and ye shall not fulfil the lust of the flesh. *Gal. 5:16.*

Forth in Thy Name, O Lord, I go,
My daily labor to pursue,
Thee, only Thee, resolved to know
In all I think, or speak, or do.

The task Thy wisdom hath assigned
O let me cheerfully fulfil;
In all my works Thy presence find,
And prove Thy good and perfect
will. . . .

Thee may I set at my right hand,
Whose eyes mine inmost substance see,
And labor on at Thy command,
And offer all my works to Thee.

Give me to bear Thy easy yoke,
And every moment watch and pray;
And still to things eternal look,
And hasten to Thy glorious day:

For Thee delightfully employ
Whate'er Thy bounteous grace hath given
And run my course with even joy,
And closely walk with Thee to heaven. *Amen.*
C. *Wesley.*

O FATHER, this day may bring some hard task to our life, or some hard trial to our love. We may grow weary or sad or hopeless in our lot. But, Father, our whole life until now has been one great proof of Thy care. Bread has come for our body, thoughts to our mind, love to our heart, and all from Thee. So help us, we implore Thee, while we stand still on this side of all that the day may bring, to resolve that we will trust Thee this day to shine into any gloom of the mind, to stand by us in any trial of our love, and to give us rest in Thy good time as we need. May this day be full of a power that shall bring us near to Thee and make us more like Thee. [Robert Collyer.]

Asleep in Jesus. *1 Thess. 4:14.*

And he [Jesus] said unto him, Verily I say unto thee, To-day shalt thou be with me in Paradise. *Luke 23:43.*

I know him whom I have believed, and I am persuaded that he is able to guard that which I have committed unto him against that day. *II Tim. 1:12.*

And Jesus, crying with a loud voice, said, Father, into thy hands I commend my spirit: and having said this, he gave up the ghost. *Luke 23:46.*

I am already being offered, and the time of my departure is come. I have fought the good fight, I have finished the course, I have kept the faith: henceforth there is laid up for me the crown of righteousness, which the Lord, the righteous judge, shall give me at that day; and not to me only, but also to all them that have loved his appearing. *II Tim. 4:6–8.*

Now the laborer's task is o'er;
  Now the battle day is past;
Now upon the farther shore
  Lands the voyager at last.
Father, in Thy gracious keeping
Leave we now Thy servant sleeping.

There the sinful souls, that turn
  To the cross their dying eyes,
All the love of Christ shall learn
  At His feet in Paradise.
Father, in Thy gracious keeping
Leave we now Thy servant sleeping.

There the tears of earth are dried;
  There its hidden things are clear;
There the work of life is tried
  By a juster Judge than here.
Father, in Thy gracious keeping
Leave we now Thy servant sleeping.

"Earth to earth, and dust to dust,"
  Calmly now the words we say;
Left behind, we wait in trust
  For the resurrection day.
Father, in Thy gracious keeping
Leave we now Thy servant sleeping.

John Ellerton.

O FATHER of all, we remember before Thee those whom we love but see no longer. Grant them Thy peace; let light perpetual shine upon them; and in Thy loving wisdom and almighty power work in them the good purpose of Thy perfect will; through Jesus Christ our Lord. [*New Every Morning.*]

Verily, verily, I say unto you, If ye shall ask anything of the Father, he will give it you in my name. Hitherto have ye asked nothing in my name: ask, and ye shall receive. *John 16:23, 24.*

If ye then, being evil, know how to give good gifts unto your children, how much more shall your heavenly Father give the Holy Spirit to them that ask him? *Luke 11:13.*

And this is the boldness which we have toward him, that, if we ask anything according to his will, he heareth us: and if we know that he heareth us . . . we know that we have the petitions which we have asked of him. *I John 5:14, 15.*

Sometimes when you need rest most you are too restless to lie down and take it. Then compel yourself to lie down and to lie still. Often, in ten minutes the compulsion fades into consent and you sleep, and rise a new man. So, if you are averse to prayer, pray the more.

Forsyth.

Intercession may grow monotonous. It is so largely given to bearing the burdens, sins, sorrows, needs of others; — to pleading for the overthrow of great evils and the success of righteous causes; — and it is not easy to labor every day in unselfish prayer. There is but one way to maintain interest and power, viz: by communion with Christ and personal meditation on the needs of those whom we help by prayer.

We must not conceive of prayer as an overcoming of God's reluctance, but as a laying hold of his highest willingness. *Trench.*

O LORD, the God of Israel, there is no God like thee, in heaven above, or on earth beneath; who keepest covenant and lovingkindness with thy servants, that walk before thee with all their heart. . . . Have thou respect unto the prayer of thy servant, and to his supplication, O Lord my God, to hearken unto the cry and to the prayer which thy servant prayeth before thee this day. . . . Forgive thy people who have sinned against thee, and all their transgressions wherein they have transgressed against thee. Hear thou [their prayers and their supplications] in heaven Thy dwelling-place; and when thou hearest, forgive. Amen. [Solomon (I Kings 8:23, 28, 50, 30).]

We would not have you ignorant, brethren, concerning them that fall asleep; that ye sorrow not, even as the rest, who have no hope. For if we believe that Jesus died and rose again, even so them also that are fallen asleep in Jesus will God bring with him. *1 Thess. 4:13, 14.*

I came out from the Father, and am come into the world: again, I leave the world, and go unto the Father. *John 16:28.*

And I saw, and I heard a voice of many angels round about the throne and the living creatures and the elders; and the number of them was ten thousand times ten thousand, and thousands of thousands. *Rev. 5:11.*

They whose course on earth is o'er,
Think they of their brethren more?
They before the Throne who bow
Feel they for their brethren now?

Yea, the dead in Christ have still
Part in all our joy and ill;
Keeping all our steps in view
Guiding them, it may be, too.

We by enemies distrest, —
They in Paradise at rest;
We the captives, they the freed, —
We and they are one indeed.

One in all we seek or shun,
One because our Lord is One,
One in heart and one in love
We below and they above.

J. M. Neale.

Living simply as if we were in the presence of an innumerable company, and as if those who thought of us most and did us most good when we saw them had not ceased to think of us because their thoughts have become freer and more loving, have not ceased to do us good since they have learnt that the great blessing is to do good.   *F. D. Maurice.*

Our heavenly father, we rejoice in the blessed communion of all Thy saints, wherein Thou givest us also to have part. . . . O let the cloud of witnesses, the innumerable company of those who have gone before and entered into rest, be to us for an example of godly life, and even now may we be refreshed with their joy; that so with patience we may run the race that yet remains before us, looking unto Jesus the author and finisher of our faith, and obtain an entrance into the everlasting Kingdom, the glorious assembly of the saints, and with them ever worship and adore Thy glorious Name, world without end. Amen. [*Prayers,* Compiled by Page and Laidlaw.]

The commandment, which was unto life, this I found to be unto death: for sin, finding occasion, through the commandment beguiled me, and through it slew me. So that the law is holy, and the commandment holy, and righteous, and good. Did then that which is good become death unto me? God forbid. But sin, that it might be shown to be sin, by working death to me through that which is good; — that through the commandment sin might become exceeding sinful. *Rom. 7:10–13.*

Let us . . . lay aside every weight, and the sin which doth so easily beset us. *Heb. 12:1.*

Where sin abounded, grace did abound more exceedingly: that, as sin reigned in death, even so might grace reign through righteousness unto eternal life through Jesus Christ our Lord. *Rom. 5:20, 21.*

> My thoughts turn backward over the long way
> The kindly years have led me. I have learned
> The way is hard to him who seeks to climb,
> And finds no place to rest below the stars.
> I have not known a day without a cloud,
> Nor have I known a night without a star.
> For always love is near, and prayer is heard,
> And faith and hope abide, when senses fail,
> And turn the ebbing sands of life to gold.
> Evening draws on; why mourn the parting day?
> The sunset is as radiant as the dawn,
> Nor doth the world's horizon bound the sky
> Earth's day of toil is measured by the sun:
> The lights of heaven appear when day is done.
>
> *J. Ritchie Smith.*

I BLESS Thee, O Heavenly Father, Father of my Lord Jesus Christ, for that Thou hast vouchsafed to remember me a poor creature. O Father of mercies and God of all comfort, thanks be unto Thee, who sometime with Thy comfort refreshed me, unworthy as I am of all comfort. I will always bless and glorify Thee forever and ever. Ah, Lord God, Thou holy lover of my soul, when Thou comest into my heart, all that is within me shall rejoice. [Thomas à Kempis.]

THE MASTER OF THE WORLD

From the rising of the sun unto the going down of the same Jehovah's name is to be praised. *Ps. 113:3.*

Wherefore also God highly exalted him, and gave unto him the name which is above every name; that in the name of Jesus every knee should bow, of things in heaven and things on earth and things under the earth, and that every tongue should confess that Jesus Christ is Lord, to the glory of God the Father. *Phil. 2:9–11.*

The day Thou gavest, Lord, is ended,
The darkness falls at Thy behest;
To Thee our morning hymns ascended,
Thy praise shall hallow now our rest.

We thank Thee that Thy Church unsleeping,
While earth rolls onward into light,
Through all the world her watch is keeping,
And rests not now by day or night.

As o'er each continent and island
The dawn leads on another day,
The voice of prayer is never silent,
Nor dies the strain of praise away.

The sun that bids us rest is waking
Our brethren 'neath the western sky,
And hour by hour fresh lips are making
Thy wondrous doings heard on high.

So be it, Lord; Thy throne shall never,
Like earth's proud empires, pass away;
But stand, and rule, and grow forever,
Till all Thy creatures own Thy sway.

John Ellerton.

O GOD, who hast made of one blood all nations of men to dwell on the face of the earth, and didst send Thy blessed Son, Jesus Christ, to preach peace to them that are far off and to them that are nigh: grant that all the peoples of the world may feel after Thee and find Thee; and hasten, O Lord, the fulfillment of Thy promise to pour out Thy Spirit upon all flesh: through Jesus Christ our Lord. . . .

O God of unchangeable power and eternal light, look favorably on Thy whole Church, that wonderful and sacred mystery: and, by the tranquil operation of Thy perpetual providence, carry out the work of man's salvation. [*New Every Morning.*]

LAMBS AND KIDS

And if his oblation be of the flock, of the sheep, or of the goats, for a burnt-offering; he shall offer it a male without blemish. *Lev. 1:10.*

And ye shall offer one he-goat for a sin-offering, and two he-lambs a year old for a sacrifice of peace-offerings. *Lev. 23:19.*

And the wolf shall dwell with the lamb, and the leopard shall lie down with the kid; . . . and a little child shall lead them. *Isa. 11:6.*

" He saves the sheep, the goats He doth not save."
So rang Tertullian's sentence, on the side
Of that unpitying Phrygian sect which cried
" Him can no fount of fresh forgiveness lave

" Who sins, once wash'd by the baptismal wave."
So spake the fierce Tertullian. But she sigh'd,
The infant Church! Of love she felt the tide
Stream on her from her Lord's yet recent grave.

And then she smiled and in the Catacombs
With eye suffused but heart inspired true
On those walls subterranean where she hid

Her head mid ignominy, death, and tombs,
She her Good Shepherd's hasty image drew —
And on His shoulders not a lamb, a kid.
Matthew Arnold.

*W*E most earnestly beseech Thee, O Thou Lover of mankind, to bless all Thy people, the flocks of Thy fold. Send down into our hearts the peace of heaven, and grant us also the peace of this life. Give life to the souls of all of us, and let no deadly sin prevail against us, or any of Thy people. Deliver all who are in trouble, for Thou art our God, who settest the captives free; who givest hope to the hopeless, and help to the helpless; who liftest up the fallen; and who art the Haven of the shipwrecked. Give Thy pity, pardon, and refreshment to every Christian soul, whether in affliction or error. Preserve us, in our pilgrimage through this life, from hurt and danger, and grant that we may end our lives as Christians, well-pleasing to Thee and free from sin, and that we may have our portion and lot with all Thy saints. [*Liturgy of St. Mark.*]

EACH MAN'S WORK

We must work the works of him that sent me, while it is day: the night cometh, when no man can work. *John 9:4.*

To each one his work. *Mark 13:34.*

I glorified thee on the earth, having accomplished the work which thou hast given me to do. *John 17:4.*

Verily, verily, I say unto you, He that believeth on me, the works that I do shall he do also; and greater works than these shall he do; because I go unto the Father. *John 14:12.*

Each man's work shall be made manifest: for the day shall declare it, because it is revealed in fire; and the fire itself shall prove each man's work of what sort it is. If any man's work shall abide which he built thereon, he shall receive a reward. *1 Cor. 3:13, 14.*

> Let me but do my work from day to day,
>   In field or forest, at the desk or loom,
>   In roaring market-place or tranquil room;
> Let me but find it in my heart to say,
> When vagrant wishes beckon me astray,
>   " This is my work; my blessing, not my doom;
>   " Of all who live, I am the one by whom
> " This work can best be done in the right way."
>
> Then shall I see it not too great, nor small,
>   To suit my spirit and to prove my powers;
>   Then shall I cheerful greet the labouring hours,
> And cheerful turn, when the long shadows fall
> At eventide, to play and love and rest,
> Because I know for me my work is best.
>
> Henry van Dyke.

*B*EHOLD, O God, our strivings after a truer and more abiding order. Give us visions which bring back a lost glory to the earth, and dreams which foreshadow that better order which Thou hast prepared for us. Scatter every excuse of frailty and unworthiness; consecrate us all with a heavenly mission; and give us grace according to our day, gladly to welcome and gratefully to fulfil it; through Jesus Christ our Lord. [*New Every Morning.*]

CHRIST GROWS ON MAN

And many more believed because of his word; and they said to the woman, Now we believe, not because of thy speaking: for we have heard for ourselves, and know that this is indeed the Saviour of the world. *John 4:41, 42.*

We beheld his glory. *John 1:14.*

Jesus said therefore unto the twelve, Would ye also go away? Simon Peter answered him, Lord, to whom shall we go? thou hast the words of eternal life. *John 6:67, 68.*

We were eyewitnesses of his majesty. *II Peter 1:16.*

Human characters are always reduced in their eminence and the impression of awe they have raised by a closer and more complete acquaintance. Weakness and blemish are discovered by familiarity. Admiration lets in qualifiers: on approach the halo dims a little. But it was not so with Christ. With His disciples in closest terms of intercourse for three whole years, their brother, friend, teacher, monitor, guest, fellow-traveller, seen by them under all conditions of public ministry and private society, where the ambition of show or pride of power, or the ill nature provoked by annoyance, or the vanity drawn out by confidence would most certainly be reducing Him to the criticism of persons most unsophisticated, . . . He is visibly raising their sense of His degree and quality; becoming a greater wonder and holier mystery, and gathering to His Person feelings of reverence and awe at once more general and more sacred. Familiarity breeds a kind of apotheosis, and the man becomes divinity in simply being known.   *Horace Bushnell.*

WE offer unto Thee, O God, our Father, our hosannas and our alleluias for Thine everlasting and exhaustless love, and we thank Thee that the Dayspring from on high hath visited us. . . . We thank Thee that Thou hast permitted us to behold Thy glory in the Face of Jesus Christ, our Lord. We come to adore Him and to rejoice that He was made manifest unto us as our Saviour and our King. . . . We thank Thee for all His great work, for His ministry upon earth. We thank Thee for His intercession and that we have the promise that we shall at last sit upon the throne of His glory, redeemed by His grace.   [L. Clarke Seelye.]

Whether therefore ye eat, or drink, or whatsoever ye do, do all to the glory of God. *I Cor. 10:31.*

Hath not the potter a right over the clay, from the same lump to make one part a vessel unto honor, and another unto dishonor? *Rom. 9:21.*

One thing I do. *Phil. 3:13.*

Inasmuch as ye did it unto one of these my brethren, even these least, ye did it unto me. *Matt. 25:40.*

I know how to be abased, and I know also how to abound: in everything and in all things have I learned the secret both to be filled and to be hungry, both to abound and to be in want. I can do all things in him that strengtheneth me. *Phil. 4:12, 13.*

> All service ranks the same with God:
> If now, as formerly He trod
> Paradise, His presence fills
> Our earth, each only as God wills
> Can work — God's puppets, best and worst,
> Are we; there is no last nor first.
>
> Say not "a small event!" Why "small"?
> Costs it more pain that this, ye call
> A "great event," should come to pass,
> Than that? Untwine me from the mass
> Of deeds which make up life, one deed
> Power shall fall short in or exceed!   *Browning.*

*W*E come unto Thee, O God our Father, with hearts troubled by the memory and the burden of our offences: of that which we ought to have done, but have not done; of that which we ought to have spoken but have not spoken; of our misjudgment of values; our treating lightly what we ought to have taken seriously; our failure to hear Thee in still small voices. Of these things and of all our sins remembered and forgotten, we repent and turn to Thee. Graciously forgive us; purify and strengthen our hearts; that we may walk steadfastly and uprightly before Thee all our days, in the love and service of Jesus Christ our Lord. [*New Every Morning* (Altered).]

Behold what manner of love the Father hath bestowed upon us, that we should be called children of God; and such we are . . . and it is not yet made manifest what we shall be. We know that if he shall be manifested, we shall be like him; for we shall see him even as he is. *1 John 3:1, 2.*

We know and have believed the love which God hath in us. God is love; and he that abideth in love abideth in God, and God abideth in him. . . . We love, because he first loved us. *1 John 4:16, 19.*

As for me, I will behold thy face in righteousness: I shall be satisfied, when I awake, with thy likeness. *Ps. 17:15, A. V.*

> No! love which on earth, amid all the shows of it,
> Has ever been the sole good of life in it.
> The love, ever growing there, spite of the strife in it,
> Shall arise, made perfect, from death's repose of it!
> And I shall behold Thee, face to face,
> O God, and in Thy light retrace
> How in all I loved here, still wast Thou!
> Whom, pressing to then, as I fain would now,
> I shall find as able to satiate
> The love, Thy gift, as my spirit's wonder
> Thou art able to quicken and sublimate,
> With this sky of Thine that I now walk under,
> And glory in Thee for, as I gaze
> Thus, thus! oh, let men keep their ways
> Of seeking Thee in a narrow shrine —
> Be this my way. And this *is* mine.
>
> *Browning.*

*F*ATHER, we thank Thee today for the simplicity of this relationship between our souls and Thine: ourselves, foolish, inconsequent, feeble; Thyself wise, stable, omnipotent. We know with certainty complete and irrefragable, that here in Thee are power, patience, wisdom, grace for all our need, and love that joyfully receives, redeems, uplifts and purifies. O Father God, here once again, a worthless gift, we give ourselves to Thee, Thy happy, grateful children, eager to do Thy work for Thee this day. [J. S. Hoyland (Abbreviated).]

When I lie down, I say, When shall I arise, and the night be gone? And I am full of tossings to and fro unto the dawning of the day. *Job 7:4.*

Weeping may tarry for the night, but joy cometh in the morning. *Ps. 30:5.*

In the day-time also he led them with a cloud, and all the night with a light of fire. *Ps. 78:14.*

There shall be no night there. *Rev. 21:25.*

> Night hath no wings to him that cannot sleep:
> And Time seems then not for to flie but creep;
> Slowly her chariot drives, as if that she
> Had broke her wheels, or crakt her axeltree.
> Just so it is with me, who list'ning, pray
> The winds to blow the tedious night away,
> That I might see the cheerful, peeping day.
> Sick is my heart: O Saviour, do Thou please
> To make my bed soft in my sicknesses;
> Lighten my candle, so that I beneath
> Sleep not forever in the vaults of death:
> Let me Thy voice betimes i' th' morning heare.
> Call, and I'll come: say Thou the when and where.
> Draw me but first, and after Thee I'll run
> And make no one stop till my race be done.   ***Herrick.***

*B*ESTOW Thy light upon us, O Lord, so that, being rid of the darkness of our hearts, we may attain unto the true Light; through Jesus Christ, who is the Light of the world. [*Sarum Breviary.*]

Let Thy mercy, O Lord, be upon us, and the brightness of Thy Spirit illumine our inward souls, that He may kindle our cold hearts, and light up our dark minds: Who abideth ever more with Thee in Thy glory. [*Mozarabic Liturgy.*]

Almighty and everlasting God, at evening, and morning and noon day, we humbly beseech Thee that Thou wouldst drive from our hearts the darkness of sin and make us to come to the true Light, which is Christ; through the same Jesus Christ Thy Son. [*Gelasian Sacramentary.*]

THE FULFILLMENT OF HEAVEN

The morning stars sang together, and all the sons of God shouted for joy. *Job 38:7.*

I will sing a new song unto thee, O God. *Ps. 144:9.*

And they sing the song of Moses the servant of God, and the song of the Lamb. *Rev. 15:3.*

For we know that if the earthly house of our tabernacle be dissolved, we have a building from God, a house not made with hands, eternal, in the heavens. *II Cor. 5:1.*

Therefore to whom turn I but to Thee, the ineffable Name?
  Builder and maker, Thou, of houses not made with hands!
What, have fear of change from Thee who art ever the same?
  Doubt that Thy power can fill the heart that Thy power expands?
There shall never be one lost good! What was, shall live as before;
  The evil is null, is naught, is silence implying sound;
What was good shall be good, with, for evil, so much good more;
  On the earth the broken arcs; in the heaven a perfect round.

All we have willed or hoped or dreamed of good shall exist;
  Not its semblance, but itself; no beauty, nor good, nor power
Whose voice has gone forth, but each survives for the melodist
  When eternity affirms the conception of an hour.
The high that proved too high, the heroic for earth too hard,
  The passion that left the ground to lose itself in the sky,
Are music sent up to God by the lover and the bard;
  Enough that He heard it once: we shall hear it by and by.
                                                    Browning.

We render unto Thee our thanksgiving, O Lord our God, Father of our Lord and Saviour Jesus Christ, by all means, at all times, in all places. Whereinsoever we have sinned against Thee, in word, or deed, or thought, be Thou pleased in Thy love and goodness to forgive, and forsake us not. O God, in whom we hope, neither lead us into temptation, but deliver us from the evil one and from his works and in the life to come fulfill and complete all that has been broken and fragmentary here on earth. By the grace and compassion of Thine only begotten Son, Jesus Christ. Amen. [*Liturgy of St. Mark* (Altered).]

Brethren, I count not myself yet to have laid hold: but one thing I do, forgetting the things which are behind, and stretching forward to the things which are before, I press on toward the goal unto the prize of the high calling of God in Christ Jesus. *Phil. 3:13, 14.*

What then? only that in every way, whether in pretence or in truth, Christ is proclaimed; and therein I rejoice, yea, and will rejoice. *Phil. 1:18.*

Peter therefore seeing him saith to Jesus, Lord, and what shall this man do? Jesus saith unto him, If I will that he tarry till I come, what is that to thee? follow thou me. *John 21:21, 22.*

Let the thick curtain fall
I better know than all
How little I have gained
How vast the unattained.
Others shall sing the song
Others shall right the wrong,
Finish what I begin
And all I fail of win.

What matter, I or they?
Mine or another's day
So the right word be said,
And life the sweeter made?
Ring bells in unreared steeples
The joy of unborn peoples,
Sound trumpets far off blown,
Your triumph is my own.

Whittier.

Passionately fierce the voice of God is pleading,
 Pleading with men to arm them for the fight,
See how those hands, majestically bleeding,
 Call us to rout the armies of the night. . . .

Peace does not mean the end of all our striving,
 Joy does not mean the drying of our tears,
Peace is the power that comes to souls arriving,
 Up to the light where God Himself appears.

G. A. Studdert-Kennedy.

O LORD, grant me heavenly wisdom. Make me pure of heart and humble and loving. Help me to rejoice in the success of others and in all good achievement of other men which carries forward Thy purposes for mankind. Enable me to enter in some measure into Thy suffering, O Father, whose Son died upon a cross and to be a fellow-builder with Thee of Thy Kingdom of righteousness and peace. [*The Cloud of Witnesses* (Altered).]

GOD'S FORGIVING GOODNESS

And Jehovah passed by before him, and proclaimed, Jehovah, Jehovah, a God merciful and gracious, slow to anger, and abundant in lovingkindness and truth; keeping lovingkindness for thousands, forgiving iniquity and transgression and sin; and that will by no means clear the guilty. *Ex. 34:6, 7.*

And be ye kind one to another, tenderhearted, forgiving each other, even as God also in Christ forgave you. *Eph. 4:32.*

Festus: Or, say he erred, —
Save him, dear God; it will be like Thee: bathe him
In light and life! Thou art not made like us;
We should be wroth in such a case; but Thou
Forgivest — so, forgive these passionate thoughts
Which come unsought and will not pass away!
I know Thee, who hast kept my path, and made
Light for me in the darkness, tempering sorrow
So that it reached me like a solemn joy;
It were too strange that I should doubt Thy love. . . .

Paracelsus: If Thou shalt please, dear God, if Thou shalt please!
We are so weak, we know our motives least
In their confused beginning. If at first
I sought . . . but wherefore bare my heart to Thee?
I know Thy mercy; and already thoughts
Flock fast about my soul to comfort it,
And intimate I cannot wholly fail,
For love and praise would clasp me willingly
Could I resolve to seek them. Thou art good,
And I should be content. *Browning.*

Glory be to Thee, O Heavenly Father, for our being, and preservation, health and strength, understanding and memory, friends and benefactors, and for all our abilities of mind and body. . . . Glory be to Thee, O Lord, O Blessed Saviour, for those ordinary gifts by which sincere Christians have in all ages been enabled to work out their salvation, for all the spiritual strength and support, comfort and illumination which we receive from Thee, and for all Thy preserving, restraining and sanctifying grace. [Bishop Ken.]

For ye died, and your life is hid with Christ in God. When Christ, who is our life, shall be manifested, then shall ye also with him be manifested in glory. *Col. 3:3, 4.*

For to me to live is Christ, and to die is gain. But if to live in the flesh, — if this shall bring fruit from my work, then what I shall choose I know not. But I am in a strait betwixt the two, having the desire to depart and be with Christ; for it is very far better. *Phil. 1:21–23.*

As therefore ye received Christ Jesus the Lord, so walk in him, rooted and builded up in him, and established in your faith, even as ye were taught, abounding in thanksgiving. . . . In him dwelleth all the fulness of the Godhead bodily, and in him ye are made full. *Col. 2:6, 7, 9, 10.*

Jesus, I live to Thee,
  The Loveliest and Best;
My life in Thee, Thy life in me,
  In Thy blest love I rest.

Whether to live or die,
  I know not which is best;
To live in Thee is bliss to me,
  To die is endless rest.

Jesus, I die to Thee,
  Whenever death shall come;
To die in Thee is life to me
  In my eternal home.

Living or dying, Lord,
  I ask but to be Thine;
My life in Thee, Thy life in me,
  Makes heaven forever mine.
      Henry Harbaugh.

ALMIGHTY GOD, who through Thine only begotten Son Jesus Christ, hath overcome death and opened unto us the gate of everlasting life: we humbly beseech Thee that, as by Thy special grace directing us, Thou dost put into our minds good desires, so by Thy continual help we may bring the same to good effect: through Jesus Christ our Lord, who liveth and reigneth with Thee and the Holy Spirit, ever one God, world without end. [*New Every Morning.*]

HOPE

I know him whom I have believed, and I am persuaded that he is able to guard that which I have committed unto him against that day. *II Tim. 1:12.*

It is good that a man should hope and quietly wait for the salvation of Jehovah. *Lam. 3:26.*

Why art thou cast down, O my soul? And why art thou disquieted within me? Hope thou in God; for I shall yet praise him for the help of his countenance. *Ps. 42:5.*

Who in hope believed against hope. *Rom. 4:18.*

I faint, O Father, and I call to Thee.
A weakling child, a famished soul in stress.
Take Thou my hand, and may I feel the press
Of Thine own hand to lead and comfort me.

Far from Thy fruitful path I long have trod,
Through the bleak chaos of the world's desire
Where hearts with stifled hope may not aspire
To share the guidance of a gracious God:

Where broken wrecks on the lone shore are strewn,
Where vagrant souls grope blindly on the way,
Where tired, faltering feet in anguish stray,
And black and changeless night envelops noon.

How bright at first the painted prospect seemed!
How swiftly did my hungry feet pursue
The rosy phantom which hath changed its hue
And left instead an aimlessness undreamed.

From out the falseness and the wanton sin
Of that which lures with smiling pleasantness,
I look to Thee, O Master, in distress,
And feel there is a kindled hope within.

William M. Graffius.

*H*ELP Thou mine unbelief, O God, give me greater patience in my hope, and make me more constant in my love. In love, let me believe, and in believing, let me love; and in loving and believing let me hope for a more perfect love and a more unwavering faith, through Jesus Christ, my Lord. [John Baillie.]

THE PRAYER OF THE KNIGHTS
OF PEACE

Let a man so account of us, as of ministers of Christ, and stewards of the mysteries of God. . . . Even unto this present hour we both hunger, and thirst, and are naked, and are buffeted, and have no certain dwelling-place; and we toil, working with our own hands: being reviled, we bless; being persecuted, we endure; being defamed, we entreat. *I Cor. 4:1, 11–13.*

To the weak I became weak, that I might gain the weak: I am become all things to all men, that I may by all means save some. And I do all things for the gospel's sake. *I Cor. 9:22, 23.*

O Lord, make me an instrument of Thy peace!
Where hate is, may I bring love;
Where offence has been given or taken, may I bring pardon;
Where there is discord, may I bring fellowship;
Where there is error, may I bring truth;
Where there is doubt, may I bring faith;
Where there is despair, may I bring hope;
Where there is darkness, may I bring light;
Where there is sadness, may I bring joy;
Master, let me seek rather to console than to be consoled;
To understand than to be understood;
To love rather than to be loved;
For it is in giving that I receive,
In forgetting myself that I find myself;
In pardoning that I receive pardon;
In dying that I am born again to the life eternal.
St. Francis of Assisi.

*F*OR the eternal love, ever seeking fuller entrance into our hearts; for the grace which is sufficient for all our needs; for the faith that overcometh the world; for the joy no man can take from us; for the peace that passeth all understanding; for the hope which is set before us, and for the promise of our Father's house, we thank Thee, O God. And, above all, for our adorable Lord, the King and Head of the Church, the Lord and Master of our lives, who ever liveth, and who must reign until all things are gathered into one in Him. [*Prayers for Students.*]

If I have withheld the poor from their desire, . . . or have eaten my morsel alone, . . . if I have seen any perish for want of clothing, or that the needy had no covering . . . then let my shoulder fall from the shoulder-blade, and mine arm be broken from the bone. *Job 31:16 f.*

The kingdom of heaven is at hand. Heal the sick, raise the dead, cleanse the lepers, cast out demons: freely ye received, freely give. *Matt. 10:7, 8.*

> " If I have eaten my morsel alone "—
> The patriarch spoke in scorn;
> What would he think of the Church,
> Were he shown Heathendom, huge, forlorn,
> Godless, Christless, with soul unfed,
> While the Church's ailment is fullness of bread,
>   Eating her morsel alone? . . .
>
> Ever of them who have largest dower
> Shall Heaven require the more;
> Ours is affluence, knowledge, power,
> Ocean from shore to shore;
> And East and West in our ears have said,
> " Give us, give us your living Bread ";
>   Yet we eat our morsel alone.
>
> " Freely, as ye have received, so give,"
> He bade, who hath given us all;
> How shall the soul in us longer live,
> Deaf to their starving call,
> For whom the Blood of the Lord was shed,
> And His Body broken to give them Bread,
>   If we eat our morsel alone? *Wm. Alexander, Primate of Ire.*

O GOD, who hast given unto Thy servants diversities of gifts by the same Spirit, and hast taught us by Thy holy apostle that all our doings without charity are nothing worth; be pleased to bless and prosper all who love and serve their fellow-men with a pure heart fervently, remembering the poor, healing the sick, comforting the sorrowful, teaching the ignorant, and lifting up the afflicted. [*The Book of Common Worship,* Revised.]

THE BURIED LIFE

Jesus looked upon him, and said, Thou art Simon the son of John: thou shalt be called Cephas (which is by interpretation, Peter). *John 1:42.*

Christ in you, the hope of glory. *Col. 1:27.*

In the autumn of 1881 the following was posted on the billboards of East London by Canon Barnett, of Toynbee Hall:

There is a poem on " The Buried Life " of which I am often reminded. Your lives are busy, useful, honest; but your faces are anxious and you are not all you want to be. There is within you another life, a buried life, which does not get free. In old days it got free through old forms of religion, and then men had peace and were not afraid of anybody or anything. We cannot go back to the old forms — they are gone with the old times and in the presence of the new learning of our days. Many therefore have given up religion altogether and carry about a buried life. It is buried but it is not dead. When it really hears God's voice it will rise. Men will live spiritual as well as honest lives. They will rest on Some One greater than themselves and have peace. I don't think this life will be stirred by excitement or by irrational preaching — and not always by rational preaching; I believe that in the quiet of a place full of good memories, in the sound of fine music, in the sympathy of fellow seekers, we may better wait God's call. St. Jude's Church in Commercial Street will thus be open from 8:30 to 9:30 on Sunday evenings. Will you come and give yourself even ten minutes? It may be that as you listen to the silence, to the music, or to the worship of others, God will speak and that the buried life will arise and that you will have peace.

SAVE us today, O Christ, into more likeness to Thee: Save us into Thy life of service for others, Thy utter self-sacrifice, Thy pity for the poor and weak, Thy scorn for all deceit and pride, Thy joy in little children, in simple natural beauty, Thy disregard of pain and shame and loss, Thy zeal for God, Thy passionate desire to show Him forth, Thy high resolve to pay the last sore price upon the Cross that men might live: Plant in us, Christ, this life today, base though we be, and live it forth Thyself in us — not unto bliss eternal for ourselves alone but that our brethren may have life, joy, freedom, truth. [J. S. Hoyland (Altered).]

THE POTTER'S WHEEL

O Jehovah, thou art our Father; we are the clay, and thou our potter; and we all are the work of thy hand. *Isa. 64:8.*

Now in a great house there are not only vessels of gold and of silver, but also of wood and of earth; and some unto honor and some unto dishonor. If a man therefore purge himself from these, he shall be a vessel unto honor, sanctified, meet for the master's use. *II Tim. 2:20, 21.*

Fool! All that is, at all,
Lasts ever, past recall;
Earth changes, but thy soul and God stand sure:
What entered into thee,
That was, is, and shall be:
Time's wheel runs back or stops: Potter and clay endure.

He fixed thee 'mid this dance
Of plastic circumstance,
This Present, thou, forsooth would fain arrest:
Machinery just meant
To give thy soul its bent,
Try thee and turn thee forth, sufficiently impressed. . . .

Look not thou down but up!
To uses of a cup,
The festal board, lamp's flash and trumpet's peal,
The new wine's foaming flow,
The Master's lips aglow!
Thou, heaven's consummate cup, what needst thou with earth's wheel?
Browning.

O LORD, by all Thy dealings with us, whether of joy or pain, let us be brought to Thee. Let us value no treatment of Thy grace simply because it makes us happy or because it makes us sad; but may all that Thou sendest us bring us to Thee, that knowing Thy perfectness, we may be sure in every disappointment that Thou art still loving us, in every darkness that Thou art still enlightening us, and in every enforced idleness that Thou art still using us; yea, in every death that Thou art giving us life. [Channing, Knight, and Brooks.]

According to his [God's] own purpose and grace, which was given us in Christ Jesus before times eternal, but hath now been manifested by the appearing of our Saviour Christ Jesus, who abolished death, and brought life and immortality to light through the gospel. *II Tim. 1:9, 10.*

Neither death, nor life, . . . shall be able to separate us from the love of God, which is in Christ Jesus our Lord. *Rom. 8:38, 39.*

He that heareth my word, and believeth him that sent me, hath eternal life, and cometh not into judgment, but hath passed out of death into life. *John 5:24.*

We know that we have passed out of death into life, because we love the brethren. He that loveth not abideth in death. *1 John 3:14.*

> There is no death! What seems so is transition
>   This life of mortal breath
> Is but a suburb of the life Elysian
>   Whose portal we call death.
>
> She is not dead — the child of our affection —
>   But gone into that school
> Where she no longer needs our poor protection
>   And Christ Himself doth rule. . . .
>
> Day after day we think what she is doing
>   In those bright realms of air
> Year after year, her tender steps pursuing
>   Behold her grown more fair.
>
> Thus do we walk with her and keep unbroken
>   The bond which nature gives
> Thinking that our remembrance though unspoken,
>   May reach her where she lives.   *Longfellow.*

O ALMIGHTY GOD, who hast knit together Thine elect in one communion and fellowship, in the mystical body of Thy Son Christ our Lord; Grant us grace so to follow Thy blessed saints in all virtuous and godly living, that we may come to those unspeakable joys which Thou hast prepared for those who unfeignedly love Thee; through Jesus Christ our Lord. [*The Book of Common Prayer.*]

GOD AT WORK ON US

We all, with unveiled face beholding as in a mirror the glory of the Lord, are transformed into the same image from glory to glory, even as from the Lord the Spirit. *II Cor. 3:18.*

And the God of all grace, who called you unto his eternal glory in Christ, after that ye have suffered a little while, shall himself perfect, establish, strengthen you. *I Peter 5:10.*

See, saith he, that thou make all things according to the pattern that was showed thee in the mount. *Heb. 8:5.*

It is God who worketh in you. *Phil. 2:13.*

We are his workmanship. *Eph. 2:10.*

Children of yesterday, heirs of tomorrow,
What are you weaving? Labor and sorrow?
Look at your loom again! Faster and faster
Fly the great shuttles prepared by the Master!
    Life's in the loom.
    Room for it — Room!

Children of yesterday, heirs of tomorrow,
Lighten the labor and sweeten the sorrow.
Now while the shuttles fly faster and faster
Up and be at it, at work for the Master!
    He stands at your loom.
    Room for Him — Room!

Children of yesterday, heirs of tomorrow,
Look at your fabric of labor and sorrow.
Seamy and dark with despair and disaster,
Turn it and lo! — the design of the Master!
    The Lord's at the loom.
    Room for Him — Room!   *Mary A. Lathbury.*

O GOD, who alone canst order the unruly wills and affections of sinful men, give us such a measure of Thy grace that, forgetting those things which are behind and reaching forth unto those things which are before, we may press toward the mark of Thy high calling of us in Christ Jesus, being assured that Thou who hast begun a good work in us will perfect the same and bring us at last to the likeness of Him whom having not seen we love.

Where is the flock that was given thee, thy beautiful flock? *Jer. 13:20.*

We are unprofitable servants. *Luke 17:10.*

What I have written I have written. *John 19:22.*

That which is crooked cannot be made straight; and that which is wanting cannot be numbered. *Eccl. 1:15.*

Hitherto hath the Lord helped us. *I Sam. 7:12.*

> Late, late, so late! and dark the night and chill!
> Late, late, so late! but we can enter still.
> Too late, too late! ye cannot enter now.
>
> No light had we; for that we do repent,
> And learning this, the bridegroom will relent.
> Too late, too late! ye cannot enter now.
>
> No light! so late! and dark and chill the night!
> O, let us in, that we may find the light!
> Too late, too late! ye cannot enter now.
>
> Have we not heard the bridegroom is so sweet?
> O, let us in, though late, to kiss his feet!
> No, no, too late! ye cannot enter now. *Tennyson.*

O GOD our Father, we who are children of time come to Thee who art above time. For us the days that are past are past beyond recall and what we have written on life's page we may not erase. But our past is still present to Thee and Thou canst undo what is beyond our power to change. Thou canst restore the wasted years. And we bring them to Thee — all the time past of our lives. Take it into Thy moulding hands. What was amiss, do Thou amend. What was faulty do Thou fulfill. We bless Thee for forgiveness but we ask for more, even that Thou shouldst annul the evil that we have done and accomplish the good in which we failed. We thank Thee that Thou art ever open to our cry, that none can come to Thee too late, that the door of the Father's house is never closed to any child who would come home. Father, we come bringing our marred lives for Thy remaking, our stained hands for Thy cleansing, our tired feet for Thy rest, our wearied hearts for Thy peace. [R. E. S.]

THE BEYOND

In my Father's house are many mansions; if it were not so, I would have told you; for I go to prepare a place for you. And if I go and prepare a place for you, I come again, and will receive you unto myself; that where I am, there ye may be also. *John 14:2, 3.*

Our citizenship is in heaven. *Phil. 3:20.*

Ye are come unto mount Zion, and unto the city of the living God, the heavenly Jerusalem, and to innumerable hosts of angels, to the general assembly and church of the firstborn who are enrolled in heaven, and to God the Judge of all, and to the spirits of just men made perfect. *Heb. 12:22, 23.*

It seemeth such a little way to me
  Across to that strange country — the Beyond;
And yet not strange, for it has grown to be
  The home of those of whom I am most fond;
They make it seem familiar and most dear,
  As journeying friends bring distant regions near. . . .

And so for me there is no sting to death,
  And so the grave has lost its victory.
It is but crossing — with abated breath.
  And white, set face — a little strip of sea,
To find the loved ones waiting on the shore,
  More beautiful, more precious than before.
                                        E. W. Wilcox.

LORD of all worlds, we bless Thy Name for all those who have entered into their rest and reached the Promised Land, where Thou art seen face to face. Give us grace to be followers of them, as they followed in the footsteps of Thy Holy Son. Keep alive in us the memory of our beloved whom Thou hast called out of this world, and make it powerful to subdue every unworthy thought and wish. Grant that every remembrance that turns our hearts to the unseen may lead them upward to Thee, till we also come to the eternal rest which Thou hast prepared for Thy people, through Jesus Christ. [F. J. A. Hort (Altered).]

THE FULFILLMENT OF LIFE

Be thou sober in all things, suffer hardship, do the work of an evangelist, fulfil thy ministry. For I am already being offered, and the time of my departure is come. *II Tim. 4:5, 6.*

And these all, having had witness borne to them through their faith, received not the promise, God having provided some better thing concerning us, that apart from us they should not be made perfect. *Heb. 11:39, 40.*

Beloved, no new commandment write I unto you, but an old commandment which ye had from the beginning: the old commandment is the word which ye heard. *I John 2:7.*

You gathered round me when the long call sounded;
   You stood beside the river while I crossed;
I saw the busy years God gave, full-rounded,
   And counted then no God-ward labor lost.

For you, my children, ever were the guerdon
   Of what I willed, God-led, and strove to be,
Out-spending brain and body for the burden
   God gave me, — to arouse my kind to see.

To see straight through to truth, sun-clear, unclouded;
   To see my neighbor's need, my own forgot;
To see the cloud-rift, and the hills unshrouded;
   To see the whiteness, rather than the blot.

In you shall be the sure, complete out-working
   Of all I longed that other men should see:
You, in the schooling yet, no labor shirking,
   I, where the vision opens wide to me.

You saw that day the shadow, — I, the glory;
   You dimly grope, — I walk where life-ways blend;
Oh, far beyond the dream of song or story,
   Believe me, sweeps the vision in the end!   *P. E. Howard.*

OUR Father, unto Thee in the light of our Saviour's blessed Life, we would lift our souls. We thank Thee for that true Light shining in our world with still increasing brightness. We thank Thee for all who have walked therein, and especially for those near to us and dear, in whose lives we have seen this excellent glory and beauty. [Rufus Ellis.]

THE TWO IN ONE

Mary hath chosen the good part, which shall not be taken away from her. *Luke 10:42.*

The peace of God, which passeth all understanding, shall guard your hearts and your thoughts in Christ Jesus. *Phil. 4:7.*

Now the Martha of her stiffened to her load,
　Down-weighing, of relentless daily care
Now she straightened upright, would not bend nor break,
　But held herself all iron standing there.

When the Mary of her called unto her soul
　And made a moan and cried to it in vain:
" Oh this woman — look! She fretteth overmuch
　And leaves no space for me; Lord, I complain."

But the Martha of her listened with the sigh
　Of those too weary or too strong to rest:
" Tell who taketh then this burden if I cease
　And empty both my hands upon my breast."

O a soul divided is a soul forespent.
　She went still asking, " Is it I? Or I? "
Low forever through the silence Mary spake,
　And Martha, sad and sure did make reply.

Till the irony and harmony of death
　Made out of these a concord high and sweet
When the Martha of the woman toiling, passed
　Estranged from ease, she sought her Master's feet.

" Now my turn has come, my turn at last." she cried,
　" My time to worship, listening to Thy Word."
Oh, but calm beyond her, fair above her still
　The Mary of her knelt before her Lord.　　*E. S. P. Ward.*

*T*HOU, O dearest Jesus, art the Head of the Church, the beginning and the first born from the dead: in all things Thou hast the preeminence, and it pleased the Father that in Thee should all fulness dwell. Kingdoms are in love with Thee: Kings lay their crowns and sceptres at Thy feet, and Queens are Thy handmaids, and wash the feet of Thy servants. [Jeremy Taylor.]

THE LIVING BREAD

Verily, verily, I say unto you, Except ye eat the flesh of the Son of man and drink his blood, ye have not life in yourselves. He that eateth my flesh and drinketh my blood hath eternal life; and I will raise him up at the last day. For my flesh is meat indeed, and my blood is drink indeed. He that eateth my flesh and drinketh my blood abideth in me, and I in him. As the living Father sent me, and I live because of the Father; so he that eateth me, he also shall live because of me. This is the bread which came down out of heaven: not as the fathers ate, and died; he that eateth this bread shall live forever. *John 6:53–58.*

'Twas August and the fierce sun overhead
   Smote on the squalid streets of Bethnal Green,
   And the pale weaver, through his windows seen
In Spitalfields, look't thrice dispirited.
I met a preacher there I knew and said:
   " Ill and o'er-worked, how fare you in this scene? "
   " Bravely," said he; " for I of late have been
Much cheer'd with thoughts of Christ the Living Bread."
O human soul! as long as thou canst so
   Set up a mark of everlasting light,
Above the howling senses' ebb and flow,
To cheer thee and to right thee if thou roam —
   Not with lost toil thou labourest through the night!
Thou mak'st the heaven thou hop'st indeed thy home.
                         Matthew Arnold.

GRANT, O Lord, that we may be cleansed from all pettiness and self-seeking, from all preference for ease and comfort; fill us with the spirit of unselfishness and unweary service, that we may bring life and hope and new vigor to others who are in need of help and cheer. . . .

Bless us, O God, with the vision of Thy being and beauty, that in the strength of it we may work without haste and without rest, and set our hearts at liberty, we pray Thee, from the service of ourselves, and let it be our meat and drink, fed by Thy bread, to do Thy will: through Jesus Christ our Lord. [*A Book of Prayers for Students* (Altered).]

Christ is all, and in all. *Col. 3:11.*

Jesus saith unto him, I am the way, and the truth, and the life. *John 14:6.*

My God shall supply every need of yours according to his riches in glory in Christ Jesus. *Phil. 4:19.*

The unsearchable riches of Christ; . . . the riches of his glory. *Eph. 3:8, 16.*

All things are yours; whether Paul, or Apollos, or Cephas, or the world, or life, or death, or things present, or things to come; all are yours; and ye are Christ's; and Christ is God's. *1 Cor. 3:21-23.*

He is a path if any be misled,
  He is a robe if any naked be;
If any chance to hunger, He is bread
  If any be a bondman, He is free;
To blind men light He is; to sick men health;
To dead men life, and to the needy wealth;
A pleasure without loss, a treasure without stealth.
                              Giles Fletcher.

There are in this loud stunning tide
  Of human care and crime
With whom the melodies abide
  Of the everlasting chime,
Who carry music in their heart
Through dusky lane and wrangling mart.
  Plying their daily toil with busier feet
  Because their secret souls a holier strain repeat.
                              John Keble.

CHRIST, whom men saw on the mountain top transfigured with the splendour of God; Christ, whom they saw at Thy Ascension girt about with the light of heaven, Thy pierced hands stretched out in longing over the world, open our eyes to see Thee as Thou art. Help us so to know Thee that we may love Thee, so to love Thee that we may grow more like Thee, so to follow Thee that through us others may know Thee and find in Thee their hope, their life, their joy. [F. R. Barry.]

Redeeming the time. *Eph. 5:16.*

Take ye heed, watch and pray: for ye know not when the time is. *Mark 13:33.*

For everything there is a season, and a time for every purpose under heaven: a time to be born, and a time to die; a time to plant, and a time to pluck up that which is planted. *Eccl. 3:1, 2.*

And these all, having had witness borne to them through their faith, received not the promise, God having provided some better thing concerning us, that apart from us they should not be made perfect. *Heb. 11:39, 40.*

> The year departs! A blessing on its head!
> We mourn not for it, for it is not dead:
> Dead? What is that? A word to joy unknown,
> Which love abhors, and faith will never own.
> The passing breezes gone as soon as felt,
> The flakes of snow that in the soft air melt,
> The smile that sinks into a maiden's eye,
> They come, they go, they change, they do not die.
> So the old year, that fond and formal name —
> Is with us yet, another and the same.
> And are the thoughts that evermore are fleeing
> The moments that make up our being's being,
> The silent workings of unconscious love
> Or the dull hate, which clings and will not move,
> Are these less vital than the wave or wind
> Or snow that melts and leaves no trace behind?
>
> *H. Coleridge.*

O THOU whose patience we have too long tried, after so many ineffectual vows, we almost fear to repent, lest we only add one unfaithfulness more, and turn our last strength into weakness. Increase our faith that we may no longer lean on our broken will, but throw ourselves freely open unto Thee, watch Thy guiding light and follow where Thou mayst lead. Lead, Kindly Light, throughout the coming year. Lead Thou us on. In all things attune our hearts now and for all time to come to the holiness and harmony of Thy Kingdom. [James Martineau (Alt.).]

My Father, who hath given them unto me, is greater than all; and no one is able to snatch them out of the Father's hand. *John 10:29.*

I am the Alpha and the Omega, the first and the last, the beginning and the end. *Rev. 22:13.*

Behold, I make all things new. *Rev. 21:5.*

In the beginning God created the heavens and the earth. *Gen. 1:1.*

And I saw a new heaven and a new earth: for the first heaven and the first earth are passed away. . . . I will give unto him that is athirst of the fountain of the water of life freely. He that overcometh shall inherit these things; and I will be his God, and he shall be my son. *Rev. 21:1, 6, 7.*

> It's wiser being good than bad:
> It's safer being meek than fierce:
> It's fitter being sane than mad.
> My own hope is a sun will pierce
> The thickest cloud earth ever stretched;
> That after Last returns the First
> Though a wide compass round be pitched;
> That what began best can't end worst,
> Nor what God blessed once, prove accurst.
>
> *Browning.*

O LORD, who never failest to help and govern those whom Thou dost bring up in Thy stedfast fear and love; Keep us we beseech Thee, under the protection of Thy good providence, and make us to have a perpetual fear and love of Thy holy Name. Grant, we beseech Thee, merciful Lord, to Thy faithful people pardon and peace, that they may be cleansed from all their sins, and serve Thee with a quiet mind. O almighty God, who alone canst order the unruly wills and affections of sinful men; Grant unto Thy people, that they may love the thing which Thou commandest, and desire that which Thou dost promise, that so, among the sundry and manifold changes of the world, our hearts may surely there be fixed, where true joys are to be found. [*Gelasian Sacramentary.*]

I go to the Father. *John 16:10.*

Father, I desire that they also whom thou hast given me be with me where I am, that they may behold my glory. *John 17:24.*

And there shall be no curse any more: and the throne of God and of the Lamb shall be therein: and his servants shall serve him; and they shall see his face; and his name shall be on their foreheads. And there shall be night no more; and they need no light of lamp, neither light of sun; for the Lord God shall give them light: and they shall reign for ever and ever. *Rev. 22:3–5.*

> God of the living, in whose eyes,
> Unveiled Thy whole creation lies,
> All souls are Thine; we must not say
> That those are dead who pass away;
> From this our world of flesh set free
> We know them living unto Thee.
>
> Released from earthly toil and strife,
> With Thee is hidden still their life;
> Thine are their thoughts, their works, their powers,
> All Thine, and yet most truly ours;
> For well we know where'er they be,
> Our dead are living unto Thee. . . .
>
> Thy word is true, Thy will is just,
> To Thee we leave them, Lord, in trust;
> And bless Thee for the love which gave
> Thy Son to fill a human grave,
> That none might fear that world to see,
> Where all are living unto Thee.   *John Ellerton.*

*T*HE past has been Thy gift, the present is laid open to us by Thee, and the future Thou dost unroll before us as a scroll upon which still more worthy records may be written. And as we think of those whom we have loved and who have passed into the higher presence and service of God, we are confident that they have found new and higher tasks to employ their maturing energies and satisfy their expanding desires. We pray that we may be worthy to share their blessed employments and to renew our own activities in a world without end. [*The Daily Altar.*]

Glory to God in the highest, and on earth peace among men in whom he is well pleased. *Luke 2:14.*

Thy righteousness is an everlasting righteousness, and thy law is truth. *Ps. 119:142.*

God hath called us in peace. *I Cor. 7:15.*

1918

The war, in shaking the very foundation of ordered civilization has driven all thoughtful men to examine the bases of national and inter-national life.

It has become clear today both through the arbitrament of war and through the tests of rebuilding a life of peace, that neither educa-tion, science, diplomacy nor commercial prosperity when allied in material force as the ultimate power, are real foundations for the ordered development of the world's life. These things are in themselves simply the tools of the spirit that handles them.

Only in the recognition of the fact of the Fatherhood of God and of the Divine purpose for the world which are central to the message of Christianity we shall discover the ultimate foundation for the recon-struction of an ordered and harmonious life for all men.

— *From a Statement Issued After the War of 1914–1918, Signed by David Lloyd George, Prime Minister for Great Britain, R. L. Borden for Canada, W. M. Hughes for Australia, R. A. Squires for Newfound-land, W. G. Manley for New Zealand, and Louis Botha for South Africa.*

1943

Hitler, Mussolini, Hirohito. Alas!

O CHRIST, Thou hast bidden us pray for the coming of Thy Father's Kingdom, in which His righteous will shall be done on earth. We have treasured Thy words but we have forgotten their meaning, and Thy great hope has grown dim in Thy Church. We bless Thee for the inspired souls of all ages who saw afar the shining city of God, and by faith left the profit of the present to follow their vision. Help us, O Lord, in the courage of faith to seize what has come so near, that the glad day of God may dawn at last. As we have mastered nature that we might gain wealth, help us now to master the social relations of mankind that we may gain justice and a world of brothers. [W. Rauschenbusch (Alt.).]

THE BELIEVING HEART

Take heed, brethren, lest haply there shall be in any one of you an evil heart of unbelief. *Heb. 3:12.*

Upon the white sea sand there sat a pilgrim band,
Telling the losses that their lives had known;
While evening waned away from breezy cliff and bay
And the strong tides went out with weary moan.

One spoke with quivering lip of a fair-freighted ship,
With all his household to the deep gone down;
But one had wider woe for a fair face, long ago
Lost in the darker depths of a great town.

There were who mourned their youth with a most tender ruth,
For its brave hopes and memories ever green;
And one upon the West turned an eye that would not rest
For far off hills whereon its joys had been.

Some talked of vanished gold, some of proud honors told.
Some spake of friends who were their trust no more;
And one, of a green grave beside a foreign wave,
That made him sit so lonely on the shore.

But when their tales were done, there spake among them one,
A stranger seeming from all sorrow free;
"Sad losses ye have met, but mine is heavier yet
For a believing heart is gone from me."

"Alas!" these pilgrims said, "for the living and the dead,
For fortune's cruelty, for love's sure cross,
For the wrecks of land and sea! but, however it came to thee,
Thine, stranger, is life's last and heaviest loss!
For the believing heart has gone from thee."   *Frances Brown.*

O GOD, too near to be found, too simple to be conceived, too good to be believed; help us to trust, not in our knowledge of Thee, but in Thy knowledge of us; to be certain of Thee, not because we feel our thoughts of Thee are true, but because we know how far Thou dost transcend them. Turn us back from our voyages of thought to that which sent us forth. Teach us to trust not to cleverness or learning, but to that inward faith which can never be denied. Give to each of us the enlightened mind and the believing heart.   [R. E. S.]

THE NAMELESS SAINTS

Not one of them is forgotten in the sight of God. *Luke 12:6.*
The righteous shall be had in everlasting remembrance. *Ps. 112:6.*

What was his name? I do not know his name.
I only know he heard God's voice and came,
　　Brought all he had across the sea to live and work for God and me;
　　　Felled the ungracious oak;
　　　Dragged from the soil with horrid toil
　　The thrice-gnarled roots and stubborn rock;
With plenty piled the haggard mountain-side;
And at the end without memorial died.
No blaring trumpets sounded out his fame;
He lived, — he died, — I do not know his name.

No form of bronze and no memorial stones
Show me the place where lie his moldering bones.
　　Only a cheerful city stands built by his hardened hands.
　　　Only ten thousand homes
　　　Where every day the cheerful play
　　Of love and hope and courage comes.
These are his monument and these alone.
There is no form of bronze and no memorial stone.

And I?
Is there some desert or some pathless sea
Where Thou, Good God of angels, wilt send me?
　　Some oak for me to rend; some sod, some rock for me to break;
　　　Some handful of His corn to take
　　　And scatter far afield, till it, in turn, shall yield
　　　Its hundredfold of grains of gold
　　To feed the waiting children of my God?
Show me the desert, Father, or the sea.
Is it Thine enterprise? Great God, send me.
And though this body lie where ocean rolls,
Count me among all Faithful Souls.　　　　*Edward Everett Hale.*

*W*E give thanks to Thee, O Lord, for all saints and servants of
Thine, who have done justly, loved mercy, and walked humbly with
their God. [*The Book of Common Worship,* Revised.]

Giving thanks unto the Father, who made us meet to be partakers of the inheritance of the saints in light; who delivered us out of the power of darkness, and translated us into the kingdom of the Son of his love. *Col. 1:12, 13.*

God is light, and in him is no darkness at all. If we say that we have fellowship with him and walk in the darkness, we lie, and do not the truth: but if we walk in the light, as he is in the light, we have fellowship one with another, and the blood of Jesus his Son cleanseth us from all sin. *I John 1:5-7.*

> Christ as a light
> Illumine and guide me!
> Christ as a shield, o'ershadow and cover me!
> Christ be under me! Christ be over me!
> Christ be beside me
> On left hand and right!
> Christ be before me, behind me, about me!
> Christ this day be within and without me!
>
> Christ the lowly and meek,
> Christ, the all-powerful, be
> In the heart of each to whom I speak
> In the mouth of each who speaks to me!
> In all who draw near me,
> Or see me or hear me! . . .
>
> Salvation dwells with the Lord,
> With Christ the Omnipotent Word,
> From generation to generation,
> Grant us, O Lord, Thy grace and salvation!
>
> *Saint Patrick.*

O THOU who art the true Sun of the world, evermore rising and never going down, who by Thy most wholesome appearing and sight dost nourish and make joyful all things, as well that are in heaven, as also that are on earth, we beseech Thee mercifully and favorably to shine into our hearts, that the night and darkness of sin and the mists of error on every side be driven away. [Erasmus.]

And as they were coming down from the mountain, he charged them that they should tell no man what things they had seen, save when the Son of man should have risen again from the dead. *Mark 9:9.*

And straightway the leprosy departed from him, and he was made clean. And he strictly charged him, and straightway sent him out, and saith unto him, See thou say nothing to any man. *Mark 1:42–44.*

Let it be the hidden man of the heart, in the incorruptible apparel of a meek and quiet spirit. *1 Peter 3:4.*

> In strenuous hope I wrought,
> And hope seem'd still betray'd.
> Lastly I said
> "I have labored through the night, nor yet
> Have taken aught,
> But at Thy word I will again cast forth the net!"
> And, lo, I caught
> (Oh, quite unlike and quite beyond my thought,)
> Not the quick shining harvest of the sea,
> For food, my wish.
> But Thee.
> Then, hiding even in me,
> As hid was Simon's coin within the fish,
> Thou sigh'd'st, with joy, "Be dumb,
> Or speak but of forgotten things to far off times to come."
> *Coventry Patmore.*

O LORD of Light, to whom all things are open and from whom no secrets are hid, forgive whatever of evil or of shame Thou dost see in our hearts, and accept our grateful praise for the love of Thee which is hidden there, for all the longings for purity and holiness of which none other knows, but which are known to Thee. We thank Thee for the imagination of Thy face, for the sweet trysts with Thy grace, for the confidences between us and Thee alone, for Thy close companionship in our solitudes, for the words unspoken to which we listen, for the things which eye hath not seen nor ear heard, but which are so surely revealed — all in the hidden place of our hearts where we meet, Thou and I, dear Lord of Light, and Life and Love.

The word of the Lord abideth for ever. *1 Peter 1:25.*
The word of our God shall stand forever. *Isa. 40:8.*
The word of God is not bound. *II Tim. 2:9.*
The word of God is living, and active. *Heb. 4:12.*
And the scripture cannot be broken. *John 10:35.*

> Last eve I passed beside a blacksmith's door,
>   And heard the anvil ring the vesper chime;
> Then looking in, I saw upon the floor
>   Old hammers, worn with beating years of time.
>
> "How many anvils have you had," said I,
>   "To wear and batter all these hammers so?"
> "Just one," he said, then said with twinkling eye,
>   "The anvil wears the hammers out, you know."
>
> And so, I thought, the anvil of God's word,
>   For ages skeptic blows have beat upon;
> Yet, though the noise of falling blows was heard,
>   The anvil is unharmed the hammers gone.

We account the Scriptures of God to be the sublime philosophy.
Sir Isaac Newton.

The Bible has God for its author; salvation for its end; and truth without any mixture of error for its matter. *Locke.*

The Bible is true. It would have been as easy for a mole to have written Sir Isaac Newton's treatise on Optics, as for uninspired men to have written the Bible. *John Randolph, of Roanoke.*

Blessed Lord, who hast caused all Holy Scriptures to be written for our learning; grant that we may in such wise hear them, read, mark, and learn, and inwardly digest them, that by patience and comfort of thy Holy Word, we may embrace and ever hold fast the blessed hope of everlasting life, which thou hast given us in our Saviour Jesus Christ. [*The Book of Common Prayer.*]

It is the spirit that giveth life; the flesh profiteth nothing: the words that I have spoken unto you are spirit, and are life. *John 6:63.*

Simon Peter answered him, Lord, to whom shall we go? thou hast the words of eternal life. *John 6:68.*

The words which thou gavest me I have given unto them; and they received them, and knew of a truth that I came forth from thee, and they believed that thou didst send me. *John 17:8.*

And the Word became flesh, and dwelt among us (and we beheld his glory, glory as of the only begotten from the Father), full of grace and truth. *John 1:14.*

Jesus originated no series of well-concerted plans; He neither contrived nor put in motion any extended machinery; He entered into no correspondence with parties in His own country and in other regions of the world, in order to spread His influence and obtain co-operation. Even the few who were His constant companions and were warmly attached to His person were not, in His lifetime, imbued with His sentiments, and were not prepared to take up His work in His Spirit after He was gone. He constituted no society with its name, design and laws all definitely fixed and formally established. He had no time to construct and to organize — His life was too short — and almost all He did was to speak. He spoke in familiar conversation with His friends, or at the wayside to passers-by, or to those who chose to consult Him, or to large assemblies as opportunity offered. He left behind Him a few spoken truths — not a line or word of writing — and a certain spirit incarnated in His principles and breathed out from His life: and then He died.

Young, The Christ of History.

MERCIFUL and most loving God, by whose will and bountiful gift, Jesus Christ our Lord, humbled Himself that He might exalt mankind, and became flesh that He might renew in us the Divine image, grant unto us the inheritance of the meek, perfect in us Thy likeness, and bring us at last to rejoice in beholding Thy beauty, and with all Thy saints to glorify Thy grace, who hast given Thine only begotten Son to be the Saviour of the world. [*Gallican Liturgy* (Altered).]

SEEING AND SERVING CHRIST
IN MEN

But when he saw the multitudes, he was moved with compassion for them, because they were distressed and scattered, as sheep not having a shepherd. *Matt. 9:36.*

And when he drew nigh, he saw the city and wept over it, saying, If thou hadst known in this day, even thou, the things which belong unto peace! but now they are hid from thine eyes. *Luke 19:41, 42.*

> From a shop window that grand face surveys
>   The street's gay, piteous pageant; sad and great,
> Set like a prophet in the market place,
>   A man of sorrows and grief's intimate,
> He sees the old hypocrisy and shame
> Meanness and pride surge past him still the same.
>
> His dream was one with God's — a people freed:
>   A race of slaves his wistful eyes behold,
> Shackled with ignorance and scourged by greed —
>   Yet in those eyes the dreams have not grown cold.
> A younger brother of the Crucified
> He trusts in man the God for whom he died.
>
> Father, we pray Thee, in this holy place
>   Here in the city's turbulent midstream
> That we may turn from that majestic face
>   Touched with the patient passion of Thy dream
> In the marred flotsam of the crowd to see
> Thy miracle of possibility.
>   *Amy Josephine Burr* (on the Bust of Lincoln by
>   Borglum in a New York Shop Window).

*L*ORD, who knowest all things, and lovest all men better than we know, Thine is might and wisdom and love to save us. As our fathers called unto Thee, and were holpen, and were led along the ways Thou sawest good, so in all time of need, from all evil, the evil of our time and our hearts, deliver us, Lord.   [Rowland Williams.]

Suffer me that I may feel the pillars whereupon the house resteth. *Judg. 16:26.*

Watch ye, stand fast in the faith, quit you like men, be strong. *1 Cor. 16:13.*

Wherefore take up the whole armor of God, that ye may be able to withstand in the evil day, and, having done all, to stand. Stand therefore, having girded your loins with truth. *Eph. 6:13, 14.*

Behold I lay in Zion a chief corner stone, elect, precious: and he that believeth on him shall not be put to shame. *1 Peter 2:6.*

Jehovah seeth not as man seeth; for man looketh on the outward appearance, but Jehovah looketh on the heart. *1 Sam. 16:7.*

> Beneath the edifice that men call Me,
>   Whose minarets attract the setting sun,
> Whose portals to the passer-by are free,
>   Abides another one.
>
> The heartbeat of the organ sounds not there,
>   To jar the heavy silence of the soul;
> Nor low amen of acolytes at prayer,
>   Nor bells that ring or toll.
>
> Unsought, undreamed, save by the solemn few,
>   Who with a lantern lit of love descend,
> To find the buried arches grim and true,
>   On which the walls depend!
>   *Martha Gilbert Dickinson.*

LIFT upon us the light of Thy countenance, O God, that we may rejoice and be glad in Thee; and send into our souls the purifying gift of Thy pardon, that our sins may be utterly removed from us, and we may go forth with a clean spirit, a joyful courage, and strength sufficient for our needs, to meet whatever thou hast appointed for us during this day. And grant, O most merciful Lord, that we may neither forget the precepts and the promises of Thy holy word, nor depart in thought, or word, or deed from the obedient faith of Thy true children in Jesus Christ. [*The Book of Common Prayer.*]

Giving no occasion of stumbling in anything, that our ministration be not blamed; but in everything commending ourselves, as ministers of God, in much patience, in afflictions, in necessities, in distresses, in stripes, in imprisonments, in tumults, in labors, in watchings, in fastings; in pureness, in knowledge, in longsuffering, in kindness, in the Holy Spirit, in love unfeigned, in the word of truth, in the power of God; by the armor of righteousness on the right hand and on the left, by glory and dishonor, by evil report and good report; as deceivers, and yet true; as unknown, and yet well known; as dying, and behold, we live; as chastened, and not killed; as sorrowful, yet always rejoicing; as poor, yet making many rich; as having nothing, and yet possessing all things. *II Cor. 6:3-10.*

How happy is he born and taught
That serveth not another's will,
Whose armor is his honest thought
And simple truth his utmost skill;

Whose passions not his masters are,
Whose soul is still prepared for death,
Not tied unto the world with care
Of public fame or private breath;

Who envies none that chance doth raise
Or vice; who never understood
How deepest wounds are given by praise,
Nor rules of state, but rules of good;

Who hath his life from rumors freed;
Whose conscience is his strong retreat;
Whose state can neither flatterers feed,
Nor ruin make accusers great;

Who God doth late and early pray
More of His grace than gifts to lend,
And entertains the harmless day
With a well-chosen book or friend;

This man is freed from servile bands
Of hope to rise, or fear to fall;
Lord of himself, though not of lands;
And having nothing, yet hath all.
Henry Wotton.

Almighty God, who art the only source of health and healing, the spirit of calm, and the central peace of the universe, grant to us, Thy children, such a consciousness of Thy indwelling presence as may give us utter confidence in Thee. In all pain and weariness and anxiety may we throw ourselves upon Thy besetting care, that, knowing ourselves fenced about by Thy loving omnipotence, we may permit Thee to give us heart and strength and peace; through Jesus Christ our Lord.

THE PRESENCE

Lo, I am with you always, even unto the end of the world. *Matt. 28:20.*

Peter and they that were with him were heavy with sleep: but when they were fully awake, they saw his glory. *Luke 9:32.*

And Elisha prayed, and said, Jehovah, I pray thee, open his eyes, that he may see. And Jehovah opened the eyes of the young man; and he saw: and, behold, the mountain was full of horses and chariots of fire round about Elisha. *II Kings 6:17.*

No man hath seen God at any time; the only begotten Son, who is in the bosom of the Father, he hath declared him. *John 1:18.*

I gaze aloof
At the tissued roof
When time and space are the warp
    and woof;
Which the King of Kings
Like a curtain flings
O'er the dreadfulness of eternal things.

But if I could see
As in truth they be —
The glories which encircle me,

I should lightly hold
This tissued fold
With its marvelous curtain of blue and
    gold.

For soon the whole,
Like a parchéd scroll,
Shall before my amazéd eyes uproll;
And without a screen,
At one burst be seen
The Presence in which I have always
    been.

T. Whytehead.

O BLESSED Jesus Christ, who didst bid all those who carry heavy burdens to come unto Thee, refresh us with Thy Presence and Thy power. Quiet our understandings, and give ease to our hearts by bringing us close to things infinite and eternal. Open to us the mind of God, that in His light we may see light. And crown Thy choice of us to be Thy servants by making us springs of strength and joy and sources of light and life, to those whom Thou hast sent us to serve, for Thy love and mercy's sake.

THE VOICE IN THE GARDEN

And they heard the voice of Jehovah God walking in the garden in the cool of the day. *Gen. 3:8.*

Jehovah hath comforted Zion; he hath comforted all her waste places, and hath made her wilderness like Eden, and her desert like the garden of Jehovah; joy and gladness shall be found therein, thanksgiving, and the voice of melody. *Isa. 51:3.*

She, supposing him to be the gardener. *John 20:15.*

> Speak to my heart through gardens, till I see
> The shame of service rendered grudgingly;
> Turn from the selfishness that could forget
> A life time were too short to pay my debt,
> Beholding how from bud to petal-fall,
> Proud poppies flame with joy at giving all.
>
> Out of the grace of gardens, make me wise
> To learn as larkspur mirrors mist-blue skies,
> Here in my place, Thy holy ground, I, too,
> May lift a life that as a mirror true
> Reflects the beauty of that Blessed One,
> Who in a garden prayed, " Thy will be done! "
>
> Teach me in dewy silences to know
> On the prunéd bush the loveliest roses grow,
> That when the shears of sorrow shall be laid
> Against my life, serene and unafraid,
> A sturdier faith shall flower there, and be
> A richer crimson in my love to Thee.
> *Molly Anderson Haley.*

Lord, let me not forget *Thy* share in life's garden! Let me remember to make all its fruits " fruits of the Spirit "! Let me not ask only if the tree is good for food, or pleasant to the eyes, or a source of human dignity; let me inquire also if it can minister to Love! If I forget that, I am not just to Thee; I am stealing Thy part of the fruit. [George Matheson.]

THE GLORY OF THE VENTURE

Jehoshaphat made ships of Tarshish to go to Ophir for gold: but they went not; for the ships were broken at Ezion-geber. *1 Kings 22:48.*

And all a wreck from stern to bow. . . .
And those could hear (who knew to hear)
Its ever-daring witness clear:
"Whoe'er beneath this headland steer!
The ship-wrecked has good words of cheer.
Say that I did not make my port —
Say that I was the typhoon's sport
The gnashing Scylla's hungry prey —
Till under fathom-depths I lay.
Say that my timbers rot and rot
On strands by merchantmen forgot,
In coves the salt sea hath forsook.
It matters not what fate o'ertook,
Stranger, your long gone sailor peer.
I say, ' Set sail, nor hark to Fear '!
Think only, when my ship went down,
That other ships of fair renown
Unto their destined havens came,
Whereof the waves still shout their fame.
I did not make my port, but yet
The glorious risk cannot forget!
So, stranger, I do counsel thee,
Give thy whole heart unto the sea.
Even the shipwrecked more prevail
Than they who never flung a sail."

Edith M. Thomas.

GRANT unto us, Almighty God, Thy peace that passeth understanding, that we amid the storms and trouble of this our life, may rest in Thee, knowing that all things are in Thee, under Thy care, governed by Thy will, guarded by Thy love; so that with a quiet heart we may see the storms of life, the cloud and the thick darkness; ever rejoicing to know that the darkness and the light are both alike to Thee. Guide, guard and govern us even to the end, that none of us may fail to lay hold upon the immortal life. [George Dawson.]

Passing along by the sea of Galilee he saw Simon and Andrew the brother of Simon casting a net in the sea; for they were fishers. And Jesus said unto them, Come ye after me, and I will make you to become fishers of men. And straightway they left the nets, and followed him. *Mark 1:16–18.*

And Simon answered and said, Master. we toiled all night, and took nothing; but at thy word I will let down the nets. *Luke 5:5.*

I owned a little boat a while ago
And sailed a Morning Sea without a fear,
And whither any breeze might fairly blow
I'd steer the little craft afar or near.
Mine was the boat, and mine the air, and mine the Sea, not mine, a
    care. . . .

One day there passed along the silent shore,
While I my net was casting in the Sea,
A man, who spoke as never man before;
I followed Him, — new life begun in me.
Mine was the boat, but His the voice, and His the call, yet mine, the
    choice. . . .

Once from His boat He taught the curious throng,
Then bade me let down nets out in the Sea;
I murmured, but obeyed, nor was it long
Before the catch amazed and humbled me.
His was the boat, and His the skill, and His the catch, and His, my will.
                                         J. A. Richards.

ALMIGHTY GOD, Merciful Father, who art the giver of all good, enable me to return Thee due thanks for Thy great mercies, for relief from diseases, for all the comforts and alleviations which Thou hast provided; and O my gracious God, make me truly thankful for the call by which Thou hast awakened my conscience, and summoned me to Repentance. Let not Thy call, O Lord, be forgotten or Thy summons neglected, but let the residue of my life, whatever it shall be, be passed in true contrition, and diligent obedience. [Samuel Johnson.]

THE SONG OF JEHOVAH

Jehovah is my strength and song, and he is become my salvation: This is my God, and I will praise him; my father's God, and I will exalt him. *Ex. 15:2.*

And when the burnt-offering began, the song of Jehovah began also. *II Chron. 29:27.*

Yet Jehovah will command his lovingkindness in the daytime; and in the night his song shall be with me, even a prayer unto the God of my life. *Ps. 42:8.*

Ye shall have a song as in the night when a holy feast is kept; and gladness of heart, as when one goeth with a pipe to come unto the mountain of Jehovah, to the Rock of Israel. *Isa. 30:29.*

There is a song so thrilling,
So far all songs excelling,
   That he who sings it, sings it oft again.

No mortal did invent it,
But God by angels sent it,
   So deep and earnest, yet so sweet and plain.

The love that it revealeth
All earthly sorrows healeth;
   They flee like mist before the break of day.

When, O my soul, thou learnest,
This song of songs in earnest,
   Thy care and sorrows all shall pass away.

Lover of our souls,
Come into these cold and empty hearts of ours,
Come to fill them with light, warmth and love,
With the heavenly music,
With the sound of the eternal harmony,
With the footfall of the saints that rejoice in Thy bliss. . . .
Come, our Lord, Thou Lover of our souls,
Come to purify and uplift our failing hearts,
Come to impart to us the eternal joy of those that are in bliss with Thee.
                                  J. S. Hoyland.

SERVING CHRIST IN COMMON THINGS

Whatsoever ye do, in word or in deed, do all in the name of the Lord Jesus, giving thanks to God the Father through him. *Col. 3:17.*

Whatsoever thy hand findeth to do, do it with thy might. *Eccl. 9:10.*

Not with eye-service, as men-pleasers, but in singleness of heart, fearing the Lord: whatsoever ye do, work heartily, as unto the Lord, and not unto men; knowing that from the Lord ye shall receive the recompense of the inheritance: ye serve the Lord Christ. *Col. 3:22.*

Lord of all pots and pans and things, since I've no time
  to be
A saint by doing lovely things, or watching late with
  Thee,
Or dreaming in the dawn light, or storming Heaven's gates,
Make me a saint by getting meals, and washing up the
  plates.

Although I must have Martha's bonds, I have a Mary mind;
And when I black the boots and shoes, Thy sandals, Lord,
  I find.
I think of how they trod the earth, what time I scrub
  the floor.
Accept this meditation, Lord, I haven't time for more.

Warm all the kitchen with Thy love, and light it with
  Thy peace.
Forgive me all my worrying, and make all grumbling cease.
Thou who didst love and give men food, in room, or by
  the sea,
Accept this service that I do — I do it unto Thee.   *M. K. H.*

O GOD our Father, gracious and merciful, give us such vision of the duties of our common life that we may see in them altars of daily sacraments where our souls may become lamps, refilled and illuminated by Thee. . . . Plant in us Thy Spirit that we may see the beauties of our common life and interpret them in a godly walk with our fellows; through Jesus Christ our Lord. [Peter Ainslie.]

RULES OF WAR

Suffer hardship with me, as a good soldier of Christ Jesus. No soldier on service entangleth himself in the affairs of this life; that he may please him who enrolled him as a soldier. *II Tim. 2:3, 4.*

Finally, be strong in the Lord, and in the strength of his might. Put on the whole armor of God, that ye may be able to stand against the wiles of the devil. *Eph. 6:10, 11.*

Defeat is a purely moral result.
Strategy is only the result of character and common sense.
Whatever is done in an army should always aim at increasing and strengthening that moral strength.
There is no victory without battle. " Victory is the price of blood. One must accept the formula or not wage war." (Clausewitz.)
Nowhere can better models be found than in the actions of Napoleon who made use of that wonderful military power in order to triumph by

Taking advantage of human emotions
Maneuvering masses of men
Giving to operations the most crushing nature ever known.

The mass absorbs for war all the physical and moral resources of the nation.
Of all mistakes only one is disgraceful — inaction.
Napoleon always marched straight to his goal without in any way bothering about the strategic plan of the enemy. *Marshal Foch.*

O THOU Divine Spirit, let me find my strength in Thee. I need Thee that I may be strong everywhere. I want both a pillar of fire and a pillar of cloud; a refuge from the night of adversity, and a shield from the day of prosperity. I can find them in Thee. Thou hast proved Thy power both over the night and over the day. Come into my heart and Thy power shall be my power. I shall be victorious over all circumstances, at home in all scenes, restful in all fortunes. I shall have power to tread upon scorpions, and they shall do me no hurt. Neither the enemies without nor the foes within the citadel of my own mind and will shall be able to harm me in Thy protection. And with Thy help I shall conquer every adversary. [*A Prayer Book for Soldiers and Sailors* (Altered).]

A little while, and ye behold me no more; and again a little while, and ye shall see me. . . . Jesus perceived that they were desirous to ask him, and he said unto them, Do ye inquire among yourselves concerning this, that I said, A little while, and ye behold me not, and again a little while, and ye shall see me? Verily, verily, I say unto you, that ye shall weep and lament, but the world shall rejoice: ye shall be sorrowful, but your sorrow shall be turned into joy. . . . And ye therefore now have sorrow: but I will see you again, and your heart shall rejoice, and your joy no one taketh away from you. *John 16:16, 19, 20, 22.*

> When I consider Life, and its few years —
> A wisp of fog betwixt us and the sun:
> A call to battle, and the battle done
> Ere the last echo dies within our ears;
> A rose choked in the grass; an hour of fears;
> The gusts that past a darkened shore do beat;
> The burst of music down an unlistening street —
> I wonder at the idleness of tears.
> Ye old, old dead, and ye of yesternight,
> Chieftains, and bards, and keepers of the sheep,
> By every cup of sorrow that you had,
> Loose me from tears and make me see aright
> How each hath back what once he stayed to weep;
> Homer his sight, David his little lad!
> *Lizette Woodworth Reese.*

O LORD, our Hiding-place, grant us wisdom, we pray Thee, to seek no hiding-place out of Thee in life or in death. Now hide us in Thine own Presence from the provoking of all men, and keep us from the strife of tongues. Make us meek, humble, patient, and teach us to seek peace and ensue it. O Lord, Thou Lover of souls, we beseech Thee to give courage to Thy soldiers, wisdom to the perplexed, endurance to sufferers, fresh vigour and interest in life to those who have lost heart, a sense of Thy Presence to the lonely, comfort to the dying, and a clear vision of Thy truth to those who are seeking Thee; for the sake of Jesus Christ our Lord. [Christina G. Rossetti.]

THE CONSTANT FRIEND

Lo, I am with you always, even unto the end of the world. *Matt. 28:20.*

They went forth, . . . the Lord working with them. *Mark 16:20.*

Your life is hid with Christ in God. *Col. 3:3.*

And the night following the Lord stood by him, and said, Be of good cheer. *Acts 23:11.*

In a very humble cot,
In a rather quiet spot,
In the suds and in the soap,
Worked a woman full of hope;
Working, singing, all alone,
In a sort of undertone:
" With the Saviour for a friend,
He will keep me to the end."

Sometimes happening along,
I had heard the semisong,
And I often used to smile,
More in sympathy than guile;
But I never said a word
In regard to what I heard,
As she sang about her friend
Who would keep her to the end.

Not in sorrow nor in glee
Working all day long was she,
As her children, three or four,
Played around her on the floor;
But in monotones the song
She was humming all day long:
" With the Saviour for a friend,
He will keep me to the end." . . .

Just a trifle lonesome she,
Just as poor as poor could be;
But her spirits always rose,
Like the bubbles in the clothes,
And though widowed and alone,
Cheered her with a monotone,
Of a Saviour and a friend
Who would keep her to the end.

I have seen her rub and scrub,
On the washboard in the tub,
While the baby, sopped in suds,
Rolled and tumbled in the duds;
Or was paddling in the pools,
With old scissors stuck in spools;
She still humming of her friend
Who would keep her to the end.

Human hopes and human creeds
Have their root in human needs;
And I would not wish to strip
From that washerwoman's lip
Any song that she can sing,
Any hope that song can bring;
For the woman has a friend
Who will keep her to the end.

Eugene F. Ware ("Ironquill").

We yield Thee hearty thanks, O Lord our God, for Thy great goodness to us. Mercifully assist us in every duty each one of us has to do, and vouchsafe to be our Companion every day, from morning to night, and night to morning; that we may love Thy presence and walk in it vigilantly. [James Skinner.]

And after the wind an earthquake; . . . and after the earthquake a fire; . . . and after the fire a still small voice. *I Kings 19:11 f.*

And they came with haste, and found both Mary and Joseph, and the babe lying in the manger. *Luke 2:16.*

Well done, thou good servant: because thou wast found faithful in a very little, have thou authority over ten cities. *Luke 19:17.*

> I come in the little things,
> Saith the Lord;
> Not borne on morning wings
> Of majesty; but I have set My Feet
> Amidst the delicate and bladed wheat
> That springs triumphant in the furrowed sod.
> There do I dwell, in weakness and in power;
> Not broken or divided, saith our God!
> In your straight garden plot I come to flower;
> About your porch My Vine
> Meek, fruitful, doth entwine:
> Waits, at the threshold, Love's appointed hour. . . .
>
> I come in the little things,
> Saith the Lord;
> My starry wings
> I do forsake,
> Love's highway of humility to take:
> Meekly I fit my stature to your need.
> In beggar's part
> About your gates I shall not cease to plead —
> As man, to speak with man —
> Till by such art
> I shall achieve My Immemorial Plan;
> Pass the low lintel of the human heart.   *E. Underhill.*

Nothing, O Lord, is liker to Thy holy nature than the mind that is settled in quietness. Thou hast called us into that quietness and peace of Thine, from out of the turmoils of this world, as it were from out of storms into a haven, which is such a peace as the world cannot give and as passeth all capacity of man. [*A Book of Christian Prayers.*]

THE ANVIL OF GOD

And the God of all grace, who called you unto his eternal glory in Christ, after that ye have suffered a little while, shall himself perfect, establish, strengthen you. *1 Peter 5:10.*

All chastening seemeth for the present to be not joyous but grievous; yet afterward it yieldeth peaceable fruit unto them that have been exercised thereby. *Heb. 12:11.*

> Pain's furnace-heat within me quivers,
>   God's breath upon the flame doth blow;
> And all my heart in anguish shivers,
>   And trembles at the fiery glow:
> And yet I whisper, "As God will!"
> And in His hottest fire hold still.
>
> He comes, and lays my heart, all heated,
>   On the hard anvil, minded so
> Into His own fair shape to beat it
>   With His great hammer, blow on blow!
> And yet I whisper, "As God will!"
> And at His heaviest blows hold still. . . .
>
> Why should I murmur? for the sorrow
>   Thus only longer-lived would be;
> Its end may come, and will, to-morrow,
>   When God has done His work in me.
> So I say, trusting, "As God will!"
> And trusting to the end, hold still.   *Julius Sturm.*

Remember, O most pitying Father, what this frail and feeble work of Thine hands can bear without fainting; nothing indeed of itself, but all things in Thee, if strengthened by Thy grace. Wherefore, grant me strength, that I may suffer and endure; patience alone I ask. Lord, give me this, and behold my heart is ready. O God, my heart is ready to receive whatsoever shall be laid upon me. Grant that in my patience I may possess my soul; to that end may I often look upon the face of Christ, Thy Son, that as He hath suffered such terrible things in the flesh, I may endeavor to be armed with the same mind. Wherefore I commit my strength unto Thee, O Lord; for Thou art my Strength and my Refuge. [*Treasury of Devotion.*]

DEEP ANSWERETH TO DEEP

And I heard a voice from heaven, as the voice of many waters, and as the voice of a great thunder: and the voice which I heard was as the voice of harpers harping with their harps. *Rev. 14:2.*

Deep calleth unto deep at the noise of thy waterfalls: all thy waves and thy billows are gone over me. Yet Jehovah will command his lovingkindness in the daytime; and in the night his song shall be with me, even a prayer unto the God of my life. *Ps. 42:7, 8.*

Lord, I thank Thee who hast wounded, for the mercy that abounded,
  For the multitudinous mercy flowing forward like a sea,
For the deeps that rolling o'er me arched into an arm that bore me,
  For the thunder-step of time that woke Thy peace, eternity.

And I thank Thee that the thunder never woke one word of wonder,
  Only hushed the murmurous thought and drove rebellion far away,
That the wrath revealed outside me showed a rest where I might hide me
  Till the inward clouds rejoined the outer darkness black as they.

Therefore, Thee I praise forever, merciful Taker, mighty Giver,
  Taking but to give, and giving none but Thou to take away,
And if darker clouds encrust Thee, though Thou slay me, I will trust
    Thee,
  For Thy hurt is simple healing, and Thy darkness simple day.
                                                    R. W. Barbour.

*L*ORD, help me to keep my love! Whatever else I lose, may I never lose that! Though all the lights go out from my life, let not this torch be extinguished! There is a peace which comes by the death of patience — by ceasing any longer to wait or to expect. There is a peace which is not patience, because it looks for nothing, longs for nothing, prays for nothing — a peace which is painless because it is numb, and is free from struggle because it is dead. I would not have that gift, O my Father! . . . Bring me the peace of pulsation, the calm of courage, the endurance that springs from energy. Bring me the fortitude of fervour, the repose through inner radiance, the tenacity that is born of trust! Bring me the silence that comes from serenity, the gentleness that is bred of joy, the quiet that has sprung from quickened faith! When I hear *Thee* in the whirlwind, there will be a great calm. [Matheson.]

THE ONLY NAME

But when they perceived that he was a Jew, all with one voice about the space of two hours cried out, Great is Diana of the Ephesians. *Acts 19:34.*

Wherefore also God highly exalted him, and gave unto him the name which is above every name; that in the name of Jesus every knee should bow, of things in heaven and things on earth and things under the earth, and that every tongue should confess that Jesus Christ is Lord, to the glory of God the Father. *Phil. 2:9–11.*

If we this day are examined concerning a good deed done to an impotent man, by what means this man is made whole; be it known unto you all, and to all the people of Israel, that in the name of Jesus Christ of Nazareth, whom ye crucified, whom God raised from the dead, even in him doth this man stand here before you whole. He is the stone . . . set at nought of you the builders, which was made the head of the corner. And in none other is there salvation: for neither is there any other name under heaven, that is given among men, wherein we must be saved. *Acts 4:9–12.*

And he hath on his garment and on his thigh a name written, King of Kings, and Lord of Lords. *Rev. 19:16.*

Diana of the Ephesians

For her, three noisy hours of fierce acclaim
When shook the theatre with craftsmen's cheers;
For Him her worshippers maligned, a Name
That claims the clamors of the endless years.
The Sunday School Times.

O LORD, make bare Thy Holy Arm in the eyes of all the nations, that all the ends of the world may see Thy salvation; show forth Thy righteousness openly in the sight of the heathen, that the Kingdom of Thy Christ may be established over all mankind; hasten the coming of the end when He shall deliver up the Kingdom unto Thee, and having put down all rule, and authority, and power, and put all things under His feet, He Himself shall be subject unto Thee, and with Thee, in the unity of the Holy Ghost, Three Persons in One God, shall be our All in all forever. [*A Chain of Prayer Across the Ages.*]

OUR DEEPEST NEED

Be ye doers of the word, and not hearers only. *James 1:22.*

I bow my knees unto the Father, . . . that he would grant you, according to the riches of his glory, that ye may be strengthened with power through his Spirit in the inward man. *Eph. 3:14, 16.*

Be strong in the Lord, and in the strength of his might. *Eph. 6:10.*

Lord, not for light in darkness do we pray,
Not that the veil be lifted from our eyes,
Nor that the slow ascension of our day
    Be otherwise.

Not for a clearer vision of the things
Whereof the fashioning shall make us great,
Nor for remission of the peril and stings
    Of time and fate. . . .

We know the paths wherein our feet should press,
Across our hearts are written thy decrees.
Yet now, O Lord, be merciful to bless
    With more than these.

Grant us the will to fashion as we feel,
Grant us the strength to labor as we know,
Grant us the purpose, ribbed and edged with steel,
    To strike the blow.

Knowledge we ask not — knowledge thou hast lent,
But Lord, the will — there lies our bitter need,
Give us to build above the deep intent
    The deed, the deed.   *John Drinkwater.*

O LORD, . . . we have no right to be of the goodly fellowship of Thy tried veterans; we cannot yet march with their sure tread, nor fight with their blithe confidence. But let us continue in Thy host, though but lagging in the rear, till by the discipline of Thy training and the inspiration of Thy leadership, and our comradeship with Thy saints, we come to make good soldiers under Thy banner which goes before us into victory, through Jesus Christ our Lord. [*A Book of Prayers for Students.*]

Whatsoever thy hand findeth to do, do it with thy might. *Eccl. 9:10.*

And Jehovah looked upon him, and said, Go in this thy might, and save Israel from the hand of Midian: have not I sent thee? *Judg. 6:14.*

Not by might, nor by power, but by my Spirit, saith Jehovah of hosts. *Zech. 4:6.*

> Here we are, gentlemen; here's the whole gang of us,
>   Pretty near through with the job we are on;
> Size up our work — it will give you the hang of us —
>   South to Balboa and north to Colon.
> Yes, the canal is our letter of reference;
>   Look at Culebra and glance at Gatun;
> What can we do for you — got any preference,
>   Wireless to Saturn or bridge to the moon?
>
> Don't send us back to a life that is flat again,
>   We who have shattered a continent's spine;
> Office work — Lord, but we couldn't do that again!
>   Haven't you something that's more in our line?
> Got any river they say isn't crossable?
>   Got any mountains that can't be cut through?
> We specialize in the wholly impossible,
>   Doing things "nobody ever could do!"
>   *Berton Braley,* "The Panama Canal Builders' Song."

REVEAL to me, O Lord, that fire which burns and yet does not consume — the fire of love! My life will be consumed *without* the burning of that fire. It is want of enthusiasm that kills me, wears me away. My soul dies through lack of burning. I never really live unless I catch fire. . . . I am never so weary as when I am aimless, never so fatigued as when I have nothing to do. Set fire to my heart, O Lord. Kindle me into the love of humanity! Inflame me with the passion to make my brother glad. . . . Lay on my heart the burden of the bondsman, the troubles of the toiler, the weights of the weary. Help me to live in the experience of human struggle. [George Matheson.]

THE EYES OF THE HEART

I thank thee, O Father, Lord of heaven and earth, that thou didst hide these things from the wise and understanding, and didst reveal them unto babes: yea, Father, for so it was well-pleasing in thy sight. *Matt. 11:25.*

Having the eyes of your heart enlightened. *Eph. 1:18.*

We speak God's wisdom in a mystery, even the wisdom that hath been hidden, which God foreordained before the worlds unto our glory: which none of the rulers of this world hath known: for had they known it, they would not have crucified the Lord of glory. *1 Cor. 2:7, 8.*

O World, thou choosest not the better part!
It is not wisdom to be only wise,
And on the inward vision close the eyes.
But it is wisdom to believe the heart.
Columbus found a world, and had no chart,
Save one that faith deciphered in the skies;
To trust the soul's invincible surmise
Was all his science and his only art.
Our knowledge is a torch of smoky pine
That lights the pathway but one step ahead
Across a void of mystery and dread.
Bid, then, the tender light of faith to shine
By which alone the mortal heart is led
Unto the thinking of the thought divine.
George Santayana.

O THOU who dwellest in light unapproachable, with whom is no darkness at all, open our eyes, we beseech Thee, to the beauty and meaning of the world by which we are encompassed. May we not be content to rest upon the surface of things, but behind the garment wherewith Thou dost clothe Thyself, catch the outline of a divine form, and above the silence of our unanswered questions, hear the beating of a divine heart. Spirit of wisdom and truth, grant us Thy light, that whatever influence the day may bring — sorrow or joy, success or failure — we may receive it as Thy gift and be thankful. [William Adams Brown.]

BORNE BY OUR BURDENS

Bear ye one another's burdens, and so fulfil the law of Christ. *Gal. 6:2.*

Jesus . . . for the joy that was set before him endured the cross, despising shame. *Heb. 12:2.*

Two are better than one, because they have a good reward for their labor. For if they fall, the one will lift up his fellow; but woe to him that is alone when he falleth, and hath not another to lift him up. *Eccl. 4:9, 10.*

A mountain traveler, the story runs,
Grown dull and spent with fighting wind and snow,
Would have sunk down and yielded. But his foot
Struck a prone something, and his chill heart leaped
To find half buried there, and breathing still,
Another who had laid him down to die.
Strong with the other's need, he drew the load
Across his back, and struggled, battle-warmed,
To friends and safety.

Thus the weaker's need
Worked through the stronger, for the weal of both.
The struggle seems a hopeless one at times,
O God our Father, and the blood grows cold.
Grant that some weaker brother in the way
Make us forget our need at sight of his,
And quicken our dull pulses with his weight:
For only thus, our Father, comes the strength
To climb the narrow path that leads to Thee.   *S. S. Times.*

O GOD, Thou mightiest worker of the universe, source of all strength and author of all unity, we pray Thee for our brothers, the individual workers of the nation. As their work binds them together in common toil and danger, may their hearts be knit together in a strong sense of their common interests and destiny. Help us to realize that the injury of one is the smart of all, and that the welfare of all must be the aim of every one. Teach all men to keep step in a steady onward march and each man in his own way to fulfil the law of Christ by bearing the common burdens. [Walter Rauschenbusch (Altered).]

Whoso shall receive one such little child in my name receiveth me: but whoso shall cause one of these little ones that believe on me to stumble, it is profitable for him that a great millstone should be hanged about his neck, and that he should be sunk in the depth of the sea. *Matt. 18:5, 6.*

The young children ask bread, and no man breaketh it unto them. *Lam. 4:4.*

Weep for yourselves, and for your children. *Luke 23:28.*

Two Litanies

Softly rose the litany:
  "Suffer them to come to me;
These my Father's chosen be,
  All the little children."
Where the faithful knelt in prayer,
To their Father singing, there
Trembled on the scented air
  Voices of the children.

Where the wheels of traffic groaned,
Men of Mammon, high enthroned,
Other litany intoned
  For the little children;
Fiercely swelling, loud and strong,
Raucous rang their savage song
Where the chaffering traders throng:
  "Suffer, little children!"

"These the gates of wealth unbar,
These upbear our triumph's car,
These our choicest chattels are —
  Suffer, little children!
Little hands must heap our gains,
Little backs must bear our pains,
Little wrists be wrapped in chains —
  Suffer, little children!

"Little faces, pinched and old,
Little fingers blue with cold,
Little lives ground into gold —
  Suffer, little children!"
Clacking looms make quick reply,
Whirring wheels took up the cry,
Echoing back hell's litany:
  "Suffer, little children!"
          George I. Knapp.

O GOD whose heart is as the heart of a child, hear us as we pray for these Thy children who are suffering through the sin and hatred and stupidity of us men and women. In Thy mercy restore to them that which we have taken from them. . . . And grant to all who tend and teach them faith to believe that Thou art able to do this, and patient wisdom to co-operate with Thee, for the sake of Jesus Christ who, taking the little children in His arms, blessed them and said, "Of such is the Kingdom of heaven." Amen. [*A Book of Prayers for Students.*]

He [John] was the lamp that burneth and shineth; and ye were willing to rejoice for a season in his light. *John 5:35.*

He was not the light, but came that he might bear witness of the light. There was the true light. *John 1:8, 9.*

Ye yourselves bear me witness, that I said, I am not the Christ, but, that I am sent before him. . . . He must increase, but I must decrease. *John 3:28, 30.*

Again therefore Jesus spake unto them, saying, I am the light of the world: he that followeth me shall not walk in the darkness, but shall have the light of life. *John 8:12.*

The path of the righteous is as the dawning light, that shineth more and more unto the perfect day. *Prov. 4:18.*

The sun shall be no more thy light by day; neither for brightness shall the moon give light unto thee: but Jehovah will be unto thee an everlasting light, and thy God thy glory. *Isa. 60:19.*

"He Must Increase, But I Decrease."

Burn thou candle, sure and slow,
Burn on downward, even so.
Shining, and fore'er consumed,
Wasting, and forever doomed,
Lasting through thy little night,

Going out at morning's light,
Having place, then put away,
Soon forgot in light of day;
Lower, lower, and now done; —
Shine Thou greater, brighter Sun!
H. W. F.

O LORD, Thou greatest and most sure Light, from whence this light of the day and sun doth spring; O Light which dost lighten every man that cometh into the world; O Light, which knowest no night nor evening, but art always a mid-day most clear and fair, without whom all is most dark darkness, by whom all things are most splendent; O Thou Wisdom of the eternal Father of mercies, lighten our minds, that we may only see those things that please Thee, and may be blinded to all other things. Grant that we may walk in Thy ways this day, and that nothing else may be light unto us. Lighten our eyes, O Lord, that we sleep not in death, lest our enemy say, " I have prevailed against him "; for the sake of Jesus Christ Thy Son our Lord. Amen. [*Christian Prayers.*]

THE CHERUBS AND THE SAINT

Then shall the King say unto them on his right hand, Come, ye blessed of my Father, inherit the kingdom prepared for you from the foundation of the world: for I was hungry, and ye gave me to eat; I was thirsty, and ye gave me to drink; I was a stranger, and ye took me in; naked, and ye clothed me; I was sick, and ye visited me; I was in prison, and ye came unto me. *Matt. 25:34–36.*

To the weak, I became weak, that I might gain the weak: I am become all things to all men, that I may by all means save some. And I do all things for the gospel's sake, that I may be a joint partaker thereof. *I Cor. 9:22, 23.*

The Ballad of the Saint

The little cherubs whispered,
 "What strange new soul is this
Who cometh with a robe besmirched
 Unto the place of Bliss?"
Then spake the eldest angel,
 "The robe he wears is fair
The groping fingers of the poor
 Have held and blessed him there."

The little cherub whispered,
 "Who comes to be our guest
With dust upon his garment's hem
 And stains upon his breast?"
Then spake the eldest angel,
 "Most lovely is the stain,
The tears of those he comforted
 Who may not weep again."

The little cherub whispered,
 "What strange new soul is he
Who cometh with a burden here
 And bears it tenderly?"
Then spake the eldest angel,
 "He bears his life's rewards
The burden of men's broken hearts
 To place before the Lord.

"The dust upon his garment's hem
 My lips shall bow to it.
The stains upon the breast of him
 Are gems thrice exquisite.
O foolish little cherub,
 What truth is this ye miss?
There comes no saint to Paradise
 Who does not come like this."
 Theodosia Garrison.

O LORD, give us more charity, more self-denial, more likeness to Thee. Teach us to sacrifice our comforts to others, and our desires for the sake of doing good. Make us kindly in thought, gentle in word, generous in deed. Teach us that it is better to minister than to be ministered unto, better to give than to receive, better to forget ourselves than to put ourselves forward. And unto Thee, O Lord of love, be glory and praise forever. [*New Every Morning.*]

THE SCRIPTURES

Every scripture inspired of God is also profitable for teaching, for reproof, for correction, for instruction which is in righteousness: that the man of God may be complete, furnished completely unto every good work. *II Tim. 3:16, 17.*

They believed the scripture, and the word which Jesus had said. *John 2:22.*

Ye do err, not knowing the scriptures. *Matt. 22:29.*

Whatsoever things were written aforetime were written for our learning, that through patience and through comfort of the scriptures we might have hope. *Rom. 15:4.*

> When I am tired, the Bible is my bed;
> Or in the dark, the Bible is my light;
> When I am hungry, it is vital bread;
> Or fearful, it is armor for the fight.
> When I am sick, 'tis healing medicine;
> Or lonely, thronging friends I find therein.
>
> If I would work, the Bible is my tool;
> Or play, it is a harp of happy sound;
> If I am ignorant, it is my school;
> If I am sinking, it is solid ground.
> If I am cold, the Bible is my fire;
> And it is wings, if boldly I aspire.
>
> Does gloom oppress? the Bible is a sun;
> Or ugliness? it is a garden fair.
> Am I athirst? how cool its currents run!
> Or stifled? what a vivifying air!
> Since thus thou givest of thyself to me,
> How should I give myself, great Book to thee?

ALMIGHTY and Most Merciful God, who hast given the Bible to be the revelation of Thy great love to man, and of Thy power and will to save him; grant that our study of it may not be made in vain by the callousness or carelessness of our hearts, but that by it we may be confirmed in penitence, lifted to hope, made strong for service, and above all filled with the true knowledge of Thee and of Thy Son Jesus Christ. [George Adam Smith.]

Finally, brethren, pray for us, that the word of the Lord may run and be glorified, even as also it is with you. *Il Thess. 3:1.*

We also pray always for you, that our God may count you worthy of your calling, and fulfil every desire of goodness and every work of faith, with power; that the name of our Lord Jesus may be glorified in you, and ye in him, according to the grace of our God and the Lord Jesus Christ. *Il Thess. 1:11, 12.*

I cannot tell why there should come to me
A thought of someone miles and years away,
In swift insistence on the memory,
Unless there be a need that I should pray.

We are too busy even to spare a thought
For days together of some friends away;
Perhaps God does it for us: and we ought
To read His signal as a sign to pray.

Perhaps just then my friend has fiercer fight;
A more appalling weakness — a decay
Of courage, darkness, some lost sense of light.
And so in case he needs my prayer, I pray.

Dear, do the same for me! If I intrude
Unasked upon you, on some crowded day;
Give me a moment's prayer, as interlude,
Be very sure I need it; therefore pray.
Marianne Farningham.

O LORD of love, who art not far from any of Thy children, watch with Thy care those who are far away from us; be Thou about their path; be Thou within their hearts; be Thou their defense upon their right hand. Give them unfailing trust in Thee; grant them power against temptation; qualify them for whatever task Thou givest them to do; deliver them from the snare of setting duty aside; make it their joy to do Thy will. Let not distance break the bonds of love which bind them to us and to Thee, but knit us closer in Thy love, for the sake of Jesus Christ our Lord. [Boyd Carpenter.]

Thou, Jehovah, hast not forsaken them that seek thee. *Ps. 9:10.*
I . . . meditate on thee in the night-watches. *Ps. 63:6.*
With my soul have I desired thee in the night. *Isa. 26:9.*

Then the earth shook and trembled. . . . Thick darkness was under his feet. . . . He was seen upon the wings of the wind. And he made darkness pavilions round about him. *II Sam. 22:8, 10–12.*

If I say, Surely the darkness shall overwhelm me, and the light about me shall be night; even the darkness hideth not from thee, but the night shineth as the day: the darkness and the light are both alike to thee. *Ps. 139:11, 12.*

In a Subway Express

I who have lost the stars, the sod,
For chilling pace and cheerless light,
Have made my meeting place with God
A new and nether night,

Have found a lane where thunder fills
Loud caverns tremulous; and these
Atone me for my reverend hills
And moonlight silences.

A figment in the crowded dark
Where men sit muted by the roar,
I ride upon the whirring spark
Beneath the city's floor.

In this dim firmament the stars
Whirl by in blazing files and tiers;
Kin meteors graze our flying bars
Amid the spinning spheres,

Speed, speed, until the quivering rails
Flash silver where the headlight gleams,
As when on lakes the moon impales
The waves upon its beams.

Life throbs about me, yet I stand
Out gazing on majestic Power;
Death rides with me, on either hand,
In my communion hour.

You that 'neath country skies can pray,
Scoff not at me — the city clod;
My only respite of the day
Is this wild ride — with God.

Chester Firkins.

*A*LMIGHTY GOD, our Light in darkness, our Strength in weakness, our Hope in sinfulness, and our Eternal Home, be unto us merciful, long-suffering and patient, that we who be slow of growth, may hope to come at last to Thy likeness, and being upheld by Thee may by Thy mercy go from strength to strength, until, through the waste and dreariness, through the joy and duty of this earthly life having safely passed, we through the fulness of Thy mercy may come into the land of the eternal peace. [George Dawson.]

And Abraham . . . called there on the name of Jehovah, the Everlasting God. *Gen. 21:33.*

Everlasting Father. *Isa. 9:6.*

An everlasting rock. *Isa. 26:4.*

Everlasting joy. *Isa. 35:10.*

Everlasting salvation. *Isa. 45:17.*

Everlasting lovingkindness. *Isa. 54:8.*

Thy sun shall no more go down, neither shall thy moon withdraw itself; for Jehovah will be thine everlasting light. *Isa. 60:20.*

He abideth faithful. *II Tim. 2:13.*

There is no time to take one's ease,
For to sit still and be at peace:
Oh, whirling wheel of Time, be still,
Let me be quiet if you will!

Yet still it turns so giddily,
So fast the years and seasons fly,
Dazed with the noise and speed I run
And stay me on the Changeless One.

I stay myself on Him who stays
Ever the same through nights and days:
The One Unchangeable for aye
That was and will be the one Stay,

O'er whom Eternity will pass
But as an image in a glass;
To whom a million years are nought,
I stay myself on a great Thought,

I stay myself on the great Quiet
After the noise and the riot:
Or in a garnished chamber sit
Far from the tumult of the street.

Oh, wheel of Time, turn round apace!
But I have found a resting place,
You will not trouble me again
In the great peace where I attain.
Katherine Tynan Hinkson.

*A*LMIGHTY, Everlasting and Faithful God who alone gavest us the breath of life and alone canst keep alive in us the breathing of holy desires, who art from everlasting to everlasting the unchanging and ever loving God, we beseech Thee for Thy compassion's sake, to sanctify all our thoughts and endeavors, that we may neither begin any action without a pure intention nor continue it without Thy blessing; and grant that having the eyes of our understanding purged to behold things invisible and unseen, we may in heart be inspired with Thy wisdom, and in work be upheld by Thy strength, and in the end be accepted of Thee. [Rowland Williams (Altered).]

They . . . are at their wits' end. Then they cry unto Jehovah in their trouble, and he bringeth them out of their distresses. *Ps. 107:27 f.*

What time I am afraid, I will put my trust in thee. *Ps. 56:3.*

I sought Jehovah, and he answered me, and delivered me from all my fears. *Ps. 34:4.*

God is my salvation; I will trust, and will not be afraid. *Isa. 12:2.*

Fear not, little flock. *Luke 12:32.*

Fear not: only believe. *Luke 8:50.*

Fear not; I am the first and the last, and the Living one; and I was dead, and behold, I am alive for evermore, and I have the keys of death and of Hades. *Rev. 1:17, 18.*

My sorrow had pierced me through; it throbbed in my heart like a thorn:
This way and that I stared, as a bird with a broken limb
Hearing the hounds strong feet thrust imminent through the corn,
So to my God I turned: and I had forgotten Him.

Into the night I breathed a prayer like a soaring fire: —
So to the wind-swept cliff the resonant rocket streams, —
And it struck its mark I know, for I felt my flying desire
Strain, like a rope drawn home, and catch in the land of dreams.

What was the answer? This — the horrible depth of night,
And deeper, as ever I fear, the huge cliff's mountainous shade,
While the frail boat cracks and grinds, and never a star in sight
And the seething waves smite fiercer; and yet I am not afraid.
Arthur Christopher Benson.

*F*ATHER, whose life is within me and whose love is ever about me, grant that Thy life may be manifested in my life today, and every day, as with gladness of heart, without haste or confusion of thought, I go about my daily tasks, conscious through Thee of ability to meet every rightful demand, seeing the larger meaning of little things and finding beauty everywhere. And now I would enter into the secret place of Thy presence, that hidden in Thee my soul may be refreshed with a sense of Thy sheltering care and all my energies quickened into newness of life.

AFTER THE NIGHT, THE DAY

Watchman, what of the night? The watchman said, The morning cometh, and also the night: if ye will inquire, inquire ye: turn ye, come. *Isa. 21:11, 12.*

And I saw the heaven opened. . . . And I saw an angel standing in the sun. *Rev. 19:11, 17.*

The darkness is passing away, and the true light already shineth. . . . He that loveth his brother abideth in the light, and there is no occasion of stumbling in him. *I John 2:8, 10.*

What of the night, O Watcher?
　Yes, what of it?
A star has risen: and the wind blows strong
The night is dark
　But God is there above it.
The night is dark: the Night is dark and long.

What of the night, O Watcher?
　Is it other?
I see a gleam, a thorn of light, a thong,
The night is dark
　The morning comes, my Brother.
The night is dark: the Night is dark and long.

What now, what now, O Watcher?
　Red as slaughter
The Darkness dies. The Light comes swift and strong.
　The night was long.
　What sayest thou, my Daughter?
The night was dark: the Night was dark and long.
                                    Madison Julius Cawein.

Grant unto us, O God, that when our vision fails and our understanding is darkened, when the ways of life seem hard and the light of life is gone, we too may see heaven opened. Then may our distrust be quieted and our confidence and living trust in Thee be made sure: and as children, knowing they are loved, cared for, guarded, kept, may we with quiet mind at all times put our trust in Thee. So may we face life without fear, and death without fainting, and in the darkest night be surest of the dawn.

And he went down with them, and came to Nazareth; and he was subject unto them: and his mother kept all these sayings in her heart. *Luke 2:51.*

If I then, the Lord and the Teacher, have washed your feet, ye also ought to wash one another's feet. *John 13:14.*

Which is greater, he that sitteth at meat, or he that serveth? is not he that sitteth at meat? but I am in the midst of you as he that serveth. *Luke 22:27.*

Learn of me; for I am meek and lowly in heart. *Matt. 11:29.*

Christ also pleased not himself. *Rom. 15:3.*

The measure of the stature of the fulness of Christ. *Eph. 4:13.*

> Wouldst thou be chief? Then lowly serve.
>   Wouldst thou go up? Go down;
> But go as low as e'er you will,
> The Highest has been lower still.
> *The Glasgow Witness.*

The martyrs shook the powers of darkness with the irresistible power of weakness. *John Milton.*

*A*LMIGHTY GOD, we commend to Thee our families and our children. Dwell in our homes, we beseech Thee; protect our dwellings from all evil, both outwardly and inwardly, and fill them with peace and holiness. May they be schools of goodness in which, learning fidelity in small duties, we shall be fitted to fulfill our calling to tasks great and difficult. Make our homes like the home in Nazareth and make us like Him who grew up there to do in all things that which pleased Thee. We pray for all who are dear to us, that they may be delivered from all the dangers of this present life, and kept by Thy grace unto salvation. And O most loving Father, we remember with undying affection those whom death has taken and who sleep in Jesus. United in one household of faith and love, may we live in the blessed hope, that when the day dawns and the shadows flee away, we shall meet with them and all Thy redeemed, in Thy presence, where there is fulness of joy; through Jesus Christ our Lord. [*The Book of Common Worship,* Revised (Altered).]

And Jesus said . . . If thou canst! All things are possible to him that believeth. Straightway the father of the child cried out, and said, I believe; help thou mine unbelief. *Mark 9:23, 24.*

God commendeth his own love toward us, in that, while we were yet sinners, Christ died for us. *Rom. 5:8.*

The sick man answered . . . , Sir, I have no man, when the water is troubled, to put me into the pool: but while I am coming, another steppeth down before me. Jesus saith unto him, Arise, take up thy bed and walk. *John 5:7, 8.*

> Because I see Thee not, oh, seek Thou me!
>   Because my lips are dumb, oh, hear the cry
>   I do not utter as Thou passest by,
> And from my life-long bondage set me free!
> Because content I perish, far from Thee
>   Oh seize me, snatch me from my fate, and try
>   My soul in Thy consuming fire! Draw nigh
> And let me, blinded, Thy salvation see.
> If I were pouring at Thy feet my tears
>   If I were clamoring to see Thy face,
>   I should not need Thee, Lord, as now I need,
> Whose dumb, dead soul knows neither hopes nor fears,
>   Nor dreads the outer darkness of this place: —
>   *Because* I seek not, pray not, give Thou heed.
> > *Louise Chandler Moulton.*

O INFINITE GOD, the brightness of whose face is often shrouded from my mortal gaze, I thank Thee that Thou didst send Thy Son Jesus Christ to be a light in a dark world. O Christ, Thou Light of Light, I thank Thee that in Thy most holy life Thou didst pierce the eternal mystery as with a great shaft of heavenly light, so that in seeing Thee we see Him whom no man hath seen at any time.

And if still I cannot find Thee, O God, then let me search my heart and know whether it is not rather I who am blind than Thou who art obscure, and I who am fleeing from Thee rather than Thou from me; and let me confess this my sins before Thee and seek Thy pardon in Jesus Christ my Lord. [John Baillie.]

Grace to you and peace be multiplied in the knowledge of God and of Jesus our Lord; seeing that his divine power hath granted unto us all things that pertain unto life and godliness, through the knowledge of him that called us by his own glory and virtue; whereby he hath granted unto us his precious and exceeding great promises; that through these ye may become partakers of the divine nature, having escaped from the corruption that is in the world by lust. *II Peter 1:2–4.*

Jesus who didst touch the leper,
　Deliver us from antipathies.
Who didst dwell among the Nazarenes,
　Deliver us from incompatibility.
Who didst eat with some that washed not before meat,
　Deliver us from fastidiousness.
Who didst not promise the right hand or the left,
　Deliver us from favoritism.
Who didst condone Samaritan inhospitality,
　Deliver us from affront-taking.
Who didst provide the sacred didrachma,
　Deliver us from offense-giving.
Who having called, didst recall Saint Peter,
　Deliver us from soreness.
Who didst love active Martha and contemplative Mary,
　Deliver us from respect of persons.
Deliver us today while it is called today,
　Thou who givest us today and promisest us not tomorrow.

O MOST gracious and loving Father, purify our souls from everything that may hide Thee from us. Let us feel Thy quickening power flowing through us, building us up into strength and sweetness. Consecrate our talents, our time, and our thoughts to Thy holy service. Strengthen us in body and in spirit that we may become living channels of Thy truth and Thy love. Help us to realize that Thou art present with us at all times and in all places, so that we may with perfect faith entrust ourselves and all that are dear to us to Thy never-failing care through Jesus Christ our Lord.

The boat was now in the midst of the sea, distressed by the waves; for the wind was contrary. And in the fourth watch of the night he came unto them, walking upon the sea. *Matt. 14:24, 25.*

Then he arose, and rebuked the winds and the sea; and there was a great calm. And the men marvelled, saying, What manner of man is this, that even the winds and the sea obey him? *Matt. 8:26, 27.*

And Jesus came to them and spake unto them, saying, All authority hath been given unto me in heaven and on earth. *Matt. 28:18.*

We were eyewitnesses of his majesty. *II Peter 1:16.*

Lord Christ came walking,
　Walking on the Sea,
All the little wind-swept waves
　Leaping to His knee.
Lord Christ was beautiful
　In His mastery.

I would wait a thousand years,
　Forfeiting delight,
Just to see the Lord Christ
　Coming in the night.
Through the dim and clouded stars
　Marvellously bright.

And the Hand that framed the spheres
　Would be stretched to me,
Oh, in all the radiant night
　One Face to see, —
Lord Christ, beautiful
　In His majesty.

Marion Couthouy Smith.

THOU art witness unto me, O God, that nothing can comfort me, no creature can give me rest, but Thou only, my God, whom I long to contemplate everlastingly. Be Thou favorable unto me, O Merciful Jesus, sweet and gracious Lord, and grant to me, Thy poor needy creature, to feel if it be but a small portion of Thy hearty love, and to see, though it be in part, something more of Thy beauty, that my faith may become more strong, my hope in Thy goodness may be increased, and that charity once kindled within me after the tasting of Thy heavenly manna, may never decay. Thy mercy is able to grant me the grace which I long for, and in the day when it shall please Thee to visit me most mercifully with Thy loving presence. [Thomas à Kempis (Altered).]

Truly the light is sweet, and a pleasant thing it is for the eyes to behold the sun. *Eccl. 11:7.*

Blessed be Jehovah that hath given rest unto his people Israel, according to all that he promised: there hath not failed one word of all his good promise. *I Kings 8:56.*

Godliness is profitable for all things, having promise of the life which now is, and of that which is to come. *I Tim. 4:8.*

According to his promise, we look for new heavens and a new earth, wherein dwelleth righteousness. *II Peter 3:13.*

And we have the word of prophecy made more sure; whereunto ye do well that ye take heed, as unto a lamp shining in a dark place, until the day dawn, and the day-star arise in your hearts. *II Peter 1:19.*

Upon the sadness of the sea
The sunset broods regretfully;
From the far lonely spaces, slow
Withdraws the wistful afterglow.

So out of life the splendor dies;
So darken all the happy skies;
So gathers twilight, cold and stern,
But overhead the planets burn.

And up the east another day
Shall chase the bitter dark away;
What tho' your eyes with tears be wet?
The sunrise never failed us yet.

The blush of dawn may yet restore
Our light, and hope and joy once more.
Sad soul, take comfort, nor forget
That sunrise never failed us yet!
Celia Thaxter.

MAY God Almighty, who by the Incarnation of His only begotten Son drove away the darkness of the world, and by His glorious Birth enlightened this day, drive away from us the darkness of sins, and enlighten our hearts with the light of Christian graces. And may He who willed that the great day of His most holy Birth should be told to the shepherds by an angel, pour upon us the refreshing shower of His blessing, and guide us, Himself being our shepherd, to the pastures of everlasting joy. And may He who through His incarnation united earthly things with heavenly, fill us with the sweetness of inward peace and goodwill, and make us partakers with the heavenly host: for the glory of His great Name. Amen. [*Treasury of Devotion.*]

BE AMBITIOUS TO BE QUIET

Be silent, all flesh, before Jehovah. *Zech. 2:13.*

We command and exhort in the Lord Jesus Christ, that with quietness they work, and eat their own bread. *II Thess. 3:12.*

And the work of righteousness shall be peace; and the effect of righteousness, quietness and confidence for ever. And my people shall abide in a peaceable habitation, and in safe dwellings, and in quiet resting-places. *Isa. 32:17, 18.*

That we may lead a tranquil and quiet life in all godliness and gravity. *I Tim. 2:2.*

He will not cry, nor lift up his voice, nor cause it to be heard in the street. *Isa. 42:2.*

> Why fret you at your work because
>   The deaf world does not hear and praise?
> Were it so bad, O workman true,
>   To work in silence all your days?
>
> I hear the traffic in the street,
>   But not the white worlds o'er the town:
> I heard the gun at sunset roar,
>   I did not hear the sun go down.
>
> Are work and workmen greater when
>   The trumpet blows their fame abroad?
> Nowhere on earth is found the man
>   Who works as silently as God.
>   *Samuel Valentine Cole.*

O LORD GOD and Father, Thou knowest how blind we are to Thy presence, how dead to Thy purpose and how deaf to Thy call; grant us to feel Thy guiding hand through all the scattered details of our daily life, in all the tumult to hear Thy still small voice, and in all dimness of our spirits to have a sense of Thine everlasting arms upbearing us, so that being willing to spend and be spent in Thy service, we may accomplish all that Thou wouldest, and at the last find fulfilment in the perfect freedom of Thy sole sovereignty. [*A Book of Prayers for Students.*]

THE DREAM THAT IS NO DREAM

The grace of God hath appeared bringing salvation to all men, instructing us, to the intent that, denying ungodliness and worldly lusts, we should live soberly and righteously and godly in this present world; looking for the blessed hope and appearing of the glory of the great God and our Saviour Jesus Christ. *Titus 2:11–13.*

For this cause I bow my knees unto the Father, from whom every family in heaven and on earth is named, that he would grant you, according to the riches of his glory, that ye may be strengthened with power through his Spirit in the inward man; that Christ may dwell in your hearts through faith; to the end that ye, being rooted and grounded in love, may be strong to apprehend with all the saints what is the breadth and length and height and depth, and to know the love of Christ which passeth knowledge, that ye may be filled unto all the fulness of God. *Eph. 3:14–19.*

> Thou art the quiet at the end of day.
> Thou art the peace no storms may ever mar.
> Thou art the light that cannot fade away —
> Lost be the path in darkness, Thou the star.
> Once as a dream that youth had held unreal,
> Now as a dream more real than all you see;
> Thou only — yet the symbol and the seal
> Of dreams eternal that shall come through Thee.

O LORD, in whose hands are all the issues of life, teach us how to use all that Thou hast given us. Show us how to live to the uttermost, so that we may truly know the meaning of work and love and prayer, of loyalty and of joy. Show us how to use every second of time, every ounce of strength, and every resource of energy. Forgive the wastage of the past, the indolence, the wrong attitudes, the darkness of self. Let us open all our heart and mind to Thee and receive from Thee the strength and the power, the wisdom and the joy that Thou hast promised and that Thou alone canst give. And these things that we need, O Father, we ask in ever fuller and deeper measure for those whom Thou hast given us. Thou wilt show us the path of life. In Thy presence is fullness of joy. [E. B. S.]

WE ARE ABLE IF!

With God all things are possible. *Matt. 19:26.*

All things are possible to him that believeth. *Mark 9:23.*

I endure all things. *II Tim. 2:10.*

Greater is he that is in you than he that is in the world. *I John 4:4.*

Apart from me ye can do nothing. *John 15:5.*

I can do all things in him that strengtheneth me. *Phil. 4:13.*

Somebody said that it couldn't be done
　But he with a chuckle replied,
That "maybe it couldn't," but he'd be the one
　Who wouldn't say no, till he'd tried.
So he buckled right in with the trace of a grin
　On his face. If he worried he hid it.
He started to sing as he tackled the thing
　That couldn't be done, and he did it. . . .

There are thousands to tell you it cannot be done.
　There are thousands to prophesy failure;
There are thousands to point out to you, one by one,
　The dangers that wait to assail you:
But just buckle in with a bit of a grin,
　Then take off your coat and go to it;
Just start in to sing as you tackle the thing
　That "cannot be done," and you'll do it.

Edgar Guest.

O GOD our Father, deliver us from the foolishness of self-confidence, from all boasting and vanity, from pride of energy and false notions of success. Teach us that our springs are not in ourselves but in Thee, that so far from being able to do what we will, we can neither will nor do any good except by Thy grace and with Thy help, that it is when we are weak in ourselves that we are strong in Thee, that Thy power is made perfect in our conscious lack of power that compels us to lay our helplessness on Thy strength. Here may we find our rest and feel, pouring through all our impotence, the tides of Thy mighty Spirit, for Thine is the kingdom, the power and glory. [R. E. S.]

HEAVEN AND EARTH AND
GOD'S GLORY

They shall dwell securely in the wilderness, and sleep in the woods. And I will make them and the places round about my hill a blessing; and I will cause the shower to come down in its season; there shall be showers of blessing. *Ezek. 34:25, 26.*

Feed thy people with thy rod, the flock of thy heritage, which dwell solitarily, in the forest in the midst of Carmel. *Micah 7:14.*

Lo, we heard of it in Ephrathah: we found it in the field of the wood. *Ps. 132:6.*

The wilderness and the dry land shall be glad; and the desert shall rejoice, and blossom as the rose. . . . They shall see the glory of Jehovah, the excellency of our God. *Isa. 35:1, 2.*

> Dim woodlands made him wiser far
> Than those who thresh their barren thought
> With flails of knowledge dearly bought,
> Till all his soul shone like a star
> That flames at fringe of heaven's bar
> Where breaks the surf of space unseen
> Against Time's veil which hangs between
> Heaven's wonders and the things that are.
> *Sturmer, On Richard Jefferies'* Story of My Heart.

CREATOR SPIRIT, who broodest everlastingly over the lands and waters of earth, enduing them with forms and colors which no human skill can copy, give me today, I beseech Thee, the mind and heart to rejoice in Thy creation.

Forbid that I should walk through Thy beautiful world with unseeing eyes. And above all give me grace to use these beauties of earth without me and this stirring of life within me as means whereby my soul may rise from creature to Creator, and from nature to nature's God.

O Thou whose divine tenderness doth ever outsoar the narrow loves and charities of earth, grant me today a kind and gentle heart towards all things that live, remembering that what I do unto the least of these His brethren I do unto Jesus Christ my Lord. [John Baillie (Abbreviated).]

HEIGHT AND HUMILITY

When thou art bidden, go and sit down in the lowest place; that when he that hath bidden thee cometh, he may say to thee, Friend, go up higher: then shalt thou have glory in the presence of all that sit at meat with thee. For every one that exalteth himself shall be humbled; and he that humbleth himself shall be exalted. *Luke 14:10, 11.*

The Son of man came not to be ministered unto, but to minister, and to give his life a ransom for many. *Matt. 20:28.*

He that is the greater among you, let him become as the younger; and he that is chief, as he that doth serve. For which is greater, he that sitteth at meat, or he that serveth? Is not he that sitteth at meat? but I am in the midst of you as he that serveth. *Luke 22:26, 27.*

But emptied himself, taking the form of a servant, . . . he humbled himself, becoming obedient even unto death. . . . Wherefore also God highly exalted him. *Phil. 2:7–9.*

If I then, the Lord and the Teacher, have washed your feet, ye also ought to wash one another's feet. For I have given you an example, that ye also should do as I have done to you. Verily, verily, I say unto you, A servant is not greater than his lord: neither one that is sent greater than he that sent him. *John 13:14–16.*

Wouldst thou the holy hill ascend
    And see the Father's face?
To all His children lowly bend
    And seek the humblest place.

Thus humbly doing on the earth
    What things the lofty scorn
Thou shalt assert the lofty birth
    Of all the lowly-born.
                George Macdonald.

O LORD JESUS CHRIST, Son of the Father, who though Thou wast rich didst become poor that we through Thy poverty might be made rich, who didst lay aside the glory which Thou hadst before the world was and didst become flesh, humbling Thyself to be the servant of man, and submitting even in Thy humility to the shame and suffering of the Cross, forgive us for our selfishness and our foolish pride, and grant us grace, forsaking our old ways, to follow Thee in lowliness of mind, each esteeming other better than ourselves, and looking not on our own things but on the things of others, and seeking in love to serve all who are in need.

THE GREAT DISCIPLINARIAN

Now I know in part; but then shall I know fully even as also I was fully known. *I Cor. 13:12.*

I know that this shall turn out to my salvation, through your supplication and the supply of the Spirit of Jesus Christ. *Phil. 1:19.*

Thy rod and thy staff, they comfort me. *Ps. 23:4.*

No man hath beheld God at any time: if we love one another, God abideth in us, and his love is perfected in us. *I John 4:12.*

All chastening seemeth for the present to be not joyous but grievous; yet afterward it yieldeth peaceable fruit unto them that are exercised thereby, even the fruit of righteousness. *Heb. 12:11.*

> We know Thee, each in part —
>   A portion small
> But love Thee, as Thou art —
>   The All in All:
> For Reason and the rays thereof
> Are starlight to the noon of Love.
>
> *John B. Tabb.*

Hear me, O God,
A broken heart
Is my best part;
Use still Thy rod
That I may prove
Therein Thy love.

If Thou hadst not
Been stern to me,
But left me free,
I had forgot
Myself and Thee.
Ben Jonson.

O LORD, by all Thy dealings with us, whether of joy or pain, of light or darkness, let us be brought to Thee. Let us value no treatment of Thy grace simply because it makes us happy or because it makes us sad, because it gives us or denies us what we want; but may all that Thou sendest us bring us to Thee, that knowing Thy perfectness we may be sure in every disappointment that Thou art still loving us, and in every darkness that Thou art still enlightening us, and in every enforced idleness that Thou art still using us; yea, in every death Thou art giving us life, as in His death Thou didst give life to Thy Son our Saviour, Jesus Christ. [Phillips Brooks.]

Verily I say unto you, Inasmuch as ye did it unto one of these my brethren, even these least, ye did it unto me. *Matt. 25:40.*

He saved others; himself he cannot save. *Mark 15:31.*

And pray one for another. *James 5:16.*

We preach not ourselves, but Christ Jesus as Lord, and ourselves as your servants for Jesus' sake. Seeing it is God, that said, Light shall shine out of darkness, who shined in our hearts, to give the light of the knowledge of the glory of God in the face of Jesus Christ. *II Cor. 4:5, 6.*

We all, with unveiled face beholding as in a mirror the glory of the Lord, are transformed into the same image from glory to glory, even as from the Lord the Spirit. *II Cor. 3:18.*

> One prayed in vain to trace the vision blest
> That shone upon his heart by night and day.
> But homely duties in his dwelling prest
> And hungry hearts that would not turn away
> And cares that still his eager hands bade stay.
> The canvas never knew the pictured face
> But year by year while yet the vision shone
> An angel near him wondering bent to trace
> On his own life the Master's image grown
> And unto men made known. *Mabel Earle.*

O THOU ever-blessed fountain of life, I bless Thee that Thou hast infused into me Thine own vital breath so that I am become a living soul. It is my earnest desire that I may not only live but grow, grow in grace and in the knowledge of my Lord and Saviour Jesus Christ. May I grow in patience and fortitude of soul, in humility and zeal, in spirituality and a heavenly disposition of mind and in loving and unselfish service of others. As Thou knowest I hunger and thirst after righteousness, make me whatever Thou wouldest delight to see me. Draw on my soul by the gentle influence of Thy gracious Spirit every trace and every feature which Thine eye, O heavenly Father, may survey with pleasure and which Thou mayst acknowledge as Thine own image. I ask and hope it through Him of whose fulness we have all received. [Philip Doddridge (Altered).]

GOD'S WILL OF PEACE

Oh that thou hadst hearkened to my commandments! then had thy peace been as a river, and thy righteousness as the waves of the sea. *Isa. 48:18.*

Behold, my servant, whom I uphold; my chosen, in whom my soul delighteth: I have put my Spirit upon him; he will bring forth justice to the Gentiles. He will not cry, nor lift up his voice, nor cause it to be heard in the street. . . . He will not fail nor be discouraged, till he have set justice in the earth; and the isles shall wait for his law. *Isa. 42:1, 2, 4.*

Calm soul of all things; Make it mine
  To feel amid the city's jar,
That there abides a peace of Thine
  Man did not make and cannot mar.

The will to neither strive nor cry
  The power to feel with others give!
Calm, calm me more! Nor let me die
  Before I had begun to live.
               Matthew Arnold.

Built on a Rock the Church doth stand
Even when temples are falling.
Crumbled have spires in every land
Bells still are chiming and calling,
Calling the young and old to rest
But above all the soul distressed
Longing for rest everlasting.

Surely in temples made with hands
God, the Most High, is not dwelling.
High above earth His Temple stands
All earthly temples excelling.
Yet He whom heavens cannot contain
Chose to abide on earth with men,
Built in our bodies His temple.
            N. V. S. Grundtvig.

*W*E confess, O God, that we have not obeyed the injunction of Thy Son, our Lord, to place first and foremost in all things the coming of Thy Kingdom. Give us, we beseech Thee, to realize in how many ways we have thwarted Thy will and thereby delayed Thy purpose. Help us to take the standard of heaven for the measure of earth, and to contrast the perfect obedience of those who are before the throne of God, and serve Him day and night in His temple, with the contradiction of Thy purposes all around us and within us. Help us to consider how far we can amend these things and bring the peace and joy and love of heaven into the life of earth and change earth's discord into the complete harmony of the song of the redeemed. We thank Thee that this is Thy will, and that against Thy purpose and the triumph of Thy Church the gates of hell cannot prevail. [Henry S. Lunn (Altered).]

And a man of God came near and spake unto the king of Israel, and said, Thus saith Jehovah, Because the Syrians have said, Jehovah is a god of the hills, but he is not a god of the valleys; therefore will I deliver all this great multitude into thy hand, and ye shall know that I am Jehovah. *I Kings 20:28.*

Lo, I am with you always, even unto the end of the world. *Matt. 28:20.*

I am persuaded, that neither death, nor life, nor angels, nor principalities, nor things present, nor things to come, nor powers, nor height, nor depth, nor any other creature, shall be able to separate us from the love of God, which is in Christ Jesus our Lord. *Rom. 8:38, 39.*

> Our eyes look up to those who stand
>   Vicegerents of Thy stainless sway,
> Heroes and saints at Thy right hand,
>   Thy priests and kings of glory they.
> Not ours to tread the path they trod,
>   Splendid and sharp, still stretching higher;
> Not ours to lay before our God
>   The crowns they snatched from flood and fire.
>
> Yet through the daily dazing toil,
>   The crowding tasks of hand and brain,
> Keep pure our lips, Lord Christ, from soil,
>   Keep pure our lives from sordid gain.
> Come to the level of our days,
>   The lowly hours of dust and din,
> And in the valley-lands upraise
>   Thy kingdom over self and sin.   *Mabel Earle.*

O GOD, who through the mighty Resurrection of Thy Son Jesus Christ our Lord from the dead hast delivered us from the power of darkness and brought us into the Kingdom of Thy love; grant, we beseech Thee, that as by His death He has recalled us into life, so by His Presence ever abiding in us He may raise us to the joy of eternal victory; through Him who for our sakes died and conquered death and rose again and is ever with us in power and great glory, even the same Jesus Christ. [*The Kingdom, the Power and the Glory* (Altered.)]

As for me, I shall behold thy face in righteousness; I shall be satisfied, when I awake, with beholding thy form. *Ps. 17:15.*

Thomas answered and said unto him, My Lord and my God. Jesus saith unto him, Because thou hast seen me thou hast believed: blessed are they that have not seen, and yet have believed. *John 20:28, 29.*

And they said to the woman, Now we believe, not because of thy speaking: for we have heard for ourselves, and know that this is indeed the Saviour of the world. *John 4:42.*

Let not your heart be troubled: believe in God, believe also in me. . . . Peace I leave with you; my peace I give unto you: not as the world giveth, give I unto you. Let not your heart be troubled, neither let it be fearful. *John 14:1, 27.*

The word which he sent unto the children of Israel, preaching good tidings of peace by Jesus Christ (he is Lord of all) — that saying ye . . . know. *Acts 10:36, 37.*

He is our peace. *Eph. 2:14.*

The peace of God, which passeth all understanding, shall guard your hearts and your thoughts in Christ Jesus. *Phil. 4:7.*

Thou shalt know Him when He comes,
Not by any din of drums,
Nor the vantage of His airs
Nor by anything He wears,
Neither by His crown
Nor His gown.
But His presence known shall be
By the holy harmony
Which His coming makes in thee.

O GOD, who art peace everlasting, whose chosen reward is the gift of peace and who hast taught us that the peacemakers are Thy children; pour Thy peace into our souls that everything discordant may utterly vanish, and all that makes for peace be loved and sought by us always through Jesus Christ our Lord. [*Mozarabic.*]

O Thou who art the light of the minds that know Thee, the life of the souls that love Thee, and the strength of the hearts that serve Thee; help us so to know Thee that we may truly love Thee; so to love Thee that we may fully serve Thee whom to serve is perfect freedom: through Jesus Christ our Lord. [*Gelasian Sacramentary.*]

Rejoice, O young man, in thy youth, and let thy heart cheer thee in the days of thy youth, and walk in the ways of thy heart, and in the sight of thine eyes. . . . Remember also thy Creator in the days of thy youth, before the evil days come. *Eccl. 11:9; 12:1.*

And he went down with them, and came to Nazareth; and he was subject unto them: and his mother kept all these sayings in her heart. And Jesus advanced in wisdom and stature, and in favor with God and men. *Luke 2:51, 52.*

I have fought the good fight, I have finished the course, I have kept the faith. *II Tim. 4:7.*

We are more than conquerors through him that loved us. *Rom. 8:37.*

God who created me
  Nimble and light of limb,
In three elements free,
  To run, to ride, to swim:
Not when the sense is dim,
  But now from the heart of joy,
I would remember Him:
  Take the thanks of a boy.

Jesus, King and Lord,
  Whose are my foes to fight,
Gird me with Thy sword
  Swift and sharp and bright.
Thee would I serve if I might:
  And conquer if I can,
From day dawn till night,
  Take the strength of a man.
         H. C. Beeching.

*M*ost heartily do we thank Thee, O Lord, for Thy mercies of every kind, and Thy loving care over all Thy creatures. We bless Thee for the gift of life, for Thy protection round about us, for Thy guiding hand upon us, and the many tokens of Thy love; especially for the saving knowledge of Thy dear Son our Saviour, and for the living presence of Thy Spirit, our Comforter. We thank Thee for friendship and duty; for health and strength; for precious memories and good hopes; for the joys that cheer us and for the trials that teach us to trust in Thee; for the courage of Christ our Captain and Companion. O heavenly Father, make us wise unto a right use of all Thy gracious benefits and blessings, and so direct and sustain us that in word and deed we may show gratitude to Thee and do Thy perfect will, through Jesus Christ, our Lord. [*The Book of Common Worship,* Revised (Altered).]

THE TEACHING OF THE TREES

The God of our fathers raised up Jesus, whom ye slew, hanging him on a tree. *Acts 5:30.*

Now from the fig tree learn her parable. *Matt. 24:32.*

Blessed are they that wash their robes, that they may have the right to come to the tree of life, and may enter in by the gates unto the city. *Rev. 22:14.*

Hurt not the earth, neither the sea, nor the trees, till we shall have sealed the servants of our God on their foreheads. *Rev. 7:3.*

The earth is full of the lovingkindness of Jehovah. *Ps. 33:5.*

His glory is above the earth and the heavens. *Ps. 148:13.*

> O dreamy, gloomy, friendly Trees,
>   I came along your narrow track
> To bring my gifts unto your knees
>   And gifts did you give back;
> For when I brought this heart that burns —
>   These thoughts that bitterly repine —
> And laid them here among the ferns
>   And the hum of boughs divine,
> Ye, vastest breathers of the air,
>   Shook down with slow and mighty poise
> Your coolness on the human care,
>   Your wonder on its toys,
> Your greenness on the heart's despair,
>   Your darkness on its noise.   *Herbert Trench.*

O GOD, who hast made this fair world and given it to all men richly to enjoy, help me never to grow dull to all its wonder. Because so many of its glories are familiar, let me not forget how wonderful they are. Keep my eyes open to the beauty of blue sky, to the changing pageant of the clouds, to the silver mystery of moonlight and to the majesty of silent stars. May I feel in every sunrise a miracle of life and light renewed, and in every sunset a pledge of Thine unfading light without which we cannot face the dark. So may no single day be common, but may each one bring the benediction of its immortal brightness to my soul, through Jesus Christ our Lord. [W. Russell Bowie.]

When he drew near to the gate of the city, behold, there was carried out one that was dead, the only son of his mother, and she was a widow. *Luke 7:12.*

And behold, there came a man named Jairus, and he was a ruler of the synagogue: and he fell down at Jesus' feet, and besought him to come into his house; for he had an only daughter, about twelve years of age, and she was dying. *Luke 8:41, 42.*

Make thee mourning, as for an only son, most bitter lamentation. *Jer. 6:26.* Read *Gen. 22:1–14; 1 Kings 17:17–24.*

A widow — she had only one!
A puny and decrepit son;
   But, day and night,
Though fretful oft, and weak and small,
A loving child, he was her all —
   The Widow's Mite.

The Widow's Mite — aye, so sustained,
She battled onward, nor complained,
   Though friends were fewer;
And while she toiled for daily fare,
A little crutch upon the stair
   Was music to her.

I saw her then; and now I see
That, though resigned and cheerful, she
   Has sorrowed much:
She has — He gave it tenderly —
Much faith; and, carefully laid by,
   A little crutch.   *Frederick Locker-Lampson.*

*A*LMIGHTY and Everlasting God, the Comfort of the sad and the Strength of sufferers, let the prayers of those that cry out of any tribulation come unto Thee; that all may rejoice to find that Thy mercy is present with them in their afflictions. Remember the poor and needy, the childless and all those who once had an only child, for Thou also, O Father, didst have an Only Child who died.

And he hath said unto me, My grace is sufficient for thee: for my power is made perfect in weakness. Most gladly therefore will I rather glory in my weaknesses, that the power of Christ may rest upon me. Wherefore I take pleasure in weaknesses, in injuries, in necessities, in persecutions, in distresses, for Christ's sake: for when I am weak, then am I strong. *II Cor. 12:9, 10.*

Over against W. E. Henley's braggart lines which he entitled "Invictus" ("Unconquered"), are to be set Dorothea Day's verses, "The Captain," which might be entitled "More than Conqueror":

Invictus

Out of the night that covers me,
Black as the pit from pole to pole,
I thank whatever gods may be
For my unconquerable soul.

In the fell clutch of circumstance
I have not winced or cried aloud.
Under the bludgeoning of chance
My head is bloody, but unbowed.

Beyond this place of wrath and tears
Looms but the horror of the shade,
And yet the menace of the grave
Finds and shall find me unafraid.

It matters not how strait the gate,
How charged with punishment the
  scroll,
I am the master of my fate
I am the captain of my soul.

The Captain

Out of the light that dazzles me,
Bright as the sun from pole to pole
I thank the God I know to be
For Christ — the Conqueror of my
  soul.

Since His the sway of circumstance
I would not wince, nor cry aloud.
Under that rule which men call
  chance,
My head, with joy, is humbly bowed.

Beyond this place of sin and tears,
That life with Him — and His the aid
That, spite the menace of the years,
Keeps, and will keep me, unafraid.

I have no fear though strait the gate:
He cleared from punishment the
  scroll.
Christ is the Master of my fate!
Christ is the Captain of my soul.

*N*ow unto him that is able to do exceeding abundantly above all that we ask or think, according to the power that worketh in us, unto Him be the glory in the church and in Christ Jesus unto all generations for ever and ever.

THE LORD'S SONG

The Lord's song. *Ps. 137:4.*

And they sing the song of Moses the servant of God, and the song of the Lamb. *Rev. 15:3.*

Jehovah is my strength and my song. *Ex. 15:2.*

He hath put a new song in my mouth. *Ps. 40:3.*

In the night his song shall be with me. *Ps. 42:8.*

None other Lamb, none other Name,
   None other Hope in heaven or earth or sea,
None other Hiding Place from guilt and shame,
   None beside Thee.

My faith burns low, my hope burns low;
   Only my heart's desire cries out in me,
By the deep thunder of its want and woe,
   Cries out to Thee.

Lord, Thou art Life, though I be dead;
   Love's Fire Thou art, however cold I be;
Nor heaven have I, nor place to lay my head,
   Nor home, but Thee.   *Christina Rossetti.*

My Father, prepare a place for the child-life that lingers in my heart! Even in the night teach me the song of the coming day. Thou hast prepared a place for my yesterday — Thou hast cancelled the dark deeds of my past. Thou hast prepared a place for today — Thou hast promised strength for the hour. But I have a need beyond my yesterday, beyond today; I have a yearning for tomorrow. Shall this be the only part of my soul for which there is no environment! Thou hast provided for memory — Thou hast suffered my heart to see its past glorified. Thou hast provided for the vision of today — Thou hast sent the energy with the emergency and the refuge with the storm. But is there to be no provision for hope, O my Father! It *cannot* be, O my Father. O my Father, it is not. Behold, the Lamb of God! He is our Light in darkness, our Song in the night, the bright and morning star, our joy and hope, the same yesterday, today, tonight, tomorrow, now and to eternity.
[George Matheson (Altered).]

The souls of the righteous are in the hand of God, and no torment shall touch them. In the eyes of the foolish they seemed to have died; and their departure was accounted to be their hurt, and their journeying away from us to be their ruin: but they are in peace. For even if in the sight of men they be punished, their hope is full of immortality; and having borne a little chastening, they shall receive great good; because God made trial of them, and found them worthy of himself. As gold in the furnace he proved them, and as a whole burnt offering he accepted them. And in the time of their visitation they shall shine. *Wisdom of Solomon 3:1-7.*

And he [Jesus] said unto him, Verily I say unto thee, To-day shalt thou be with me in Paradise. *Luke 23:43.*

> When Lazarus left his charnel-cave,
>   And home to Mary's house return'd,
>   Was this demanded — if he yearn'd
> To hear her weeping by his grave.
>
> "Where wert thou, brother, those four days?"
>   There lives no record of reply,
>   Which telling what it is to die
> Had surely added praise to praise.
>
> From every house the neighbors met,
>   The streets were fill'd with joyful sound,
>   A solemn gladness even crown'd
> The purple brows of Olivet.
>
> Behold a man raised up by Christ!
>   The rest remaineth unreveal'd;
>   He told it not; or something seal'd
> The lips of that Evangelist.   *Tennyson.*

O GOD, the God of the spirits of all flesh, in whose embrace all creatures live, in whatsoever world or condition they be, I beseech Thee for those whose name and dwelling and every need Thou knowest. Lord, vouchsafe them light and rest, peace and refreshment, joy and consolation in Paradise, in the companionship of saints, in the presence of Christ, in the ample folds of Thy great love. [A friend of Sir Henry Lunn (Altered).]

CHRIST, OUR LIFE

Christ . . . our life. *Col. 3:4.*

Your life is hid with Christ in God. *Col. 3:3.*

To me to live is Christ. *Phil. 1:21.*

Know ye not that your bodies are members of Christ? . . . He that is joined unto the Lord is one spirit. *I Cor. 6:15, 17.*

In the sight of God speak we in Christ. *II Cor. 12:19.*

Christ liveth in me. *Gal. 2:20.*

As lyre and the musician,
As thought and spoken word,
As rose and fragrant odours,
As flute and breath accord,
So deep the bond that binds me
  To Christ, my Lord.

As mother and her baby,
As traveler lost and guide,
As oil and flickering lamp-flame
Are each to each allied;
Life of my life, Christ bindeth
  Me to His side.

As lake and streaming rain fall,
As fish and waters clear,
As sun and gladdening day spring
In union close appear,
So Christ and I are holden
  In bonds how dear.

Narayan Vaman Tilak.

Lord Jesus, who didst rise from the dead to die no more; grant us so to die to sin that with Thee we may rise to newness of life. Lord Jesus, who didst raise Thy body to a new and glorious condition; grant us ever to serve Thee in purity of flesh and spirit; Lord Jesus, who didst die for our sins and rise again to be our justification; apply to us, we pray Thee, in the Sacraments of Thy grace the merits of Thy Cross and Passion. Lord Jesus, who didst promise to be with Thy disciples all days, even unto the end, grant us always to remember Thine unseen Presence and to rely upon Thine ever ready aid. Lord Jesus, come and dwell in our hearts that we may be one with Thee. Even as Thou wast in the Father and the Father was in Thee, so do Thou be one with us. [A. C. A. Hall (Altered).]

WOULD THAT HE MIGHT COME!

They shall not hurt nor destroy in all my holy mountain; for the earth shall be full of the knowledge of Jehovah, as the waters cover the sea. *Isa. 11:9.*

Behold, he cometh with the clouds; and every eye shall see him, and they that pierced him; and all the tribes of the earth shall mourn over him. *Rev. 1:7.*

They cry " He comes! "
The signs are sure, the mystic number is fulfilled,
He comes.
   We answer, O that He would come!
We want the Christ, we want a God
To burn afresh the truth upon the forehead of the world.
We want a man to walk again. . . .

O for the Christ again!
Already Christ is coming, hear ye not?
The footfalls of the Lord.
He comes, the Spirit of a riper age
When all that is not good and true shall die,
When all that's bad in custom, false in creed,
And all that makes the boor and mars the man
Shall pass away for ever. Yes, He comes
To give the world a passion for the truth,
To inspire us with a holy human love,
To make us sure that ere a man can be
A Saint, he first must be a man.

O THOU KING, Eternal, Immortal and Invisible, Thou only wise God our Saviour, hasten, we beseech Thee, the coming of Thy Kingdom upon earth and draw the whole world of mankind into willing obedience to Thy blessed reign. Overcome all the enemies of Christ and bring low every power that is exalted against Him. Cast out all the evil things which cause wars and fightings among us and let Thy Spirit rule the hearts of men in righteousness and love. Manifest Thy will, Almighty Father, in human brotherhood and bring in universal peace, through the coming and victory of Christ our Lord. [*The Book of Common Worship,* Revised (Altered).]

Then shall they also answer, saying, Lord, when saw we thee hungry, or athirst, or a stranger, or naked, or sick, or in prison, and did not minister unto thee? Then shall he answer them, saying, . . . Inasmuch as ye did it not unto one of these least, ye did it not unto me. *Matt. 25:44, 45.*

They crucify to themselves the Son of God afresh, and put him to an open shame. *Heb. 6:6.*

If a brother or sister be naked and in lack of daily food, and one of you say unto them, Go in peace, be ye warmed and filled; and yet ye give them not the things needful to the body; what doth it profit? *James 2:15, 16.*

When Jesus came to Golgotha they hanged Him on a tree,
They drave great nails through hands and feet and made a Calvary;
They crowned Him with a crown of thorns, red were His wounds and
    deep,
For those were crude and cruel days, and human flesh was cheap.

When Jesus came to Birmingham they simply passed Him by,
They never hurt a hair of Him, they only let Him die;
For men had grown more tender and they could not give Him pain.
They only just passed down the street and left Him in the rain.

Still Jesus cried, "Forgive them for they know not what they do,"
And still it rained the winter rain that drenched Him through and
    through;
The crowds went home and left the streets without a soul to see,
And Jesus crouched against a wall and cried for Calvary.

Studdert-Kennedy.

O<small>UR</small> Father, we look back on the years that are gone and shame and sorrow come upon us, for the harm we have done and the good we have failed to do rise up in our memory to accuse us. Grant that in the days still left to us we may heal that which we have hurt and do that which we should have done. Grant that for every harm we have done we may do some brave act of salvation, and that for every soul that has stumbled or gone unhelped at our fault we may bring to Thee some other one whose strength has been renewed by our love, that so Christ may be comforted. [Walter Rauschenbusch (Altered).]

And he saith unto them, Come ye yourselves apart into a desert place, and rest a while. *Mark 6:31.*

And they constrained him, saying, Abide with us; for it is toward evening, and the day is now far spent. And he went in to abide with them. *Luke 24:29.*

Your life is hid with Christ in God. *Col. 3:3.*

I am with you always. *Matt. 28:20.*

Alone with Jesus! fades the daylight slowly,
    Soft o'er the earth, shades of the evening fall,
As worn and weary with the day's temptations,
    My spirit answers to the Saviour's call.

Alone with Jesus! from the day's hard conflict,
    What have I brought that I His grace may win!
Only the burden of my sin and longing,
    Only the same heart-cry, Forgive my sin.

Alone with Jesus! He hath seen each wandering,
    Hath watched each failure from His throne above,
And yet, tonight He bids me come confiding
    In the great wealth of His unchanging love.

Alone with Jesus! here can come no sorrow;
    From pain and conflict, here my soul is free.
This be my prayer tonight: O Jesus, Saviour,
    Teach me through life to dwell alone with Thee.

*L*ET us not seek out of Thee what we can find only in Thee, O Lord, peace and rest and joy and bliss, which abide only in Thy abiding joy. Lift up our souls above the weary round of harassing thoughts to Thy Eternal Presence. Even lift up our souls to the pure, bright, serene, radiant atmosphere of Thy Presence, that there we may breathe freely, there repose in Thy Love, there be at rest from ourselves and from all things that weary us; and then to return with Thy peace to do and be what shall please Thee, and to serve our fellows in love and rest and joy. [E. B. Pusey (Altered).]

As far as the east is from the west, so far hath he removed our transgressions from us. *Ps. 103:12.*

Thou hast cast all my sins behind thy back. *Isa. 38:17.*

Thou wilt cast all their sins into the depths of the sea. *Micah 7:19.*

And their sins and their iniquities will I remember no more. *Heb. 10:17.*

If we confess our sins, he is faithful and righteous to forgive us our sins, and to cleanse us from all unrighteousness. *1 John 1:9.*

"Now I have won a marvel and a truth,"
So spake the Soul and trembled, — "dread and ruth
Together mixed; for I did sin of yore;
But this (so said I oft) was long ago, —
So put it from me far away; but, lo!
With Thee is neither After nor Before,
O Lord, and clear within the noonlight set
Of one illimitable Present, yet
Thou lookest on my fault as it were now.
So will I mourn and humble me; yet Thou
Art not as man, that oft forgives a wrong
Because he half forgets it, Time being strong
To wear the crimson of guilt's stain away: —
For Thou, forgiving, dost so in a Day
That shows it clearest, — in the boundless sea
Of Mercy and Atonement utterly,
Casting our pardoned trespasses behind, —
No more remembered, or to come to mind,
Set aside from us as East from West away."

O THOU whose love can be in the heart of man as a fire to burn up all that is shameful and evil, let me now lay hold upon Thy perfect righteousness and make it my own. Blot out all my transgressions and let my sins be covered. Lead me in battle, O God, against my secret sins. Fence round my life with a rampart of pure desire. And let Christ be formed in my heart through faith. All this I ask for his Holy Name's sake. [John Baillie (Altered).]

God is light, and in him is no darkness at all. If we say that we have fellowship with him and walk in the darkness, we lie and do not the truth: but if we walk in the light, as he is in the light, we have fellowship one with another, and the blood of Jesus his Son cleanseth us from all sin. *I John 1:5–7.*

Except Jehovah build the house, they labor in vain that build it: except Jehovah keep the city, the watchman waketh but in vain. *Ps. 127:1.*

Come unto me, all ye that labor. *Matt. 11:28.*
That our God may lighten our eyes. *Ezra 9:8.*

The mighty master Michel Angelo,
   While working with his chisel, oft was known
To place above his head a candle prone,
That every stroke should be within its glow,
That he across his art should never throw
   The shadow of himself; but carve each stone
   In free accord with promptings from the Throne
To his responsive genius here below.

So may thy love above my forehead shine
   That neither shadows of a weary mood
   Nor self-reflections of a mystic mind
Shall mar the lives God wills me to refine.
   Oh, tender spirit radiating good
   Illuminate my toil for humankind.
               Stephen Van Rensselaer Trowbridge.

GRANT unto us, O Lord, that knowledge of ourselves without which we can neither rightly repent nor seek to amend our lives. Illumine for us the ways of life and the beauty of character by which we may so judge ourselves that we may not too greatly fear Thy judgment of us. May we offer ourselves wholly and without any fear to the searching of Thy love, humbly accepting Thy rebukes and seeking only to be what Thou wouldst have us be. In His Name who knew what was in the hearts of men and knowing still loved them. [Gaius Glenn Atkins.]

A NEW LIFE

We were buried therefore with him through baptism unto death: that like as Christ was raised from the dead through the glory of the Father, so we also might walk in newness of life. *Rom. 6:4.*

If the Spirit of him that raised up Jesus from the dead dwelleth in you, he that raised up Christ Jesus from the dead shall give life also to your mortal bodies through his Spirit that dwelleth in you. *Rom. 8:11.*

If any man is in Christ, there is a new creation. *II Cor. 5:17 marg.*

Rigid I lie in a winding sheet
  Which my own hands did weave
My narrow cell is myself, *myself*
  Whose wall I may not cleave.

But in the dawn of the early morn
  A clear Voice seems to say,
"I am the Lord of the final Word —
  Ye may not say Me nay."

"Unfold your hands that your broth-
  er's need
May ever find them free,
Unbind your feet from their winding
  sheet —
Henceforth they walk with Me."

And lo, I hear! I am blind no more!
  I am no longer dumb!
Out from the doom of a self-wrought
  tomb
Pulsate with life I come.
  Rose Trumbull.

LORD of life, Thou art not the dead Christ, or we were of all men most miserable. Our tears are turned into joy as we remember Thy words: "After three days I will rise again." All hail, risen Christ! We glory in Thy triumph over death and the grave, and say: "Thanks be to God who giveth us the victory through our Lord Jesus Christ." In Thy triumph we mortals of yesterday can face death, the last enemy, rejoicing in the final and complete victory of our Lord and Saviour, Jesus Christ. Ascended Lord, fulfill in us the last promise of Christ and send upon us, we beseech Thee, the power of the Holy Spirit, that we may be witnesses to all men of Thy power, the Crucified, to lead captivity captive, and to receive gifts for men, and to give to man life in abundance, Almighty God, who commanded the light to shine out of darkness, shine in our hearts to give the light of the knowledge of the glory of God in the face of our Risen and Ascended Lord, and make us to live in Him, the living One, who was dead and lo! He is alive forevermore. [Henry S. Lunn (Altered).]

DOORS

I am the door; by me if any man enter in, he shall be saved, and shall go in and go out, and shall find pasture. *John 10:9.*

A great door and effectual is opened unto me, and there are many adversaries. *I Cor. 16:9.*

I came to Troas for the gospel of Christ, and . . . a door was opened unto me in the Lord. *II Cor. 2:12.*

These things saith he that is holy, he that is true, he that hath the key of David, he that openeth and none shall shut, and that shutteth and none openeth: I know thy works (behold, I have set before thee a door opened, which none can shut). *Rev. 3:7, 8.*

Behold, I stand at the door and knock: if any man hear my voice and open the door, I will come in to him, and will sup with him, and he with me. *Rev. 3:20.*

> I am the Door that nevermore shall close
> Though time run out his sands, and ocean's roar
> In silence sinks where pale oblivion flows —
> I am the Door.
> By Me ye shall go in, by Me shall store
> Your wealth in heavenly mansions of repose —
> By Me not going out forevermore.
> Beyond all sound or silence ocean knows,
> Beyond all wrecks that sands of time deplore;
> Beyond the dawn that through death's orient glows —
> I am the Door.   *William James.*

O THOU Divine Spirit that, in all events of life, art knocking at the door of my heart, help me to respond to Thee. I would have my heart open at all times to receive Thee, — at morning, noon and night; in spring and summer and winter. Knock and I shall open unto Thee. I am the door. Knock upon me.

And, blessed Lord, Thou art the Door, the Door to truth and life and love and joy. Thou art the Door of God. I do not need to knock. I need only to come and Thou art worthy to receive me. Thou art the Door of home, my home with God forever, my home in God here today. Give me grace to enter into Thee and through Thee now. [George Matheson (Altered).]

THE FULFILLING OF LOVE
AND LIGHT

For as the rain cometh down and the snow from heaven, and returneth not thither, but watereth the earth, and maketh it bring forth and bud, and giveth seed to the sower and bread to the eater; so shall my word be that goeth forth out of my mouth: it shall not return unto me void, but it shall accomplish that which I please, and it shall prosper in the thing whereto I sent it. *Isa. 55:10, 11.*

In the morning sow thy seed, and in the evening withhold not thy hand; for thou knowest not which shall prosper, whether this or that, or whether they both shall be alike good. *Eccl. 11:6.*

Through love be servants one to another. *Gal. 5:13.*

A pilgrim journeyed o'er life's way —
  The path was steep and long:
He bore his burden mournfully,
  When, lo! he heard love's song;
And though he ne'er the singer knew,
With joy he did his way pursue.

A traveller journeyed in the night:
  The way was dark and drear;
He knew not whence to seek a light,
  When, lo! a ray most clear:
And though by unseen hand 'twas held
The darkness was at once dispelled.

The singer sang her song, nor knew
  The joy its singing lent.
The hand that held the light so true
Ne'er knew of rays it sent,
Yet such is Love's most perfect way,
That no good deed shall e'er decay.
         Lillian Olive Huey.

O FATHER, that there may be in me such love and light for the help of other lives, I make my prayer the words of this "Invocation":

Eternal Light, throughout all ages shining,
  Shine once again upon this heart of mine;
Thy flaming glory knoweth no declining —
  Rekindle now my waning light by Thine.
         [Dwight J. Bradley.]

WARFARE

Fight the good fight of the faith, lay hold on the life eternal. *1 Tim. 6:12.*

And they overcame him because of the blood of the Lamb, and because of the word of their testimony; and they loved not their life even unto death. *Rev. 12:11.*

The prophets: who through faith subdued kingdoms, wrought righteousness, obtained promises, stopped the mouths of lions, quenched the power of fire, escaped the edge of the sword, from weakness were made strong, waxed mighty in war, turned to flight armies of aliens. *Heb. 11:32–34.*

O ye who dare go forth with God,
Behold His flag unfurled
And hear His trumpets' challenge ring
Across the answering world,
For His great war with sin and shame,
Though coward hearts refuse,
Go, draw the sword that in His name
You shall find strength to use.

The citadels He bids you storm
Are walled with ancient wrong;
The foes He bids you shock against
Are insolent and strong.
Where fleshly lusts and greed for gain
Make dens for souls to die,
For rescue from that poisoned pain
The bitter voices cry.

The bitter voice goes up to God
From the dark house of shame,
'Mid iron wheels of driving toil
And from the men they maim:
From every stricken child who lies
In some foul room and drear,
From those who watch with sodden eyes
To whom no hope comes near.

Where sordidness and pain and sin
Cry for the avenging sword,
Where selfish ease and indolence
Call for the blazing word:
There God's clear trumpet summons those
Who dare to face the wrong,
And launch against His Spirit's foes
The strength which He makes strong.
W. R. Bowie.

O GOD, who maketh the frail children of men to be Thy glad soldiers in the conquest of sin and misery, breathe Thy Spirit, we pray Thee, into the people of this land and all countries that they may come together in faith and fellowship, and stand up as an exceeding great army for the deliverance of the oppressed and for the triumph of Thy Kingdom. Through Jesus Christ our Master.

OUR SAVIOUR JESUS CHRIST

There is born to you this day in the city of David a Saviour, who is Christ the Lord. *Luke 2:11.*

When the kindness of God our Saviour, and his love toward man, appeared, not by works done in righteousness, which we did ourselves, but according to his mercy he saved us, through the washing of regeneration and renewing of the Holy Spirit, which he poured out upon us richly, through Jesus Christ our Saviour; that, being justified by his grace, we might be made heirs according to the hope of eternal life. *Titus 3:4-7.*

I am not skilled to understand,
What God hath willed, what God
    hath planned,
I only know at God's right hand
Stands One who is my Saviour.

I take God at His word and deed,
Christ died to save me, this I read;
And in my heart I feel a need
Of Him to be my Saviour.

I am poor; oblation have I none,
None for a Saviour but Himself alone.
Whate'er I render Thee, from Thee it came;
And if I give my body to the flame,
My patience, love and energy divine
Of heart and soul and spirit, all are Thine.
Oh vain attempt to expurge the mighty score!
The more I pay, I owe Thee still the more.
                Madame Guyon.

O GOD, our Father, teach us by the suffering of Thy Son, our Saviour, how we, being troubled in spirit, may come, if we will, into the realm of Thy power. Deliver us from all bitterness, from all hopelessness in failure and enable us to face each day with sweetness and purity of soul, patience of mind, and steadiness of will. In full confidence of Thy love do we lift up our prayer, knowing that Thou art equal to all our needs. Save us from selfishness and self-pity and help us to be mindful of others who are called upon to suffer. As we are strengthened by Thy grace, may we be a source of strength to those who also walk through the valley of the shadow; in the name of Christ our Lord. [Whitney S. K. Yeaple (Altered).]

LIFE UNTO GOD

We are debtors, not to the flesh, to live after the flesh: for if ye live after the flesh, ye must die; but if by the Spirit ye put to death the deeds of the body, ye shall live. For as many as are led by the Spirit of God, these are sons of God. *Rom. 8:12–14.*

If I could live to God for just one day
    One blessed day, from early dawn of light
    Till purple twilight deepened into night —
    A day of faith unfaltering, trust complete
    Of love unfeigned and perfect charity,
Of hope undimmed, of courage past dismay,
    Of heavenly peace, patient humility —
    No hint of duty to constrain my feet,
    No dream of ease to lull to listlessness,
    Within my heart no root of bitterness,
No yielding to temptation's subtle sway —
    Methinks in that one day would so expand
    My soul to meet such holy, high demand,
    That never, never more could hold me bound
    This shrivelling husk of self that wraps me round.
So might I henceforth live to God alway.
                   Susan E. Gammon.

O THOU who art the Way, the Truth and the Life, who didst come in the flesh of humanity that we who are of this flesh might have life abundantly in Thee, help us to accept Thee and Thy gift. Be Thou our life today. May the mind that was in Thee be in us, that every thought of ours this day may be in captivity to Thine obedience. May our wills conform in all things small and great to Thy will. May we walk in the light, as Thou art in the light, and, cleansed from all sin by Thy blood, may we have fellowship one with another in home and in work today, and fellowship above all and through all with Thee. As Thou didst invite Thy first disciples to come to Thee and to go with Thee, and to abide where Thou didst abide, so may we hear Thy call to us today and straightway rise up to follow Thee in all the moments of this day, that it may be filled with the holiness and peace and strength and joy of Thy presence. [R. E. S.]

Comfort one another. *1 Thess. 4:18.*

Blessed be the God and Father of our Lord Jesus Christ, the Father of mercies and God of all comfort; who comforteth us in all our affliction, that we may be able to comfort them that are in any affliction, through the comfort wherewith we ourselves are comforted of God. *II Cor. 1:3, 4.*

Thy rod and thy staff, they comfort me. *Ps. 23:4.*

Be ye kind one to another, tenderhearted, forgiving each other, even as God also in Christ forgave you. *Eph. 4:32.*

> Comfort one another
> For the way is often dreary
> And the feet are often weary
>   And the heart is very sad.
> There is heavy burden-bearing
> When it seems that none are caring,
>   And we half forget that ever we were glad.
>
> Comfort one another
> With the handclasp, close and tender;
> With the sweetness love can render,
>   And the look of friendly eyes.
> Do not wait with grace unspoken
> While life's daily bread is broken;
>   Gentle speech is oft like manna from the skies.

BLESSED JESUS, who didst bid all those who carry heavy burdens to come unto Thee, refresh us with Thy Presence and Thy power. Quiet our understandings and lay Thy comfort on our hearts by bringing us close to things infinite and eternal, to Thyself, the infinite and eternal Son of the Father. Open to us the Mind of God, that in Thy Light we may see light and in Thy peace find rest. Crown Thy choice of us to be Thy servants by making us springs of strength and joy for those whom Thou hast sent us to serve. Help us to comfort others with the comfort wherewith we ourselves have been comforted of God. Set our hearts at liberty from the service of ourselves and let it be our meat and drink as it was Thine to do the will of God. [*A Book of Prayers for Students* (Altered).]

Thy King cometh unto thee. *Matt. 21:5.*

Keep the commandment, without spot, without reproach, until the appearing of our Lord Jesus Christ: which in its own times he shall show, who is the blessed and only Potentate, the King of kings, and Lord of lords; who only hath immortality, dwelling in light unapproachable; whom no man hath seen, nor can see: to whom be honor and power eternal. *1 Tim. 6:14-16.*

Christ may dwell in your hearts. *Eph. 3:17.*

For thus saith the high and lofty One that inhabiteth eternity, whose name is Holy: I dwell in the high and holy place, with him also that is of a contrite and humble spirit, to revive the spirit of the humble, and to revive the heart of the contrite. *Isa. 57:15.*

King Jesus is a Gentle Man —
  Gentle in work an' deed;
His words fa' lik the early dew;
  He breaks nae bruised reed.
He didna scorn the sinfu' lass
  That longed for peace wi' heav'n;
He saw her tears, He read her heart,
  An' sent her hame forgiv'n.
    We'll hae nae King but Jesus!
    We've throned Him in our
      very hearts,
    And canna let Him gang.

An' Jesus is our Saviour;
  He saves us ane an' a':
He kens oor sorrows, bears oor sins,

An's never far awa';
For tho' in heaven He has His hame,
  Wi' saint an' seraphim,
His Kingdom is in human heart,
  We'll hae nae King but Him.
    We'll hae nae King but Jesus
    We've waited for Him lang
    He hauds oor hearts, we maunna
      pairt —
    We canna let Him gang.

We'll hae nae King but Jesus!
  We've made oor holy tryste;
God help us aye to keep it true:
  Nae King, nae King but Christ.

O LORD GOD, our Heavenly Father, we thank Thee for Thy grace that Thou hast sent us Thy Son, and hast appointed Him to be the King of righteousness, and our Saviour and Redeemer, who should rescue us from the dominion of darkness, and bestow on us righteousness, salvation and blessedness. May He take up His abode among us and within us, and may we ever continue in His kingdom and allegiance. [*The Riga Prayer Book.*]

I will arise and go to my father. . . . But while he was yet afar off, his father saw him, and ran, and fell on his neck. *Luke 15:18, 20.*

Herein is love, not that we loved God, but that he loved us, and sent his Son to be the propitiation for our sins. . . . We love, because he first loved us. *1 John 4:10, 19.*

Christ also suffered . . . that he might bring us to God. *1 Peter 3:18.*

It is God who worketh in you. *Phil. 2:13.*

> I will arise and to my Father go;
>   This very hour the journey is begun.
> I start to reach the blissful goal, and lo,
>   My spirit at one bound her race has run.
> For seeking God and finding Him are one:
> He feeds the rillets that towards Him flow.
>   It is the Father who first seeks the son,
> And moves all heavenward movement, swift or slow.
> I dare not pride myself on finding Him,
>   I dare not dream a single step was mine:
> His was the vigor in the palsied limb —
>   His the electric fire along the line —
> When drowning, His the untaught power to swim,
>   Float o'er the surge, and grasp the Rock Divine.
>   *John Charles Earle.*

I GIVE Thee humble thanks, O heavenly Father, that Thou hast vouchsafed to call me to the knowledge of Thy peace and to faith in Thee. May my whole life be one thanksgiving unto Thee for all which Thou hast given and for all which Thou hast forgiven; for Thy call to me when I was thoughtless of Thee, for the constraint of Thy love which sought me ere I loved Thee, for all Thine open and Thy hidden blessings, and for those which in my negligence I have passed over, for every gift of nature or of grace, for my power of loving; for all which Thou hast yet in store for me, for everything whether joy or sorrow, whereby Thou art drawing me to Thyself. There and there only would I be, in Thy loving care and Presence, O my Father God. [*Prayers from Ancient and Modern Sources* (Altered).]

CLEAVING TO TRUTH

With my soul have I desired thee in the night; yea, with my spirit within me will I seek thee earnestly. *Isa. 26:9.*

And now, . . . little children, abide in him; that, if he shall be manifested, we may have boldness, and not be ashamed before him at his coming. *I John 2:28.*

Abhor that which is evil; cleave to that which is good. *Rom. 12:9.*

Thou shalt love the Lord thy God with all thy heart, and with all thy soul, and with all thy mind, and with all thy strength. *Mark 12:30.*

Now in life's breezy morning
  Here on life's sunny shore,
To all the powers of falsehood
  We vow eternal war.

Eternal hate to falsehood:
  And then as needs must be,
O Truth, O Lady peerless,
  Eternal love to thee.

All fair things that seem true things
  Our hearts shall aye receive,
Not overquick to seize them,
  Nor overloath to leave:

Not overloath or hasty
  To leave them or to seize,
Not eager still to wander,
  Nor clinging still to ease.

But one vow links us ever
  That whatso'er shall be,
Nor life, nor death shall sever
  Our souls, O Truth, from Thee.   *Ernest Myers.*

O GOD, Thou infinite and solemn Presence; if we have not had Thee in all our thoughts, it is that we are not pure enough to see Thee. We have pleased ourselves instead of serving Thee; we have lived in this world without remembering that it is Thine. We have fled with coward spirit from the earnest battle of life, and have made a shameful peace with our temptations. We have believed rather the flatteries of selfish desire, than the stern voice of duty and the inspiration of true affection. . . .

Enlarge our souls with a divine charity that we may hope all things, believe all things, endure all things, and become messengers of Thy healing mercy to the grievances and infirmities of men. [James Martineau.]

Brethren, even if a man be overtaken in any trespass, ye who are spiritual, restore such a one in a spirit of gentleness; looking to thyself, lest thou also be tempted. Bear ye one another's burdens, and so fulfil the law of Christ. *Gal. 6:1, 2.*

Woe to him that is alone when he falleth, and hath not another to lift him up. *Eccl. 4:10.*

And I looked, and there was none to help; and I wondered that there was none to uphold. *Isa. 63:5.*

Through love be servants one to another. For the whole law is fulfilled in one word, even in this: Thou shalt love thy neighbor as thyself. *Gal. 5:13, 14.*

> If you were toiling up a weary hill,
>   Bearing a load beyond your strength to bear,
> Straining each nerve untiringly, and still
>   Stumbling and losing foothold here and there;
> And each one passing by would do so much
>   And give one upward lift and go their way,
> Would not the slight, reiterated touch
>   Of help and kindness lighten all the day?
>
> There is no little and there is no much;
>   We weigh and measure and define in vain;
> A look, a word, a light responsive touch
>   Can be the minister of joy to pain.
> A man can die of hunger walled in gold;
>   A crumb may quicken hope to stronger breath.
> And every day we give or we withhold
>   Some little thing that tells for life or death.

MAY Thy most holy will be done by me and by all pilgrims here below, in the perfect performance of Thy precepts, and all Thy good pleasure, as readily and constantly all the days and moments of our life on earth, as it is done by the blessed. Out of the boundless treasury of Thy mercy pardon us all the sins we have committed in thought, word, deed or by omission, against Thee and against our neighbors, as we forgive all their offences. [Father Christ Mayer.]

For all this I laid to my heart, even to explore all this: that the righteous, and the wise, and their works, are in the hand of God. *Eccl. 9:1.*

My times are in thy hand. *Ps. 31:15.*

Into thy hand I commend my spirit. *Ps. 31:5.*

There shall thy hand lead me, and thy right hand shall hold me. *Ps. 139:10.*

Humble yourselves therefore under the mighty hand of God. *1 Peter 5:6.*

The judgment of God is according to truth. *Rom. 2:2.*

Lay Thy hand upon me
  When I fall asleep,
Through the silent hours
  Close beside me keep:
Then the Prince of Darkness,
  Ruler of the air
Will not dare to touch me
  If Thy hand is there.

Lay Thy hand upon me,
  Tenderly restrain
All too eager longings
  Every impulse vain:
Calm my spirit's chafing
  Restless with long care:
Murmurs melt in silence
  When Thy hand is there.

Lay Thy hand upon me
  When I rashly stray
Into paths forbidden,
  Choosing my own way.
Oh! how much correction,
  Lord, I have to bear
Yet must take it meekly,
  For Thy hand is there.

Lead me now and always
  Even to the last,
Till the way is ended
  And the darkness past:
Till I reach the glory
  I was born to share,
This its crown and centre,
  That my Lord is there.

C. M. Noel.

LORD, make me to know Thee aright, that I may more and more love, and enjoy, and possess Thee. And since in the life here below, I can not fully attain this blessedness, let it at least grow in me day by day, until it all be fulfilled at last in the life to come. Here be the knowledge of Thee increased, and there let it be perfected. Here let my love to Thee grow, and there let it ripen; that my joy being here great in hope, may there in fruition be made perfect. Through Jesus Christ our Lord. [Saint Anselm.]

When a man voweth a vow unto Jehovah, or sweareth an oath to bind his soul with a bond, he shall not break his word. *Num. 30:2.*

When thou shalt vow a vow unto Jehovah thy God, thou shalt not be slack to pay it: for Jehovah thy God will surely require it of thee. *Deut. 23:21.*

He is faithful and righteous to forgive us our sins. *1 John 1:9.*

Said I not so, that I would sin no more?
    Witness my God, I did;
Yet I am run again upon the score:
    My faults cannot be hid.
What shall I do? Make vows and break them still?
    'Twill be but labor lost;
My good cannot prevail against mine ill:
    The bus'ness will be crost.

O say not so: thou canst not tell what strength
    Thy God may give thee at the length;
Renew thy vows, and if thou keep the last,
    Thy God will pardon all the past. . . .

Thy God hath not denied thee all,
    While He permits thee but to call:
Call to thy God for grace to keep
    Thy vows; and if thou break them, weep.
Weep for thy broken vows, and vow again:
Vows made with tears cannot be made in vain.
    Then once again
I vow to mend my ways;
    Lord, say "Amen,"
And Thine be all the praise.   *George Herbert.*

ALMIGHTY and merciful God, the Fountain of all goodness, who knowest the thoughts of our hearts, we confess unto Thee that we have sinned against Thee, and done evil in Thy sight. Wash us, we beseech Thee, from the stains of our past sins, and give us grace and power to put away all hurtful things; so that, being delivered from the bondage of sin, we may bring forth worthy fruits of repentance. [Alcuin.]

I am in a strait betwixt the two, having the desire to depart and be with Christ; for it is very far better: yet to abide in the flesh is more needful for your sake. *Phil. 1:23, 24.*

Whether we live, we live unto the Lord; or whether we die, we die unto the Lord: whether we live therefore, or die, we are the Lord's. *Rom. 14:8.*

> I know not which to choose; whether to live
> A little longer here or to depart.
> That would be sweet, to be at rest, to toil
> No more; no more feel pain, to have no griefs,
> No anxious fears, nor for myself, nor others, —
> That would be sweet: and sweeter still to have
> No more to sin, affection or desire.
> But to be near, and feel that nearness near
> Unto my Lord; to have a thrilling sense
> Of blessedness, the eternity of joy
> At hand yet greater, safe, forever safe.
> So to be resting would be sweet. And yet
> To live for Christ, to live to do His pleasure:
> To fight the fight, clad in His panoply,
> Knowing that He looks on the while, and smiles
> By love unfathomable ever moved.
> To go and tell to others of His grace
> The bliss unutterable of the life
> That is in Him,
> Surely a life so spent is blessedness,
> And all too little to repay His love. . . .
> Which shall I choose? — living to live to Christ,
> Or dying, die to Him, — which shall I choose?
> Whichever of the twain more to Thy glory be
> *That,* Lord, I pray Thou wilt appoint for me.   *H. Swinney.*

I THANK Thee, O Lord, that Thou hast so set eternity within my heart that no earthly thing can ever satisfy me wholly. I thank Thee that every present joy is so mixed with sadness and unrest as to lead my mind upwards to the contemplation of a more perfect blessedness. [John Baillie.]

THE DOUBLE SEARCH

The Son of man came to seek and to save that which was lost. *Luke 19:10.*

What man of you, having a hundred sheep, and having lost one of them, doth not leave the ninety and nine in the wilderness, and go after that which is lost, until he find it? *Luke 15:4.*

He is a rewarder of them that seek after him. *Heb. 11:6.*

They . . . say unto him, All are seeking thee. *Mark 1:37.*

They . . . came to Capernaum, seeking Jesus. *John 6:24.*

I am found of them that sought me not. *Isa. 65:1.*

There are two gone out on the starless wild
  Gone out 'neath the desert night:
Earth's sad and weary and homeless child,
  And Heaven's fair Lord of Light.

And one is seeking forlorn and blind,
  Can give to his loss no name;
But the Other knows well what He stoops to find —
  Knows well what He comes to claim.

Though the hills are dark, though the torrents roll,
  By each must his path be trod;
Both seek, for the Saviour has lost the soul,
  And the soul has lost its God. . . .

I can hear the sound of their nearing feet
  By a sure attraction drawn;
Those night-long seekers shall timely meet
  As the darkness dies in the dawn.

*A*LMIGHTY GOD, we give Thee thanks for the mighty yearning of the human heart for the coming of a Saviour, and the constant promise of Thy Word that He was to come. We bless Thee for the tribute that we can pay to Him from our very sense of need and dependence, and that our own hearts can so answer from their wilderness, the cry, " Prepare ye the way of the Lord." O God, prepare Thou the way in us now, and may we welcome anew Thy Holy Child. [Samuel Osgood.]

CHRIST'S HANDS AND OURS

In all things I gave you an example, that so laboring ye ought to help the weak, and to remember the words of the Lord Jesus, that he himself said, It is more blessed to give than to receive. *Acts 20:35.*

Hereby know we love, because he laid down his life for us: and we ought to lay down our lives for the brethren. *I John 3:16.*

Herein is love, not that we loved God, but that he loved us, and sent his Son to be the propitiation for our sins. Beloved, if God so loved us, we also ought to love one another. *I John 4:10, 11.*

Be perfected; be comforted; be of the same mind; live in peace: and the God of love and peace shall be with you. *II Cor. 13:11.*

A pair of little hands I see,
Two chubby infant hands so wee,
Clutching sweet Mary's face in glee.

Two boyish hands, sturdy and brown
Holding the plane in Nazareth town
In Joseph's shop as the sun goes down.

Two hands of a youth older grown
Folded in prayer by a rugged stone
Out on the hill top, all alone.

A young man's hands, toil marked
  and strong,
Seeking to aid in the restless throng
The helpless victims of sin and wrong.

Two tired hands 'neath the olive tree
In the Garden of grey Gethsemane
Clasped for my sins in agony.

Two hands outstretched on a cross of
  wood,
From cruel nail wounds red with
  blood
Bringing a lost world back to God.

O hands of my Crucified Christ divine
Take into Thine own these hands of mine
And teach them to serve with a love like Thine.

Bell Mona Menzies.

O BLESSED LORD, who hast commanded us to love one another, grant us grace that having received Thine undeserved bounty, we may love every one in Thee and for Thee. We implore Thy clemency for all; but especially for the friends whom Thy love has given to us. Love Thou them, O Thou Fountain of love, and make them to love Thee with all their heart, that they may will, and speak and do those things only which are pleasing to Thee. [Saint Anselm.]

Come unto me, all ye that labor and are heavy laden, and I will give you rest. Take my yoke upon you, and learn of me; for I am meek and lowly in heart: and ye shall find rest unto your souls. *Matt. 11:28.*

Surely goodness and lovingkindness shall follow me all the days of my life. *Ps. 23:6.*

The path of the righteous is as the dawning light, that shineth more and more unto the perfect day. *Prov. 4:18.*

When passing southward I may cross the line
Between the Arctic and Atlantic Oceans,
I may not tell by any tests of mine,
By any startling signs or strange commotions
    Across my track.
But if the days grow sweeter one by one,
And e'en the icebergs melt their hardened faces,
If sailors linger, basking in the sun,
I know I must have made the change of places
    Some distance back.

When answering timidly my Master's call,
I passed the bourne of life in coming to Him,
When in my love for Him I gave up all,
The very moment when I thought I knew Him,
    I cannot tell.
But as unceasingly I feel His love,
As this cold heart is melted to o'erflowing,
As now so clear the light shines from above,
I marvel at the change and press on, knowing
    That all is well.

Lᴏʀᴅ, I thank Thee that Thy love constraineth me. I thank Thee that, in the great labyrinth of life, Thou waitest not for my consent to lead me. I thank Thee that Thou leadest me by a way which I know not, by a way which is above the level of my poor understanding. . . . Protect me from the impetuous desires of my nature — desires as short-lived as they are impetuous. Ask me not where I would like to go; tell me where to go; lead me in Thine own way; hold me in Thine own light. Amen.   [George Matheson.]

LIFE THROUGH DEATH

All chastening seemeth for the present to be not joyous but grievous; yet afterward it yieldeth peaceable fruit unto them that have been exercised thereby, even the fruit of righteousness. *Heb. 12:11.*

Beneath the cover of the sod
The lily heard the call of God:
Within its bulb so strangely sweet
Answering pulse began to beat.
The earth lay damply, dark and cold
And held the smell of grave and mold,
But never did the lily say:
"Oh, who shall roll the stone away?"
It heard the call, the call of God,
And up through prison house of sod
It came from burial place of gloom
To find its perfect life in bloom!

O soul of mine, cling not to earth!
God calls thee to the glad new birth;
No coverlid of death or sod
Can keep thee from the will of God.
Thus things that seem to shut out day
Shall at God's voice be rolled away,
And thou shalt find that night and gloom
Were meant to help thy joy to bloom!
That through the ministry of death
We reach the ecstasy of breath!
O Soul of mine, God's voice is sweet,
O fuller life, I feel thy beat;
I rise through night and death and sod
To wake and find myself with God.

Mary McGee Snell.

*H*ELP us, O God of our life, to bear our pain as Thy beloved Son bore His trials and passion, so that we may gather strength out of weakness and suffering and consecrate our sorrows even as He did. [*A Prayer Book for Soldiers and Sailors.*]

Verily, verily, I say unto you, If ye shall ask anything of the Father, he will give it you in my name. *John 16:23.*

Your sins are forgiven you for his name's sake. *I John 2:12.*

Dear Lord . . . as evening shades around me fall,
    One prayer I make:
Blot out the faults and failures of this day,
    For Jesus' sake.

For His dear sake who trod alone for me,
    Through weary days,
The paths of earthly sorrow, pain, and loss, —
    Such dreary ways, —
Who carried all my sins upon the cross,
    That I might take
All joy forevermore; through Him I ask, —
    For Jesus' sake.

No other name have I with which to plead
    At heaven's gate,
When, worn with failures oft and sore mistakes,
    I sadly wait;
But lo! all clouds and darkness disappear,
    And sunlight wakes;
Sweet peace comes down in answer to my plea, —
    " For Jesus' sake."

And so, as twilight shadows deeper fall,
    And night comes on,
I bring to Him the seeming failures all,
    The victories won:
And through His mighty love and boundless grace,
    New strength I take;
While God's own hand wipes all the tears away, —
    For Jesus' sake.   *Ella M. Parks.*

O FATHER of our Lord Jesus Christ, who didst send Thy Son to suffer and die for us on this earth, make us truly and sincerely thankful for this and for all Thine other benefits; and for Thy long suffering with the sins and sorrows of men we thank Thee, O Lord. [*A Book of Prayers for Students* (Altered).]

Go out quickly into the streets and lanes of the city, and bring in hither the poor and maimed and blind and lame. And the servant said, Lord, what thou didst command is done, and yet there is room. And the lord said unto the servant, Go out into the highways and hedges and constrain them to come in, that my house may be filled. *Luke 14:21–23.*

> Our Lord made His feast and had three friends,
> The Lord at the head of the table spread,
> Welcomes whoso attends.

"Upon a threshold," quoth one guest, "a woman wept with child at breast."
"A felon whispered," quoth one guest, "asking where the hunted rest."
"From an alley," quoth one guest, "whined a fool, disease-distressed."

> Our Lord's eye burns with the wrath of heaven.
> "Ye shall not dine, ye friends of Mine
> Save as we number seven."

"Find yon mother," saith the Lord, "straightway fetch her to My board."
"Find the hunted," saith the Lord, "fetch him as My closest ward."
"Find yon alley," saith the Lord, "fetch the beggar you abhorred."

> "My table is spread for the lost and the least.
> Bring hither the three who are dear to Me
> Without them none shall feast."

O GOD, Thou great Redeemer of mankind, our hearts are tender in the thought of Thee, for in all the afflictions of our race, Thou hast been afflicted, and in the sufferings of Thy people it was Thy body that was crucified. Thou hast been wounded by our transgressions and bruised by our iniquities, and all our sins are laid at last on Thee. Amid the groaning of creation we behold Thy Spirit in travail till the sons of God shall be born in freedom and holiness. . . .

Fill us now with hunger and thirst for justice that we may bear glad tidings to the poor and set at liberty all who are in the prison house of want and sin. [Walter Rauschenbusch.]

And ye shall call upon me, and ye shall go and pray unto me, and I will hearken unto you. And ye shall seek me, and find me, when ye shall search for me with all your heart. *Jer. 29:12.*

> Jesus went up into the hills to pray,
>   Did He?
> Sure, and I can't do that;
> Here with Pat, bless him —
> Down on his back for more than a year
> Ever since the wreck on the " G,"
> With taking in washing every day.
> All I can do
> Is to steal around to old St. Bridget's
> On Seventh Avenue.
> And do you think the Lord minds?
> Faith, the hills are beautiful green.
>   *Arthur B. Heeb*

A garden so well watered before morn
Is hotly up, that not the swart sun's blaze,
Down beating with unmitigated rays,
Nor scorching winds from arid deserts borne,
Shall quite prevail to leave it bare and shorn
Of its green beauty, shall not quite prevail
That all its morning freshness shall exhale,
Till evening and the evening dews return —
A blessing such as this our hearts might reap,
The freshness of the garden they might share,
Through the long day an heavenly freshness keep,
If knowing how the day and the day's glare
Must beat upon them, we would largely steep
And water them betimes with dews of prayer. *Trench.*

O ALMIGHTY GOD, from whom every good prayer cometh, and who pourest out on all who desire it the spirit of grace and supplication; deliver us when we draw nigh to Thee from coldness of heart and wanderings of mind, that with steadfast thoughts and kindled affections we may worship Thee in spirit and in truth, through Jesus Christ our Lord. [William Bright.]

I WILL NOT FEAR

The Lord is my shepherd; I shall not want. He maketh me to lie down in green pastures; he leadeth me beside still waters. . . . Yea, though I walk through the valley of the shadow of death, I will fear no evil; for thou art with me. *Ps. 23:1, 2, 4.*

And the sea is no more. . . . And death shall be no more. . . . There shall be no night there. *Rev. 21:1, 4, 25.*

As always, so now also Christ shall be magnified in my body, whether by life, or by death. *Phil. 1:20.*

Our Saviour Christ Jesus, who abolished death, and brought life and immortality to light through the gospel. *II Tim. 1:10.*

> Dawn and the bounding sea,
> Dawn with its rapture free;
> I stand on the cliffs by the wind-swept shore,
> Where wanton the waves o'er the drifted sands,
> Caressing each dune with their foamy hands, —
> This life I adore and its conquering roar
> Rolls out from the far-off, flashing gates
> Of dawn on the wild blue sea,
> Dawn, with its rapture free.
>
> Night and the moaning sea,
> Night, and eternity;
> I am borne in the dark to the water's edge,
> My shroud is clutched by the hands of the tide —
> The chill wind shrieks, and from far and wide
> Comes the groan of the surge on each hidden ledge;
> But a Light shines clear, and I cease to fear
> Night, and the endless sea
> Night, and eternity. *John Theodore Troth.*

O MERCIFUL GOD, the Father of our Lord Jesus Christ, who is the Resurrection and the Life: in whom whosoever believeth, shall live, though he die; and whosoever liveth, and believeth in Him, shall not die eternally; . . . We humbly beseech Thee, O Father, to raise us from the death of sin unto the life of righteousness; that, when we shall depart this life, we may rest in Him. [*A Prayer Book for Soldiers and Sailors.*]

Now then do it. *II Sam. 3:18.*

Ever learning, and never able to come to the knowledge of the truth. *II Tim. 3:7.*

One thing I do, forgetting the things which are behind, and stretching forward to the things which are before, I press on. *Phil. 3:13, 14.*

One thing thou lackest. *Mark 10:21.*

What prayer, O God, shall I send up tonight,
  Kneeling here a suppliant, with bowed head?
For I tonight would pray that, in Thy sight,
  The things I need the least remain unsaid,
  Only the one great need of all be hallowéd.

I do not pray for purposes and plans;
  Of these I have had many, and have still;
The finger of God's holy hand slow scans
  The rhythm of my life and finds a fill
  Of these, — all honorable, — not one among them ill.

Oh not for purposes and plans I pray;
  My life is glutted with ambitions vast
Each treading on the heels of each; — but may
  I plead for constancy and strength to cast
  Some single resolution to the last
  Point of success or failure, — ere my day be past.

ALMIGHTY GOD and Heavenly Father, who by Thy divine Providence, hast appointed for each one of us our work in life, and hast commanded that we should not be slothful in business, but fervent in spirit, serving Thee, help us always to remember that our work is Thy appointment, and to do it heartily as unto Thee. Preserve us from slothfulness, and make us to live with loins girded and lamps burning, that, whensoever our Lord may come, we may be found striving earnestly to perfect the work that Thou hast given us to do; through the same Jesus Christ our Saviour. [Dean Goulburn.]

For everything there is a season, and a time for every purpose under heaven: a time to be born, and a time to die; a time to plant, and a time to pluck up that which is planted. *Eccl. 3:1, 2.*

Fire and hail, snow and vapor; stormy wind, fulfilling his word; mountains and all hills; fruitful trees and all cedars; . . . both young men and virgins; old men and children: Let them praise the name of Jehovah. *Ps. 148:8, 9, 12, 13.*

And we know that to them that love God all things work together for good, even to them that are called according to his purpose. *Rom. 8:28.*

If all my year were summer, could I know
What my Lord means by His " made white as snow "?
If all my days were sunny, could I say
" In His fair land He'll wipe all tears away "?

If I were never weary, could I keep
Close to my heart, " He gives His lov'd sleep "?
Were no graves mine, might not I come to deem
The life eternal but a baseless dream?

My winter, yea my tears, my weariness,
Even my graves may be His way to bliss;
I call them ills, yet surely that can be
Nothing but good that shows my Lord to me.

O THOU whose secret is with the reverent and humble soul, save us from intellectual pride and the weakness of a selfish judgment. We would see things as they are and not merely as they affect ourselves. We would see them steadily and as a whole and with Thy light shining upon them. We would have a wise and modest estimate of our own power and live in full contact with all things, high and true and good. Teach us our failings and faults, give us courage to acknowledge them and by Thy grace enable us to overcome them. Lift us above the unstable currents of our self-will, and establish us on the rock of Thy purposes. [John Hunter.]

CHRIST AND WOMANHOOD

She . . . called Mary her sister secretly, saying, The Teacher is here, and calleth thee. *John 11:28.*

God sent forth his Son, born of a woman. *Gal. 4:4.*

And the women, who had come with him out of Galilee, followed after, and beheld the tomb, and how his body was laid. And they returned, and prepared spices and ointments. And on the sabbath they rested according to the commandment. But on the first day of the week, at early dawn, they came unto the tomb, bringing the spices which they had prepared. *Luke 23:55 to 24:1.*

> O woman hearts, that keep the days of old
>   In living memory, can you stand back
>   When Christ calls? Shall the Heavenly Master lack
> The serving love which is your life's fine gold? . . .
>
> Do you forget who bade the morning break,
>   And snapped the fetters of the iron years?
>   The Saviour calls for service: from your fears
> Rise, girt with faith, and work for His dear sake.

O GOD, our Father, we thank Thee that Thine only-begotten Son took our nature upon Him and was born of a Virgin, that He grew up under a mother's loving care and that on His cross He made sure of a home for her with His dearest friend. We thank Thee for His constant tenderness toward all women and for His first meeting on the Resurrection morning. We thank Thee for His influence through all the centuries in protecting women from wrong, in securing justice and equality, in opening the paths of service. And we thank Thee for the faith and devotion with which women in all ages and in all lands have answered Thy love in Him, and in fidelity and sacrifice fulfilled Thy will. Wherever they still suffer injustice and wrong we pray Thee to deliver them. Wherever their power is wasted on inferior ends, recall them to their great mission. Help them as they mould the future in the child life that is in their care, to believe in the possibility of Thy Kingdom and to train for its citizenship that which Thou hast entrusted to them, in the Name of Thy Holy Child Jesus. [R. E. S.]

Be ye stedfast, unmovable, always abounding in the work of the Lord, forasmuch as ye know that your labor is not vain in the Lord. *I Cor. 15:58.*

Work out your own salvation with fear and trembling; for it is God who worketh in you. *Phil. 2:12, 13.*

We must work the works of him that sent me, while it is day: the night cometh, when no man can work. *John 9:4.*

To talk with God no breath is lost,
  Talk on, talk on;
To walk with God no strength is lost,
  Walk on, walk on;
To grind the axe no work is lost,
  Grind on, grind on;
The work is quicker, better done,
Nor needing half the strength laid
    on —
  Grind on, grind on.

Martha stood, but Mary sat,
Martha murmured much at that,
Martha cared but Mary heard,
Listening to the Master's Word,
And the Lord her choice preferred,
  Sit on, hear on;
  Work without God is labor lost,
  Work on, work on;
Full soon you'll learn it to your cost,
  Toil on, toil on;

    Little is much when God is in it,
      Much is little everywhere,
    Man's busiest day is not worth God's minute,
      If God the labor do not share.
    Go work with God, and nothing's lost,
    Who works with Him does best and most,
      Work on, work on.

O LORD, forasmuch as all our strength is in Thee, grant unto us this grace, that we may allow Thee to do whatsoever Thou wilt; and that our doing may be to lie still in Thy hand that Thou mayest do with us that thing only which is most pleasing to Thee. Do Thou adorn us with holy virtues, giving unto us humbleness of mind, purity of heart, and all those gifts and graces which Thou knowest to be needful for us, and whatsoever Thou wouldst have to be in us, whether in body or soul; that so we may be able the better to please Thee, the more worthily and faithfully to serve Thee, and the more perfectly to love Thee. [Ludovicus Palma.]

Lo, I am with you always, even unto the end of the world. *Matt. 28:20.*

Fear not; for I am with thee: I will bring thy seed from the east, and gather thee from the west; I will say to the north, Give up; and to the south, Keep not back; bring my sons from far, and my daughters from the end of the earth. *Isa. 43:5, 6.*

Hills of the North, rejoice
  River and mountain spring
Hark to the advent voice
  Valley and lowland sing
Though absent long your Lord is nigh
He judgment brings and victory.

Lands of the East, awake
  Soon shall your sons be free
The sleep of ages, break
  And rise to liberty
On your far hills, long cold and grey,
Has dawned the everlasting day.

Isles of the Southern seas
  Deep in your coral caves
Pent be each warring breeze
  Lull'd by your restless waves
He comes to reign with boundless
    sway
And make your wastes His great
    highway.

Shores of the utmost West
  Ye that have waited long
Unvisited, unblest,
  Break forth to swelling song;
High raise the note that Jesus died,
Yet lives and reigns — the Crucified!

Shout, while ye journey home
  Songs be in every mouth;
Lo, from the North we come,
  From East and West and South:
City of God, the bond are free:
We come to live and reign with Thee.
            Charles Edward Oakley.

O GOD, who hast made the most glorious Name of our Lord Jesus Christ, Thine only-begotten Son, to be exceedingly precious and supremely lovable to Thy faithful servants, and a protection against all evil; mercifully grant that all who devoutly venerate this Name of Jesus on earth may in this life receive the sweetness of Holy Comfort and in the life to come attain the joy of great gladness and never-ending praise; through the same Jesus Christ our Lord. [*The Devotional Companion.*]

Whosoever would become great among you, shall be your minister; and whosoever would be first among you, shall be servant of all. For the Son of man also came not to be ministered unto, but to minister, and to give his life a ransom for many. *Mark 10:43-45.*

Let no man seek his own, but each his neighbor's good. *I Cor. 10:24.*

Love . . . seeketh not its own. *I Cor. 13:4, 5.*

> One knelt within a world of care
> And sin, and lifted up his prayer:
> "I ask Thee, Lord, for health and power
> To meet the duties of each hour;
> For peace from care, for daily food,
> For life prolonged and filled with good." . . .
>
> But as he prayed, lo! at his side
> Stood the thorn-crowned Christ, and sighed:
> "O blind disciple, — came I then
> To bless the selfishness of men? . . .
>
> "My gift is sacrifice; my blood
> Was shed for human brotherhood, . . .
> Come, leave thy selfish hopes, and see
> Thy birthright of humanity! . . .
> Spend and be spent, yearn, suffer, give,
> And in thy brethren learn to live."

O LORD, give us more charity, more self-denial, more likeness to Thee. Teach us to sacrifice our comforts to others and our likings for the sake of doing good. Help us to think of others rather than ourselves, in honor and service preferring one another. Make us kindly in thought, gentle in word, generous in deed. Teach us that it is better to give than to receive, better to forget ourselves than to put ourselves forward; better to minister than to be ministered unto. Especially make us unselfish, mindful of others in our prayers. Enroll us in the school of faithful intercession. And unto Thee, the God of Love, be all glory and praise, both now and forevermore. [Henry Alford.]

THE TEACHER AND HIS ASSISTANTS

And he [God] gave some to be . . . teachers. *Eph. 4:11.*

Whosoever shall do and teach them [these least commandments], he shall be called great in the kingdom of heaven. *Matt. 5:19.*

I was appointed . . . a teacher . . . in faith and truth. *1 Tim. 2:7.*

And the teachers shall shine as the brightness of the firmament; and they that turn many to righteousness as the stars for ever and ever. *Dan. 12:3 and margin.*

It were well for him if a millstone were hanged about his neck, and he were thrown into the sea, rather than that he should cause one of these little ones to stumble. *Luke 17:2.*

> A moment more and they will gather — some
> With faces shy, and some with eager smiles;
> With welcoming eyes, and all the little wiles
> That speak of love and trust though lips are dumb.
> Soon this hushed room will quicken with the hum
> Of many voices, and these narrow aisles
> Will feel the tread of softly-walking files —
> Only a moment more and they will come.
> O, I am glad today that I may stand
> Again within the walls of this glad place:
> Dwelling once more in Life's bright borderland,
> A tenant in Youth's country for a space;
> Holding awhile sweet Childhood by the hand —
> Teacher of little children, by God's grace!
>
> *Marion B. Craig.*

WE beseech Thee to hear us, O Lord, for all teachers, that they may find in Christ the continual renewal and deepening of spirit which they need; for those with no love for children or teaching that they may not cause any little child to stumble or to miss Thy gracious will. Lead every teacher to the Great Teacher to learn of Him patience, wisdom, skill, understanding, sympathy, tenderness and strength. And may every school be a true home for the child-spirit, bathing it in true affection and opening wide its door to Thee, the Source and Giver of life. [*A Book of Prayers for Students* (Altered).]

And Jehovah God called unto the man, and said unto him, Where art thou? And he said, I heard thy voice in the garden, and I was afraid. *Gen. 3:9, 10.*

There is no fear in love: but perfect love casteth out fear. *I John 4:18.*

Whose children ye now are, if ye do well, and are not afraid with any terror. *I Peter 3:6 and margin.*

> I am afraid of silence, when, if spoken,
>   A word would save a soul from scandal's flame;
> Afraid of speech, if what I say might fasten
>   The stain of calumny upon a name. . . .
>
> I am afraid of plenty, when my brother
>   Is not invited to the feast I spread;
> I am afraid of fasting, when my hunger
>   Craves not the riches of the Living Bread!
>
> I am afraid to let Love's altar candles
>   Grow dim and flicker for the want of care;
> I am afraid to let hate's flaring torches
>   Burn high within the secret place of prayer.
>
> I am afraid to bind what should be broken;
>   Afraid to break what evermore should stay —
> O Gracious Courage, keep me ever fearing
>   To hear "Depart" upon the Judgment Day!
>   *Anna Rozilla Craver.*

O FATHER of mercies and God of all comforts, who by Thy Blessed Son hast declared that all sins shall be forgiven unto the sons of men upon their true repentance, let this most comfortable word support us Thy servants against the temptations of the devil. Though our sins are great, they cannot be too great for Thy mercy, which is infinite. O give us true repentance for all the errors of our life past, and stedfast faith in Thy Son Jesus Christ, that our sins may be done away by Thy mercy; through the merits of the same Jesus Christ our Lord, that thus all fear may go from us save the fear of missing Thy will and displeasing Thee. [Bishop Thomas Wilson (Altered).]

THESE LITTLE ONES

And whosoever shall give to drink unto one of these little ones a cup of cold water only, in the name of a disciple, verily I say unto you he shall in no wise lose his reward. *Matt. 10:42.*

See that ye despise not one of these little ones. *Matt. 18:10.*

Because of one small, low-laid head all crowned
    With golden hair,
Forevermore all fair young brows to me
    A halo wear;
I kiss them reverently. Alas! I know
    The pain I bear. . . .

Because of little pallid lips, which once
    My name did call,
No childish voice in vain appeal upon
    My ears doth fall;
I count it all my joy their joys to share
    And sorrows small.

Because of little dimpled hands
    Which folded lie,
All little hands henceforth to me do have
    A pleading cry;
I clasp them as they were small wandering birds
    Lured home to fly.

Because of little death-cold feet, for earth's
    Rough roads unmeet,
I'd journey leagues to save from sin or harm
    Such little feet,
And count the lowliest service done for them
    So sacred — sweet!

DEAR LORD, who didst become a child for love of us, grant Thy loving pity to all children under age who labor for daily wages in this land of ours or anywhere in Thy world. Touch the hearts of those who through thoughtlessness or love of gain consider not their weak and tender years. Assist the passing of just laws in their behalf, free them from their bondage, and bring them to the joyful inheritance of the children of God, for Thy Name's sake. [*S. C. H. C.*]

BEYOND PEACE

And it came to pass, when Moses came down from mount Sinai with the two tables of the testimony in Moses' hand, when he came down from the mount, that Moses knew not that the skin of his face shone by reason of his [God's] speaking with him. *Ex. 34:29*

I know a man in Christ, fourteen years ago (whether in the body, I know not; or whether out of the body, I know not; God knoweth), such a one caught up even to the third heaven. And I know such a man (whether in the body, or apart from the body, I know not; God knoweth), how that he was caught up into Paradise, and heard unspeakable words, which it is not lawful for a man to utter. *II Cor. 12:2-4.*

Who has known heights and depths, shall not again
Know peace — not as the calm heart knows
Low ivied walls; a garden close;
The old enchantment of a rose.
And though he tread the humble ways of men,
He shall not speak the common tongue again.

Who has known heights, shall bear forevermore
An incommunicable thing
That hurts his heart, as if a wing
Beat at the portal, challenging;
And yet — lured by the gleam his vision wore —
Who once has trodden stars seeks peace no more.
Eleanor Davidson.

On this new day we come to Thee, gracious Father, to thank Thee for life and all the good it holds for us. Thou hast revealed to us a destiny far more wonderful than our utmost dreams could have pictured. Give us courage, we pray Thee, to fulfill this high purpose by obedience to Thy will, and consecration to the holy ends of life. Aid us in our endeavors after the best that the present and the future can bring. With spirit undismayed may we follow after the ideals of righteousness and true holiness, never losing sight of the light that leads us on. We ask for the sake of Christ, in whom we have seen the depths and the heights of Love's possibility and Life's. [*The Daily Altar* (Altered).]

I am the light of the world: he that followeth me shall not walk in the darkness, but shall have the light of life. *John 8:12.*

Ye are the light of the world. A city set on a hill cannot be hid. Neither do men light a lamp, and put it under the bushel, but on the stand; and it shineth unto all that are in the house. Even so let your light shine before men; that they may see your good works, and glorify your Father who is in heaven. *Matt. 5:14–16.*

I have set thee for a light of the Gentiles. *Acts 13:47.*

His lamp am I, to shine where He shall say;
And lamps are not for sunny rooms, nor for the light of day,
But for dark places of the earth,
Where shame, and wrong, and crime have birth;
And for the murky twilight ray,
Where wandering sheep have gone astray,
And where the lamp of faith grows dim,
And souls are groping after Him.
And as sometimes a flame we find,
Bright shining through the night,
So dark, we cannot see the lamp
But only see the light;
So may we shine, His love the flame,
That souls may glorify His Name. *Annie Johnson Flint.*

O GOD, who art the Fountain of Light and Author of all knowledge, vouchsafe, we beseech Thee, to enlighten our understanding, and to remove from us all darkness of sin and ignorance. [*S. C. H. C.*]

O God, who art the source of life and light and dost nourish and gladden all things in heaven and earth: we beseech Thee mercifully to shine in our hearts: that the night and darkness of sin, and the mists of error on every side, being driven away by the brightness of Thy light, we may all our life walk without stumbling, as in the day, and being pure and clean from the works of darkness, may abound in all good works which Thou hast prepared for us to walk in; through Jesus Christ our Lord. [*New Every Morning.*]

Every one to his service and to his burden. *Num. 4:19.*

Bear ye one another's burdens, and so fulfil the law of Christ. . . . Each man shall bear his own burden. *Gal. 6:2, 5.*

Cast thy burden upon Jehovah, and he will sustain thee. *Ps. 55:22.*

My yoke is easy, and my burden is light. *Matt. 11:30.*

> The camel kneels at break of day
> To have his guide replace his load
> Then rises up anew to take
>   The desert road.
>
> So thou shouldst kneel at morning's dawn
> That God may give thee daily care:
> Assured that He no load too great
>   Will make thee bear.
>
> The camel at the close of day
> Kneels down upon the sandy plain,
> To have his burden lifted off
>   And rest again.
>
> My soul, thou too shouldst to thy knees
> When daylight draweth to a close,
> And let Thy Master lift the load
>   And grant repose.

O LORD, our Saviour, who hast warned us that Thou wilt require much of those to whom much is given: Grant that we whose lot Thou hast cast in so goodly a heritage may strive together the more abundantly by prayer, by almsgiving and by every other appointed means to extend to others what we so richly enjoy; and as we have entered into the labors of other men, so to labor that in their turn other men may enter into ours, to the fulfilling of Thy holy will and our own everlasting salvation. [*Intercessions for the Church.*]

MY HOME IS GOD

Ye are come unto mount Zion, and unto the city of the living God, . . . and to God the Judge of all, and to . . . Jesus. *Heb. 12:22-24.*

Jesus saith unto him, I am the way, and the truth, and the life: no one cometh unto the Father, but by me. *John 14:6.*

There is therefore now no condemnation to them that are in Christ Jesus. *Rom. 8:1.*

"My Home is God Himself." Christ brought me there.
I laid me down within His mighty arms;
He took me up and safe from all alarms,
He bore me where "no foot but His hath trod,"
And bade me dwell in Him, rejoicing there.
O holy place! O Home divinely fair!
And I, God's little one, abiding there.

"My Home is God Himself"; it was not always so!
A long, long road I traveled night and day,
And sought to find within myself some way,
Aught I could do, or feel, to bring me near;
Self-effort failed, and I was filled with fear,
And then I found Christ was the Only Way,
That I must come to Him and in Him stay,
And God had told me so.   *F. Brook.*

ALMIGHTY LORD, merciful Father, vouchsafe to accept the thanks which I now presume to offer Thee. Grant, O Lord, that as my days are multiplied, my good resolutions may be strengthened, my power of resisting temptations increased, and my struggles with snares and obstructions invigorated. Be at home in my mind. May my mind's true home be in Thee. Grant me true repentance of my past life, and as I draw nearer and nearer to the grave, strengthen my faith, enliven my hope, extend my charity, and purify my desires, and so help me by Thy Holy Spirit that when it shall be Thy pleasure to call me hence, I may be received to everlasting happiness in the true and everlasting home of the soul in Thee, for the sake of Thy Son Jesus Christ our Lord. Amen. [Samuel Johnson (Altered).]

My grace is sufficient for thee: for my power is made perfect in weakness. *II Cor. 12:9.*

As thy days, so shall thy strength be. *Deut. 33:25.*

Thou wilt deal bountifully with me. *Ps. 142:7.*

If any of you lacketh wisdom, let him ask of God, who giveth to all liberally and upbraideth not; and it shall be given him. *James 1:5.*

My God shall supply every need of yours according to his riches in glory in Christ Jesus. *Phil. 4:19.*

> He giveth more grace when the burdens grow greater.
> He sendeth more strength when the labors increase.
> To added affliction He addeth His mercy,
> To multiplied trials, His multiplied peace.
>
> When we have exhausted our store of endurance,
> When our strength has failed ere the day is half done,
> When we reach the end of our hoarded resources,
> Our Father's full giving has only begun.
>
> His love has no limits. His grace has no measure.
> His power no boundary known unto men.
> For out of His infinite riches in Jesus,
> He giveth, and giveth, and giveth, again.
>
> *Annie Johnson Flint.*

O HOLY GOD, in whom is all goodness, Whose pity and mercy made Thee to descend from the high throne down into this world, the valley of woe and weeping, and here to take our nature, and in that nature to suffer pain and death, to bring our souls to Thy Kingdom, Merciful Lord, forgive us all our sins that we have done, thought and said. O glorious Trinity, send us cleanness of heart and purity of soul; restore us with Thy Holy Spirit, and strengthen us with Thy might, that we may always withstand evil temptations. Comfort us with Thy Holy Ghost, and fill us with grace and charity, that we may henceforth live virtuously and love Thee with all our heart, with all our might and with all our soul, so that we may never offend Thee, but ever follow Thy pleasure in will, word, thought and deed. Now grant us this, good Lord, that art Infinite, which eternally shall endure; through Jesus Christ Thy Son. [Richard Rolle.]

A BETTER COUNTRY

I am in a strait betwixt the two, having the desire to depart and be with Christ; for it is very far better. *Phil. 1:23.*

In my Father's house are many mansions; if it were not so, I would have told you; for I go to prepare a place for you. . . . I . . . will receive you unto myself; that where I am, there ye may be also. *John 14:2, 3.*

And his delight shall be in the fear of the Lord. *Isa. 11:3.*

They desire a better country, that is, a heavenly: wherefore God is not ashamed of them, to be called their God; for he hath prepared for them a city. *Heb. 11:16.*

> We asked that he might live: Eternal Love
> From out the fullness of His boundless store
> Hath granted him to share the life above,
> Alive forever more.
>
> We asked for health: and faith can almost see
> His radiant face, his movements swift and strong;
> With every power quickened, joyously
> His soul is breathing song.
>
> We prayed at last, that he again might come
> To see the home that he had held so dear:
> And peacefully he reached a fairer Home,
> And dearer — but not here.
>
> O Wisdom infinite and Love supreme!
> This light on sorrow, care and doubt is thrown,
> Beyond our prayers, our hopes, our brightest dream,
> What God doth give His own.   *Mary Isabella Forsyth.*

O ETERNAL LORD GOD, who holdest all souls in life: we beseech Thee to shed forth upon Thy whole Church, in Paradise and on earth, the bright beams of Thy light and heavenly comfort: and grant that, following the good example of those who have served Thee here and are now at rest, we may at the last enter with them into the fulness of Thine unending joy: through Jesus Christ our Lord. [*New Every Morning.*]

READY!

Jehovah called Samuel: and he said, Here am I. *1 Sam. 3:4.*

And I heard the voice of the Lord, saying, Whom shall I send, and who will go for us? Then I said, Here am I; send me. *Isa. 6:8.*

Now there was a certain disciple at Damascus, named Ananias; and the Lord said unto him in a vision, Ananias. And he said, Behold, I am here, Lord. *Acts 9:10.*

I am debtor both to Greeks and to Barbarians, both to the wise and to the foolish. So, as much as in me is, I am ready. *Rom. 1:14, 15.*

Ready unto every good work. *Titus 3:1.*

Still, as of old, Thy precious word
Is by the nations dimly heard;
The hearts its holiness hath stirred
  Are weak and few;
Wise men the secret dare not tell;
Still in Thy temple slumbers well
Good Eli: Oh, like Samuel —
  Lord, here am I!

Few years, no wisdom, no renown,
Only my life can I lay down;
Only my heart, Lord! to Thy throne
  I bring! and pray
That child of Thine I may go forth,
And spread glad tidings through the earth,
And teach sad hearts to know Thy worth —
  Lord, here am I! . . .

I ask no heaven till earth be Thine,
Nor glory-crown while work of mine
Remaineth here; when earth shall shine
  Among the stars,
Her sins wiped out, her captives free,
Her voice a music unto Thee,
  For crown, new work give Thou to me —
  Lord, here am I!

O LORD, my Maker and Protector, . . . while it shall please Thee to continue me in this world where much is to be done and little is to be known, teach me by Thy Holy Spirit to withdraw my mind from unprofitable and dangerous enquiries, from difficulties vainly curious, and doubts impossible to be solved. Let me rejoice in the light which Thou hast imparted, let me serve Thee with active zeal, and humble confidence, and wait with patient expectation for the time in which the soul which Thou receivest, shall be satisfied with knowledge. [Samuel Johnson.]

The precepts of Jehovah are right, rejoicing the heart. *Ps. 19:8.*

When the son hath done that which is lawful and right, and hath kept all my statutes, and hath done them, he shall surely live. *Ezek. 18:19.*

Asa did right. *I Kings 15:11.* Jehoshaphat did right. *I Kings 22:42, 43.* Jehoash did right. *II Kings 12:2.* Amaziah did right. *II Kings 14:1, 3.* Azariah did right. *II Kings 15:1, 3.* Jotham did right. *II Kings 15:32, 34.* Hezekiah did right. *II Kings 18:1, 3.* Josiah did right. *II Kings 22:1, 2.*

> " If it is right, there is no other way."
>   Brave words to speak and braver still to live,
> A flag to guide the battle of each day,
>   A motto that will peace and courage give.
> " If it is right, there is no other way."
>   Wise words that clear the tangle from the brain.
> Pleasure may whisper, doubt may urge delay
>   And self may argue, but it speaks in vain.
> " If it is right, there is no other way."
>   This is the voice of God, the call of truth:
> Happy the man who hears it to obey
>   And follows onward, upward from his youth.
>   *Priscilla Leonard.*

O THOU who art the Father of that Son which hast awakened us and yet urgeth us out of the sleep of our sins, and exhorteth us that we become Thine, to Thee, Lord, we pray, who art the supreme Truth, for all truth that is, is from Thee. Thee we implore, O Lord who art the highest Wisdom, through Thee are wise, all those that are so. Thou art the supreme Joy, and from Thee all have become happy that are so. Thou art the highest Good, and from Thee all beauty springs. Thou art the intellectual Light, and from Thee man derives his under-standing. To Thee, O God, we call and speak. . . . We seek Thee, we follow Thee, we are ready to serve Thee; under Thy power we desire to abide, for Thou art the Sovereign of all. We pray Thee to command us as Thou wilt; through Jesus Christ Thy Son our Lord. Amen. [King Alfred.]

GOD AND OUR PROBLEMS

Casting all your anxiety upon him, because he careth for you. *1 Peter 5:7.*

Your heavenly Father feedeth them [the birds]. Are not ye of much more value than they? . . . If God doth so clothe the grass of the field, . . . shall he not much more clothe you? *Matt. 6:26, 30.*

If ye then, being evil, know how to give good gifts unto your children, how much more shall your Father who is in heaven give good things to them that ask him? *Matt. 7:11.*

O God . . . renew a right spirit within me. *Ps. 51:10.*

He led them also by a straight way. *Ps. 107:7.*

A little child with lessons all unlearned
And problems still unsolved before me stands;
With tired, puzzled face to me upturned,
She holds a slate within her outstretched hands:
"My sums are hard — I cannot think tonight:
Dear father, won't you make the answers right? "

Thus do I come to Thee, great Master, dear;
My lessons, too, are hard; my brain is weak.
Life's problems still unsolved, the way not clear,
The answers wrong — Thy wisdom would I seek,
A tired, puzzled child, I pray tonight:
"Here is my slate — O make the answers right! "
Jean Dwight Franklin.

O ETERNAL, Immortal, Invisible God, . . . we praise Thee for Thy Holy Spirit ever working in the world and revealing new truth, and for the many blessings of this life: for the glorious beauty of the world of nature; for human love; for health and strength; for the joy of friendship; and for all the manifold interests of life. Above all we thank Thee for the revelation of Thyself to man through Jesus Christ, who for us men and for our salvation was made man, who suffered and was betrayed and crucified; yet death had no dominion over Him, the author and giver of eternal life. Wherefore in praise and adoration, O Lord God Almighty, we lift up our hearts unto Thee. Amen. [*New Every Morning.*]

And we have the word of prophecy made more sure; whereunto ye do well that ye take heed, as unto a lamp shining in a dark place, until the day dawn, and the day-star arise in your hearts. *II Peter 1:19.*

I am the light of the world: he that followeth me shall not walk in the darkness, but shall have the light of life. *John 8:12.*

Thou art my hiding-place. *Ps. 32:7.*

We speak God's wisdom in a mystery, even the wisdom that hath been hidden, which God foreordained before the worlds unto our glory. *I Cor. 2:7.*

My heart gives thanks for yonder hill
That makes this valley safe and still,
That shuts from sight my onward way
And sets a limit to my day;
That keeps my thoughts so tired and
    weak
From seeking what they should not
    seek.
On that fair bound across the west
My eyes find pasturage and rest,
And of its dewy stillness drink
As do the stars upon its brink;
It shields me from the day to come
And makes the present hour my
    home. . . .

I thank Thee, Lord, that Thou dost lay
These near horizons on my way.
If I could all my journey see,
There were no charm or mystery,
No veiléd grief, no changes sweet,
No restful sense of tasks complete,
I thank Thee for the hills, the night,
For every barrier to my sight;
For every turn that blinds my eyes
To coming pain or glad surprise.

For every bound Thou settest nigh
To make me look more near, more
    high;
For mysteries too great to know;
For everything Thou dost not show.
Upon Thy limits rests my heart:
Its safe horizon, Lord, Thou art.
         Frances L. Bushnell.

O GOD, who knowest all things and from whom nothing is hid; Thou hast seen fit to limit our knowledge, and to set before us the slow learning of Thy works and ways. Grant us grace to accept the mystery of life with a humble heart. [*The Book of Common Worship,* Revised.]

THOU KNOWEST, LORD

Come unto me, all ye that labor and are heavy laden, and I will give you rest. Take my yoke upon you, and learn of me; for I am meek and lowly in heart: and ye shall find rest unto your souls. *Matt. 11:28, 29.*

Cast thy burden upon Jehovah, and he will sustain thee: he will never suffer the righteous to be moved. *Ps. 55:22.*

He hath borne our griefs, and carried our sorrows; . . . the chastisement of our peace was upon him; and with his stripes we are healed. . . . Jehovah hath laid on him the iniquity of us all. *Isa. 53:4-6.*

Christ is the end of the law unto righteousness. *Rom. 10:4.*

Now I know in part; but then shall I know fully even as also I was fully known. *1 Cor. 13:12.*

> Thou knowest, Lord, the weariness and sorrow
>   Of the sad heart that comes to Thee for rest:
> Cares of today and burdens for tomorrow,
>   Blessings implored and sins to be confessed. . . .
> I come before Thee at Thy gracious word,
>   And lay them at thy feet;
>   Thou knowest, Lord; Thou knowest, Lord.
> Therefore I come, Thy gentle call obeying,
>   And lay my sin and sorrows at Thy feet.
> On everlasting strength my weakness staying,
>   Clothed in Thy robe of righteousness complete;
> Then rising and refreshed I leave Thy throne
> And follow on to know as I am known.

S ET free, O God, our souls from all restlessness and anxiety; give us that peace and power that flow from Thee. Keep us in all perplexities and distresses, in all fears and faithlessness; that so upheld by Thy power and stayed on the rock of Thy faithfulness, we may through storm and stress abide in Thee; through Jesus Christ our Lord.

O Lord Jesus Christ, who art the way, the truth and the life: suffer us not, we pray Thee, to wander from Thee who art the way, nor to distrust Thee who art the truth, nor to rest in any other than Thee who art the life. Teach us what to do, what to believe, and wherein to take our rest. Amen. [*New Every Morning.*]

THE LIGHT OF LOVE IN THE DARK

Thou . . . settest me before thy face for ever. *Ps. 41:12.*

As for me, I shall behold thy face in righteousness. *Ps. 17:15.*

See that ye despise not one of these little ones: for I say unto you, that in heaven their angels do always behold the face of my Father who is in heaven. *Matt. 18:10.*

On this wise ye shall bless the children of Israel: ye shall say unto them, Jehovah bless thee, and keep thee: Jehovah make his face to shine upon thee, and be gracious unto thee: Jehovah lift up his countenance upon thee, and give thee peace. *Num. 6:23–26.*

I will counsel thee with mine eye upon thee. *Ps. 32:8.*

Here in my bed low-lying, eyes held so I cannot see,
Lord, art Thou there in the chamber, and is Thy Face turned towards
   me?
Dost Thou hear me cry in the darkness nor comest unto mine aid?
Thy child who is weak and helpless, and shrinking and sore afraid?

If I hear Thy voice in the silence, and know that Thou art anigh,
That Thy Face is turned towards my slumber where feeble and wan
   I lie,
I shall nestle soft on my pillow with never a thought or care,
Sure that Thy Love waits with me, that my Father is watching there.

I shall know that Thy love is bridging long hours 'twixt the dusk and
   dawn,
Till all terrors have fallen from me and the last of my fears is gone;
And 'yond the night's strange weird fancies in the dim growing light
   I see
Thy Presence merge slow through the gloaming, with Thy Face ever
   turned towards me.   *Mary M. Churchod.*

HEAVENLY Father, in whom is no darkness at all, nor any shadow that is cast by turning, forgive our feverish ways — our anxieties, our fears, our uncertainties. Open our eyes that we may see Thee, and our minds, that we may understand and know Thee. Grant unto us Thy light that we may know Thy will, and by keeping it increase our light. Grant to us that what we cannot see, we may be content to trust Thee for. [*Prayers,* Compiled by Page and Laidlaw (Abbreviated).]

And we know that to them that love God all things work together for good, even to them that are called according to his purpose. *Rom. 8:28.*

And the God of all grace, who called you unto his eternal glory in Christ, after that ye have suffered a little while, shall himself perfect, establish, strengthen you. To him be the dominion for ever and ever. *I Peter 5:10, 11.*

These things saith he that is holy, he that is true, he that hath the key of David, he that openeth and none shall shut, and that shutteth and none openeth: I know thy works (behold, I have set before thee a door opened, which none can shut). *Rev. 3:7, 8.*

On the far reef the breakers
  Recoil in shattered foam,
Yet still the sea behind them
  Urges its forces home;
Its chant of triumph surges
  Through all the thunderous din —
The wave may break in failure,
  But the tide is sure to win!

The reef is strong and cruel;
  Upon its jagged wall
One wave — a score — a hundred,
  Broken and beaten fall;

Yet in defeat they conquer,
  The sea comes flooding in —
Wave upon wave is routed,
  But the tide is sure to win.

O mighty sea! thy message
  In clinging spray is cast;
Within God's plan of progress
  It matters not at last
How wide the shores of evil,
  How strong the reefs of sin —
The wave may be defeated,
  But the tide is sure to win!
            Priscilla Leonard.

*A*LMIGHTY GOD, our Father in heaven, we rejoice in the privilege of lifting our hearts unto Thee. We seek communion with Thee because we know Thee through the ministry of Thy Son. The tendrils of our faith cluster around His cross. Therein is our inspiration to continue stedfast in faith and hope and love.

We thank Thee for a growing sense of need, for we know that they are blessed who hunger and thirst after the things of God. Grant us, we implore Thee, a supply from Thy hand that all our wants may be met. Teach us to live bravely for Thee day by day. [William Crowe (Abbreviated).]

GOD'S OTHER ROOM

Jesus said unto her, I am the resurrection, and the life: he that believeth on me, though he die, yet shall he live; and whosoever liveth and believeth on me shall never die. *John 11:25, 26.*

If we died with Christ, we believe that we shall also live with him. *Rom. 6:8.*

'Tis passing strange how nearer seems a friend
Whose home has been far distant from your own,
When you have learned that he has passed within
The mystic shrine denied as yet to us,
And sacred kept for those found worthy death.
Now, now, you say, I have him safe and near
As God is near to all who hold Him true.

But yesterday I learned that one whose face
Was beautiful in glowing womanhood
When first I knew her, two score years away,
And ever grew more beautiful, as soul
Took on new beauty in its homeward growth,
Had gained her entrance into life indeed.
Now seems she not a thousand miles away
But very near in the adjoining room!
As full of kindly interest as before,
With added powers for strength and comforting.

Nor do I have to seek me wizard test
To know she is alive and very near.
Since she's with God and God is here and now!
Nor will I rudely try to lift the latch.
'Tis God shall whisper: "Now the feast is spread,
And you may come! Full welcome to the board!"
So will I think of loving friends who now
Are living safely in God's other room. *Adelbert S. Coats.*

O ETERNAL GOD to whom do live the spirits of them that depart hence in the Lord, . . . teach me to practice their doctrine, to imitate their lives, following their example, and being united as a part of the same mystical body by the bond of the same faith, and a holy hope, and a never ceasing charity. [Jeremy Taylor.]

OUR WORK

Knew ye not that I must be in my Father's house. *Luke 2:49.*

Concerning love of the brethren ye have no need that one write unto you: for ye yourselves are taught of God to love one another; for indeed ye do it toward all the brethren that are in all Macedonia. But we exhort you, brethren, that ye abound more and more; and that ye study to be quiet, and to do your own business, and to work with your hands, even as we charged you. *1 Thess. 4:9–11.*

I rose up, and did the king's business. *Dan. 8:27.*

We must work the works of him that sent me, while it is day. *John 9:4.*

Jesus saith unto them, My meat is to do the will of him that sent me, and to accomplish his work. *John 4:34.*

> To love some one more dearly every day,
> To help a wandering child to find his way,
> To ponder o'er a noble thought and pray,
>   And smile when evening falls.
>
> To follow truth as blind men long for light,
> To do my best from dawn of day till night,
> To keep my heart fit for His holy sight,
>   And answer when He calls.
>   *Maude Louise Ray.*

O LORD, our God, today we go away one from another, but no one of us goes apart from Thee! We go back to the greatest of joys, the joy of working together with Thee for the coming of Thy kingdom on earth. May we know the love of Christ that passeth knowledge, and in knowing that love may all pride, all self-seeking, all jealousy, all suspicion, all weakness be burned out of our lives. Grant that looking unto Him we may be renewed day by day, finding in the searching of His words, and the waiting on His voice, the power that shall enable us to be His ministers in the fight against all evil, all injustice, all things that savour of death. May we know no discouragement from our own or others' failures, and may we all, with strength of body and of soul, be filled unto all the fulness of God.

And bring us not into temptation, but deliver us from the evil one. *Matt. 6:13.*

He that dwelleth in the secret place of the Most High shall abide under the shadow of the Almighty. . . . He will cover thee with his pinions, and under his wings shalt thou take refuge. *Ps. 91:1, 4.*

Let all those that take refuge in thee rejoice, let them ever shout for joy, because thou defendest them: Let them also that love thy name be joyful in thee. *Ps. 5:11.*

> Not what we have, O Lord, but what we missed:
> For shining eyes tonight Death might have kissed.
> For loving hands so dear we might not hold,
> For lips we love which might tonight be cold.
>
> For what we missed, O Lord, for what we missed;
> The child who might have wandered, Judas-kissed,
> The sin which might have found us unaware
> And entering in our hearts have flourished there.
>
> For what we missed, O Lord, for what we missed,
> We give Thee thanks; for days no blight has kissed —
> For hearts and homes tonight that by Thy grace
> Rejoice that there is not an empty place.   *Ruth Sterry.*

ALMIGHTY GOD, we beseech Thee graciously to behold this Thy family, for which our Lord Jesus Christ was contented to be betrayed, and given up into the hands of wicked men, and to suffer death upon the cross. . . .

O God, who knowest us to be set in the midst of so many and great dangers, that by reason of the frailty of our nature we cannot always stand upright; Grant to us such strength and protection, as may support us in all dangers, and carry us through all temptations. Keep us both outwardly in our bodies, and inwardly in our souls; that we may be defended from all adversities which may happen to the body, and from all evil thoughts which may assault and hurt the soul. Keep Thy Church and household continually in Thy true religion; that they who do lean only upon the hope of Thy heavenly grace may evermore be defended by Thy mighty power. [*Gregorian Sacramentary.*]

LOVE THAT IS AND THAT MAY BE

That we . . . speaking truth in love, may grow up in all things into him, who is the head, even Christ; from whom all the body fitly framed and knit together through that which every joint supplieth, according to the working in due measure of each several part, maketh the increase of the body unto the building up of itself in love. *Eph.* 4:14–16.

The Lord is not slack concerning his promise, as some count slackness; but is longsuffering to you-ward, not wishing that any should perish, but that all should come to repentance. . . . According to his promise, we look for new heavens and a new earth, wherein dwelleth righteousness. *II Peter 3:9, 13.*

And I saw no temple therein: for the Lord God the Almighty, and the Lamb, are the temple thereof. And the city hath no need of the sun, neither of the moon, to shine upon it: for the glory of God did lighten it, and the lamp thereof is the Lamb. *Rev. 21:22, 23.*

Thy grace impart! In time to be
Shall one great temple rise to Thee,
Thy Church one broad humanity.
White flowers of love its walls shall
    climb
Soft bells of peace shall ring its chime
Its days shall all be holy time.

A sweeter song shall then be heard,
Confessing in a world's accord
The inward Christ, the living Word.
That song shall swell from shore to
    shore,
One hope, one faith, one love restore
The seamless robe that Jesus wore.

WE beseech Thee, O Lord, for the gift and for the grace of Thy Holy Spirit. Give us more love to Thee and to our neighbors, more joy in worship, more peace at all times, more long-suffering. O Christ, our only Saviour, so dwell within us that we may go forth with the light of hope in our eyes, Thy Word on our tongue, and Thy love in our hearts.

Almighty God, from whom to be turned is to fall, to whom to be turned is to rise, and in whom to abide is to stand fast forever; Grant us in all our duties Thy help; in all our perplexities Thy guidance; in all our gladness Thy hallowing spirit; and in all our sorrows Thy comfort and joy. Fulfill in every contrite heart the promise of redeeming grace; forgiving all our sins and cleansing us from an evil conscience; through the perfect sacrifice of Christ our Lord.

THE GAIN OF PAIN

All chastening seemeth for the present to be not joyous but grievous; yet afterward it yieldeth peaceable fruit unto them that have been exercised thereby, even the fruit of righteousness. *Heb. 12:11.*

For it became him, for whom are all things, and through whom are all things, in bringing many sons unto glory, to make the author of their salvation perfect through sufferings. *Heb. 2:10.*

And the God of all grace, who called you unto his eternal glory in Christ, after that ye have suffered a little while, shall himself perfect, establish, strengthen you. *1 Peter 5:10.*

> The cry of men's anguish went up unto God:
> "Lord, take away pain,
> The shadow that darkens the world Thou hast made,
> The close clinging chain
> That strangles the heart, the burden that weighs
> On the wings that would soar —
> Lord, take away pain from the world Thou hast made
> That it love Thee the more."
> Then answered the Lord to the cry of His world:
> "Shall I take away pain?
> And with it the power of the soul to endure,
> Made strong by the strain?
> Shall I take away pity that knits heart to heart,
> And sacrifice high?
> Shall I take away love that redeems with a price
> And smiles at its loss
> Can ye spare from the lives that would climb unto Mine
> The Christ on His cross?"   *Julia Larned.*

*A*LMIGHTY FATHER, who in thy patience didst accept the sacrifices of men as a preparation for faith in the one offering of Jesus, we pray that this day may be a day of recollection of His passion and of Thy redeeming love. May the grace of the Cross empower us to offer our bodies a living sacrifice, holy and acceptable, a spiritual service. We would come to the Cross this day to do Thy will, O God, as He came, joyous in tribulation through our conquering Christ. [Fitzgerald S. Parker (Abbreviated).]

THE PRESENCE OF ETERNAL LIFE

And this is life eternal, that they should know thee the only true God, and him whom thou didst send, even Jesus Christ. *John 17:3.*

He that eateth my flesh and drinketh my blood hath eternal life. *John 6:54.*

I came that they may have life, and may have it abundantly. *John 10:10.*

I am the resurrection, and the life: he that believeth on me, though he die, yet shall he live; and whosoever liveth and believeth on me shall never die. *John 11:25, 26.*

In him was life; and the life was the light of men. *John 1:4.*

It will not meet us where the shadows fall
    Beside the sea that bounds the Evening Land;
It will not greet us with its first clear call
    When death has borne us to the farther strand.

It is not something yet to be revealed —
    The Everlasting Life; 'tis here and now,
Passing unseen because our eyes are sealed
    With blindness for the pride upon our brow.

It dwells not in innumerable years;
    It is the breath of God in timeless things —
The strong divine persistence that inheres
    In love's red pulses and in faith's white wings.

And if we feel it not among our strife
    In all our toiling and in all our pain —
This rhythmic pulsing of immortal life —
    Then do we work and suffer here in vain.

WE Thank Thee, O Heavenly Father, that Thou hast given Thyself to us through Jesus Christ. We bless Thee for the Light that shines upon us, and for the spiritual Bread with which our souls are fed, that Thine exceeding great and precious promises for the future are matched by Thine exceeding great and precious gifts today, that the Eternal Life that is in Christ Jesus is our glorious possession now. . . . Blessed by Thy Name for Thy goodness which is ever seeking us and offering to us in Jesus Christ the fulness of Thy Life and Love. [*The Fellowship of Prayer.*]

THERE IS WELCOME FOR SINNERS

Him that cometh to me I will in no wise cast out. *John 6:37.*

If thou, Lord, shouldest mark iniquities, O Lord, who could stand? *Ps. 130:3.*

Through this man is proclaimed unto you remission of sins: and by him every one that believeth is justified from all things. *Acts 13:38.*

I will forgive their iniquity, and their sin will I remember no more. *Jer. 31:34.*

Her sins, which are many, are forgiven; for she loved much: but to whom little is forgiven, the same loveth little. And he said unto her, Thy sins are forgiven. *Luke 7:47, 48.*

Now all the publicans and sinners were drawing near unto him to hear him. And both the Pharisees and the scribes murmured, saying, This man receiveth sinners. *Luke 15:1, 2.*

" Where are you going, heart of woe,
Pitiful heart of fear and shame? "
" A strange and lonely way I go,
Where none shall pity, none shall
    blame.
For with my sin and misery
I creep, on doubtful feet, alone.
No human heart can follow me
To mark my tears or hear my moan."
Nay — but the never-ceasing sting,
The clearness of remembering!

" What do you see, O changing face,
Alight with strange and tender
    gleams? "
"I near the hushed and holy place
Of One who gives me back my
    dreams."
" Where are your daring, eager feet —
Feet that so wild a way have trod? "
" O bitter world, no scorn I meet.
Sinful and hurt I go to God.
On my dark sin for evermore
A sinless Hand has closed the door."
      Annie Campbell Huestis.

*A*LMIGHTY and most merciful Father, we have erred and strayed from Thy ways like lost sheep, but Thou art our Shepherd and art seeking for us to bring us home from all our wanderings. Thou knowest, O God, all the weakness and sin of our hearts and the temptations we daily meet; we humbly beseech Thee to have compassion on our infirmities, to forgive and forget our sins according to Thy promises, and to give us the constant help of Thy Holy Spirit; that we may be surely restrained from all follies and blindness, and be excited to our duty and enabled to live in all thoughtfulness and purity and kindness and love.

SPECIAL DAYS

In the beginning God. *Gen. 1:1.*

I am the Alpha and the Omega, saith the Lord God. *Rev. 1:8.*

The eyes of the Lord thy God are always upon it [the land], from the beginning of the year even unto the end of the year. *Deut. 11:12.*

First, I thank my God through Jesus Christ. *Rom. 1:8.*

Who shall go up for us first . . . to fight? *Judg. 1:1.*

The New Year comes — not like the Child of glory
  To vanquish sin by helpless innocence —
No Wise Men kneel adoring at his manger,
  No Virgin breast his tender providence.

A wanderer from out Time's stormy mountain,
  Untried he comes — across the eastern hills;
New grief, new hate, new victory await him —
  His flying track the old year snowflake fills.

Thy naked thigh, anointed, is it supple?
  Gird up thy loins! Art thou Peniel shod?
Gauge well the lusty sinews of the stranger —
  A wrestler coming forth to thee from God.

Wrestling for peace, for country, love and honor —
  Wrestling alone — in combat for thy soul —
This be thy cheer should dawnlight worst or bless thee —
  Another challenge meets thee at the goal.   *Martha Dickinson.*

O GOD, we thank Thee that Thou art the timeless One, above all the changes of our mortal changefulness. From everlasting to everlasting Thou art God. And now, on what to us is a new beginning of days, we come to trust ourselves anew to Thee and Thine unchanging stedfastness. Deliver us, we pray, from the burden of past evil. Preserve for us all past good. By Thy grace confirm and establish us this day in Thine own integrity and lead us forth into the new year strengthened with might by Thy Spirit, to do Thy good and perfect and acceptable will, through Jesus Christ, Thy Son, our Lord, who is the same yesterday, today, and forever. [R. E. S.]

GETHSEMANE

Then cometh Jesus with them unto a place called Gethsemane.
. . . Then saith he unto them, My soul is exceeding sorrowful, even
unto death. *Matt. 26:36, 38.*

If any man serve me, let him follow me; and where I am,
there shall also my servant be. *John 12:26.*

A disciple is not above his teacher, nor a servant above his lord.
It is enough for the disciple that he be as his teacher, and the servant
as his lord. *Matt. 10:24, 25.*

In golden youth, when seems the
　　earth
A summer land of singing mirth,
When souls are glad and hearts are
　　light,
And not a shadow lurks in sight,
We do not know it, but there lies
Somewhere, veiled under evening
　　skies,
A garden each must some time see,
　　Gethsemane, Gethsemane,
　　Somewhere his own Gethsemane.

All those who journey, soon or late,
Must pass within the garden's gate;
Must kneel alone in darkness there,
And battle with some fierce despair.
God pity those who can not say,
"Not mine, but Thine," who only
　　pray,
"Let this cup pass," and can not see
The purpose in Gethsemane.
　　Gethsemane, Gethsemane,
　　God help us through Gethsemane!
　　　　E. W. Wilcox.

. . .

O DEAR Christ, crucified for our sins, make us to realize that in
the Cross is salvation, in the Cross is life, in the Cross is protection
against our enemies, in the Cross is infusion of heavenly sweetness, in
the Cross is strength of mind, in the Cross joy of spirit, in the Cross the
height of virtue, in the Cross perfecting of holiness; that we may therefore take up our cross and follow Thee into life everlasting. And grant
us such preparation for our cross and such perfect unity of will with
Thee as we behold with grateful and reverent awe our Lord's anguish
in Gethsemane when with strong crying and tears He prayed unto Thee
to save Him from death in the Garden that He might fulfill His mission
on the Cross and was heard for His perfect obedience and His perfect
fear. [*S. C. H. C.* (Altered).]

JESUS OF THE SCARS

And they [the soldiers] platted a crown of thorns and put it upon his head, . . . and they spat upon him, and took the reed and smote him on the head. *Matt. 27:29, 30.*

But Thomas . . . said unto them, Except I shall see in his hands the print of the nails, and put my finger into the print of the nails, and put my hand into his side, I will not believe. *John 20:24, 25.*

This is my body, which is broken for you. *1 Cor. 11:24 and margin.*

If we have never sought, we seek Thee now;
  Thine eyes burn through the dark, our only stars;
We must have sight of thorn-pricks on Thy brow,
  We must have Thee, O Jesus of the scars.

The heavens frighten us; they are too calm,
  In all the universe we have no place.
Our wounds are hurting us. Where is the balm?
  O Jesus, by Thy scars we claim Thy grace.

If, when the doors are shut, Thou drawest near,
  Only reveal those hands, that side of Thine;
We know to-day what wounds are, we have no fear,
  Show us Thy scars, we know the countersign.

The other gods were strong; but Thou wast weak;
  They rode, but Thou didst stumble to a throne;
But to our wounds only God's wounds can speak,
  And not a god has wounds, but Thou alone.

Edward Shillito.

LORD JESUS CHRIST, Thou holy and spotless Lamb of God, who didst take upon Thyself our sins, and bear them in Thy body on the cross; we bless Thee for all the burdens Thou hast borne, for all the tears Thou hast wept, for all the pains Thou hast suffered, for all Thy scars, for all the words of comfort Thou hast spoken by Thy Cross, for all Thy conflicts with the powers of darkness, and for Thine eternal victory over sin and death. With the host of the redeemed, we ascribe unto Thee power and wisdom and honor and glory and blessing, forever and ever. [*Book of Common Order* (Altered).]

Christ died for our sins according to the scriptures; and . . . he was buried; and . . . he hath been raised on the third day according to the scriptures. *1 Cor. 15:3, 4.*

Thou foolish one, that which thou thyself sowest is not quickened except it die: and that which thou sowest, thou sowest not the body that shall be, but a bare grain, it may chance of wheat, or of some other kind; but God giveth it a body even as it pleased him, and to each seed a body of its own. *1 Cor. 15:36–38.*

For if we have become united with him in the likeness of his death, we shall be also in the likeness of his resurrection. *Rom. 6:5.*

His wide Hands fashioned us white grains and red,
His Eyes with rains to swell them in their bed,
Whereby the dust-grains of our lives are fed. Alleluia.

In Earth our mother's bosom undecayed
The Seed-corn of the Flesh He took, He laid —
One white small Grain beneath a sealed rock's shade. Alleluia.

How blind that Seed lay till this autumn morn,
When faith it sprouted, blade and flower and corn
And with Its lifted Head the seal was torn. Alleluia.

Hope of men's bodies' grains both red and white —
Shrivelled and sere and void of speech and sight,
Is that blind Seed Who burst His way to light. Alleluia.

We God's red millet grains, men hold so cheap,
Innumerable beneath our grey rocks sleep,
Yet He that cared to sow us cares to reap. Alleluia.

Arthur Shearley Cripps, on Easter in South
Africa Where It Falls in the Autumn.

*W*E give thanks to Thee, O heavenly Father, who, by the appearing of Thy Son Jesus Christ to His disciples after His crucifixion, hast made known to us that death has no dominion over Him, and that with Him we may enter through death into life eternal. We praise Thee, O Christ, who hast made dying to be the pathway into the fuller life. [*New Every Morning.*]

THE RESURRECTION AND
THE LIGHT

The sun was risen upon the earth when Lot came unto Zoar. *Gen. 19:23.*

After I am raised up, I will go before you. *Matt. 26:32.*

Go quickly, and tell his disciples, He is risen from the dead; and lo, he goeth before you into Galilee; there shall ye see him. . . . And they departed quickly from the tomb with fear and great joy, . . . and behold, Jesus met them. *Matt. 28:7–9.*

But if we died with Christ, we believe that we shall also live with him; knowing that Christ being raised from the dead dieth no more; death no more hath dominion over him. . . . Even so reckon ye also yourselves to be dead unto sin, but alive unto God in Christ Jesus. *Rom. 6:8, 9, 11.*

> I got me flowers to straw Thy way,
>   I got me boughs of many a tree;
> But Thou wast up by break of day,
>   And brought'st Thy sweets along with Thee.
>
> The sunne arising in the East,
>   Though he give light, and the East perfume;
> If they should offer to contest
>   With Thy arising, they presume.
>
> Can there be any day but this,
>   Though many sunnes to shine endeavor?
> We count three hundred, but we miss:
>   There is but one, and that one ever.
>
> *George Herbert.*

O THOU, who very early in the morning, about the rising of the sun, wast pleased to leave Thy empty tomb, and return again from the dead, raise us we pray Thee, to walk in newness of life, by such daily exercise of repentance and virtue as may keep us dead unto sin, but alive unto God, through Thee, and save us. [*S. C. H. C.*]

But Mary was standing without at the tomb weeping: . . . and she beholdeth two angels in white sitting, one at the head, and one at the feet, where the body of Jesus had lain. . . . She turned herself back, and beholdeth Jesus standing, and knew not that it was Jesus. Jesus saith unto her, Woman, why weepest thou? whom seekest thou? She, supposing him to be the gardener, saith unto him, Sir, if thou hast borne him hence, tell me where thou hast laid him, and I will take him away. Jesus saith unto her, Mary. She turneth herself and saith unto him in Hebrew, Rabboni; which is to say, Teacher. *John 20:11, 12, 14–16.*

At dusk of dawn the fragrant garden slept
Full of a mystery the night had known,
When Mary entered, trembling and alone.
And as she trod the grassy way, she wept;
But from the place of deepest shadow crept
A light most radiant — there was no stone!
And the cold rock in which He rested shone
Where two archangels holy vigil kept.
Wondering she saw the flame-white seraphim
At that dark entrance bidding her rejoice,
Yet on the flowers her tears fell one by one;
Then turning comfortless in search of Him
She heard the quiet music of a Voice,
And Christ stood there against the rising sun.

Thomas S. Jones, Jr.

O THOU God and Father of our Lord Jesus Christ, we render Thee most humble and hearty thanks, that when He had descended into the grave, Thou didst not suffer Thy Holy One to see corruption, but didst show unto Him the path of life, and raise Him from the dead, and set Him at Thine own right hand in the heavenly places. Grant us grace, we beseech Thee, to apprehend with true faith the glorious mystery of our Saviour's Resurrection, and fill our hearts with joy and a lively hope, that amid all the sorrows, trials and temptations of our mortal state, and in the hour of death, we may derive strength and comfort from this sure pledge of an inheritance incorruptible and undefiled, and that fadeth not away   [Comegys.]

SHARERS OF THE RESURRECTION

We were buried therefore with him through baptism into death: that like as Christ was raised from the dead through the glory of the Father, so we also might walk in newness of life. For if we have become united with him in the likeness of his death, we shall be also in the likeness of his resurrection; knowing this, that our old man was crucified with him, that the body of sin might be done away, that so we should no longer be in bondage to sin; for he that hath died is justified from sin. But if we died with Christ, we believe that we shall also live with him. *Rom. 6:4-8.*

If then ye were raised together with Christ, seek the things that are above, where Christ is, seated on the right hand of God. *Col. 3:1.*

Good Friday in my heart! Fear and affright!
My thoughts are the Disciples when they fled,
My words the words that priests and soldier said,
My deed the spear to desecrate the dead.
And day, Thy death therein, is changed to night.

Then Easter in my heart sends up the sun,
My thoughts are Mary, when she turned to see.
My words are Peter, answering " Lov'st thou Me? "
My deeds are all Thine own drawn close to Thee,
And night and day, since Thou dost rise, are one.
Mary Elizabeth Coleridge.

O GOD, who hast brought again from the dead our Lord Jesus, the glorious Prince of Salvation with everlasting victory over hell and the grave, grant us power, we beseech Thee, to rise with Him to newness of life, that we may overcome the world with the victory of faith, and have part at last in the resurrection of the just, through the merits of the same risen Saviour, who liveth and reigneth with Thee and the Holy Spirit, ever one God, world without end. And O Thou Son of God and Son of Man, Who by Thy victory over death hast brought life and immortality to light, let us be dead with Thee to all evil and be raised with Thee, by faith in Thee, from the grave of sin and be delivered from the darkness of unbelief and quickened to a new life in Thy Spirit of righteousness and true holiness and love. [*The Book of Common Worship,* Revised (Altered).]

THE MORAL CLEANNESS OF
THE NATION

I charge thee in the sight of God, who giveth life to all things, and of Christ Jesus . . . ; that thou keep the commandment, without spot, without reproach, until the appearing of our Lord Jesus Christ: which in its own times he shall show, who is the blessed and only Potentate, the King of kings, and Lord of lords. *1 Tim. 6:13–15.*

I will turn my hand upon thee, and thoroughly purge away thy dross, and will take away all thy tin; and I will restore thy judges as at the first, and thy counsellors as at the beginning: afterward thou shalt be called The city of righteousness, a faithful town. Zion shall be redeemed with justice, and her converts with righteousness. *Isa. 1:25–27.*

And they shall call them The holy people, The redeemed of Jehovah: and thou shalt be called Sought out, A city not forsaken. *Isa. 62:12.*

Ye are an elect race, a royal priesthood, a holy nation, a people for God's own possession, that ye may show forth the excellencies of him who called you out of darkness into his marvellous light. *1 Peter 2:9.*

Judge eternal, throned in splendor,
Lord of lords and King of kings,
With Thy living fire of judgment
Purge this land of bitter things:
Solace all its wide dominion
With the healing of Thy wings. . . .

Crown, O God, Thine own endeavor;
Cleave our darkness with Thy sword:
Feed the faint and hungry heathen
With the richness of Thy Word;
Cleanse the body of this nation
Through the glory of the Lord.
Henry Scott Holland.

O THOU King eternal, immortal, invisible, Thou only wise God our Saviour; hasten, we beseech Thee, the coming of Thy kingdom upon earth, and draw the whole world of mankind into willing obedience to Thy blessed reign. Overcome all the enemies of Christ, and bring low every power that is exalted against Him. Cast out all the evil things which cause wars and fightings among us, and let Thy Spirit rule the hearts of men in righteousness and love. [*The Book of Common Worship,* Revised.]

THE NATION AND RELIGION

And Moses made haste, and bowed his head toward the earth, and worshipped. And he said, If now I have found favor in thy sight, O Lord, let the Lord, I pray thee, go in the midst of us; for it is a stiffnecked people; and pardon our iniquity and our sin, and take us for thine inheritance. *Ex.34:8, 9.*

Righteousness exalteth a nation; but sin is a reproach to any people. *Prov. 14:34.*

If any man thinketh himself to be religious, while he bridleth not his tongue but deceiveth his heart, this man's religion is vain. Pure religion and undefiled before our God and Father is this, to visit the fatherless and widows in their affliction, and to keep oneself unspotted from the world. *James 1:26, 27.*

> I say no man has ever yet been half devout enough.
> None has ever yet adored or worship'd half enough. . . .
> I say that the real and permanent grandeur of these
>   States must be their religion.
> Otherwise there is no real and permanent grandeur;
> (Nor character, nor life worthy the name without religion,
> Nor land, nor man, nor woman without religion.)
>   *Walt Whitman.*

ALMIGHTY GOD, who hast given us this good land for our heritage; we humbly beseech Thee that we may always prove ourselves a people mindful of Thy favor and glad to do Thy will. Bless our nation with honorable industry, sound learning, and pure manners. Save us from violence, discord, and confusion; from pride and arrogancy, and from every evil way. Defend our liberties, and fashion into one united people the multitudes brought hither out of many kindreds and tongues. Endue with the spirit of wisdom those to whom in Thy Name we entrust the authority of government, that there may be justice and peace at home, and that, through obedience to Thy law, we may show forth Thy praise among the nations of the earth. In the time of prosperity, fill our hearts with thankfulness, and in the day of trouble, suffer not our trust in Thee to fail; all which we ask through Jesus Christ our Lord. [*The Book of Common Worship,* Revised.]

And the angel said unto her, Fear not, Mary: for thou hast found favor with God. And behold, thou shalt conceive in thy womb, and bring forth a son, and shalt call his name Jesus. He shall be great, and shall be called the Son of the Most High: and the Lord God shall give unto him the throne of his father David: and he shall reign over the house of Jacob for ever; and of his kingdom there shall be no end. . . . The Holy Spirit shall come upon thee, and the power of the Most High shall overshadow thee: wherefore also the holy thing which is begotten shall be called the Son of God. *Luke 1:30–33, 35.*

I shall you tell a great marvel,
How an angel, for our avail,
Came to a maid, and said: "*All hail!*"
 What, heard ye not, the King of Jerusalem
 Is now born in Bethlehem?

"*All hail,*" he said, "*and full of grace,*
God is with thee now in this place,
A child thou shalt bear in little space."
 What, heard ye not, the King of Jerusalem
 Is now born in Bethlehem?

The maid answered the angel again:
"*If God will that this be sayn,*
The wordes be to me full fain."
 What, heard ye not, the King of Jerusalem
 Is now born in Bethlehem?

Now will we all, in rejoicing
That we have heard this good tiding,
To that child "*Te Deum*" sing:
 "*Te Deum laudamus.*"

O ALMIGHTY GOD who by the Birth by a Virgin of Thy Holy Child Jesus, hast given us a great Light to dawn upon our darkness, grant, we pray Thee, that in His light we may see light to the end of our days; and bestow upon us we beseech Thee that most excellent Christmas gift of charity to all men, that so the likeness of Thy Son may be formed in us, and that we may have the ever brightening hope of everlasting life; through Jesus Christ. Amen.   [Knight (Altered).]

GOD SPAKE TO MARY. TO US?

Now in the sixth month the angel Gabriel was sent from God unto a city of Galilee, named Nazareth, to a virgin . . . ; and the virgin's name was Mary. *Luke 1:26, 27.*

And Jehovah spake unto Moses face to face, as a man speaketh unto his friend. *Ex. 33:11.*

And Jehovah came, and stood, and called as at other times, Samuel, Samuel. Then Samuel said, Speak; for thy servant heareth. *I Sam. 3:10.*

In quietness and confidence shall be your strength. *Isa. 30:15.*

> God whispered and a silence fell: the world
>   Poised one expectant moment like a soul
> Who sees at heaven's threshold the unfurled
> White wings of cherubim, the sea impearled,
>   And pauses, dazed, to comprehend the whole:
> Only across all space God's whisper came
> And burned about her heart like some white flame.
>
> Then suddenly a bird's note thrilled the peace,
>   And earth again jarred noisily to life
> With a great murmur as of many seas.
> But Mary sat with hands clasped on her knees,
>   And lifted eyes with all amazement rife,
> And in her heart the rapture of the spring
> Upon its first sweet day of blossoming.   *Theodosia Garrison.*

*E*TERNAL FATHER, whom the heaven of heavens cannot contain; Thou who dost hide Thyself from the wise and prudent that Thou mayst reveal Thyself unto babes, grant unto us this day the spirit of children with their Father. There is so much in life that we cannot understand, so much that is hard to bear. We come into Thy Presence seeking at Thy call to press through the shadows. We are compassed about with mystery, the mystery of life and the mystery of death, the mystery of love and the mystery of hate, the mystery of sin and the mystery of the Cross that atones for sin. O Thou who art Thyself the Mystery of mysteries and at the same time Light of light, part the clouds that hide Thy face and reveal Thyself unto us today. [William Adams Brown.]

THE ROAD TO BETHLEHEM

And the angel of the Lord found her . . . and . . . said, . . . whence camest thou? and whither goest thou? *Gen. 16:7, 8.*

Let the righteous be glad; let them exult before God: yea, let them rejoice with gladness. Sing unto God, sing praises to his name. . . . O God, when thou wentest forth before thy people, . . . thou . . . didst confirm thine inheritance, when it was weary. God is unto us a God of deliverances. *Ps. 68:3, 4, 7, 9, 20.*

The Lord . . . is with thee whithersoever thou goest. *Josh. 1:9.*

These are they that follow the Lamb whithersoever he goeth. *Rev. 14:4.*

Blessed is the man that walketh not in the counsel of the wicked, nor standeth in the way of sinners, . . . for Jehovah knoweth the way of the righteous; but the way of the wicked shall perish. *Ps. 1:1, 6.*

Enter ye in by the narrow gate: for wide is the gate, and broad is the way, that leadeth to destruction, and many are they that enter in thereby. For narrow is the gate, and straitened the way, that leadeth unto life, and few are they that find it. *Matt. 7:13, 14.*

Let us now go even unto Bethlehem, and see this thing that is come to pass, which the Lord hath made known unto us. *Luke 2:15.*

> Men travel bravely by a thousand roads,
> Some broad and lined with palaces, some steep
> And hard and lonely, some that blindly twist
> Through tangled jungles where there is no light;
> And mostly they are travelled thoughtlessly.
> But once a year an ancient question comes
> To every traveller passing on his way,
> A question that can stab and burn and bless:
> " Is this the road that leads to Bethlehem? "

O BLESSED JESUS, who by the shining of a star didst manifest Thyself to them that sought Thee, show Thy heavenly light to us, and give us grace to follow until we find Thee; finding to rejoice in Thee and rejoicing to present to Thee ourselves, our souls and bodies for Thy service evermore for Thine honour and glory.

IN BETHLEHEM

But thou Beth-lehem Ephrathah, which art little to be among the thousands of Judah, out of thee shall one come forth unto me that is to be ruler in Israel; whose goings forth are from of old, from everlasting. *Micah 5:2.*

Oh that one would give me water to drink of the well of Bethlehem, which is by the gate! *II Sam. 23:15.*

Jesus was born in Bethlehem of Judæa. *Matt. 2:1.*

O little town, O little town,
  Upon the hills so far,
We see you like a thing sublime,
  Across the great, gray wastes of
    time,
And men go up and men go down
  But follow still the Star.

And this is humble Bethlehem
  In the Judea wild:
And this is lowly Bethlehem
  Wherein a mother smiled:
Yea, this is happy Bethlehem
  That knew the little child.

Aye, this is glorious Bethlehem
  Where He drew living breath
(Ah, precious, precious Bethlehem!
  So every mortal saith)
Who brought to all that tread the
  earth
  Life's triumph over death!

O little town, O little town,
  Upon the hills afar,
You call to us, a thing sublime
  Across the great, gray wastes of
    time
For men go up and men go down,
  But follow still the Star.
      Clinton Scollard.

P<small>REPARE</small> our hearts, O God, for the coming of Jesus Christ Thy Son. By true faith in Him as the Divine Redeemer, strengthen our loyalty and our hope, that at His appearing in glory we may welcome Him as our Risen Lord, our royal Master, the Saviour of our souls. And O, Almighty God, give us grace that we may cast away the works of darkness and put upon us the armor of light, now in the time of this mortal life in which Thy Son Jesus Christ came to visit us in great humility: that in the last day when He shall come again to judge both the quick and the dead, we may rise to the life immortal, from this lowly village of our earthly Bethlehem to the Holy City, the Heavenly Jerusalem, through Him who liveth and reigneth with Thee and the Holy Ghost now and ever. [*The Book of Common Worship*, Revised (Altered).]

And she brought forth her first-born son; and she wrapped him in swaddling clothes, and laid him in a manger, because there was no room for them in the inn. *Luke 2:7.*

Behold, I stand at the door and knock: if any man hear my voice and open the door, I will come in to him, and will sup with him, and he with me. *Rev. 3:20.*

That Christ may dwell in your hearts through faith. *Eph. 3:17.*

If a man love me, he will keep my word: and my Father will love him, and we will come unto him, and make our abode with him. *John 14:23.*

The Bethlehem Innkeeper Speaks

The inn was full. There was no room.
  And yet of course, I might have made
Arrangement. But the evening gloom
  Came on — a man must keep his trade —
  The guests were in — they all had paid.

There was no room. The inn was full.
  And it had been a busy day;
So many vexing questions pull
  A landlord's heart. All cannot stay —
  The late ones must be turned away.

The inn was full. There was no room.
  But certainly I could have done
Something if I had known for whom —
  Ah, that my door should be the one
  To shut out Mary and her Son!

B. Y. Williams.

ALMIGHTY GOD, we give Thee thanks for the mighty yearning of the human heart for the coming of a Saviour, and the constant promise of Thy word that He was to come. In our own souls we repeat the humble sighs of ancient men and ages, and own that our souls are in darkness and infirmity, without faith in him who brings God to man and man to God. . . . O God, prepare Thou the way in us now, and may we welcome anew Thy Holy Child. [Samuel Osgood.]

THE BABY AND THE MOTHER

When the fulness of the time came, God sent forth his Son, born of a woman. *Gal. 4:4.*

And the angel said unto her, Fear not, Mary: for thou hast found favor with God. And behold, thou shalt conceive in thy womb, and bring forth a son, and shalt call his name JESUS. He shall be great, and shall be called the Son of the Most High: and the Lord God shall give unto him the throne of his father David: and he shall reign over the house of Jacob for ever; and of his kingdom there shall be no end. *Luke 1:30–33.*

And Elisabeth . . . said, Blessed art thou among women, and blessed is the fruit of thy womb. And whence is this to me, that the mother of my Lord should come unto me? *Luke 1:41–43.*

Not to Jerusalem's palm-welcomed King
　　Not to the Man reviled on Calvary's height
Not to the Risen God my heart doth lift
　　In wondering awe tonight.

But to the Baby, shut from Bethlehem's inn
　　About whose feet the wondering creatures pressed,
The downy head, the little nestling hands
　　On Mary's breast.

There were so many ways Thou couldst have come, —
　　Lord of incarnate life and form Thou art —
That Thou shouldst choose to be a helpless Babe,
　　Held to a woman's heart,

Dost seem Thy tenderest miracle of love.
　　For this, more wondrous than love sacrificed,
All women, till the utmost stars grow dim
　　Must love Thee, Christ.　　*Ednah Proctor Clarke.*

*B*LESSED be Thy Name, O Jesus; Son of God and Son of Mary; born in Bethlehem to save the world from sin. Infant Redeemer, we adore Thee; Light of the world, we bow before Thee; open our hearts and enter in. [*The Book of Common Worship,* Revised.]

THE BEASTS AND THE BABY

The beasts of the field had shadow under it, and the birds of the heavens dwelt in the branches thereof, and all flesh was fed from it. *Dan. 4:12.*

The beasts of the field shall be at peace with thee. *Job 5:23.*

And I saw in the midst of the throne and of the four living creatures, and in the midst of the elders, a Lamb standing. *Rev. 5:6.*

The Son of man hath not where to lay his head. *Matt. 8:20.*

> In a rude stable cold,
> The friendly beasts their stories told:
> "I," said the donkey, shaggy and brown,
> "Carried His mother up hill and down,
> Carried her safely to Bethlehem town."
> "I," said the cow all white and red,
> "Gave Him my manger for His bed,
> Gave Him my hay to pillow His head."
> "I," said the sheep, with the curly horn,
> "Gave Him wool for His blanket warm;
> He wore my coat on Christmas Morn."
> "I," said the camel, all yellow and black,
> "Over the desert, upon my back,
> Brought Him a gift in the Wise Man's pack."
> "I," said the dove, "from my rafter high,
> Cooed Him to sleep, that He should not cry,
> We cooed Him to sleep, my mate and I."
> And every beast, by some good spell
> In the stable darkness, was able to tell
> Of the gift he gave to Emmanuel.   *Robert Davis.*

Merciful and most loving God, by whose will and bountiful gift Jesus Christ our Lord humbled Himself that He might exalt mankind; and became flesh that He might renew in us the divine image; grant unto us the inheritance of the meek, perfect in us Thy likeness, and bring us at last to rejoice in beholding Thy beauty, and, with all Thy saints, to glorify Thy grace, who hast given Thine only-begotten Son to be the Saviour of the world. [*The Book of Common Worship,* Revised.]

THE CHILD

The people that walked in darkness have seen a great light: they that dwelt in the land of the shadow of death, upon them hath the light shined. . . . For unto us a child is born, unto us a son is given; and the government shall be upon his shoulder: and his name shall be called Wonderful, Counsellor, Mighty God, Everlasting Father, Prince of Peace. Of the increase of his government and of peace there shall be no end, upon the throne of David, and upon his kingdom, to establish it, and to uphold it with justice and with righteousness from henceforth even for ever. *Isa. 9:2, 6, 7.*

You little children, in whose eyes
Undimmed the light of heaven glows,
Whose dreams are bright with paradise,
Whose souls are whiter than the snows,
From holy lips and undefiled
Breathe your soft prayer to Christ the Child!

Are you whose thinning locks are sprent
With unreturning autumn's rime,
Whose heads, like wind-worn trees, are bent
Beneath the savage storms of time —
Pray Christ the Child to be your guide
Past the dim shoal, where shadows hide!

O saving hands! O Christ, that hears
A mortal mother's lullabies;
That feels our agony and tears,
Whose bosom trembles with our sighs,
Give us pure hearts and undefiled
Make us like Thee, O Christ the child!

Leading Editorial, New York Sun, *December 25, 1897.*

*A*LMIGHTY GOD, who hast given us thy only-begotten Son to take our nature upon him, and as at this time to be born of a pure virgin; Grant that we being regenerate, and made thy children by adoption and grace, may daily be renewed by thy Holy Spirit; through the same our Lord Jesus Christ, who liveth and reigneth with thee and the same Spirit ever, one God, world without end. [*The Book of Common Prayer,* Collect for Christmas Day.]

THE LIGHT OF THE WORLD

And God said, Let there be light: and there was light. *Gen. 1:3.*

Every good gift and every perfect gift is from above, coming down from the Father of lights. *James 1:17.*

Seeing it is God, that said, Light shall shine out of darkness, who shined in our hearts, to give the light of the knowledge of the glory of God in the face of Jesus Christ. *II Cor. 4:6.*

In him was life; and the life was the light of men. *John 1:4.*

The dayspring from on high shall visit us, to shine upon them that sit in darkness and the shadow of death; to guide our feet into the way of peace. *Luke 1:78, 79.*

Light of the world, the world is dark about Thee,
  Far out on Juda's hills the night is deep;
Not yet the day is come when men shall doubt Thee,
  Not yet the hour when Thou must wake and weep.
    Sleep, little One,
    O, Lord of Glory, sleep.

Love of all heaven, love's arms are folded round Thee,
  Love's heart shall be the pillow of Thy cheek;
Not yet the day is come when men shall wound Thee,
  Not yet for shelter vainly must Thou seek.
    Rest, little One,
    So mighty, and so weak.

Lie still and rest, Thou Rest of earth and heaven;
  Rest, little hands, our hopes of bliss ye keep;
Rest, little heart, one day shalt Thou be riven,
  O new-born life, O Life Eternal, sleep.
    Far out on Juda's hills,
    The night is deep.

*A*LMIGHTY GOD, who by the birth of Thy Holy One into the world didst give Thy true light to dawn upon our darkness; grant that as Thou hast given us to believe in the mystery of His incarnation and hast made us partakers of the divine nature, so we may ever abide with Him in this world and in the glory of His Kingdom; through the same Jesus Christ our Lord.

THE DOOR WITHOUT A LOCK

And the Spirit and the bride say, Come. And he that heareth, let him say, Come. And he that is athirst, let him come: he that will, let him take the water of life freely. *Rev. 22:17.*

For God so loved the world, that he gave his only begotten Son, that whosoever believeth on him should not perish, but have eternal life. *John 3:16.*

Let us therefore draw near with boldness unto the throne of grace, that we may receive mercy, and may find grace to help us in time of need. *Heb. 4:16.*

When that our gentle Lord was born
And cradled in the hay
There rode three wise men from the East —
Three rich wise men were they —
All in the starry night they came
Their homage gifts to pay.

They gat them down from camel-back,
The cattle shed before,
And in the darkness vainly sought
A great latch on the door.
" Ho! this is strange," quoth Balthazar.
" Aye, strange," quoth Melchior.

Quoth Gaspar, " I can find no hasp:
Well hidden is the lock."
" The door," quoth Melchior, " is stout
And fast, our skill to mock."
Quoth Balthazar, " The little King
Might wake. We dare not knock."

The three wise men they sat them down
To wait for morning dawn.
The cunning wards of that old door
They thought and marvelled on.
Quoth they, " No gate in all the East
Hath bar bolts tighter drawn."

Anon there came a little lad
With lambkins for the King.
He had no key, he raised no latch,
He touched no hidden spring,
But gently pushed the silent door
And open it gan swing.

" A miracle! A miracle! "
Cried out the wise men three:
" A little child hath solved the locks
That could not opened be."
In wonder spoke the shepherd lad.
" It hath no locks," quoth he.
George M. P. Baird.

*F*ATHER in heaven, whose mercy we praise in the yearly remembrance of the birth of Thy beloved Son, Jesus Christ our Lord; grant that as we welcome our Redeemer, His presence may shed abroad, in our hearts and in our homes, the light of heavenly peace and joy. [*The Book of Common Worship,* Revised (Altered).]

THE CHILD'S LEADERSHIP

And a little child shall lead them. *Isa. 11:6.*

Verily I say unto you, Whosoever shall not receive the kingdom of God as a little child, he shall in no wise enter therein. *Mark 10:15.*

God chose the weak things of the world, that he might put to shame the things that are strong. *I Cor. 1:27.*

For God so loved the world, that he gave his only begotten Son, that whosoever believeth on him should not perish, but have eternal life. *John 3:16.*

They all were looking for a king
    To slay their foes and lift them
    high:
Thou cam'st, a little baby thing
    That made a woman cry.

O Son of Man, to right my lot
    Naught but Thy presence can avail;
Yet on the road Thy wheels are not,
    Nor on the sea Thy sail!

My how or when Thou wilt not heed,
    But come down Thine own secret stair
That Thou may'st answer all my need
    Yes, every bygone prayer.

George Macdonald.

No war or battle sound
Was heard the world around
    The idle spear and shield were high uphung.
The hookéd chariot stood
Unstain'd with hostile blood,
    The trumpet spake not to the arméd throng,
And kings sat still with awful eye
As if they surely knew their Sovereign Lord was by.

John Milton.

Almighty god, give us grace that we may cast away the works of darkness, and put upon us the armour of light, now in the time of this mortal life, in which Thy Son Jesus Christ came to visit us in great humility; that in the last day, when he shall come again in his glorious majesty to judge both the quick and the dead, we may rise to the life immortal, through him who liveth and reigneth with thee and the Holy Ghost, now and ever. [*The Book of Comon Prayer,* Collect for First Sunday in Advent.]

A SON IS GIVEN

Unto us a child is born, unto us a son is given; and the government shall be upon his shoulder: and his name shall be called Wonderful, Counsellor, Mighty God, Everlasting Father, Prince of Peace. Of the increase of his government and of peace there shall be no end. *Isa. 9:6, 7.*

Unto you it is given to know the mysteries of the kingdom. *Matt. 13:11.*

And he said unto them, Take heed what ye hear: with what measure ye mete it shall be measured unto you; and more shall be given unto you. *Mark 4:24.*

I will give you the holy and sure blessings of David. *Acts 13:34.*

I am with you always. *Matt. 28:20.*

Unto Us a Son Is Given

Given, not lent,
And not withdrawn — once sent,
This Infant of mankind, this One
Is still the little welcome Son.

Even as the cold
Keen winter grows not old,
As childhood is so fresh, foreseen,
And spring in the familiar green.

New every year,
New born and newly dear,
He comes with tidings and a song,
The ages long, the ages long;

Sudden as sweet
Come the expected feet.
All joy is young, and new all art,
And He, too, Whom we have by heart.
Alice Meynell.

M AY God Almighty, who by the Incarnation of His only begotten Son drove away the darkness of the world, and by His glorious Birth enlightened this day, drive away from us the darkness of sins, and enlighten our hearts with the light of Christian graces. And may He who willed that the great day of His most holy Birth should be told to the shepherds by an angel, pour upon us the refreshing shower of His blessing, and guide us, Himself being our Shepherd, to the pastures of everlasting joy. And may He who through His Incarnation united earthly things with heavenly, fill us with the sweetness of inward peace and goodwill, and make us partakers with the heavenly host: for the glory of His great name. Amen. [*Treasury of Devotion.*]

PEACE ON EARTH

And suddenly there was with the angel a multitude of the heavenly host praising God, and saying, Glory to God in the highest, and on earth peace among men. *Luke 2:13, 14.*

And he will judge between the nations, and will decide concerning many peoples; and they shall beat their swords into plowshares, and their spears into pruning-hooks; nation shall not lift up sword against nation, neither shall they learn war any more. *Isa. 2:4.*

And the fruit of righteousness is sown in peace for them that make peace. *James 3:18.*

Blessed are the peacemakers: for they shall be called sons of God. *Matt. 5:9.*

I heard the bells on Christmas Day,
Their old familiar carols play,
And wild and sweet the words repeat
Of peace on earth, good will to men! "

I thought how, as the days had come,
The belfries of all Christendom
Had rolled along the unbroken song
Of peace on earth, good will to men!

And in despair I bowed my head;
" There is no peace on earth," I said,
" For hate is strong, and mocks the song
Of peace on earth, good will to men! "

Then pealed the bells more loud and deep;
" God is not dead, nor doth He sleep!
The wrong shall fail, the right prevail,
With peace on earth, good will to men! "

H. W. Longfellow.

O GOD our Father, after whom the whole family in heaven and on earth is named, who hath made of one blood all the nations and hath appointed unto them the bounds of their habitation, forgive us that we have so shamefully marred our human unity and have made of the earth which Thou didst create for peace a field of conflict and war. Thou art a God of righteousness. Cleanse us from all evil and by Thy judgments overthrow all falsehood and wrong, purge away all hatreds and establish truth and peace among all men. O mighty and righteous and loving Father, do Thou intervene and do through us and for us what we have been found unable to do for ourselves. Make peace, O God, who madest man, make peace. [R. E. S.]

ALL THINGS NEW

One thing I do, forgetting the things which are behind, and stretching forward to the things which are before, I press on toward the goal unto the prize of the high calling of God in Christ Jesus. *Phil. 3:13.*

Put away, as concerning your former manner of life, the old man, that waxeth corrupt after the lusts of deceit; and that ye be renewed in the spirit of your mind, and put on the new man, that after God hath been created in righteousness and holiness of truth. *Eph. 4:22–24.*

Ring out, wild bells, to the wild sky,
  The flying cloud, the frosty light:
  The year is dying in the night;
Ring out, wild bells, and let him die.

Ring out the old, ring in the new,
  Ring, happy bells, across the snow:
  The year is going, let him go;
Ring out the false, ring in the true. . . .

Ring out a slowly dying cause,
  And ancient forms of party strife;
  Ring in the nobler modes of life,
With sweeter manners, purer laws.

Ring out the want, the care, the sin,
  The faithless coldness of the times;
  Ring out, ring out my mournful rhymes,
But ring the fuller minstrel in. . . .

Ring out old shapes of foul disease;
  Ring out the narrowing lust of gold;
Ring out the thousand wars of old,
Ring in the thousand years of peace.

Ring in the valiant man and free,
  The larger heart, the kindlier hand;
  Ring out the darkness of the land,
Ring in the Christ that is to be.
Tennyson.

ETERNAL GOD from whom nothing passeth and it is gone, and to whom no new thing can appear, we seek in Thee our refuge and strength. At the close of another year we come to Thee with our thanksgivings, and in Thy presence would we humble ourselves. We remember with grateful hearts the mercy of which we have been constant partakers through these swiftly passing days; Thou hast been our Good Shepherd and we have wanted no good thing. We bring to Thee many memories of transgression and failure, and our secret and sad confessions and in the recollections of them we would humble ourselves before Thee. Heal us with Thy stripes and be with us that we fall no more. [John Hunter (Altered).]

INDEX

INDEX

INDEX

INDEX

INDEX

ACKNOWLEDGMENTS

Grateful acknowledgment is made to the many authors and publishers who have courteously allowed their copyrighted materials to be used in this devotional guide. Where any poems and prayers appear without proper acknowledgment, it is to be understood that diligent search has been made, and is still being made, and that upon further information due credit will be given in future editions.

To the American Unitarian Association, for "My Dead," by F. L. Hosmer, p. 117.

To D. Appleton-Century Company, for "Vespers," by S. Weir Mitchell, p. 162.

To the Association Press, for prayers from *The Quiet Hour,* by William Adams Brown, on pp. 52, 78, 123, 262, 363.

To *The Atlantic Monthly,* for "The Crypt," by Martha Gilbert Dickinson, p. 245.

To The Bobbs-Merrill Company, for the poem by James Whitcomb Riley, from *Rhymes of Childhood,* copyright, 1890, 1919, p. 112.

To The Chautauqua Institution, for "Song of Hope," by Mary A. Lathbury, p. 227.

To the W. B. Conkey Company, for "Beyond," "Gethsemane," and an excerpt from a poem by Ella Wheeler Wilcox, pp. 229, 354, 63.

To Dodd, Mead & Company, for "A Warrior's Prayer," by Paul Laurence Dunbar, p. 48; "The Mystic's Prayer," "The White Peace," by William Sharp, pp. 121, 180.

To Dodd, Mead & Company, and to J. M. Dent & Sons, Ltd., for "The Wild Knight," by G. K. Chesterton, p. 156.

To Dodd, Mead & Company, and to Wilfred Meynell, for "In No Strange Land," "Lilium Regis," "The Veteran of Heaven," by Francis Thompson, pp. 91, 107, 149.

To Dorrance & Co., Inc., for the poem by John Theodore Troth, p. 321.

To Doubleday, Doran & Company, Inc., for "Citizen of the World," by Joyce Kilmer, p. 43.

To E. P. Dutton & Co., Inc., for "Approaches," "That Holy Thing," and excerpts from poems by George Macdonald, pp. 83, 98, 282, 372; "God's Anvil," by Julius Sturm, p. 257.

To E. P. Dutton & Co., Inc., and to J. M. Dent & Sons, Ltd., for the prayers from *Devotional Services,* by John Hunter, pp. 9, 12, 27, 109, 130, 323, 375.

To the Evangelical Publishers, Toronto, for the poems by Annie Johnson Flint, pp. 160, 332, 335.

ACKNOWLEDGMENTS

To Farrar & Rinehart, Inc., for "The Shadow of the Perfect Rose," by Thomas S. Jones, copyright by John L. Foley, p. 358.

To The Hampshire Bookshop, for prayers from *Prayers of the College Year,* by L. Clark Seelye, on pp. 176, 213.

To Harper & Brothers, and to Hodder & Stoughton, Ltd., for "The Unutterable Beauty," "The Suffering God," "Indifference," by G. A. Studdert-Kennedy, pp. 111, 218, 296.

To Houghton Mifflin Company, for "A Prayer," by John Drinkwater, p. 260; "Call Me Not Dead," by Richard Watson Gilder, p. 174; "The Chambered Nautilus," by Oliver Wendell Holmes, p. 99; "Follow Me," "Resignation," "Christmas Bells," by Henry Wadsworth Longfellow, pp. 132, 226, 374; "Opportunity," "The Fool's Prayer," "Life," by Edward Rowland Sill, pp. 59, 188, 192; and for prose selection from *The Christ of Today,* by G. A. Gordon, on p. 171.

To J. B. Lippincott Company, and to Messrs. Wm. Blackwood & Sons, Ltd., for "In the Cool of the Evening" and an excerpt from "A Belgian Christmas Eve," from *Collected Poems,* Vols. I, III, by Alfred Noyes, copyright, 1913-1920, on pp. 89, 139.

To Little, Brown & Company, for "The Nameless Saint," by Edward Everett Hale, p. 239.

To Dr. Francis Litz, for "The Recompense," "Christ and the Pagan," "Ave atque Vale," "All in All," by John B. Tabb, pp. 25, 119, 175, 283.

To Lothrop, Lee & Shepard Co., for the poem by Richard Burton, p. 120.

To The Macmillan Company, for "Advent," by F. W. H. Meyers, p. 32; prayers from *Secret of the Saints,* by Henry S. Lunn, on pp. 285, 300, and *Lift Up Your Hearts,* by Walter Russell Bowie, on p. 289.

To Virgil Markham, for "Man-Test" and an excerpt from a poem, both by Edwin Markham, pp. 140, 177.

To Juanita Miller, for "Columbus," by Joaquin Miller, p. 116.

To Thomas Bird Mosher, for "Tears," by Lizette Woodworth Reese, p. 254.

To John Murray, for the poems by J. A. Symonds, pp. 22, 38, and "Vitai Lampada," from *Poems New and Old,* by Sir Henry Newbolt, p. 167.

To Thomas Nelson and Sons, Ltd., for "Coming," from *Ezekiel and Other Poems,* by Barbara MacAndrew, p. 95.

To John Oxenham's Estate, for poems by John Oxenham, pp. 12, 54, 100, 164, 202.

To Oxford University Press, for "Easter in South Africa," from *Africa and Other Poems,* by Arthur Shearley Cripps, p. 356; prayers from *The Kingdom, The Power and The Glory,* pp. 21, 47 132, 286.

ACKNOWLEDGMENTS

To G. P. Putnam's Sons, for "Miracles," by Marguerite Wilkinson, p. 61.

To Mrs. Walter Rauschenbusch, for the prayers by Walter Rauschenbusch, pp. 89, 172, 237, 263, 296, 319.

To Reilly & Lee Co., for "It Couldn't Be Done," by Edgar A. Guest, p. 280.

To William E. Rudge's Sons, for "Resurgam," "The Ballad of the Saint," "The Annunciation," by Theodosia Garrison, pp. 50, 266, 363.

To Charles Scribner's Sons, for "Emancipation," by Maltbie D. Babcock, p. 159; "Margaritae Sorori," "Invictus," by William E. Henley, pp. 141, 291; "A Ballad of Trees and the Master," by Sidney Lanier, p. 51; "Two Easter Stanzas," by Vachel Lindsay, p. 109; "To a Daisy," "Unto Us a Son Is Given," by Alice Meynell, pp. 40, 373; "Faith," by George Santayana, p. 262; "Work," by Henry van Dyke, p. 212; for prayers from A Diary of Private Prayer, by John Baillie, on pp. 107, 171, 221, 274, 281, 298, 313; and for the selections from Horace Bushnell's works, on pp. 143, 213.

To The Student Christian Movement Press, Ltd., for prayers from The Divine Companionship, by J. S. Hoyland, on pp. 16, 203, 215, 224, and A Book of Prayers for Students, on pp. 51, 318.

To The Sunday School Times Publishing Company, for the poems, pp. 259, 263, 300.

To The Viking Press, Inc., for "O Black and Unknown Bards," from Saint Peter Relates an Incident, by James Weldon Johnson, copyright by the author, 1917, 1921, 1935, p. 66.

To Willett, Clark & Company, for the prayer from The Daily Altar, by Willett and Morrison, on p. 236.

To The Womans Press, for the poem by Martha Foote Crow, p. 152.

To the World Book Company, for the poem by David Starr Jordan, p. 123.

To the following authors and individual owners of copyrights for poems and prayers used: Sarah N. Cleghorn, p. 20; Daniel Henderson, p. 33; Hugh T. Kerr, p. 173; Dwight J. Bradley, p. 302; W. R. Bowie, p. 303; Edward Shillito, p. 355; Mrs. Clinton Scollard, p. 365; George M. P. Baird, p. 371.